The Compact City: A Sustainable Urban Form?

Edited by

Mike Jenks, Elizabeth Burton and
Katie Williams
Oxford Brookes University, Oxford, UK

E & FN SPON
An Imprint of Chapman & Hall

London · Glasgow · Weinheim · New York · Tokyo · Melbourne · Madras

Published by E & FN Spon, an imprint of Chapman & Hall, 2–6 Boundary Row, London SE1 8HN, UK

Chapman & Hall, 2–6 Boundary Row, London SE1 8HN, UK

Blackie Academic & Professional, Wester Cleddens Road, Bishopbriggs, Glasgow G64 2NZ, UK

Chapman & Hall, GmbH, Pappelallee 3, 69469 Weinheim, Germany

Chapman & Hall USA, 115 Fifth Avenue, New York, NY 10003, USA

Chapman & Hall Japan, ITP-Japan, Kyowa Building, 3F, 2-2-1 Hirakawacho, Chiyoda-ku, Tokyo 102, Japan

Chapman & Hall Australia, 102 Dodds Street, South Melbourne, Victoria 3205, Australia

Chapman & Hall India, R. Seshadri, 32 Second Main Road, CIT East, Madras 600 035, India

First edition 1996

© 1996 E & FN Spon

pp 45–52: *Density, Efficiency and Equality in Australian Cities*, © Hugh Stretton. This paper appears by permission of *Australian Planner*.
p 54, Fig. 1:© The British Museum.
pp 248–258: *Environmental Capacity of a Historic City*, © Peter Drummond and Corinne Swain
pp 302–317: *The Compact City and the Need to Travel*, Michael Breheny, Adrian Gurney and James Strike. © Crown copyright 1995. Published with the permission of the Controller of Her Majesty's Stationery Office. The views expressed are those of the author and do not necessarily reflect the views or policy of the Controller or of the Department of the Environment.

Printed in Great Britain at the Alden Press, Oxford

ISBN 0 419 21300 7

A catalogue record for this book is available from the British Library

∞ Printed on acid-free text paper, manufactured in accordance with ANSI/NISO Z39.48-1992 (Permanence of Paper).

The Compact City:
A Sustainable Urban
Form?

Edited by

Mike Jenks, Elizabeth Burton and
Katie Williams
Oxford Brookes University, Oxford, UK

E & FN SPON
An Imprint of Chapman & Hall

London · Glasgow · Weinheim · New York · Tokyo · Melbourne · Madras

Published by E & FN Spon, an imprint of Chapman & Hall, 2–6 Boundary Row, London SE1 8HN, UK

Chapman & Hall, 2–6 Boundary Row, London SE1 8HN, UK

Blackie Academic & Professional, Wester Cleddens Road, Bishopbriggs, Glasgow G64 2NZ, UK

Chapman & Hall, GmbH, Pappelallee 3, 69469 Weinheim, Germany

Chapman & Hall USA, 115 Fifth Avenue, New York, NY 10003, USA

Chapman & Hall Japan, ITP-Japan, Kyowa Building, 3F, 2-2-1 Hirakawacho, Chiyoda-ku, Tokyo 102, Japan

Chapman & Hall Australia, 102 Dodds Street, South Melbourne, Victoria 3205, Australia

Chapman & Hall India, R. Seshadri, 32 Second Main Road, CIT East, Madras 600 035, India

First edition 1996

© 1996 E & FN Spon

pp 45–52: *Density, Efficiency and Equality in Australian Cities*, © Hugh Stretton. This paper appears by permission of *Australian Planner*.
p 54, Fig. 1: © The British Museum.
pp 248–258: *Environmental Capacity of a Historic City*, © Peter Drummond and Corinne Swain
pp 302–317: *The Compact City and the Need to Travel*, Michael Breheny, Adrian Gurney and James Strike. © Crown copyright 1995. Published with the permission of the Controller of Her Majesty's Stationery Office. The views expressed are those of the author and do not necessarily reflect the views or policy of the Controller or of the Department of the Environment.

Printed in Great Britain at the Alden Press, Oxford

ISBN 0 419 21300 7

A catalogue record for this book is available from the British Library

∞ Printed on acid-free text paper, manufactured in accordance with ANSI/NISO Z39.48-1992 (Permanence of Paper).

Contents

Contributors

Joanna Averley
Llewelyn-Davis, London

George Barrett
ECOTEC Research and Consulting Ltd,
Birmingham

Michael Breheny
Department of Geography, University of
Reading, Reading

Elizabeth Burton
School of Architecture, Oxford Brookes
University, Oxford

Tony Burton
Council for the Protection of Rural England,
London

Patrick Clarke
Llewelyn-Davies, London

Tessa Coombes
Faculty of the Built Environment, University
of the West of England, Bristol

Will Cousins
David Lock Associates: Town Planning,
Urban Design and Development,
Milton Keynes

Martin Crookston
Llewelyn-Davies, London

Ben Croxford
The Bartlett School of Architecture,
University College London

Peter Drummond
Building Design Partnership, London

Stuart Farthing
Faculty of the Built Environment, University
of the West of England, Bristol

Charles Fulford
Drivers Jonas, London

Ray Green
Retired City Planning Officer and
Vice Chairman of the Town and Country
Planning Association

Adrian Gurney
Arup Economic and Planning, London

Mayer Hillman
Policy Studies Institute, London

Mike Jenks
School of Architecture, Oxford Brookes
University, Oxford

Jim Johnson
Edinburgh Old Town Renewal Trust,
Edinburgh

Christopher Knight
Savills: Chartered Surveyors and
International Property Consultants,
Cambridge

Peter Larkham
School of Planning, University of Central
England, Birmingham

John Littler
Research in Building Group, Department of
Architecture and Engineering,
University of Westminster, London

Lilli Matson
Council for the Protection of Rural England,
London

Peter Nijkamp
Department of Spatial Economics, Free
University of Amsterdam, Netherlands

Alan Penn
The Bartlett School of Architecture,
University College London

Richard Pratt
School of Planning, University of Central
England, Birmingham

Caitríona Ní Riain
Research in Building Group, Department of
Architecture and Engineering,
University of Westminster, London

Sytze A. Rienstra
Department of Spatial Economics, Free
University of Amsterdam, Netherlands

Ernie Scoffham
Department of Architecture, University of
Nottingham, Nottingham

Harley Sherlock
Andrews Sherlock and Partners, Chartered
Architects and Surveyors, London

Hedley Smyth
School of Construction and Earth Sciences,
Oxford Brookes University, Oxford

Hugh Stretton
Department of Economics, University of
Adelaide, Australia

James Strike
Arup Economic and Planning, London

Corinne Swain
Arup Economic and Planning, London

Louise Thomas
David Lock Associates: Town Planning,
Urban Design and Development, Milton
Keynes

Patrick N. Troy
Urban Research Program, Research School
of Social Sciences,
Australian National University, Canberra,
Australia

Brenda Vale
Department of Architecture, University of
Nottingham, Nottingham

Michael Welbank
Entec UK Ltd, London

Katie Williams
School of Architecture, Oxford Brookes
University, Oxford

Elizabeth Wilson
School of Planning, Oxford Brookes
University, Oxford

John Winter
Faculty of the Built Environment, University
of the West of England, Bristol

Acknowledgements

Producing a book of this magnitude depends on the help of many people to whom we extend our heartfelt thanks. We express our gratitude to: all the contributors, who have worked wonders in producing their chapters to our deadline; Graham Freer and Rahmat (Baio) Bayudi for the DTP and formatting of the text; Kathryn Pratley for preparing some of the illustrations; Iradj Parvaneh for photographic work; Mike O'Connell for providing research material; and Vivien Walker for secretarial assistance. In particular we would like to give our warmest thanks to Margaret Jenks, Jonathan Kemp and Bart Sheehan for their help and support during the period of intensive work involved in producing this book.

Introduction

Mike Jenks, Elizabeth Burton and Katie Williams

Compact Cities and Sustainability: *An Introduction*

> ...the year [19]95 is a symbolic marker; after which the balance seems to tilt away from anxieties about death and decay to dreams of regeneration and rebirth (Showalter, 1995, p.3)

It is less than a decade since the Brundtland report *Our Common Future* was published (World Commission on Environment and Development, WCED, 1987), and little more than three years since the Rio Declaration was signed by over 150 countries (United Nations, 1993). Within a very short time issues of sustainability and of sustainable development have become part of the mainstream. Concern about the future of the world's environment and its resources is now an established fact of life, and this has been accompanied by expressions of good intention by governments worldwide. There has been wide ranging discussion about the importance of achieving inter- and intra-generational sustainability. The debate has covered many issues related to population, agriculture and biodiversity, industry, energy consumption, global warming and pollution, equity in access to resources, and urbanism. The arguments have largely moved on from the rather doom laden scenarios of global catastrophe, towards a certain optimism that having understood the problems, solutions might be found. But it is an optimism tinged with doubt, as questions remain about how best to achieve effective solutions, and whether there is the will to implement them. While the whole range of environmental issues is important, and all are interrelated, it is the issue of urbanism that seems to provide the problems that are among the most intractable and difficult to solve. The significance of cities is not in doubt. As Elkin *et al.* (1991, p.4) observe, 'Urban centres are crucial to the functioning of the world economic order'. But although the problems are generally known, the complexity of cities, and differences in the urban experience of their inhabitants, lead to a variety of issues that make the search for effective solutions a daunting task. Nevertheless, it is a task that needs to be undertaken; a large part of the response to unsustainable development 'should come from the cities because that is where the most intense environmental damage is taking place, and it is there that many improvements can effectively be made' (White, 1994, p.109).

The sheer scale of action required to achieve sustainable cities is readily apparent. Brundtland predicted that by the year 2000 almost half of the world's population would live in urban areas (WCED, 1987, p.235). This prediction was accurate as in 1995 just over 45% of the population lived in urban areas, representing some 2.6 billion people, of which more than one billion lived in large cities of three quarters of a million people or more (World Resources Institute, WRI, 1995). By the turn of the century it has been estimated that the 40 largest cities will have populations ranging from 4.5 million in Philadelphia to 25.6 million in Mexico City (Girardet, 1992). However, urban populations are not evenly distributed, nor are cities at the same stage of development (Auty, 1995). Over 70% of the populations of economically advanced nations in North America, Europe and Oceania live in cities, yet they only account for around 28% of urban dwellers worldwide. These tend to be mature cities where growth rates are generally slow, or in decline (van den Berg *et al.*, 1982). In the developing countries just under 1.9 billion live in urban areas; furthermore, in these nations the growth rate within, and migration into, cities are high (WRI, 1995). Girardet (1992, p.185) encapsulates the difference: 'Population censuses in cities such as Sao Paulo, Cairo, Lagos, Bombay or Bangkok are out of date as soon as they have been completed. This contrasts with 'mature' cities such as London whose population has been virtually static for decades.' While sustainability concerns in the emerging nations are associated with extremes of growth and size, in the developed countries they are more to do with the loss of population and the resulting decline and decay.

It is tempting to suggest that cities in the developing world, with high growth rates which place a heavy toll on the environment, have such overwhelming problems that all our efforts to find solutions should be concentrated there. However, the relative affluence of many cities in the developed world, far from providing solutions, contributes to the problems of unsustainablity. It is in these cities that the disproportionate consumption of resources has a major global impact. On average, citizens of North America consume 16 times more energy than those in Africa, and over eight times more than citizens in Asia or South America. The same is true, to a slightly lesser extent, with the emission of greenhouse gases. Europe is also a relatively high consumer, but still only consumes about half of the energy per capita than in North America (United Nations Environment Programme, 1993; WRI, 1995). White (1994) argues that it is the richest cities that contribute to worldwide environmental degradation because of their dependency on 'an unsustainable level of resource use', which if followed by the developing nations would mean that 'we will soon experience large-scale ecosystem collapse...we must strive to develop alternative models...' (p.113)

Getting the right policies, management and form for cities will be a key factor. With such a large proportion of the world population, the concentration of environmental problems, and consumption of resources, cities clearly appear to be the most important location for action to help the goals of sustainable development. If successful policies and practical solutions can be found, then the benefits will be great.

The compact city

The problems of, and search for solutions for, cities in the developed world are the focus of this book, in particular the concept of the compact city. There is a strong link between urban form and sustainable development, but it is not simple and straightforward. It has been suggested that a sustainable city 'must be of a form and scale appropriate to walking, cycling and efficient public transport, and with a compactness that encourages social interaction.' (Elkin *et al.*, 1991, p.12). Other proponents have suggested forms that range from large concentrated centres, through ideas of decentralised but concentrated and compact settlements linked by public transport systems, to strategies for dispersal in self-sufficient communities (Haughton and Hunter, 1994). In existing cities, the concept of compaction arises through processes that intensify development and bring in more people to revitalise them. The ideas behind the compact city are an important strand in the attempt to find sustainable urban forms.

The vision of the compact city has been dominated by the model of the densely developed core of many historic European cities. These are a great attraction not just to architects, planners and urban designers, but to countless tourists who flock to see them. They are seen, often by those from outside, as ideal places to live and experience the vitality and variety of urban life. The danger is that it is a romantic vision, one which assumes a golden age that can be recaptured through urban form, leading to a sustainable and benign civility. Perhaps it is not surprising that the strongest advocate for the compact city has been the European Community (Commission of the European Communities, 1990). However, the policies proposed have been based more in theory than in practice, and the arguments are contentious. The theory is to an extent premised on urban containment, to provide a concentration of socially sustainable mixed uses, that will concentrate development and reduce the need to travel, thus reducing vehicle emissions. The promotion of the use of public transport, traffic calming, walking and cycling are often cited as solutions (Elkin *et al.*, 1991; Newman, 1994). Further reductions from harmful emissions might also accrue from more energy efficient land use planning, combined power and heating schemes, and energy efficient buildings (Nijkamp and Perrels, 1994; Owens, 1986; Owens, 1992). Higher densities may help to make the provision of amenities and facilities economically viable, enhancing social sustainability (Haughton and Hunter, 1994). But on the down side, the compact city may become overcrowded and suffer a loss of urban quality, with less open space, more congestion and pollution (Breheny, 1992a, 1992b), and may simply not represent the sort of environment in which the majority of people would wish to live if they had the choice.

With concepts and theories that are sometimes conflicting, what is needed is knowledge drawn from research and practice to provide a clearer understanding of the more complex reality. Differences between cities should mean that the compact city is not just a simplistic concept, drawing on particular reified urban forms. As Haughton and Hunter (1994, p.311) point out:

> The sustainable city is not rooted in an idealised version of past settlements, nor is it one given to a radical casting-off from its own particular cultural, economic and physical identity in the name of the latest passing fad for urban change.

5

Is the compact city, then, a romantic ideal, or is it a genuine way forward? Answers are needed with some urgency. Policies for creating higher density development, environmentally friendly design, and reduced reliance on private transport are in place in Europe, the UK and Australia. There is the likelihood of action being taken and solutions implemented, without an accurate understanding of the impacts they may have, nor how sustainable they may turn out to be. The theory would suggest beneficial outcomes, yet despite the advocacy and debate, many questions remain.

A sustainable urban form?

It is the aim of this book to address some of the questions raised about the conceptions of the compact city. The chapters that follow present many sides of the debate, in order to put forward different points of view, and to draw together both diverse and common strands of the arguments. It is by no means clear that the compact city is the best or only way forward. In presenting new thinking and research, the intention is to advance the debate, and to provide a basis for a better understanding of the concept.

Theory is considered in the first part of the book. It is argued that sustainable development is an imperative if the dire consequences of global warming are to be ameliorated. A link is made between urban forms that are often associated with the compact city, and with lifestyle changes that would be necessary to reduce dependence on the car. However, questions are raised about the form and effectiveness of the compact city concept in achieving sustainability, and whether it means concentration and centralisation, or decentralisation with some degree of autonomy. Strong arguments are put for each position and a middle way, or compromise, of intensification in cities in parallel with some green field suburban development is suggested as a possible solution. Overall it is recognised that while there may be strategic benefits, the impacts of the compact city are likely to be felt locally. Arguments address the issue of acceptability, the desires of individuals, and the wider responsibilities of the citizen and the public interest.

The focus in Part 2 turns to a more detailed consideration of social and economic issues. There are concerns about the dominance of environmental arguments for compaction, and the social and economic consequences that might arise unless they are given equal weight. The relationship between high density living and mixed use environments, and a high quality of life is examined. While such an environment may be advantageous to some groups, it may not be an improvement for all. To achieve such compact development would require investment which is only likely to come from the private sector. The debate extends to take in the views of developers, their willingness to build, and the obstacles that appear to hinder more dense development. A clear message is the need to make the intensification of cities both appealing and economically viable, if people are to be attracted back into them.

Environmental issues are covered in Part 3, particularly the connection between transport and urban form, and whether or not the claimed benefits would result from the compact city. The evidence discussed indicates, at best, only marginal gains, and counter-arguments are presented that sustainability might be better achieved with less dense, more self-sufficient settlements. It is argued that a greater impact might occur through changes in travel behaviour and more environmentally friendly technologies, than hoping for a modal change in the means of transport.

A degree of uncertainty in theory and in the particular issues surrounding the compact city debate exists, and Part 4 addresses some methodological approaches that could contribute towards a more certain knowledge base. Here it is argued that complexity and uncertainty mean that a precautionary principle should be applied in relation to the development of more compact urban forms. Theories have generally not been validated by research, and what has been done is critically reviewed; it is argued that a better co-ordination and integration of research is needed. Research is presented that breaks new ground in defining environmental capacity and in the modelling of complex urban forms to enable predictions of pollution dispersal. The final part of the book addresses the implementation of compact city concepts, and gives examples and practical advice. The role of agencies, particularly local authorities and the planning system, is discussed. The chapters here debate some of the measures used to implement and manage compact city ideas, the scale and level of implementation, and issues of legitimacy.

The book presents common as well as conflicting themes, and draws some conclusions. It shows that the concept of the compact city is a complex one, and that the debate is by no means resolved. By finally pointing to some ways forward, the hope is that the book will contribute to the 'tilt' in balance towards a more achievable and sustainable urban future.

References

Auty, R. (1995) *Patterns of Development: Resources, Policy and Economic Growth*, Edward Arnold, London.

Breheny, M (ed.) (1992a) *Sustainable Development and Urban Form*, Pion, London.

Breheny, M. (1992b) The contradictions of the compact city: a review, in *Sustainable Development and Urban Form* (ed. Breheny, M.) Pion, London.

Commission of the European Communities (1990) *Green Paper on the Urban Environment*, European Commission, Brussels.

Elkin, T., McLaren, D. and Hillman, M. (1991) *Reviving the City: Towards Sustainable Urban Development*, Friends of the Earth, London.

Girardet, H. (1992) *The Gaia Atlas of Cities*, Gaia Books, London.

Haughton, G. and Hunter, C. (1994) *Sustainable Cities*, Jessica Kingsley Publishers, London.

Newman, P. (1994) Urban design, transportation and greenhouse, in *Global Warming and the Built Environment* (eds Samuels, R. and Prasad, D.) E & FN Spon, London.

Nijkamp, P. and Perrels, A. (1994) *Sustainable Cities in Europe*, Earthscan, London.

Owens, S. (1986) *Energy Planning and Urban Form*, Pion, London.

Owens, S. (1992) Energy, environmental sustainability and land-use planning, in *Sustainable Development and Urban Form* (ed. Breheny, M.) Pion, London.

Showalter, E. (1995) Apocalypse not. *Guardian Friday Review*, 27 October, pp.2-3.

United Nations (1993) *Earth Summit Agenda 21: The UN Programme of Action from Rio*, United Nations, New York.

United Nations Environment Programme (1993) *Environmental Data Report 1993-4*, Blackwells Publishers, Oxford.

van den Berg, L., Drewett, R., Klaassen, L., Rossi, A. and Vijverberg, C. (1982) *Urban Europe: A Study of Growth and Decline*, Pergamon Press, Oxford.

White, R. (1994) Strategic decisions for sustainable urban development in the Third World. *Third World Planning Review*, **16(2)**, pp.103-16.

World Commission on Environment and Development (1987) *Our Common Future*, Oxford University Press, Oxford.

World Resources Institute (1995) *World Resources 1994-5*, Oxford University Press, Oxford.

Part One
Compact City Theory

Part 1
Compact City Theory
Introduction

The relationship between urban form and sustainability is currently one of the most hotly debated issues on the international environmental agenda. The way that cities should be developed in the future, and the effect that their form can have on resource depletion and social and economic sustainability, are central to this debate. The chapters in Part 1 add to this argument by presenting theoretical perspectives on what Welbank has described as *The Search for a Sustainable Urban Form*. Collectively the chapters form an overview of the theoretical advances in the compact city debate and present thinking on the best option for future urban development; but taken individually they offer strong, and often conflicting, opinions about the benefits and, importantly, the costs of urban compaction.

At one extreme of the debate, there are those who believe that compact cities are an important component of a sustainable future. Hillman, for example, argues that compacting the city is one way of reducing travel distances, and therefore reducing emissions and greenhouse gases, thus curbing global warming. He concedes that living at higher densities will have implications for individual lifestyles, but does not believe that these will be negative. By reducing consumption of fossil fuels, he argues, urban residents could enjoy, amongst other things, lower transport expenditure, less pollution and lower heating costs.

There are then those who believe in what Breheny terms a 'compromise' position, who favour neither extreme centralisation nor decentralisation solutions (Breheny, Scoffham and Vale, and Thomas and Cousins). Breheny suggests that many of the benefits of centralisation may not stand up to scrutiny, and he questions whether the local 'pain' suffered by urban dwellers will be worth the 'gain' to sustainability; especially as some of the gains are questionable. He then advocates a position which supports both the merits of centralisation, for example urban containment and urban regeneration, and the benefits of the 'inevitable decentralisation' to towns and suburbs which offer a range of public facilities.

A similar 'compromise' position is held by Scoffham and Vale, and Thomas and Cousins. Scoffham and Vale dismiss extreme centralisation and propose instead that individual neighbourhoods should develop, each with a strong local identity and control over local resources. For them 'compact' refers more to the degree of autonomy a neighbourhood has, than to its physical form. Thomas and Cousins question the compact city in the light of current economic trends, environmental objectives, aspirations to quality of life and political reality, and conclude that the compact city is 'unsuccessful, undesirable and unworkable'. In a similar vein to Scoffham and Vale they advocate a decentralised urban form which is physically and 'virtually' compact; where local compactness is complemented by regional compactness, and where the routes between settlements are so efficient that travel times and distances are reduced.

Finally, there are those who argue against the process of compaction on the grounds that it is unsustainable, and unacceptable to urban and suburban residents, for the simple reason that the claimed benefits are outweighed by losses to the social, economic and natural environment. Stretton epitomises this view with his critique of urban compaction in Australia. He argues that there is too much to be lost from urban consolidation, and that solutions lie in reforming transport systems, rather than re-structuring cities.

The divergence in opinion in these chapters indicates that the implementation of the compact city needs to be treated with extreme caution. Welbank has argued that in Europe and the UK the search for a sustainable urban form has, to a certain extent, been 'founded on conviction rather than rationality'. This conviction is grounded in the assumption that the changes needed to bring about strategic benefits will also bring about local improvements, particularly in the quality of urban life. This issue is explored by Williams *et al.* in a review of the process of urban intensification. They conclude that for the compact city to be acceptable, the benefits must be evident at the local level; only by understanding and managing the inherent problems of adopting strategic aims, which have implications for every neighbourhood, will intensification be acceptable to those already living in cities.

The chapters in Part 1 illustrate that whilst the search for the most appropriate urban form has a long history, as a search for a sustainable form the challenge is fairly new. They also show that this search has yet to find conclusively either in favour of, or against, the compact city. What is clear, however, is that only by rigorous investigation and continued questioning and testing of assumptions, will the implications of sustainability for our towns and cities be understood. These chapters strikingly illustrate the complexity and liveliness of the debate.

Michael Breheny

Centrists, Decentrists and Compromisers: *Views on the Future of Urban Form*

Introduction

The sustainable development imperative has revived a forgotten, or discredited, idea: that planning ought to be done, or can be done, on a big scale. Up to the 1960s planning had a long, and reasonably creditable, history of visionary ideas. After that date, the public lost confidence in planners, and planners lost confidence in themselves. Subsequently, pragmatism has ruled. However, there is now a fascinating debate underway about the role of planning in promoting sustainable development, and - here we have the big idea - about which urban forms will most effectively deliver greater environmental protection. Viewed as a narrow environmental debate, the issue is profoundly important. But when the broader economic, social and cultural repercussions are taken into account, it soon becomes apparent that nothing less than the future of western lifestyles is at stake.

This debate is not the preserve of unworldly academics. It is taking place at inter-governmental, governmental, and local government levels across the world. Following the Brundtland Commission report of 1987 (World Commission on Environment and Development, 1987), the notion that the natural environment should become a political priority - under the 'sustainable development' banner - has taken hold to a remarkable degree. In many countries there have been profound changes in policies and in political and popular attitudes, as commitment to the sustainable development idea has increased. The fundamental question in all places, however, has been how to deliver major environmental improvements. One common answer seems to be to use planning systems to achieve these gains; and, in turn, to use those planning systems to achieve greater urban compaction. Thus, a legitimate, indeed profound, research question is whether such compaction - 'the compact city' - will deliver the gains demanded by the politicians.

The political urgency of this debate is demonstrated by the fact that we have a rare case of politicians racing ahead of academics, pressing for specific policies before the research community is able to say with any confidence which policies will have what effects. Perhaps this arises because national governments are keen to meet - and be seen to meet - international environmental obligations.

Although, as we will see, the debate is tending to favour heavily one solution, the scope of the debate can be usefully summarised by classifying stances initially into two groups: 'decentrists', who favour urban decentralisation, largely as a reaction to the problems of the industrial cities; and 'centrists', who believe in the virtues of high density cities and decry urban sprawl.

The decentrist and centrist views of urban form have long histories, albeit that the motives for their promotion in the past have been somewhat different from those driving the current debate. These histories are important, however, because although they do not cast much direct light on the sustainability question, they do put that question into a wider context. They also act as a reminder that decisions made on environmental grounds will have broader - economic, social, and cultural - repercussions that must not be ignored. There is a danger at present that the sheer weight of the environmental argument will swamp all other considerations. Indeed, for some this is the hope.

Thus, the review presented here will (a) reflect briefly and selectively on the histories of the decentrist and centrist arguments, and (b) outline the contemporary debate, focusing as it does on the environmental issues. In the historical review the decentrist and centrist approaches will be considered in turn. In the contemporary review, the two will be considered together. This is because the current promotion of one or the other consists largely in criticism of the opposite position, to a much greater degree than in the past. This makes for a slightly messy presentation, but does allow the richness of the interplay of ideas between the two stances to emerge. When the decentrist and centrist positions have been reviewed, it will be argued in conclusion that the existence of a third stance ought to be recognised: a conscious middle line in this debate - the 'compromise' view.

The weight attached in this review to various positions reflects the material readily available to the author. Thus, it has a strong Anglo-American flavour, with a bias in favour of the British material. In turn, within the British literature there is an inevitable focus on projects with which the author is particularly familiar or has been involved. Thus, the perspective is partial, perhaps even narrow. However, it is hoped that the coverage is sufficient to map the boundaries of the debate.

Historical advocacy of centrism and decentrism: radiant city, garden city or Broadacres?

Different protagonists in the centrist versus decentrist debate over the years have had different motives. The mainstream concern has been with the quality of urban and rural life and, to a lesser extent, the aesthetics of urbanity. As Hall (1988) says, the history of 20th century planning 'represents a reaction to the evils of the nineteenth-century city' (p.7). From Howard, Geddes, Wright, and Le Corbusier, through to Mumford and Osborn and many followers, this was the motive. In the post-1945 period, with the cities appearing to be rather less evil and the problems being increasingly of 20th century origin, planning motives became more diverse, more specific and less visionary. Nevertheless, centrist and decentrist camps remained clear, and, as we will see, the occasional big idea did emerge, through to the early 1970s.

Many wonderful histories of planning have been written. The ideas and practices explained below have all been covered thoroughly and expertly elsewhere (for example, Hall, 1988; Fishman, 1977). Indeed, this review relies heavily on these sources. What is different here, however, is the attempt to see elements of this planning history directly in terms of the decentrist versus centrist debate.

It is difficult to know where to start in reviewing the history of discussions about appropriate urban forms. It is probably fair to say that the decentrist view has the longer pedigree. Conscious practical town planning developed in Europe and North America in reaction to the squalor of the towns and cities thrown up by the Industrial Revolution. Although this reaction included initiatives within those towns and cities, it also spawned decentralised solutions. In the UK these took the form of private, philanthropic ventures from the early 19th century onwards, most obviously at New Lanark, Saltaire, Port Sunlight, Bournville, and New Earswick. The common denominator of all of these initiatives was a desire to plan for communities in healthy and efficient surroundings, away from the disease and congestion of the industrial towns. These planned communities made only a minor dent in the dominant process of urban centralisation, which continued in Europe until the immediate post-1945 period. Nevertheless, they are important in this history because they established, for the first time, the idea that there might be a conscious alternative to centripetal urbanisation.

The most important period in the history of the debate about urban form was from 1898 through to 1935. During this period the boundaries of the debate were mapped out. The extreme cases were both proposed in full in 1935; by Le Corbusier the arch-centrist, and Frank Lloyd Wright the champion decentrist. Both had the benefit of being able to reflect on the work of Ebenezer Howard, in terms of his ideas and their practical application at Letchworth, Welwyn Garden City and Hampstead Garden Suburb. In fact, both felt the need to propose antidotes to Howard's influential views. The following brief historical review will be built around these three contributions; because they all proposed big, total solutions to the urban problem, and also because they represent the extreme position. Other contributions to the debate can be built fruitfully around the three defining views of planning history's most important 'seers' (Hall, 1992).

Placed alongside the extremes of La Ville Radieuse and Broadacres City, Howard's Garden City proposal seems to hold the middle ground. Indeed, later it will be suggested that Howard ought to be regarded not as a centrist or decentrist, but as a representative of a compromise position. However, others, and most obviously Jane Jacobs, have cast him firmly as a villainous decentrist; indeed, as *the* villain.

The order in which these three sets of solutions should be reviewed is not obvious. The extremes of Le Corbusier and Wright might be presented first, in order to demonstrate that Howard is best cast in the middle ground rather than as the decentrist villain portrayed by some commentators. The alternative is a more obvious chronological coverage, because this both reflects the sequence of ideas and allows the work of Le Corbusier and Wright to be seen, in part, as a reaction to Howard. The latter approach is adopted, with Howard and Wright, considered as decentrists, followed by Le Corbusier as the classic centrist.

Decentrists in planning history

As we will see later, both Wright and Le Corbusier were presenting antidotes to the profoundly influential ideas of Ebenezer Howard: 'the most important single character in this entire tale' (Hall, 1988, p.87). Howard, a stenographer by trade, became an amateur social reformer, pondering the large social and economic issues of the 1880s and 1890s, but with a particular concern with the urban squalor created by rapid industrialisation. To him the cities were 'ulcers on the very face of our beautiful island' (Fishman, 1977, p.38).

Howard concluded that 'Radical hopes for a cooperative civilization could be fulfilled only in small communities embedded in a decentralized society' (Fishman, 1977, p.37). He acknowledged that the cities did have some attractive characteristics. Hence, Howard was looking for a marriage of the best of town and country. The famous three magnet diagram asked the question: 'the people: where will they go?'. The answer was to 'town-country', or the 'garden city'. Howard's garden cities would accommodate 32,000 people, at a density of approximately 25-30 people per acre; a density level that Fishman (1977, p.42) suggests might have been borrowed from Dr Richardson's 1876 plan for *Hygeia: A City of Health*, and Hall (1988, p.93) says was higher than that in the historical city of London. The 1898 version of Howard's book showed groups of garden cities, linked by railways, all forming a polycentric Social City (Hall, 1988, p.92). Residential areas, each built around a school, would be separated from industrial areas. The central area would have civic buildings, a park and an arcade or 'crystal palace' containing shops. The town would occupy 1,000 acres, surrounded by a 5,000 acre belt of agricultural land. This belt would provide the town with produce, but would also act as a green belt, preventing the town from spilling into adjacent countryside. Thus, despite Howard's view that 'every man, every woman, every child should have ample space in which to live, to move, and to develop' (Fishman, 1977, p.45), the solution is one of contained decentralisation. This point is important for present purposes. It places Howard at some considerable distance from the arch-decentrists.

Howard's legacy is well known. Letchworth and Welwyn Garden City became direct, practical, and ultimately very successful, applications of his ideas. Howard's Garden City Association established a forum for the promotion of garden city principles that continues through to the present in the form of the Town and Country Planning Association. The postwar new towns programme in Britain had a direct lineage back to Howard, as, arguably, did such programmes around the world. Even the burst of proposals for privately-funded new settlements in the UK in the 1980s (Breheny, Gent and Lock, 1993) can be claimed to have roots in Howard's modest book.

Powerful advocates of Howard's ideas carried the torch through a large part of the 20th century. Most notable amongst these were Lewis Mumford and Fredric Osborn, who were willing to take on all-comers in the long-running debate about appropriate urban forms. The mutual development of their ideas is revealed in their fascinating published letters (Hughes, 1971). Apart from an ongoing disagreement over housing densities - Osborn favoured marginally lower densities than Mumford - they consistently promoted moderate decentralisation, new towns, and urban regeneration, while opposing extreme centrist and decentrist views. In their respective countries they were very influential, but felt that they were generally fighting a losing battle.

To centrists at least, Ebenezer Howard and his followers represent one clear decentrist camp. However, Frank Lloyd Wright represents much more clearly the extreme case:

Wright wanted the whole United States to become a nation of individuals. His planned city, which he called 'Broadacres', took decentralization beyond the small community (Howard's ideal) to the individual family home. Wright believed that individuality must be founded on individual ownership. Decentralization would make it possible for everyone to live his chosen lifestyle on his own land. (Fishman, 1977, p.9)

Wright's advocacy stemmed from a mixture of ideology and simple acceptance of the inevitable. In the 1920s Wright saw that the motor car and electricity would loosen cities, enabling them to spread out into the countryside. Here was an opportunity to use new technology to take people back to the land, for them to reclaim their native birthright. For him the basic living unit was to be the homestead, with factories, schools and stores scattered across a fundamentally agricultural landscape. The new technologies would emancipate Americans from ties with the city: each citizen would have 'all forms of production, distribution, self-improvement, enjoyment within the radius of, say, ten to twenty miles of his own home' (Wright, 1945, quoted in Hall, 1988, p.288). Like Howard and Le Corbusier he hated the industrial city and industrial capital. But unlike Howard, who wanted cooperative socialism, and Le Corbusier who favoured centralised control, Wright - in the Jeffersonian, pioneer tradition - wished to free individuals to live and work in the countryside. As Hall (1988, p.287) says, Wright did not wish to marry town and country, he wished to merge them.

The Broadacres vision was not, however, meant to be a decentralised free-for-all. It was to be planned and it was to be controlled aesthetically. However, Wright was correct in anticipating the popularity of his decentralised vision; he was wrong in assuming that it would be planned. From the 1920s onwards a variety of forces combined to create massive suburbanisation, and later counter-urbanisation, in the United States.

An important thread in planning history that spans virtually the whole of the period reviewed to date is that of regional planning. In principle, the advocacy of regional scale planning implies neither a centrist nor decentrist stance. However, there is little doubt that ardent centrists have regarded the regional planning movement as decentrist in effect. This movement is usually traced from French 19th century geographers through Patrick Geddes and many subsequent proponents including Patrick Abercrombie, and Lewis Mumford and the Regional Planning Association of America. The consistent theme was the need to put any locality into a wider economic, social and physical context. This led to the idea of the civic or regional survey, and to planning at a city region scale. The grandest practical manifestations of these ideas were Thomas Adams' Regional Plan of New York of 1927-31 and Abercrombie's Greater London Plan of 1945. The overall drift of the regionalist argument was generally to accept the inevitability of centrifugal forces, and to plan for it accordingly. The centrist critics, however, most notably Jane Jacobs, have argued that one is either with them or against them. They have no truck with the middle ground. Thus, by virtue of accommodating, if not promoting, decentralisation, the regionalists would have been cast as confirmed decentrists.

Centrists in planning history
Le Corbusier, reviled in recent years as the inspiration for the disastrous high-

rise programmes of the 1960s, may be due for rehabilitation: as a champion of the centrists. Le Corbusier was very much a maverick, for his solution to the same - Victorian city - problem as perceived by Howard, Wright and many others was to increase rather than reduce urban densities: 'to decongest the centres of our cities by increasing their density' (Hall, 1988, p.207). High tower blocks would increase open space and improve circulation. This was all to be done by total clearance, the 'urban surgery' to which Jane Jacobs (1962) took such exception even before the idea was taken up with such vigour across the world in the 1960s. Le Corbusier's ideas were at their most advanced in La Ville Radieuse of 1935. This was a collectivist city, with everyone living in giant high-rise blocks, in apartments built according to rigid space norms. By this time, Le Corbusier was concerned not just with urban surgery, but also with new high-rise cities in open countryside.

Although Le Corbusier was singularly unsuccessful as a practising architect, his legacy of ideas had profound effects, most notably in the building of Chandigarh, and influencing the design of Brasilia, the new capitals of Punjab and Brazil. Hall (1988) charts the effects in Britain, both on theory and practice. In the postwar period, the students and staff of the Architectural Association in London took up Le Corbusier's ideas with what Osborn described to Mumford in 1952 as 'animal unreason' (Hughes, 1971, p.205). The consequence was a stream of proposals for high-rise blocks, many of which were implemented in the 1960s: the monuments 'from generations of AA graduates, were scattered across the face of urban England' (Hall, 1988, p.222).

But the centrist movement was wider still. One of its most vociferous advocates in the UK in the postwar period was Ian Nairn. Nairn, an architectural journalist, produced two influential special issues of *Architectural Review* in the 1950s, each of which railed against the 'creeping mildew' of urban sprawl. The first piece, *Outrage* (Nairn, 1955), issued a prophecy of doom:

> the prophecy that if what is called development is allowed to multiply at the present rate, then by the end of the century Britain will consist of isolated oases of preserved monuments in a desert of wire, concrete roads, cosy plots and bungalows. There will be no distinction between town and country. (1955, p.365)

Nairn's fear was of creeping suburbia, but also of the disappearance of the distinction between town and country as the new, crude suburban trappings - 'the excreta of suburbia' - were adopted everywhere. The planners were largely to blame for the promotion of 'subtopia' (suburb + utopia) because of their adherence to a policy of low density dispersal, on the grounds that 'England was of unlimited size' (p.367). He was concerned that subtopia would produce subtopians: people so inured to the new ways that they would lose all critical faculties.

The *Outrage* polemic was followed a year later by a second paper: *Counter-Attack Against Subtopia* (Nairn, 1956). This second paper in fact consists of a series of contributions, each offering ideas by which the 'outrage' of subtopia might be countered. Nairn himself offers an ABC of aesthetic control. A paper entitled *Oversprawl* by Elizabeth Denby was prescient in questioning the continuing validity of dispersal from the major cities and towns. Her exhortation might have come from a modern-day centrist: 'The time is ripe - over-ripe - for looking back into the towns and particularly into the old industrial areas, redeveloping according to human needs - that is, planning with, not for (or against!) the people' (Denby, 1956, p.427).

The 'looking back into the towns' philosophy was taken yet further by the *Architectural Review*, which published in 1971 a vision of the high density city - *Civilia* (de Wofle, 1971) - that would be the antidote to suburbia and to the advocates of planned decentralisation. The *Civilia* book despised the dominant decentrist stance, blamed largely on Mumford and Osborn, arguing in the most aggressive way that society has a natural centripetal tendency, which had been disturbed temporarily by the recoil from the Victorian city. Sudjic (1992) describes the proposal as the 'highest and the most absurd point of the campaign for congestion, an urban fantasy launched at a moment when all but the most myopic had realised that suburban life was an overwhelmingly popular choice for those who could afford it, and that every restriction on development outside the city simply raised the price of decent housing.' (p.12).

Despite Sudjic's criticisms, today's centrists might take a fruitful look at *Civilia*. The overall logic is very fashionable: deplore sprawl and the car, promote urban regeneration and high urban densities. Indeed, one of the features of the book is now a much vaunted solution: the 'multi-centred city', in which new, intensive transport and activity nodes are created within suburban areas. All of this is in *Civilia*. It is also contained in more extreme form in Dantzig and Saaty's (1973) proposal for a 'compact city', aimed at reducing urban sprawl and preserving open countryside. A quarter of a million people would live in a two mile wide, eight-level tapering cylinder. In a climate-controlled interior, travel distances between horizontal and vertical destinations would be very low, and energy consumption would be minimised. Steadman (1979), in a review of urban form and energy consumption, is sceptical about Dantzig and Saaty's claims about the energy efficiency of their proposal.

Perhaps the most articulate of the centrists during the 1960s was Jane Jacobs (1962). Whilst she can be placed fairly and squarely in the urbanist camp, her advocacy of centrism had very different and specific roots. Her enemies were the classic decentrists, such as Mumford and Howard. Howard started the rot, having 'set spinning powerful and city-destroying ideas' (p.18) in his advocacy of garden cities.

But her enemies also included the centrist urban surgeons, like Le Corbusier, who wanted a clean sweep in the cities. They were criticised for their crude physical solutions, and also for their egotistical authoritarianism. She wanted to retain the urban vitality and diversity that she found in her New York neighbourhood. She advocated high urban densities on the grounds that density creates diversity; and that diversity creates the richness of urban life that she enjoyed in New York. Her views did eventually prevail to some degree. The backlash that followed the wholesale urban renewal of the 1960s favoured physical rehabilitation and the retention of established communities. Sudjic (1992) suggests that Jacobs' view of urban life was coloured both by a neighbourhood - even if it was as cosy as she suggests, which he doubts - that was the exception not the rule, and by a mis-placed romanticism: 'Hudson Street was clearly never the soft focus idyll that Jacobs portrays.' (p.25).

The fundamental contradiction in Jacobs' work is that she failed to accept that big problems - the decline of cities and the dominance of urban sprawl - require big solutions. No amount of neighbourhood protection and promotion of diversity could reverse the decentralisation trends that she so despised. They might help, but no more.

Fishman (1977) concludes his elegant critique of Le Corbusier, Howard and Wright by arguing that by the 1970s planners had lost faith in the one thing that united all three: a belief that a solution to the urban problem can be found. Planners had become mere pragmatists, either no longer interested in 'big' ideas or convinced that the big idea is that there should be no such idea. Fishman's parting remarks, however, were prescient. He anticipated that energy crises and uncontrolled urban sprawl would eventually necessitate a return to serious, large scale planning; that the anti-planning strategies of Jacobs and others cannot be effective:

> The ideal cities of Howard, Wright and Le Corbusier have not been pushed aside by more up-to-date solutions. They have been superseded by the belief that no such 'solution' exists...There is now a widespread reaction against the idea of large-scale planning. Its most profound source, I believe, is the loss of confidence in the reality of a common good or purpose which can become the basis of city life. (1977, p.267)

Perhaps we have now found just such a common good: sustainable development! This constitutes a big problem, somewhat equivalent to the 19th century industrial city problem faced by the 'seers'. The big idea in response is the compact city.

The contemporary debate: urban compaction or decentralisation?
The contemporary debate on urban form was sparked off in the late 1980s as it became clear that planning, and hence urban form, would be central to the promotion of sustainable development. Suddenly, urban compaction became the order of the day. The decentrist view, having stolen the debate for so long, has now become distinctly unfashionable as the debate focuses on environmental sustainability. Nevertheless, there are bands of protagonists. At the risk of over-simplifying matters, these latter-day decentrists can be split into two groups:

- The 'free-marketeers', who claim that it is interference by planners in land markets that causes problems, and that market solutions will optimise urban forms.
- The 'good-lifers', who argue for a lifestyle that is decentralised, both geographically and institutionally, and a return to 'rural values'.

The centrists hold sway, however, in the current debate. The particular motives differ a little in different countries, but all are driven by the sustainability imperative. The two dominant motives are global warming, and hence the reduction of pollution, and the loss of open countryside to urban uses.

The logic behind the first motive is that stricter urban containment will reduce the need for travel - which is the fastest growing and least controlled contributor to global warming - by facilitating shorter journeys and inducing greater supply and use of public transport. Thus, the use of non-renewable fuels will be reduced along with harmful emissions. This argument reflects the weight given to concerns over global warming in the current passion for environmental sustainability; and, in turn, the concern over the growing contribution of transport to CO_2 and other pollutants. The second, but generally subsidiary, motive is that urban containment might deliver other environmental benefits, such as reductions in loss of open land and valuable habitats. Interestingly, another motive is the improved quality of urban life that would result from higher densities in cities. This particular concern is interesting because it is a centrist motive that is common to the current and earlier debates. Just as it was much disputed earlier, so it is now.

The centrist view is being promoted academically and politically. Because the focus of the debate is now on technical questions, rather than the less tangible focus of the historic discussions, much of the concern is to gather or challenge evidence. Opinion still matters, but the quest for hard evidence dominates.

Evidence on decentralisation

Much of the evidence adduced in this debate relates to the merits and demerits of compaction. Breheny (1995b), however, has argued that a fundamental set of prior questions has largely been ignored. These concern the degree to which urban decentralisation is continuing, and, if it is, the power of the trend. An understanding of the causes of decentralisation is crucial in any attempt to slow or halt it. Rapid urban decentralisation has been a feature of most Western countries from the second world war onwards, and earlier in the United States. The nature of this decentralisation has differed in different countries. In the United States, Canada, Japan and Australia it has tended to take the form of massive suburbanisation, creating at its extreme form The 100 Mile City (Sudjic, 1992). It is this massive sprawl that is now so reviled by centrist commentators in the US. In European countries, decentralisation has taken the form of suburbanisation of larger cities and towns, but also of growth of smaller towns and villages down the urban hierarchy: a process sometimes referred to as 'counter-urbanisation'. This discontinuous growth results in part from the existence of sacrosanct green belts around the larger cities.

Interestingly, census evidence across Europe for the 1980s shows that this process of decentralisation is no longer pervasive. It persists in some countries, but seems to have been countered by modest renewed urbanisation in others. This may be good news for the modern centrists. The evidence for the UK, however, suggests that the process of decentralisation continues. The absolute scale of change has slowed down, but the geography remains clear. An official urban typology is used in the UK to monitor change in the urban hierarchy. Fig. 1 shows percentage employment change for the period 1981-91 for each type. The logic could not be neater. The largest losses are in the older industrial cities, and the largest gains in the most rural categories. A similar, if slightly less clear, pattern is shown by population change. The centrist task in the UK, then, is to turn around this clear process of decentralisation. It seems like a tall order. This is particularly so when the powerful forces underlying the changing space economy are taken into account, and with a planning system that is often accused of being able to do little more than tinker with the market.

The neglect of these questions about decentralisation is rather surprising because there is a solid body of literature on decentralisation, or more particularly on the extreme version of counter-urbanisation (see for example, Cheshire and Hay, 1986, Champion; 1989). This literature, by and large, has not been related to the urban compaction literature.

Urban densities

In the absence of any great concern with the direction and strength of decentralisation, the quest for hard evidence in the compaction debate focuses on two issues: the effects of urban densities and urban size on travel, and hence on emissions. In other words, are there specific urban forms that will induce less travel? Or, given the strength of commitment to the idea, will the compact city induce less travel? If the evidence does show that higher densities and larger towns and cities do generate significantly less travel, then urban decentralisation is the villain, and compaction the solution.

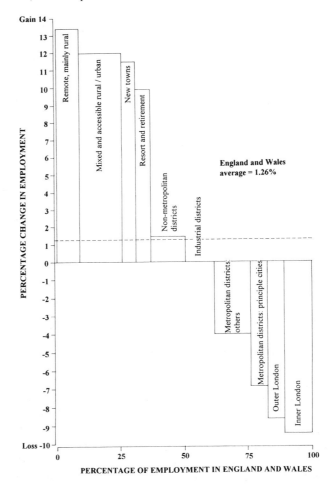

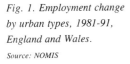

Fig. 1. Employment change by urban types, 1981-91, England and Wales.

Source: NOMIS

   Much of the technical case for compact cities has revolved around the supposedly lower levels of travel, and hence lower levels of fuel consumption and emissions, associated with high urban densities. Central to the debate has been the work of the Australian academics Newman and Kenworthy (1989a; 1989b; and Newman, 1992). For a number of large cities around the world, they have related petroleum consumption per capita to population density. They found a consistent pattern with higher densities being associated with lower fuel

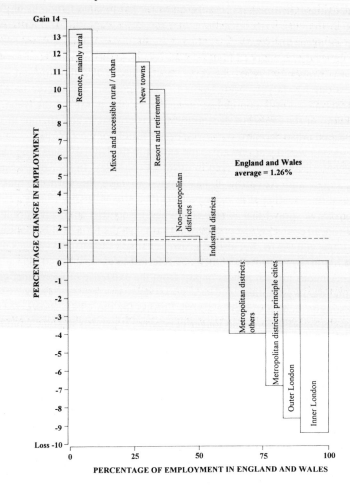

consumption. The cities with the lowest densities, and hence the highest consumption rates, were in the United States. European cities were relatively fuel-efficient, but Hong Kong, with very high densities and a large mass transit system, was by far the most efficient. The conclusion from the exercise was that, if fuel consumption and emissions are to be reduced, there is a need for policies to promote urban compaction and public transport. A similar message emerged from the ECOTEC (1993) study for the UK Government. This also produced evidence to suggest that higher densities are associated with less travel. Table 1 shows a neat inverse correlation between total distances travelled per week and population density. Car travel accounts largely for the differences. People living at the lowest densities travel twice as far by car each week as those living at the highest densities. Given the high political priority afforded to questions of global warming in the sustainability debate, and the knowledge that transport is the fastest growing contributor to CO_2 emissions, the Newman and Kenworthy and ECOTEC message has been accepted readily. Nevertheless, although accepted politically, the message remains controversial in the academic world.

Density (Persons per hectare)	All Modes	Car	Local Bus	Rail	Walk	Other
Under 1	206.3	159.3	5.2	8.9	4.0	28.8
1 - 4.99	190.5	146.7	7.7	9.1	4.9	21.9
5 - 14.99	176.2	131.7	8.6	12.3	4.3	18.2
15 - 29.99	152.6	105.4	9.6	10.2	6.6	20.6
30 - 49.99	143.2	100.4	9.9	10.8	6.4	15.5
50 and +	129.2	79.9	11.9	15.2	6.7	15.4
All Areas	159.6	113.8	9.3	11.3	5.9	19.1

Table 1. Density and distance travelled per person per week by mode (km): UK 1985/1986.
Source: ECOTEC (1993), Table 6

Data exclude trips less than 1.6km and only refer to the main mode used for a trip.

As might be expected, the strongest free-marketeers - and by obvious extension, decentrists - come from the United States. In the planning field, Gordon and Richardson and colleagues have been both the most active promoters of this line and the strongest critics of the now fashionable growth management and anti-sprawl campaigns in the US. Their contribution to the debate consists of both promoting the efficacy of markets generally (e.g. Richardson and Gordon, 1993) and a critique of the Newman and Kenworthy work (Gordon and Richardson, 1989), as described above. Obviously, they object to Newman and Kenworthy's reliance on intervention to resolve urban problems, preferring to leave the market to determine optimum solutions. The likelihood is, they argue, that market mechanisms will produce polycentric cities, with relatively low energy consumption and congestion. They are deeply sceptical about the prospects for massive public investment in transit systems, pointing to the immense subsidies required to support large scale systems around the world.

Gordon and Richardson also object to the Newman and Kenworthy work on empirical grounds. In the United States they have found that commuting distances have tended to remain stable or fall in recent years, despite continuing decentralisation. This arises, they argue, because of the co-relocation of people and jobs. Thus, most work - and now non-work - trips are from suburb to suburb (see also, Gordon, Kumar and Richardson, 1989; Gordon, Richardson and Jun, 1991; Bae, 1993). This observation is supported by Levinson and Kumar (1994), who find that travel times have remained stable, and attribute this to the 'rational locator'. In contrast, Spence and Frost (1995) have found that in the UK, despite changes in locations of both homes and workplaces, the characteristics of work travel seem enduring, but with average trips being longer.

The Newman and Kenworthy work has been criticised for focusing too heavily on the single variable of density, when other factors, some intertwined with density, are likely to be important in explaining travel behaviour. Gomez-Ibanez (1991), in a review of Newman and Kenworthy's (1989a) sourcebook, pursues this point. In particular he argues that household income and gasoline price are important determinants of such behaviour. Likewise, he points out that the relationship between income and density may make it difficult to identify clearly the link between density and gasoline consumption. This latter point has been made in a preliminary study of densities and modal split by Breheny (1995a). Gomez-Ibanez (1991) also makes a rare but fundamental point: the costs of radical containment policies - in terms of economic losses, reduced quality of life etc. - have not been weighed against the supposed environmental gains. For deep-green environmentalists these losses are acceptable by definition. But for most policy-makers a degree of balance - and hence an understanding of gains and losses - will be required. Hall (1991), who as Director of the Town and Country Planning Association represents an unbroken line of new town advocates stretching back to Howard, takes Newman and Kenworthy to task on a number of counts. He criticises their naive review of density issues, and argues that travel distances and modal splits are as much to do with urban structures as urban densities. He also regards their criticism of the 'Anglo-Saxon pastoral or anti-urban tradition' as being simplistic. He says that they fail to justify the claim that low density living dampens the 'higher aspects' of human communities. Most importantly, Hall argues that the authors - along with many others, one might add - do not appreciate that even with higher urban densities, a substantial proportion of future housing development will have to take place outside existing urban boundaries, a point stressed by Breheny, Gent and Lock (1993).

Newman and Kenworthy (1992) have responded to their critics by stressing the importance of the role of planning in addressing these issues. They make the point that land use planning - and hence a focus on densities - is likely to remain a major tool for reducing urban energy consumption because of governmental fear of economic measures, and particularly prices. This logic certainly applies in the UK, where there is a heavy focus on the planning system and a reluctance on the part of government to address pricing mechanisms (although the consumption tax on petroleum is set to rise each year at 5% above the rate of inflation). Indeed, the most direct policy initiative, *Planning Policy Guidance 13* (PPG13) on land use and transport, is aimed at reducing the *need* for travel. This acknowledges the fact that, without price rises, the propensity or 'inclination' to travel, as Owens (1995) puts it, will not reduce. Thus, there is in place one part of a two part policy: the need to travel will be reduced, but price mechanisms to reduce inclination are awaited. Newman and Kenworthy are rather dismissive of their opponents' empirical evidence, suggesting that a focus on just US cities can be misleading; 'heaven help us' they say if Los Angeles is held up as a model

(Newman and Kenworthy, 1992, p.360).

Herskowitz (1992) and Bourne (1992) have supported the Australians. The former suggests that, despite Gordon and Richardson's evidence, urban sprawl continues to aggravate transportation problems. Bourne is unwilling to allow market planning to determine the future form and health of cities. He suspects that the continued promotion of urban dispersal will contribute to 'the evolution of future urban forms that are increasingly inefficient and socially inequitable.' (Bourne, 1992, p.513).

Urban size

Relative to the debate on urban densities, the link between urban size and transport energy consumption has received little attention. The ECOTEC (1993) study mentioned above did address this issue. Using empirical evidence for the UK, it concluded that urban size is negatively correlated with transport energy consumption. The average weekly distance travelled per person in the UK rises down the urban hierarchy, with residents of the most rural areas travelling twice as far as those in the largest cities. Virtually all of the difference is accounted for by car travel. Although public transport usage accounts for a very small proportion of overall travel, the highest levels of patronage are in the most urban areas. This logic clearly supports a policy of urban compaction, because this would tend to halt or slow down urban decentralisation. In principle this process seems to be profoundly unsustainable, with people and jobs moving to areas where car-borne travel is necessarily high, and away from the places where such travel is lower and public transport provision is highest.

The obvious answer, in line with the views of Newman and Kenworthy (1989a), seems to be greater compaction, preventing development at the more profligate end of the urban hierarchy. However, Breheny (1995b) has tested this logic. He has tried to simulate the total transport energy consumption in Great Britain at 1991, given knowledge of population levels by urban type, average mileage per capita in each urban type, and consumption rates per kilometre. He then simulates the equivalent energy consumption as if no urban decentralisation had occurred for the 30 years from 1961; this being a crude equivalent to a draconian policy of allowing no further decentralisation over the next 30 years. The result is an energy saving per week nationally of 2.5%. This is hardly the scale of savings politicians are expecting when asking the planning system to take the lead in confronting the sustainability problem. Breheny (1995b) warns that the gains to be made from compaction policies may be trivial relative to the 'pain' - in terms, for example, of unpopular restrictions on movement - required to deliver such policies. Perhaps one problem in the whole debate is that politicians are reluctant to specify, and professionals and academics unwilling to predict, expected environmental gains from compaction policies.

Nevertheless, national governments around the world, and the European Union, are committed to policies of urban containment. The UK Government has promoted this approach in, for example, the *UK Strategy for Sustainable Development* (UK Government, 1994) and in PPG13 on transport (Department of the Environment and Department of Transport, 1994). The latter - drawing very much on the ECOTEC (1993) study - calls specifically for higher urban densities in general and for exceptionally high densities around public transport nodes. Amongst other policies, this radical document proposes the following under the heading of

'Planning for Less Travel':

Development plans should aim to reduce the need to travel, especially by car, by:

- influencing the location of different types of development relative to transport provision (and vice versa); and
- fostering forms of development which encourage walking, cycling and public transport use (para 1.7).

PPG13, which provides a series of detailed policies designed to induce less travel, is a radical document, and one which overturns much government thinking on planning and transport policy. The overall effect of the policies is to promote much stronger urban containment, to promote, in effect, the 'compact city'.

Other centrists adopt a broader advocacy of urban containment. They are conscious of the energy-saving possibilities of containment, but choose also to stress other potential merits. The Council for the Protection of Rural England (1992; 1993), for example, has reiterated a long-standing grievance: that planning policies are using up open land at an unacceptable rate. They argue that current plans for the accommodation of new housing development alone will lead to an environmental disaster. Consultants Llewelyn-Davies (1994) also argue that greater urban intensification is necessary to safeguard precious open countryside. They attempt to demonstrate how higher housing densities can be achieved without loss of quality of life. Interestingly, this report demonstrates that higher housing densities are very dependent on the degree to which off-street parking is provided on housing developments. In turn, the prospects of reducing off-street parking are dependent on the scope for on-street parking. In turn again, on-street parking is dependent on car ownership. The logic seems to suggest that high residential densities can only be achieved in poorer areas with low car ownership. An innocuous-sounding policy - higher densities - thus seems to have marked distributional effects. There may be a valuable warning here: that the effectiveness of grand urban sustainability strategies may rest or fall on the degree to which modest-sounding initiatives - densities, car parking standards, mixed uses - can be made to 'stick'.

The major practical focus for the urban form debate in Britain in the immediate future will be the accommodation of housing development. In recent years central government has required regional planners to plan for regional housing allocations as derived from government-produced household forecasts. This allocation process has been very controversial, particularly in pressured southern England, where there is great resistance to further development. To date, the Government view has prevailed despite confrontations with a number of county councils. All counties have been required to plan for the housing level allocated to them in regional planning guidance. In 1995, however, a new set of household forecasts (Department of the Environment, 1995) added nearly one million households to the previous forecast of 2.5 million additional households in England over the 1991-2011 period. The prospect of finding land to accommodate the implied extra houses fills local planners and politicians with dread. Environmentalists have argued that the household forecasts are too high and that, even if correct, they need not be converted directly into an additional housing demand. This view has to be countered, however, by the fact that over the last decade or so all official forecasts have tended to underestimate not overestimate household growth. The likelihood, then, is that the forecasts are realistic and additional housing provision has to be made (Breheny, 1995c).

The big question, of course, is where to put this additional housing. The environmentalist centrists (for example, the Council for the Protection of Rural England) will argue for urban infill and the protection of open countryside. A moderate decentrist line - from the Town and Country Planning Association, for example - will argue that new settlements should have a role. There is no obvious extreme decentrist view. The Government, sensitive to - or even frightened of - this issue is encouraging debate about household numbers and their physical accommodation. This issue is a real test of strength for the centrist and decentrist camps in Britain.

Urban compaction and the market

The question of the direction and strength of urban decentralisation, raised above, is but one example of the potential clash between planning policy and the market. In principle such clashes might arise in the case of both centrist and decentrist policies. In practice, given the general dominance of decentralisation trends, it is centrist policies that are most likely to go against the grain of the market, as Gordon and Richardson (1989) have argued in the United States. Little attempt has been made in the current urban form debate to gauge the degree of likely practical confrontation between policy and the market. Two studies that begin to approach the issue are those by Breheny, Gurney and Strike (1995) and Fulford (1995). The former study considers the problems of implementing PPG13 on land use and transport, from the perspective of both local authorities and the private sector.

In the case of the private sector, it is evident that there will be some resistance to policies that run counter to the logic of the property market. The chief fear is that sustainable development policies, as in PPG13, will not be sustained by governments. Thus, any concessions to PPG13 now might leave investors with 'inferior' property (with, say, low parking provision or mixed uses) when the policy regime relaxes in the future. The issue is not immediate for many property interests because of substantial pipelines of planning permissions granted before sustainable development was discovered. Interestingly, those property and business interests that have low stocks of permissions, such as retailers, have resisted changes in policy but have also adopted new coping strategies (such as new in-town 'metro-stores'). Fulford (1995) has interviewed house-building companies to gain their views on urban compaction policies. Surprisingly, given their record of preference for greenfield sites, he found these companies to be less antagonistic towards the prospect of operating on urban infill sites than might be expected. In contrast, Breheny, Gurney and Strike (1995) found office developers to be extremely wary of urban brownfield sites, to the point of avoiding them at all costs - unless, that is, some of those costs were to be heavily subsidised.

The free-marketeer group of decentrists will argue that resistance from the property market to policies that are against the market grain is inevitable. Indeed, they will argue that it is desirable. For them, the market is the best and most efficient device for resolving our urban problems. This group indirectly supports decentralisation by arguing for a relaxation of planning policy, which they say is to blame for high land and property prices. The case of Gordon and Richardson has already been explained. Less directly associated with the compaction debate is the camp represented by, for example, Evans (1991), Cheshire and Sheppard (1995), and Simmie (1993). They argue in favour of a relaxation of planning controls in order that land and property prices be reduced. As a straight economic case, this argument is disputed. As planning policy, it flies in the face of everything that the British planning system stands for. This system has, at its root, the assumption that the use and development of land should be controlled. The power of the state to do this since the 1947 Planning Act is a bedrock of the whole planning system, and one much copied around the world. Planners accept the effects on land and property prices, if true, to be a regrettable but acceptable consequence. The group of economists favouring relaxation of planning control for this reason, tend, in turn, to ignore both the benefits of the planning system and the effects of the decentralisation that would inevitably result from their proposals. Unlike their fellow free-marketeers Gordon and Richardson, they do not address these effects.

Quality of life

In addition to the search for hard empirical evidence to support their stance, modern day centrists are also trying to base their case on the superiority of high density urban living. It is crucial that they can demonstrate that higher densities are compatible with a high quality of urban life; and to demonstrate this to a public that is voting with its feet for low density, suburban or ex-urban lifestyles.

The resulting revival of interest in urban culture and quality of life has served to revive interest in Jane Jacobs. Her ideas now warrant particular attention because, despite her overly-romantic notions of the city, many of those ideas have come full circle. On a more prosaic level, as has been demonstrated, questions of urban residential densities are very much part of the current compaction debate (Breheny, 1995a). Likewise, mixed uses are suddenly fashionable. But there is also a new romanticism.

The European Commission (Commission of the European Communities, 1990) has attempted to argue that containment will deliver both environmental and quality of life benefits. This document has been treated with suspicion by a number of commentators, who find it difficult to reconcile the image of the Italian hill town that the authors clearly have in mind with the reality of inner or suburban areas of cities across Europe. The naivety of the report is also demonstrated when the contempt for suburban areas shown by the authors is compared to the inevitability - no matter how our cities are changed - that most urban dwellers will continue to live in such areas. Other commentators (Yanarella and Levine, 1992, for example) also see the Italian hill town as the ideal to which we might aspire as we focus on the compact city. The architect Richard Rogers in his 1995 Reith lectures has promoted the compact city, with the same 'pavement-cafe' view of urban life. Culture in cities, including the promotion of diversity (Parkinson and Bianchini, 1993; Montgomery, 1995), has become a serious policy issue. Sennett's (1970) desire that urban residents should feel 'uncomfortable' is now echoed in the idea that it is their 'edge' that makes cities exciting. It is a neat play on words that for many people it is the very existence of urban 'edge' that is driving them to 'edge cities' (Garreau, 1991).

The creation or re-creation of small, intimate neighbourhoods is also part of this renewed interest in community-level solutions. Proposals take the form of new urban villages or free-standing new settlements in the UK (Urban Villages Group, 1992; Breheny, Gent and Lock, 1993) or equivalent 'neo-traditionalist' developments in the United States. In the latter case, the movement has gained considerable momentum, under the 'new urbanism' label. The development of the small community of Seaside, Florida, designed by Duany and Plater-Zyberk, has created considerable interest (Mohney and Easterling, 1991), as have the ideas of Calthorpe (1993). He promotes both regional planning, to encompass problems of decaying cities and dispersed suburbs, and Transit-Oriented Development, along the lines advocated by the Dutch for some time. Bourne (1995) suggests that 'new urbanism' is as yet little more than a fad in North America, but that it does reflect a new twist to the contemporary planning debate.

Quality of life is the prime motivation for the second group of modern decentrists identified above - the good lifers. This group might in turn be split into two factions. There is the very rare, but rather exotic, anarchist tendency. In the UK a version of this view has been expressed over a long period by Colin Ward, who traces the lineage back to Kropotkin, to the early 'beards and sandals' residents at Letchworth, and to the residents of the inter-war plotlands scattered across the UK and in some cases still thriving (although sadly one of the more famous plotlands - Jaywick Sands in Essex - has recently suffered physical and social disintegration). Perhaps the 'new age travellers' represent a peripatetic version of this group.

The second, more mainstream group of good lifers (for example, Robertson, 1990; Green and Holliday, 1991; and Holliday, 1994) argue, against the grain, that the answer to our problems is decentralised living - geographically and institutionally - and a focus on 'rural values'. In this case, the argument is not for planned garden cities, but for geographically dispersed communities in which households have enough land to become near self-sufficient in crop production; this is a solution owing more to Wright than Kropotkin. It is now assumed that such decentralised living would supplement traditional rural values with the optimum use of telecommunications: the often discussed, but slow to emerge, 'electronic cottage' model of life. There is evidence of increased telecommuting, but the popular view that new technology will 'unglue' the cities is in dispute. Richardson, Gillespie and Cornford (1995), for example, suggest that the case is over-stated, while Handy and Mokhtarian (1995) find confusing evidence of the scale of telecommuting in the United States.

Conclusion: centrists, decentrists or compromisers?

There is, then, a long history of views on the appropriate form of urban development. Throughout the 20th century these views have tended to polarise between clear decentrist and centrist camps (see Table 2). From the turn of the century onwards, factions have tended to rally around, and elaborate on, the classic stances of Howard, Wright and Le Corbusier. A clear lineage can be traced for each of the camps through to the late 1960s and early 1970s. Big ideas, however, went out of favour at that time. Now that a big problem - sustainable development - and a big solution - the compact city - have emerged, the debate has been revived. The old factions have been re-formed and are presenting their cases with as much vigour as was the case sixty years ago. But does the answer have to lie at one extreme or the other? Will town and country only survive under a decentrist or centrist regime? Could they survive satisfactorily under a middle line, a compromise?

Compromise positions are never very fashionable. This may be why advocates of a position between the centrists and the decentrists have been slow to emerge. Nevertheless, this slowness is surprising, because it is clear that there are merits to be taken from each of the extreme positions and demerits to be discarded. The compromise position results not from any ideological stance, but from a realisation that - for anyone wishing to adopt a realistic stance - this mixture of merits and demerits precludes the unbridled advocacy of either of the extremes.

| | Centrists | | Decentrists | |
	Solution	Protagonist	Solution	Protagonist
1800			New Lanark	Robert Owen
1850			Saltaire	Titus Salt
			Bournville	George Cadbury
			Port Sunlight	William Lever
1900			Garden Cities movement	Ebenezer Howard
1935	La Villa Radieuse	Le Corbusier	Broadacres City: A new Community Plan	Frank Lloyd Wright
1955	Counter-attack against 'Subtopia'	Nairn	New Towns movement	Mumford, Osborn TCPA
1960	Urban Diversity	Jacobs, Sennett		
1970	Civilia	de Wofle		
1975	Compact city	Dantzig & Saaty		
1990	Compact city	National governments	Market solutions	Gordon & Richardson Evans, Cheshire, Simmie
		Newman & Kenworthy ECOTEC, CPRE, FOE	'Good life'	Robertson, Green & Holliday

Table 2. A selection of historical Centrist and Decentrist proposals.

The case against the centrists rests on four main points: first, the likelihood that it will not deliver the environmental benefits claimed; second, the probable impossibility of halting urban decentralisation, whether it is regarded as desirable or not; third, that some greenfield development is inevitable even with compaction policies; and fourth, that higher urban densities are unlikely to bring about the high quality of life that the centrists promise. On the first point, although some reduction in energy consumption might be expected from compaction, evidence presented above suggests that the gains will be very modest compared to the discomfort likely to be caused by the necessary draconian policies. As Breheny (1995b) puts it, the policies designed to reduce travel 'had better be worth it'. He concludes that they probably will not be worth it, demonstrating that only marginal savings in fuel consumption and hence emissions would result from such containment policies. On the second point, it is clear that urban decentralisation, in the UK at least, continues apace, despite a continuing planning regime of containment. During the period 1981-91 something like 1.2 million people moved to rural and semi-rural areas. Although this might not be a pure expression of locational preference, it obviously does reflect a major desire for lifestyles in such areas. It also implies that strict containment policies are likely to be very unpopular.

On point three, while the extreme centrist case argues that all future urban development should be contained within existing urban boundaries, the truth is that some greenfield development is inevitable. Breheny, Gent and Lock (1993), in reviewing alternative ways of accommodating development, conclude that unless much tougher containment policies are introduced - at the very time when concerns are being expressed over urban intensification - it is inevitable that significant greenfield development will take place in the UK. The third case against the centrists is that, arguably, urban quality of life will deteriorate with higher densities, not improve as they suggest. This case suggests that the majority of people, in the UK at least, gain satisfaction from living at moderately low densities. Resources permitting, they will choose to avoid the kinds of densities now being advocated by the centrists. Clearly, there are groups of people - of particular ages, occupations and levels of income - who may choose high density, urban living. Likewise, there are high density urban areas - usually historically and architecturally interesting and socially exclusive - that remain popular through time. However, these people and these areas are very much the exception. Many people who do live in high density urban areas, as in inner rings, are more likely to be trapped by virtue of employment opportunities and the availability of rented housing than they are to have made a conscious decision to live there. There is now a concern that in some urban areas, and most particularly in suburbs, a consequence of past containment policies has been 'town cramming'. This suggests that policies aimed at preventing development in the countryside have pushed pressures back on urban areas, resulting in the loss of urban green spaces, and increased congestion. Thus, the argument goes, protection of the countryside and the quality of life of rural dwellers has lowered the quality of life of urban dwellers.

The case against the extreme decentrists has been articulated - albeit to extremes - by the centrists. If the energy consumption argument does not stand - as Breheny (1995b) has suggested - then the land loss argument probably does stand. Although the CPRE (1992; 1993) has tended to exaggerate the annual loss of open land to development, the case is generally valid nevertheless. Although the dispersed electronic cottage model is different from the suburbanisation to which the centrists object, it is unlikely to be any more acceptable. Millions of people developing their one acre plots in the countryside is not an attractive proposition. Also, it is not at all clear that the full benefits of telecommunications - on which much of the modern decentrist case rests - will ever be available in every small town and hamlet. Another profound argument against the decentrists is the ongoing fear that continuing decentralisation will further sap the lifeblood of cities: the Jane Jacobs argument. There is abundant evidence that if planning policies allowed it, there would be greater decentralisation of business activity from our cities than is the case. A more relaxed attitude to decentralisation would hasten the demise of the cities.

Given the merits and demerits of the centrist and decentrist cases, a compromise position has many attractions. From the centrist case it can adopt continued, indeed tougher, containment, urban regeneration strategies, and a whole range of new intra-urban environmental initiatives. There will be environmental gains, but not at the expense of quality of life. From the decentrist case it can allow for the controlled direction of inevitable decentralisation - to suburbs and towns able to support a full range of facilities and public transport, and to sites that cause the least environmental damage. It takes account of the grain of the market, without being subservient to it. It might allow for some development in the form of environmentally-conscious new settlements.

This compromise position is rarely espoused in the current, compaction-dominated debate. However, there are a few adherents to this middle ground. This is the general line taken, for example, by the TCPA (Blowers, 1993) in their promotion of the 'sustainable social city' (Breheny and Rookwood, 1993), a label deliberately invoking memories of Ebenezer Howard. Indeed, rather than representing an extreme decentrist position, as portrayed by Jane Jacobs and others, Howard's views fall close to this compromise position. He did favour urban regeneration; he did favour protection of the countryside; he did favour containment; and he did want to marry the best of town and country. Hooper (1994) and Lock (1991; 1995) are other advocates of this position. Hooper reviews the extremes of the urban form debate and concludes, very unfashionably, that suburban development is much maligned. It has, he argues, played, and will yet play, a relatively successful role in our towns and cities. Lock rehearses the gains and losses from more intensive use of urban areas, and concludes that there is 'still nothing gained from overcrowding', a play on the title of a famous pamphlet by Raymond Unwin - Howard's architect at Letchworth - of 1912.

One of Hall's (1992) parting shots in his review of the 'seers' of planning history was that they tended to ignore the practicalities of the real world. The unwillingness of extreme advocates now - particularly the centrists - to see the modern day practicalities is evidence that we have come full circle. The desire for the big idea has returned. However, the world is now more complex and political than it was when Howard, Wright, and Le Corbusier were in full flow. Even if sustainability gives us a motive for the big idea, that idea necessarily has to be tempered by a dose of realism. The compromise line might seem like a little idea; perhaps properly packaged it could be big.

References

Bae, C-H. (1993) Air quality and travel behaviour - untying the knot. *Journal of the American Planning Association*, **59 (1)**, pp.65-74.

Blowers, A. (ed.) (1993) *Planning for a Sustainable Environment*, Earthscan, London.

Bourne, L. (1992) Self-fulfilling prophecies? decentralization, inner city decline, and the quality of urban life. *Journal of the American Planning Association*, **58 (4)**, pp.509-13.

Bourne, L. (1995) *Reinventing the Suburbs: Old Myths and New Realities*, paper presented to the annual conference of the Institute of British Geographers, Newcastle-Upon-Tyne, UK.

Breheny, M. (1995a) *Urban Densities and Sustainable Development*, paper presented to the annual conference of the Institute of British Geographers, Newcastle-Upon-Tyne, England, January.

Breheny, M. (1995b) Compact cities and transport energy consumption. *Transactions of the Institute of British Geographers NS*, **20 (1)**, pp.81-101.

Breheny, M. (1995c) The housing numbers game - again. *Town and Country Planning*, **64 (7)**, pp.170-72.

Breheny, M., Gent, T. and Lock, D. (1993) *Alternative Development Patterns: New Settlements*, HMSO, London.

Breheny, M., Gurney, A. and Strike, J. (1995) This Volume, pp323-338.

Breheny, M. and Rookwood, R. (1993) Planning the sustainable city region, in *Planning for a Sustainable Environment* (ed. Blowers, A.) Earthscan, London.

Calthorpe, P. (1993) *The Next American Metropolis: Ecology, Community, and the American Dream*, Princeton Architectural Press, New York.

Champion, A. (1989) Counterurbanization in Britain. *Geographical Journal*, **155 (1)**, pp.52-9.

Cheshire, P. and Hay, D. (1986) The development of the European urban system, in *The Future of the Metropolis* (ed. H-J. Ewers) Walter de Gruyer and Co., Berlin, pp.120-41.Commission of the European Communities (1990) *Green Paper on the Urban Environment*, European Commission, Brussels.

Cheshire, P. and Sheppard, S. (1995) On the price of land and the value of amenities. *Economica*, **62 (246)**, pp.247-67.

Council for the Protection of Rural England (1992) *The Lost Land*, Council for the Protection of Rural England, London.

Council for the Protection of Rural England (1993) *The Regional Lost Land*, Council for the Protection of Rural England, London.

Dantzig, G. and Saaty, T. (1973) *Compact City: A Plan for a Liveable Urban Environment*, Freeman, San Francisco.

Denby, E. (1956) Oversprawl, in *Counter-Attack Against Subtopia* (ed. I. Nairn) The Architectural Press, London, pp.427-34.

Department of the Environment (1994) *PPG13 Transport*, HMSO, London.

Department of the Environment (1995) Projections of Households in England to 2016, HMSO, London.

de Wofle, I. (ed.) (1971) *Civilia: The End of Suburban Man - A Challenge to Semidetesia*, The Architectural Press, London.

ECOTEC (1993) *Reducing Transport Emissions Through Planning*, HMSO, London.

Evans, A. (1991) Rabbit hutches on postage stamps. *Urban Studies*, **28 (6)**, pp.853-70.

Fishman, R. (1977) *Urban Utopias in the Twentieth Century: Ebenezer Howard, Frank Lloyd Wright, and Le Corbusier*, Basic Books, New York.

Fulford, C. (1995) This volume, pp.131-43.

Garreau, J. (1991) *Edge City: Life on the New Frontier*, Doubleday, New York.

Gomez-Ibanez, J. (1991) A global view of automobile dependence - review of Newman, P. and Kenworthy, J. *Cities and Automobile Dependence: A Sourcebook. Journal of the American Planning Association*, **57 (3)**, pp.376-79.

Gordon, P. and Richardson, H. (1989) Gasoline consumption and cities - a reply. *Journal of the American Planning Association*, **55 (3)**, pp.342-5.

Gordon, P., Kumar, A. and Richardson, H. (1989) Congestion, changing metropolitan structure, and city size in the United States. *International Regional Science Review*, **12 (1)**, pp.45-6.

Gordon, P., Richardson, H. and Jun, M. (1991) The commuting paradox - evidence from the top twenty. *Journal of the American Planning Association*, **57 (4)**, pp.416-20.

Green, R. and Holliday, J. (1991) *Country Planning - A Time For Action*, Town and Country Planning Association, London.

Hall, D. (1991) Altogether misguided and dangerous - a review of Newman and Kenworthy (1989). *Town and Country Planning*, **60 (11/12)**, pp.350-51.

Hall, P. (1988) *Cities of Tomorrow*, Basil Blackwell, Oxford.

Hall, P. (1992) *Urban and Regional Planning*, Third Edition, Routledge, London.

Handy, S. and Mokhtarian, P. (1995) Planning for telecommuting: measurement and policy issues. *Journal of the American Planning Association*, **61 (1)**, pp.99-111.

Herskowitz, D. (1992) Letter to the editor: the commuting paradox - a reply. *Journal of the American Planning Association*, **58 (2)**, p.244.

Holliday, J. (1994) The new urban realm. *Town and Country Planning*, **63 (10)**, pp.259-61.

Hooper, A. (1994) Land availability and the suburban option. *Town and Country Planning*, **63 (9)**, pp.239-42.

Hughes, M. (ed.) (1971) *The Letters of Lewis Mumford and Frederic J. Osborn: A Transatlantic Dialogue*, Adams and Dart, Bath.

Jacobs, J. (1962) *The Death and Life of Great American Cities*, Jonathan Cape, London.

Levinson, D. and Kumar, A. (1994) The rational locator: why travel times have remained stable. *Journal of the American Planning Association*, **70 (3)**, pp.319-32.

Llewelyn-Davies (1994) *Providing More Homes in Urban Areas*, SAUS Publications, University of Bristol, Bristol.

Lock, D. (1991) Still nothing gained by overcrowding. *Town and Country Planning*, **60 (11/12)**, pp.337-39.

Lock, D. (1995) Room for more within city limits? *Town and Country Planning*, **64 (7)**, pp.173-76.

Mohney, D. and Easterling, K. (1991) *Seaside: Making a Town in America*, Princeton Architectural Press, New York.

Montgomery, J. (1995) Urban vitality and the culture of cities. *Planning Practice and Research*, **10 (2)**, pp.101-09.

Nairn, I. (1955) *Outrage*, The Architectural Press, London.

Nairn, I. (1956) *Counter-Attack Against Subtopia*, The Architectural Press, London.

Newman, P. (1992) The compact city - an Australian perspective. *Built Environment,* **18 (4)**, pp.285-300.

Newman, P. and Kenworthy, J. (1989a) *Cities and Automobile Dependence: A Sourcebook*, Gower, Aldershot and Brookfield, Victoria.

Newman, P. and Kenworthy, J. (1989b) Gasoline consumption and cities - a comparison of US cities with a global survey. *Journal of the American Planning Association,* **55 (1)**, pp.24-37.

Newman, P. and Kenworthy, J. (1992) Is there a role for physical planners? *Journal of the American Planning Association,* **58 (3)**, pp.353-62.

Owens, S. (1995) Transport, land-use planning and climate change: what prospects for new policies in the UK? *Journal of Transport Geography*, **3 (2)**, pp.143-

45.

Parkinson, M. and Bianchini, F. (eds) (1993) *Cultural Policy and Urban Regeneration*, Manchester University Press, Manchester.

Richardson, H. and Gordon, P. (1993) Market planning: oxymoron or common sense? *Journal of the American Planning Association*, **59 (3)**, pp.347-52.

Richardson, R., Gillespie, A. and Cornford, J. (1995) Low marks for rural home work, *Town and Country Planning*, **64 (3)**, pp.82-84.

Robertson, J. (1990) Alternative futures for cities, in *The Living City: Towards a Sustainable Future* (eds D. Cadman and G. Payne), Routledge, London.

Sennett, R. (1970) *The Uses of Disorder: Personal Identity and City Life*, Alfred A. Knopf, New York.

Simmie, J. (1993) *Planning at the Crossroads*, University College Press, London.

Spence, N. and Frost, M. (1995) Work travel responses to changing workplaces and changing residences, in *Cities in Competition: The Emergence of Productive and Sustainable Cities for the 21st Century* (eds J. Brotchie, M. Batty, P. Hall and P. Newton) Longman Cheshire, Melbourne, pp.359-81.

Steadman, P. (1979) Energy and patterns of land use, in *Energy Conservation Through Building Design* (ed. D. Watson) McGraw-Hill, New York, pp.245-60.

Sudjic, D. (1992) *The 100 Mile City*, Andre Deutsch, London.

UK Government (1994) *Sustainable Development: The UK Strategy*, Cmnd 2426, HMSO, London.

Urban Villages Group (1992) *Urban Villages*, Urban Villages Group, London.

Yanarella, E. and Levine, R. (1992) The sustainable cities manifesto: pretext, text and post-text. *Built Environment*, **18 (4)**, pp.301-13.

World Commission on Environment and Development (1987) *Our Common Future*, Oxford University Press, Oxford.

Mayer Hillman
In Favour of the Compact City

Introduction

The growing geographical spread of patterns of activity this century, accelerating at an alarming rate in the last few decades, reflects both the effects of the wider ownership of motor vehicles and planning changes interacting with this. It reflects too public perceptions of accessible catchments: within the time people are prepared to devote to travel, those with their own form of motorised transport have been able to choose more distant locations than was previously possible when choice was limited to non-motorised modes, in combination with public transport. And commerce and industry have been able to increase the size of their individual outlets whilst reducing their number, in order to achieve internal economies of scale and, in the process, extending not only their own patterns of transport activity areally but also those of their customers.

Most of these newly adopted patterns, particularly in suburban, urban fringe and rural locations, are car- and lorry-dependent, and cannot realistically be served by bus or rail. They are largely antithetical to such concepts as self-sufficiency and containment, energy efficiency and community enterprise. Indeed, it is almost as if there has been a conspiracy to curtail options for making the transition to sustainable activity patterns and lifestyles.

Half a century ago in the UK, passenger mileage by bus was twice that by car, whereas now passenger mileage by car is 14 times that by bus. Cycle mileage, which exceeded car mileage then, is now exceeded by it, by a factor of 75. And though there is no record of changes in the extent of mileage on foot during this same period, over the last 20 years alone, it has fallen from 40% to 30% of all journeys. Furthermore the transport sector currently accounts for a third of all primary energy consumption, and this figure is rising at an alarming rate.

Damaging outcomes

The rise in car ownership and use, steady decline in walking and cycling, and poorer public transport services have led to a worsening of the situation in respect of most of the economic, social and environmental measures that could be used to monitor progress in this domain of public policy. In appraisals of public policy, the adverse effects are only partially appreciated because many of them are not susceptible to valuation in monetary terms and have not therefore featured prominently. These adverse effects manifest themselves in crucial areas affecting the quality of life:

- The difficulty that people without a car - the majority of the population - have in meeting daily needs which are dependent on non-motorised and public forms of transport.
- Congestion spreading to more roads, and for longer periods of the day, with attendant waste of travel time and resources.
- The fear and anxiety generated by the growing volume and speed of traffic, owing to the perceived risk of death and injury in traffic accidents; then requiring the exercise of ever greater vigilance by pedestrians, and deterring would-be cyclists from taking to the road.
- The intimidating and severance effects of traffic on community life, limiting the former range of functions of the street to only that of acting as a channel for motor vehicles.
- The dispersal of an increasing proportion of activity beyond the confines of the local neighbourhood.
- The spread of noise from all traffic sources - road, rail and air.
- Exposure to air pollution, contributing to ill-health, especially respiratory diseases.
- Disincentives to cycling and walking, which, if they form a major part of the routine of getting about in daily life, are the most effective ways for the majority of the population to keep fit.

Social polarisation has tended to increase, with the more vulnerable members of society worse affected. This is true by income, as poorer people are less likely to be able to afford to own and run a car, and public transport fares have risen more sharply than have the costs of car use. In addition, poorer people are likely to live in the least desirable neighbourhoods: in outer suburbs, on heavily trafficked roads, and in inner urban areas subject to road building or road widening. Polarisation can also be seen in terms of gender. For instance, women, especially those who are more elderly, are less inclined to go out after dark. Not surprisingly, pavements become increasingly denuded of the pedestrians who might provide the reassurance of 'safety in numbers'.

Social polarisation by age is also apparent. A particularly effective litmus test that can be employed to illustrate this is to consider the impact on children of the growing motorisation of modern society. Most live in car-owning households and have been able to benefit from their parents' access, compared to that of previous generations, to a greater spread of opportunities, such as choice of schools, extra-curricular activity and leisure activities. However, parents feel obliged to restrict their children's independence because of growing concerns about risks outside the home, and the greater distances that have to be covered to school and leisure destinations which used to be more local. Children's lives are becoming increasingly conducted under adult surveillance, which may have disturbing effects on their physical, social and emotional development - as well as imposing a time-consuming burden on the lives of the parents, usually mothers, who see the escorting of their able-bodied children as an unavoidable element of child-rearing for many years.

An explanation for these outcomes

How can these highly unsatisfactory consequences, which run so counter to furthering the objectives of a civilised society, be accounted for, apparently with the tacit acceptance of the great majority of the population? There appear to be four crucial reasons.

The first is that it is now judged perfectly reasonable to reach decisions about where to travel and what mode to use entirely from a self-interest perspective, and without any regard for the effects on the quality of other people's lives, on community health or on the physical environment. The public interest is not taken into account as a moderating element - indeed it has been fading fast in recent decades.

The source of the problem is that, whilst the adverse effects of any one of these decisions are only marginal, there are now 30 million licence-holders in this country, on average driving 30 kilometres a day. Marginal effects? Moreover, a fallacious judgement is made that the car has just been replacing journeys previously made by other means, overlooking the fact that car ownership alters perceptions of accessible geographical catchments of possible activity, which consequently leads to journeys over longer distances which perhaps can only be made by car.

The second reason is that, in spite of the obvious benefits of encouraging as many journeys as possible to be made on foot or cycle, these modes are treated as peripheral to transport policy. How else can one explain Ministers of Transport in recent years repeatedly referring to a spurious statistic that 90% of journeys are made by car. It is clear that, because non-motorised journeys tend to be short, they are considered unimportant.

Allied to this error of judgement is the exaggeration of the role of public transport as the way out of the impasse created by the growth of car dependence. This overlooks the fact that, for instance in the last 20 years, for every passenger mile lost to public transport, 18 more have been made by car; and in the last 10 years, 28 more. In other words, most current car mileage was not previously made by public transport. The error then results in chasing an ephemeral objective in the belief that the situation can be reversed by sufficiently high investment in public transport: calls are made from many quarters for high investment in rail to provide a substitute for the car, although rail accounts for less than two per cent of all journeys.

The third reason is the gross inappropriateness of indicators used to measure success in this domain - rising car ownership, lengthening motorway mileage, reduced road deaths (as if that can be interpreted as stemming from safer roads), a flourishing vehicle manufacturing industry, more holidays taken in distant locations, and perhaps most damagingly, GDP as the measure of prosperity.

The public has been persuaded that governments can build their way out of the difficulties and crises induced by the growing demand for travelling further and faster by motorised means. It is assumed that transport investment should be largely directed to meeting that objective rather than that of promoting shorter and more local travel. It is only recently that the belief that constructing more motorways and by-passes, when the national economy can afford them, has been recognised as mistaken - perhaps informed by the simple yet critical calculation by John Adams that the increase in traffic forecast by the Department of Transport for the year 2025 would require construction of the equivalent of over 250 lanes of motorway from London to Edinburgh - simply to accommodate it parked nose to tail!

The fourth reason, allied to the first, is that motorists, and to a large extent non-motorists, seem unaware both of the extent of damage from the growing motorisation of our lives, and of the overwhelming benefits of reversing this process rather than just slowing it down. They are persuaded in the main that more traffic reflects a vigorous economy and social progress. Moreover, contrary to the evidence, episodes of high air pollution and, associated with these, increases in consultations with doctors, hospital attendance, and death, are not seen to be the consequences of their own decisions. Instead, insofar as the general public is aware of the contribution it is making to ill-health and damage to the environment, it takes comfort from the fact that the government does not appear to view the situation with any real degree of alarm, and that the palliative steps it is taking are an adequate and sufficient response to ensure that matters do not get out of hand.

It is seen to be the responsibility of central and local government to control and regulate planning change in the light of the transport implications of different residential densities and scales and locations of new developments. With the connivance of government, the public has been able to shield itself from any serious questioning of the efficacy of car-dependent lifestyles. The benefits of many of the measures adopted to offset some of the adverse effects of these lifestyles in terms of the damage per unit of transport activity have been overtaken by the costs from the larger number of units: overall, social and environmental damage have continued to rise.

As part of this public mind-set, the evidence on the unsustainability of our lifestyles is largely disregarded. High levels of consumption of finite energy resources - and the production of greenhouse gas emissions - lie at the heart of the problem. Cheap fuel, and the absence of policies appropriate to minimising the environmental harm that its consumption causes, have led to more sprawl, greater distances between the origin and destinations of journeys, more traffic and associated environmental degradation and despoliation, ever-increasing demand for investment in the transport infrastructure, rising migration from inner city to suburban and rural locations, a general loss of community feeling and, with it, more crime and social alienation.

Justification for the compact city

As if this litany was insufficient grounds for advocating the promotion of forms of settlement with the least need for energy-intensive patterns of activity, the issue of global warming now represents the ultimate justification for it; it is an imperative over-arching all aspects of policy on sustainable futures. Concern about global warming was highlighted by the Inter-Governmental Panel on Climate Change (IPCC) in 1990, 1992, and again in 1995. The consensus of its climate scientists' Working Group is that a reduction of carbon emissions of between 60% and 80% is essential if the risk of serious and possibly catastrophic ecological damage to the planet is to be avoided in the next century.

What the Working Group did not say is that such a scale of reduction will clearly have to vary according to a principle other than one of average. People in the Third World contribute far less, as their consumption of resources in any lifetime is often only a fraction of that in the affluent West. On a per capita basis - and there are neither moral grounds for, nor political prospect of, obtaining international agreement on any other basis - the UK will have to cut its emissions by well over 90%. And even this may prove insufficient in the face of the considerable future increase in world population in developing countries, which are in the process of industrialising their economies in ways that require intensive use of fossil fuels and therefore intensive output of greenhouse gas emissions.

It is salutary to note that primary energy consumption in the rapidly developing economies of China, India and Indonesia has increased by 60% in the last ten years alone. Nor can we be certain that no countries will renege on undertakings given following any international agreement to limit emissions.

Implications for politicians

How have governments around the world responded to the problem of climate change? Some have taken it more seriously than others. Most appear to believe or hope that it will require no more than some belt-tightening. Others cling to the view that the climate scientists could prove to be wrong and that we will be able to proceed along the *gradus ad parnassum* towards an ever-expanding economy and hedonistic lifestyle which have become the prime goals of their policies, irrespective of the evidence of their unsustainability, let alone their damaging effects. When pressed to admit that time may be up, politicians have shielded themselves behind a claim that the necessary resolute action cannot be imposed on an unwilling public which is not yet prepared to alter its lifestyle. Their instincts are not to take too seriously evidence which has longer term implications, such as the substantial increase in the number of households in recent years, which is forecast to rise even more in the next 20 years (without that being accounted for by a rise in population), in light of the energy inefficiency of small households per capita. We can carry on, it is implied, oblivious of the increasingly likely fact that we no longer have a choice if climate change is to be averted.

An allied problem for politicians is that success has to be achieved in the face of another target, namely economic growth. Given the fairly close link between this growth and fossil fuel use, the per capita reduction in carbon emissions seems even more implausible. In view of their time horizons, politicians prefer to subscribe to the view that economic growth and consumerism in the forms which we have witnessed over many decades are the primary route to improving public welfare, and to protecting the environment, and are compatible with responsible stewardship of the planet; it is easier for them to maintain this fiction in the short term as they cannot afford to see their responsibilities extending to consideration of the effects of their decisions in the longer term.

For fear of alienating the public by starting to take the radical measures implicit in meeting the IPCC target, European governments have sought to show their common resolve by undertaking to contain carbon dioxide emissions at 1990 levels by the end of the decade - a 0% response to the over 90% one called for! In the UK, this target looks likely to be easily achieved owing to the switching of fuels from coal to gas for electricity generation, the reduction in fuel needed by industry - as more activity has transferred from manufacturing to the service sector - and the effects of the economic recession of the last seven years, rather than from improvements in the efficiency with which fuels are used, for instance by getting more miles from a gallon of petrol.

If European governments imagine that the current world recession, as measured by the conventional indicator of GNP, is alarming, they need to prepare themselves for a far more catastrophic outcome. When the penny drops, the sound will be deafening. It is clear that changes entailing substantial rather than modest alterations to our current lifestyles, for example those dependent on car and air travel, heating poorly insulated homes and offices, and on short-life and energy-inefficient consumer so-called durables, are called for; they have only been able to be adopted because the ecological implications have been largely ignored. It is perhaps unsurprising, but no less disturbing, that these governments have fought shy of facing the public with the facts, owing to their aversion to proposing political change which interferes with the way we conduct ourselves at present.

Implications for individual lifestyles

How are the lifestyle changes to be effected in a democratic society, given that governments look increasingly likely to have to take action which does not necessarily command broad public support? Rising affluence which has generated more leisure time and surplus money has fuelled an acquisitive society. People have been encouraged to subscribe to the cosy view - and act on it - that an assured route to improving the quality of life is to raise material standards by discarding the old and buying the new.

Any massive reduction in our individual greenhouse gas emissions will require dramatic changes which can only be made with an exceptional environmental education and public information programme if government *diktat* will not have to prevail over the democratic decision-making process, particularly as failure could result in future generations being left with a legacy of climate change on an appalling scale.

What does the reduction of over 90% in these emissions referred to earlier mean for the typical UK household when related to its current annual average carbon dioxide emissions of about 27 tonnes? Clearly, the household 'ration' of about 2.5 tonnes will only stretch to the most essential of energy-intensive activities. At present, the share of the average household for electricity generation alone is 10.8 tonnes; for industry, it is 5.7 tonnes; for transport, mainly car use, it is 4.3 tonnes; and for domestic uses, mainly heating, it is 3.4 tonnes. To live within the budget will require extremely well-insulated and energy-efficient homes, little, if any, commuting by car, in all likelihood no travel by air, and the purchase and use of commodities which are very frugal in the consumption of energy, both in manufacture and in use, unless its source is non-renewable.

The changes needed to reduce emissions are, fortuitously, required for a variety of other reasons: lowering our consumption of fossil fuels will improve the quality of life. The reductions will bring in their wake sustainable lifestyles, with much less transport expenditure, lower heating and lighting costs, more self-reliance, less pollution, more community activity, much less motorised travel and far more cycling and walking, and thereby better health and increased longevity.

Implications for planners

Anyone given the task of formulating a rational policy for the fabric, pattern of settlement, and movement systems of our towns and cities - against the background of the ecological imperative noted above, as well as the need to further economic, social, health and local environmental objectives - would certainly recognise the desirability of promoting industrial and commercial practices and the adoption of personal lifestyles conducive to a rapid and marked decline in the use of fossil fuels, in whatever areas that is possible. Herein lies the virtue of the compact city, the characteristics of which are associated with lower energy inputs for transport and heating purposes in particular.

There can be little doubt that making our cities more sustainable in the future requires a holistic approach to reducing demand for space and water heating, power and lighting and use of motorised transport, and increasing self-sufficiency in lifestyle practices. What is exciting is that there is a common thread within many of the elements of that approach. These elements include:

- Settlement patterns and housing forms with low energy requirements; a diversity of land uses, and housing densities and layouts which allow for economy in the provision of shared heating and waste disposal services.
- Planning control, which has as one of its primary functions an assessment of the implications of any development from the perspective of energy consumption.
- Public facilities and adequate open space at a scale and location which reduce the need for motorised travel (fuel consumption is three times as high in the lowest as compared with the highest density areas, partly owing to their different socio-economic circumstances but also because consumption per car is over 50% higher).
- Transport strategies which give priority to walking and cycling and then, and only then, promote public transport use, which entail lower speeds and stricter standards on noise and pollution, and which recognise that streets also have a function as a focus for social life.

The elements of this approach have to cover improved access to facilities used in daily life, more flexible use of buildings, more recycling, and more use of land for growing food. These elements can be more easily met in the compact city. In a greenfield location, it is relatively easy to design, as indeed was proposed by the author of this paper nearly 40 years ago, inspired by the early conviction that the quality of urban life would be enhanced if the need for motor travel could be minimised. That logically pointed to a linear form, with high density areas of residential population, space-extensive land uses located beyond these areas, mixed land uses, a pedestrian-oriented movement system within walking distance of its axes, along which are located public and commercial facilities, and which carry the public transport system. Regrettably, it failed to recognise the role of the bicycle!

Such a model contains within it the elements that can be applied to restructuring existing cities along similar lines and with similar objectives, in terms of thrift in the consumption of fossil fuels by its inhabitants and the associated benefits of optimal use of human resources, nurturing community values, conviviality, and the quality of life generally.

Conclusions

Our actions can demean or enhance the lives of others and the state of the world. We delude ourselves that, in a world finite in the context of its capacity to soak up greenhouse gas emissions, let alone to provide limitless resources, the aggregation of individual preferences leads to an optimal outcome: the reality in such a world is that if some people have more than their fair share, others must inevitably have less. The issue of climate change is an ecological imperative which could be described as the most critical challenge facing all the professions whose work affects the energy characteristics of urban settlements.

Most of us like to believe that we care about the future. Consider then being accountable to our grandchildren for our actions - or inaction. The history of this century, and the accumulating evidence of the early effects of climate change and its tragic ecological consequences, would make the response 'We did not know what was happening' wholly inadmissible. We must now set about drastically lowering our material standards of living in order to be able to pass over the planet to them in at least as wholesome a state as we had it passed on to us. The compact city is one way of responding to the challenge of 'thinking globally and acting locally'!

References

Texts used in the preparation of this chapter:

British Petroleum Company (1995) *BP Statistical Review of World Energy 1995,* BP, London.

Elkin, T., McLaren, D. and Hillman, M. (1991) *Reviving the City: Towards Sustainable Urban Development,* Friends of the Earth with The Policy Studies Institute, London.

Elkins, P., Hillman, M. and Hutchison, R. (1992) *Wealth Beyond Measure: An Atlas of New Economics,* Gaia Books Ltd, London.

Harman, R. and Hillman, M. (1983) Getting about locally, in *Decision-Making in Britain: Transport,* The Open University Press, Milton Keynes.

Hillman, M. (1957) Project for a linear new town. *Architects' Journal,* 4 April; *Community Planning Review,* **Vol.VII, No.3,** September, pp.136-140 Community Planning Associations of Canada.

Hillman, M. (1970) *Mobility in New Towns,* PhD Dissertation, University of Edinburgh.

Hillman, M. (1984) *Conservation's Contribution to UK Self Sufficiency,* Heinemann Educational Books, London.

Hillman, M. (1992) *The Incompatibility of Growth in the Transport Sector and Environmentally-Sustainable Futures,* The Cambridge Econometrics Annual Conference on Transport, Communications and the 21st Century, Fitzwilliam College, Cambridge.

Hillman, M. (1992) Cities, transport and the health of the citizen. *Environment, Traffic and Urban Planning,* European Academy of the Urban Environment, Berlin.

Hillman, M. (1992) *Cycling: Towards Health and Safety,* a report from the British Medical Association, Oxford University Press, Oxford.

Hillman, M. (1993) Social goals for transport policy, in *Health and Wellbeing: A Reader,* Macmillan, in association with The Open University, London.

Hillman, M. (ed.) (1993) *Children, Transport and the Quality of Life,* Policy

Studies Institute, London.

Hillman, M. (1994) Curbing car use: the dangers of exaggerating the future role of public transport. *Transportation Planning Systems,* **Vol. 2** No.4, pp.21-30.

Hillman, M. (in press) *Environmental Perspectives and the Quality of Life, 1995-2010, United Kingdom,* A report for the European Foundation for the Improvement of Working and Living Conditions.

Hillman, M. and Bollard, A. (1985) *Less Fuel, More Jobs: The Promotion of Energy Conservation in Buildings,* Policy Studies Institute, London.

Hillman, M. and Potter, C. (1978) Movement systems in British new towns, in *International Urban Growth Policies: New Town Contribution* (G. Golany ed) John Wiley and sons, USA.

Hillman, M. and Whalley, A. (1983) *Energy and Personal Travel: Obstacles to Conservation,* Policy Studies Institute, London.

Joint Memorandum by Political and Economic Planning and the Council for Protection of Rural England (CPRE) to House of Commons Select Committee Inquiry on Energy Conservation, First Report on Science and Technology, Session 1974-75, May 1975, HMSO, 1975.

Hugh Stretton
Density, Efficiency and Equality in Australian Cities

Introduction
The safety, equity and environmental effects of Australia's urban transport need to be improved. Should we do that directly by reforming the transport, or indirectly by rebuilding the cities more compactly?

People who want to reduce the demand for powered transport indirectly, by rebuilding the cities in more compact form, argue from comparisons which have been researched most extensively by Peter Newman and his colleagues at Murdoch University (Newman, 1992). Australian cities average about a quarter of the population density of European cities, and per head of population they have:

- about twice the kilometres of private motoring
- about four times the length of roads
- three quarters of the public transport route length, but only half the passenger kilometres, and much less than half the number of passenger journeys
- about a quarter as many journeys on foot or by bike.

Altogether we make 12% of our recorded urban journeys by foot, bike and public transport, where the European figure is 46%.

Those figures are generally taken to indicate that our system is comparatively expensive and inefficient. But one implication of the figures suggests that the Australian arrangements may be more efficient than the European: we enjoy four times the urban space per head, with only 18% more travel time and 64% more travel mileage than the Europeans. A relatively small increase of travel time and distance thus buys a fourfold increase of space. Some of that is road and parking space, but most of it is private house and garden space, school playgrounds, public parks and playing fields, golf courses, tennis courts and other recreational spaces. So if the space is worth having, we get it at much lower travel time and infrastructure cost per hectare than Europeans pay for their urban space.

Nevertheless our own sprawling Australian cities are accused of being environmentally unsustainable, economically inefficient, inequitable, and unsociable. We can unpack these charges in turn.

Environment

About 10% of Australia's energy use fuels urban car travel. If we could halve that, and consequently have to fuel some more public transport, we might save 3% of national energy use. We could save a little more than that by contriving for all our private motoring in town and country the average 30% improvement of fuel efficiency that is now technically feasible (Rooney, 1993).

Further gains are possible by limiting the size and power of vehicles. If we reformed the cars and converted the cities to European density we might save 6 or 7% of total energy use. But less than half of that would come from the higher density, and some of that gain would be reduced by the energy cost of rebuilding the cities and of servicing high buildings, and the environmental cost of losing some home production of fruit and vegetables and flowers. There is also some evidence that people with gardens care more for the natural environment than flat-dwellers do, and bring up children with more concern for it.

There is thus a modest gain in sustainability to be won by reducing the private motoring use of fuel. But increasing residential density may not be the best way, or even a possible way, to do it.

Economy

The claim that Australian cities are less economically efficient than denser cities relies on childish accounting tricks. The Australian Government and most economists make housing and urban infrastructure look unproductive by refusing to notice their products. First, public infrastructure is part of the capital which every private producer and every household uses - but neither public nor private accounts ever say so. One result is that all accounts of the productivity and rates of return to private capital overstate the private and understate the public capital contribution to private output. Second, household capital - house, equipment, garden, car - is the capital for more than a third of the national output of material goods and services. Properly estimated, that capital averages about the same productivity as our public and private sector capital does. But our authorities do not measure its output, do not know how the output varies with the amount or distribution of the capital employed, do not include it in their accounts of national product, and do not compare it with the household output of other countries. They do not compare what a densely housed English family can produce for themselves in a tower flat over a vandalised car park with what they can, and do, produce for themselves as emigrants to a house and garden in an Australian suburb.

Castles doubted the OECD story that the Japanese are now richer than Australians, he used available household expenditure and time use surveys to arrive at comparisons of productivity and material standards of living in Australian and Japanese cities (Castles, 1992). Tokyo has about five times the population density of Sydney. How productive are Japanese and Australian workers, and what will their wages buy? Australians have always been and still are more productive per hour. (The higher Japanese money income per head of population comes from working longer hours and supporting fewer dependents.) What will the money incomes buy? Castles compares the wage price of a Sydney basket and a Tokyo basket of household necessities, mostly food. To earn the price of a year's supply of what Australians consider basic, Tokyo residents would have to work two and a half times the hours Sydney residents do: 600 hours in Tokyo, 245 in Sydney, at 1987 wages and prices. To earn the price of what Japanese households consider basic, the difference is predictably less - but not much less: people in Tokyo must still work twice the hours that Sydneysiders would have to work to buy that Japanese basket of goods at their local prices. For other goods the differences are less, but still significant and all in Sydney's favour. Very roughly speaking, an hour's work in Sydney buys about one and a half times the market goods that an hour's work in Tokyo buys. So much for the belief that more compact cities necessarily promise more efficient production of market goods.

Castles next compares the private and public space and facilities with which people can produce non-market goods and services for themselves and each other with their unpaid labour, and can occupy their time interestingly and enjoyably. A majority of Japanese share the Australian preference for a separate house and garden. But in cities, fewer achieve it, and those who do have smaller houses on smaller allotments pay much more for them. 74% of Sydney households have some sort of house and garden, compared with 35% of Tokyo households. New Sydney dwellings of all types average more than twice the floor area of new Tokyo dwellings, and those with their own allotments average more than four times the lot size. But on average, Tokyo's accommodation is more expensive than Sydney's.

What can people do for themselves away from home, in a non-market way, in their cities' public spaces and facilities? Per million of population, Sydney has 2040 public recreational sites. Tokyo has 260. The Sydney sites average more than two hectares; the Tokyo sites average less than one. Sydney has 10 times the playing fields and 19 times the tennis courts.

In debates about the future direction of Japan's development, economists as diverse as Lester Thurow in the US, Kyoko Sheridan in Australia, and in Japan a number of officers of the MITI (the Ministry of International Trade and Industry, chief planner of Japan's 'economic miracle') are arguing that the next challenge for Japan is to equip its households and neighbourhoods with Western standards of amenity and productivity: Tokyo should copy Sydney, rather than Sydney copy Tokyo. MITI's skills might achieve that with less loss of public transport than the West.

A final economic argument alleges that Australia can no longer afford to build new suburbs. Compare the $40,000 - $70,000 it is said to cost to service each new suburban allotment, with the negligible cost of connecting a new house to the under-used services of the existing city; multiply the difference by the number of additional households to be housed in the coming decades; and it is plain that we can not afford it.

I do not know how this argument has escaped the derision it deserves. If you want to compare the likely alternative costs of suburban extension and compact rebuilding you must compare the cost of new suburban services with the cost of connecting not one but some hundreds of thousands of new customers to the old urban services. That will require the reconstructing and expanding of some of them through built-up areas, which is more expensive than installing them on greenfield sites. Any substantial increase of density will require some demolition and replacement as well as infilling, and the replacement costs should be brought to account. So should the loss of quality or quantity of some existing services, if a serious increase of numbers is going to compete for space in the existing recreational spaces and asphalt yards of the old inner city schools. Then, having arrived at an honest estimate of costs, our capacity to pay should be investigated. Our grandparents, with less than half our present productivity, enabled the Australian working class to afford and acquire their first suburban houses and gardens. Now more than twice as productive, we can perfectly well afford to continue meeting the market demand for standard housing, and to supply it with standard services.

Prevailing theories also tell us that reducing investment in housing and its infrastructure will increase other investment and employment. Opposite effects are actually more likely. A sensible public investment program, sensibly financed, could contribute usefully to private employment and growth. In almost all developed economies through the last half-century the rate of economic growth has varied *with* the proportion of national income invested in housing, not inversely to it.

Altogether, market productivity, household productivity, and urban adaptability to changing industrial and household needs seem to do well at Australian urban densities. But can the same be said of social equity, or the culture and lifestyles that the cities allow?

Equity

Judgements about equity do of course vary between people with differing values; and the urban issues to be judged are complex. In the argument about density I do not think either side has a knock-down case on equitable grounds.

In European cities that are governed and serviced in a European social democratic way, most residents have good physical access to whatever the city has room for. Compared with Australian conditions, many more working, shopping, educational, service and recreational journeys can be made on foot, bike or public transport by the quarter or so of households and the half or so of the population who have no cars of their own. Their access is also cheaper than car-borne access. So for many poorer people, access to the city's attractions is both physically and financially easier than it is for many poor Australians. Ease of exit from the city is more variable. Australia has a lot of suburbs with bush or beach boundaries, but also a lot without, and a lot of those without have no ready access to bush or beach by public transport. Exit is often easier in Europe with shorter distances, better public transport and many smaller cities. But there, exit may need to be more frequent: Europeans have to leave town to reach some recreations that Australian cities have room for in town. Quite a high proportion of Australian households, including some of the poorest, have cars, and access to a wider variety of in-town open-air recreations than urban Europeans or Japanese have. Perhaps a heroic simplification would allow that dense cities can offer their poor better access, but to a narrower range of facilities, while Australian cities offer a wider variety of facilities, but worse access to some of them for people without cars.

The best of the European cities offer some of their citizens a marvellously interesting, attractive and sociable urban life. Australia has a few fashionable patches of that. But there is overwhelming evidence that Australian majorities, through most stages of life, want public and private space more than they want that dense urbanity. And Australia and New Zealand distribute that space more equally than any other country does. That is doubly equitable. It is good that most households, if they want to, can have the space to share the country's most preferred lifestyle. And in equipping people to do a good deal for themselves, house and garden forms can have special importance for households with low incomes. If you are poor and car-less in an upstairs flat in a neighbourhood without much open space - and especially if you are a child, or bringing up children - you can do a good deal less for yourself than you can do with a house and garden and shed in a suburb, with the parks and playgrounds and school grounds that Australian densities allow. Finally, if governments do succeed in imposing some higher density on Australian cities, there is not much doubt that the rich and middle classes will hang onto their houses and gardens, and it will mostly be the poorest households who lose their private space.

Community

As a fourth objection to suburban life, do the private garden, the private car and the longer travel distances isolate people in an unsociable lifestyle - watching TV, motoring to visit a few friends and relations - while more civilised Europeans and Japanese commune with more acquaintances and strangers in more crowded neighbourhoods and public spaces?

Not altogether. People watch more TV the *less* private indoor and outdoor space they have. Australians eat and drink away from home more than ever before. They join with others in more sporting and recreational activities than do the Japanese, and perhaps Europeans. Ian Halkett's studies, twenty years ago, of the extent to which public space and facilities could replace private house and garden space, found that in many respects the two were not alternatives but complements: people with most resources at home went out and made most use of public and convivial resources away from home (Halkett, 1976).

Now, in the 1990s, research of unprecedented scale, skill and sophistication is being done on the material living conditions of urban Australians, and their reasons for residential preferences and choices (Stevens and Hassan, 1990; Stevens, Baum and Hassan, 1991; McDonald, 1993; Travers and Richardson, 1993). These investigators find what Halkett found. As expected, people's experience and preferences vary with their tastes and circumstances. But a large majority of households are happy with where they live and how they live there, and specifically prefer their suburban houses and locations to denser housing forms or inner city locations. Most of them have quite a strong sense of neighbourhood and neighbourliness, and value it. Scarcely any would be helped, and a great many would lose conditions which they value highly, and use fruitfully, if they had to leave their suburban houses for inner city apartment life. Most of them could have chosen that alternative if they had wanted to.

There remain two terminal arguments - in both senses of the word - about the compact city project. First, its proponents rarely get their sums right. With economic growth and rising income, people buy themselves more space per head. Most inner suburban replacements in Australian cities replace houses, which averaged five residents and a car, with a few rows of houses or flats which average less than two people and more than one car. And with rising income, people demand and get more shopping, services, parking and recreational space in their neighbourhoods. Only where non-residential land is converted to housing is there any overall increase of population density. There is no close relationship between the density of bricks and mortar and cars, and the density of people.

Second, none of the relevant politicians intend to apply any of the coercion that would be necessary to achieve enough consolidation to have significant effects on transport costs and emissions. They will not ration new urban land. They will not compulsorily acquire occupied houses or their back yards for denser development. They will not ration internal space, as has sometimes been done in wartime, by requiring small households with big houses to take boarders or get out. They will sell some surplus schools for housing, but not the playgrounds of continuing schools, and not many public parks or playing fields. The only people they are likely to coerce are some public housing tenants.

Alternatives

The politicians must know by now that they cannot consolidate the cities by permissive or persuasive means, and they dare not coerce them. So the cities are plainly going to continue their general character and mode of growth. I do not think that is extravagant, stupid, culturally bad or economically unproductive. But its present costs in fuel consumption, pollution and road accident and injury are high and ought to be reduced. If we had the will to tame and cleanse our urban transport, what might we do?

- We could shape planning and transport policies to further improve the district re-centering of employment, shopping, services and recreations that are already in progress.
- We could improve footpath and cycle routes through many old suburbs, and plan better ones through new developments.
- We could increase taxation to finance large losses, for a time, to provide good public transport throughout the metropolis, capable of accepting a coerced shift from private transport.
- To force that shift we would have to ration car fuel or mileage, or both. The means of rationing are unpleasant, unpopular and imperfect, but they are well tried and reasonably effective. With some further cost and irritation the rations can be roughly adjusted to household and business needs.
- Finally we could reform the vehicles. If a 30% improvement in fuel efficiency is available, we could insist on as much of it as saves fuel without increasing pollutant emissions.

For most of these purposes, rationing is more equitable and effective than taxing and pricing policies.

Fantasy

A bolder strategy offering economic as well as environmental gains might combine good, temporarily subsidised public transport, with a radical plan for the automotive industry, as follows.

Over a ten year period ask the car-makers, or as many as wish to stay under the forthcoming conditions, to produce, with public financial and research support, a range of super-virtuous vehicles: from motor-assisted pedal cycles and lightweight low-powered motorbikes through electric runabouts to minimum-functional cars (like underpowered Mini Minors and Morris 1100s), with state-of-the-art fuel economy and emission-cleansing; design electric cars around a standard range of slide-in, slide-out batteries; equip service stations with one-minute battery exchange gear and recharging units. The new vehicles can be as cheaply or expensively furnished as the market demands, but they must be low-powered and long-lasting. In a staged program over the same period close the frontier to imports which do not meet the same virtuous requirements.

What might we have at the end of the transition, when the last old V8 gas-guzzler is in the museum, and the good public transport is carrying the numbers to pay its way? At worst, we would have a safer, greener, fairly unpopular passenger and light goods transport system, with some better transport than before for people without cars, and some improvements in our employment and exchange figures. At best, our car-makers might be inventive pioneers of virtuous vehicles at a time when the world is driven to follow our example: and because their vehicles would, by then, be cheap and durable, they might find big export markets in Asia and elsewhere.

I know all too well how absurdly improbable this fantasy is, and how little chance anything like it has of being adopted by our prevailing economic rationalists, tax-cutting politicians, or business leaders in their tax-evasive six litre Mercedes and Jaguar V12s. But that fantasy would actually leave us with perfectly liveable, loveable and efficient cities, more helpful to many of their poorer people than the present cities are. I know this from family life in pre-war Melbourne, when most of the passenger transport was public; and from family life in postwar Britain when most people's cars, though far from fuel-efficient, were about as small and slow and tame as virtuous, state-of-the-art, minimum functional cars could be now. We need designers like Issigonis again, who start from the dimensions of a man's body rather than his ego.

Second, Australians would rather lose their cars than lose their cars *and* their houses. However hard it may be to get them to trade their big cars for little ones and rationed mileage, or to give them up altogether, it would be harder still to get them to do it by first giving up their houses and gardens and neighbourhood parks and playing fields. I think they are right, for social and economic reasons, and also for environmental reasons. Suburban life without private cars can be quite tolerable, and without cars it promises better environmental performance than dense cities can.

This is not an excuse for doing nothing. A radical transformation of our wasteful, pollutant and accident-prone urban transport is something I believe we owe to our Australian successors and to the world at large in its task of global environmental reform.

Summary

If we and our political leaders genuinely wish to reform Australia's urban transport for local or global reasons, (1) we should reform the transport system directly, not indirectly by offering tax and price inducements, or by trying to rebuild cities compactly; (2) it needs more radical, inventive and unpopular action than we have yet considered; but (3) we should realise that reforming our transport system itself nevertheless offers the least-cost, least inequitable, and even the least unpopular way, in our Australian conditions, of significantly reducing transport harm.

By permission of *Australian Planner* this paper is drawn from a longer article called *Transport and the Structure of Australian Cities.*

References

Castles, I. (1992) Living standards in Sydney and Japanese cities - a comparison, in *The Australian Economy in the Japanese Mirror* (K. Sheriden ed.) University of Queensland Press.

Halkett, I. (1976) *The Quarter Acre Block*, Canberra AIUS, and unpublished studies of the uses of public and private space in 'medium dense' housing.

McDonald, P. (ed.) (1993) *The Australian Living Standards Study, Berwick Report, Part 1: The Household Survey*, revised edition, Australian Institute of Family Studies, Melbourne.

Newman, P. (1992) The compact city: an Australian perspective. *Built Environment,* **18**, pp.285-300.

Rooney, A. (1993) *Urban Transport and Urban Form: Planning for the 21st Century*, IIR Conference Paper, 22 March 1993.

Sheridan, K. (1993) *Governing the Japanese Economy*, Polity Press, Cambridge.

Stevens, C. and Hassan, R. (1990) *Housing and Location Preferences and the Quality of Life in Community Environments*, Flinders University, Adelaide.

Stevens, C., Baum, S. and Hassan, R. (1991) *Housing and Location Preferences Survey, Stage 2 - A Report*, Flinders University, Adelaide.

Thurow, L. (1993) *Head to Head,* Nicholas Brealey, London.

Travers, P. and Richardson, S. (1993) *Living Decently*, Oxford University Press, Melbourne.

Louise Thomas and Will Cousins

The Compact City: *A Successful, Desirable and Achievable Urban Form?*

Introduction

The debate on the ability of different forms of urban development to provide more practical and 'better' environments has a long history. From the earliest strategies for the colonisation of land for human habitation, to today's research-led and policy-driven statements on environmentally conscious activity, a wealth of material has been written propounding the benefits (and disbenefits) of various settlement forms.

The current debate in Britain, which addresses the imperative of 'sustainable development', is in many ways the late twentieth century's contribution to this on-going debate. 'Sustainable development' has become most popularly understood from its definition in the report by the Brundtland Commission as 'development which meets the needs of the present without compromising the ability of future generations to meet their own needs and aspirations' (World Commission on Environment and Development, 1987, p.47). While this definition successfully captures the essence of sustainable action, it is increasingly quoted as inferring a concept called 'sustainability' as a durable condition without any further consideration. The important aspect of this aim should be that our action in living today must continue to be relevant and workable in the future - embodying ideals and aspirations that our grandchildren's children will be happy to inherit, and that does not consume irreplaceable assets. It is important therefore to understand sustainability as action which balances the present with the future, but also with the past: 'soundly based so that it can last' (DoE, 1990, p.1).

Seen from this perspective, the search for the 'ideal' land use planning pattern which is to satisfy specific social, economic, and environmental criteria is at risk of simplifying a complex and continually unfolding topic. Therefore discussions which focus only on the 'compact city' can only represent just one facet of the debate as it stands today.

53

The compact city

What is this 'compact city'? Initial impressions evoke an intense medieval city, whose limits are clearly visible, and where the hubbub of daily activity is confined within the city's walls (Fig. 1). It is the product of a certain form, scale, and mix of activities.

Fig. 1. An image of a compact city?

Source: Girouard, M. (1985) Cities and People, p.36

Few of the supporters of the compact city describe it in ways which are explicit. McLaren (1992) in *Compact or dispersed? dilution is no solution* discusses the benefits of high population densities in compact cities. Elkin *et al.* (1991) promote the 'intensification of the use of space in the city' (p.16) with higher residential densities and centralisation, and they write that 'planners should aim for compactness and integration of land uses, for some degree of "self-containment"' (p.43). Newman and Kenworthy (1989) also demand more intensive land use, centralised activity and higher densities. Breheny (in Blowers, 1993) provides an apt summary of the 'compact city' as a high density, mixed use city, where growth is encouraged within the boundaries of existing urban areas, but with no development beyond its periphery.

Several authors describe the 'compact city' in contrast to other competing settlement patterns. Owens and Rickaby (in Breheny, 1992a) describe two key patterns: centralisation and decentralised concentration. Breheny (1992a) distinguishes between centralists, *laissez-faire* town crammers, and decentralists. Breheny *et al.* (DoE, 1993a) describe five scenarios for accommodating growth: urban infill, urban extensions, key villages, multiple village extensions, and new settlements. With 'urban infill' there is the further distinction between urban intensification (higher density land use), and the reclamation of brownfield sites (Aldous, 1992; Llewelyn-Davies, 1994). The illustration in Fig. 2 gives an indication of the form of each of these patterns.

For Breheny the case for the compact city as the solution to settlement ills and environmental imperatives is most clearly, provocatively and significantly articulated in The Commission of the European Communities *Green Paper on the Urban Environment* (CEC, 1990). 'Its advocacy of the compact city rests not just on strictly environmental criteria of energy consumption and emissions, but also on *quality of life* grounds' (Breheny, 1992b, p.139). The aim is to 'avoid escaping the problems of the city, by extending its periphery; [to] solve its problems within existing boundaries' (CEC, 1990, p.45).

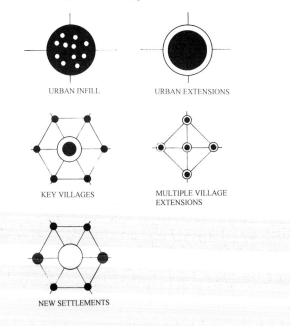

URBAN INFILL

URBAN EXTENSIONS

KEY VILLAGES

MULTIPLE VILLAGE
EXTENSIONS

NEW SETTLEMENTS

Fig. 2. Five development growth scenarios.

Source: David Lock Associates

Barton *et al.* (1995) have described the case for or against the compact city as being fought between the supporters of the CEC and the Town and Country Planning Association, who invoke the high-rise horrors of postwar urban Britain and the congested squalor of Victorian Britain, in doubting the attractions of the compact city (Blowers, 1993). Within this chapter it is not our intention to present a review of research data currently available, against which it might be possible to 'measure' the compact city, so that we could present an unbiased view of its merits. The intention instead is to provide an overview, highlighting circumstances which question the compact city as a desirable target for planners, designers and politicians with green interests.

There are arguably many ways of teasing apart the issues inherent in the compact city debate. Using economic and environmental criteria, as well as social and political reactions to sustainable development ideas, it is possible to assess the compact city. This is done with reference to economic trends, resource efficiency, and its popularity among the people and politicians who we would expect to support and to live in it.

The most obvious issues that future urban development forms will need to address are (in no particular order): accommodating growth, energy consumption, accessibility, economic viability, ecological integration and protection, political achievability, popular aspirations of quality of life and the burden of proof of success.

The reputation of the compact city is already widespread and its benefits are cited as: less car dependency, low emissions, reduced energy consumption, better public transportation services, increased overall accessibility, the re-use of infrastructure and previously developed land, the rejuvenation of existing urban areas and urban vitality, a high quality of life, the preservation of green space, and a *milieu* for enhanced business and trading activities (CEC, 1990; Elkin *et al.*, 1991; Engwicht, 1992; Jacobs, 1961; McLaren, 1992; Newman in Breheny, 1992b; Newman and Kenworthy, 1989; Owens and Rickaby in Breheny, 1992a; Sherlock, 1991).

However, there is evidence which suggests that these claims are at the very least romantic and dangerous, and do not reflect the hard reality of economic demands, environmental sustainability and social expectations. The overriding problem with the compact city is that it requires us to ignore the causes and effects of decentralisation, and the benefits that it might bring.

Economic demands
Employment
Fothergill *et al.* (1983) in their review of *Changes in Industrial Floorspace and Employment in Cities, Towns and Rural Areas* note that while industry was shifting from premises in cities to smaller towns or rural locations, the demand for net floorspace increased. Greater sophistication and size of machinery meant that job densities decreased, which resulted in demand for floorspace which is far less 'peopled' and on a far greater scale than before, and furthermore not commonly found within cities. More recent work by Debenham Tewson and Chinnocks (1987) charts the subsequent slight drop in industrial activity between 1974 and 1985, and the simultaneous boom in demand for warehousing, office accommodation, and retail and leisure floorspace. The scale of industrial units diminished, but new office, retail and leisure units and warehouses were far larger.

Prism Research (DoE, 1993b) found that in the case of business relocation to and from South East England, the two principle factors for movement were a complete change of premises, or the consolidation of business activities. New accommodation was in 'what were perceived as high quality amenity environments' (p.17) within two hours' travel of airports in the West, North and South West. The motivation to relocate was to escape city congestion, reduce overheads and to gain space, in addition to improving surroundings, access, and the company image. The availability of space, the lower costs of employing staff and operations, and technological advances meant that the move out of the South East or more urbanised areas was both feasible and desirable.

Advancements in telecommunications technology imply a reduced importance of physical proximity for many forms of employment. While Owens and Cope (1992) forecast that teleworking is unlikely to grow into a significant employment land use and travel factor, it cannot be denied that the telephone and fax machine have reduced the need to concentrate and centralise business communities in a more traditional manner.

The trends for larger building footprints (the ubiquitous 'shed') have not diminished significantly since these surveys were undertaken, nor has the demand for peripheral sites. The existence of the distribution industry can be witnessed on any day of the week on Britain's roads, together with the proliferation of distribution parks, within maximum EC regulation drive-times from European seaports, across the South and the Midlands. It is significant that of all employers, the distribution industry will continue to have specific location demands for efficient operations.

Factors other than the need for space, ease of distribution, and competitive operating costs may be equally influential in affecting the decentralisation of employment space. Garreau offers us a simple law of the American experience of 'Edge City', 'Whenever a company moves its headquarters, the commute of the chief executive officer always becomes shorter' (1991, p.92). Whyte (1988) concludes that this distance is typically about eight miles. This indicates two important elements in the location of new employment premises - proximity to an appropriate (suburban) workforce, and the search for the kind of unstressful environments which will attract and retain the best employees. The Royal Society of Arts' (1995) profile of 'tomorrow's companies' suggests that this quality of life will become an increasingly important factor in the future.

A glance at any town or city today will also reveal the arrival of the superstore on our townscape. While debates rage over the negative effects of the out-of-town supermarket, the success story of 'Britain's £1 billion-a-week food retailing industry' continues (Katz, 1993). The might and popularity of these commercial giants is currently too great for the compact city to cast them into exile for some time yet.

If as Sudjic writes 'work, in the widest sense, is what shapes the city' (1992, p.122), is there any correlation between the needs and demands of employers and the compact city?

Environmental expectations

Sustainability requires two key actions: resource conservation, and pollution reduction. This refers to energy efficient travel and buildings, and natural habitat preservation.

Travel

The main advantage cited of the compact centralised city, in the sustainability stakes, is its ability to reduce car dependency and fuel use, through its compactness and centre-to-periphery public transport corridors. In their research into the relationship between gasoline consumption and density in cities, Newman and Kenworthy (1989) state that the higher density traditional city is often more fuel efficient than its low density rivals. The four critical factors that act upon car dependence, and hence petrol consumption, are density, centrality, road supply, and car parking provision.

However, McLaren concedes that a large centralised city can often result in greater traffic congestion, and fuel efficiency is greatly reduced through increased travel times and slower traffic speeds. Bendixson and Platt's work on Milton Keynes states that 'the absence of congestion led to vehicle speeds that gave, per mile, high fuel-efficiency and low exhaust emissions, while the city's dispersed land-use pattern... kept down the length of trips' (1992, p.166). McLaren quotes Bozeat *et al.* who write that 'the congestion issue makes it clear that the success... in reducing emissions will depend on how far action is taken to enhance the attractiveness of public transport' (1992, p.272).

In their attack on Newman and Kenworthy's research, Gordon and Richardson (1989) dispute many of the research findings, particularly the effectiveness of a radial rail-based transport system. Increasingly complex suburb-to-suburb travel patterns, the number of trips made which are less than five miles (approximately 75% of all car trips), together with increased non-work related travel (77% of car journeys) render the traditional commute to work in the city centre almost irrelevant (Cervero, 1991; Owens and Rickaby in Breheny, 1992a; Pharoah, 1992). Breheny *et al.* conclude that 'the evidence in favour of the "centralised" city option is not clear cut' (DoE, 1993a, p.34).

Building stock

> Energy efficiency is to be promoted in a number of ways, including planning
> and site design, building design, efficient appliances, a range of energy
> management services... (Owens, 1986, p.100).

In *Energy Planning and Urban Form*, Owens explores the role of ambient energy sources and development footprints, which facilitate the use of both active and passive solar energy, in tandem with other low-tech and energy-conscious landscape features for water collection and wind protection. The orientation, density, or spatial needs of these measures imply 'that total reliance on renewable energy sources is not compatible with highly urbanised spatial structures' (1986, p.49). She advocates 'energy-flexible land use patterns' which can take advantage of combined heating and power systems, as well as low technology options.

Elkin *et al.* (1991) admit that the scope for the re-use of redundant commercial and industrial buildings, most of which are in inner cities, is limited. The principal reason for this is that they are most suited to the types of companies who have just abandoned them in search of more space. The penalty of VAT on materials and labour for conversion and refurbishment projects has meant that redevelopment is often more successful and cheaper.

Breheny *et al.* (DoE, 1993a) believe that the potentially high renovation and energy costs associated with reusing existing infrastructure and constrained urban infill land will discourage developers from pursuing urban sites given a choice. Llewelyn-Davies (1994) also outline the conditions which deter housing developers from using land which may be contaminated or more difficult to develop.

Rydin (in Breheny, 1992b) writes that the commitment to 'green' development is largely a factor of the time horizons within which investors, developers and occupiers view property; 'the timescale of development is not in tune with the needs of urban sustainability' (p.227). Demand for environmentally sensitive buildings depends on whether it is a developers' or occupiers' market, and even then the extent to which the occupier is interested in green issues. At present, this interest is still low on the list of priorities.

The green city

Breheny (1992b) pinpoints one of the major contradictions of the compact city proposal - the desire to both 'green' the city, as well as to use existing land within the city more intensively. These two pressures on urban land remain unresolved in the compact city. Calls for more containment and the development of currently derelict land can often lead to the destruction of rich natural inner city wildlife habitats.

The conflict of interests between the preservation of rural land by the CPRE, in favour of the development of urban land, and the densification of housing and resultant reductions in private garden space is, according to David Bellamy, 'one of the current biggest threats to the natural environment in the UK' (CPRE, 1993, p.154). The significance of this 'greenery' is that for many of today's city dwellers, it is some of the only natural wildlife that they experience on a regular basis. As such it is a very valuable resource to the physical and mental well-being of many people.

Social and political expectations

> One definite problem with the compac city proposal is that it requires a complete reversal of the most persistent trend in urban development in the last 50 years: that is, decentralisation.
> (Breheny and Rookwood in Blowers, 1993, p.155)

Fig. 3 illustrates this trend of decentralisation by 1992, where evidence suggests that the residential population, as well as employment in Britain's major cities, is shifting to smaller provincial towns and villages. This trend is set to continue into the next millennium, with the predicted bulge in retired, more affluent people or GLAMMIES (Greying, Leisured, Affluent, Middle-aged Spenders) moving to coastal or market towns, out of the cities (McLoughlin, 1991).

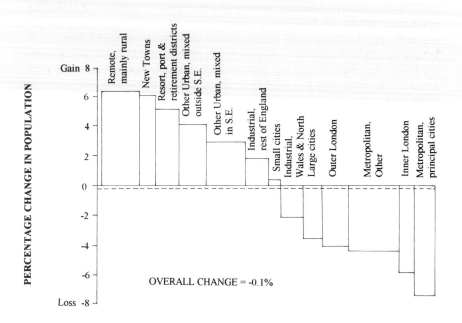

Fig. 3. Decentralisation trends. OPCS (1992)

Source: Blowers (1993), Planning for a Sustainable Environment, p.153.

Increased leisure time, the rejection of work as 'identity', and greater personal control over lifestyle decisions mean that for many people, their expectations for a certain quality of life will increase. 'Public opinion surveys suggest that most people would like the chance to live in a country setting. The Henley Centre for Forecasting predicts that more of them will get their wish by the year 2000' (McLoughlin, 1991, p.49; Robertson, and Begg and Moore in Cadman and Payne, 1990).

Worpole (1992) and Sorkin (1993) describe how leisure and popular entertainment, once the essential and irredeemable preserve of the central city, have been transformed into a private in-house activity: the video replacing the cinema and the theatre; the pizza delivery the cafe or restaurant; the compact disc player the concert; even the humble laundrette has been replaced largely by our individual washing machines! Worpole describes how the night-time attractions of the city are often overshadowed by urban fear; the urban vitality of the compact city appears to have a great deal of ground to cover.

New projections for household numbers in England suggest that the level of growth previously envisaged in some areas could rise by 29% from 1991 to 2016. This rise is a product of population growth, but also the numbers of newly created, smaller households, as the more traditional family group breaks up (DoE, 1995). The ability of the compact city to cope with this huge increase must surely put even greater pressure on existing urban land (Webb, 1995).

Llewelyn-Davies (1994) have examined the capacity for providing more homes in urban areas. The conclusion reached is that it is possible to achieve far higher densities than current standards allow, albeit in some cases with 'no public open space or street trees'. Sherlock (1991) describes many ways in which housing density can be increased using existing and new building forms. What is not apparent in his calculations is the importance of 'trade-off' or the amount that we are prepared to pay or sacrifice for something. What is to be gained from 'the stick' of increased densities, if there is no room for 'the carrot' of invigorating and ample public open space and amenities?

Gans (1991), among many others, argues that the popularity of the suburbs both in the United States and in Britain is still growing, and for many represents the continuing ideal of a higher quality of life. This is important to remember, for as we originally heard, sustainability demands the matching of environmental needs with aspirations in order to succeed and to be equitable.

Blowers (in Breheny, 1992b) doubts the political reality of weaning the majority of people out of their suburban homes and cars. Once the radical implications of sustainability are grasped, enthusiasm is 'likely to fade'. The sacrifices required of them by environmentalists will probably mean that 'people will be prepared to put up with a great deal more congestion, pollution and general environmental deterioration, so long as they continue to enjoy the freedom and comforts of modern consumerist society' (p.36).

Rydin (in Breheny, 1992b) considers that the pressure for profit will continue to overwhelm many involved in the development industry. It is not until environmental standards such as the Building Research Establishment's Environmental Assessment Method (BREEAM) are perceived by investors (who have the longest term view) as valuable marketing tools to give a 'competitive edge', that green issues will be a concern. However, this also is not reflected in the apparent preferences of owner-occupiers and mortgage companies as investors. For them, accommodation for the car and a private garden top the list of important features, with energy efficiency at the bottom.

On another level, Macnaghten *et al.* (1995), in their survey of public perceptions of sustainability, have recorded suspicion among interviewees of the need for sustainable action: 'They keep you in the dark and then come up with terms like sustainability' (p.76). For many people living in economically depressed regions, the concept of sustainability is a luxury that they have not considered. More immediate concerns were finding a job, and achieving any 'quality of life'.

How then do we tell these people that the CPRE has the right approach when they state that 'planning should not always "balance" the benefits of development against the costs to the environment... To sustain society within such capacity limits, some developments should be ruled out whatever their current benefits' (1993, p.22).

The political action required to convert popular negative 'green awareness' into positive 'green behaviour' is judged to be a long way off, requiring long term environmental policies of the sort advocated by the Green Party, and not the political parties whose popularity is more assured (Jowell *et al.*, 1992).

Conclusion

The indications are that the success, desirability and achievability of the compact city are equivocal. Yet the aspirations of the compact city proposal are well founded: increasing accessibility on foot and by energy efficient public transport, providing mobility, where the car is not essential for both daily needs and other trips, and where rural natural habitats are given greater respect.

The work of Peter Calthorpe (1993) in Fig. 4, Duany and Plater-Zyberk (1991) in Fig. 5 and the Urban Villages Group (Aldous, 1992) suggest how walkable mixed use developments of varying densities could begin to satisfy the need to balance lifestyle aspirations with more soft energy-conscious design layouts and well defined open space. However, the grain of these developments does not sit well with the realities of employment space discussed above (Audirac and Shermyen, 1991). Nor do they respond to the energy consumption implications of their separation. Fig. 6 suggests that there would be no coherent strategy for transportation working with the cluster of urban villages.

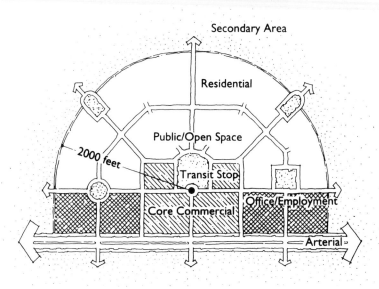

Fig. 4. Calthorpe's model of transit oriented development.
Source: Calthorpe, P. (1993), The Next American Metropolis, p.56.

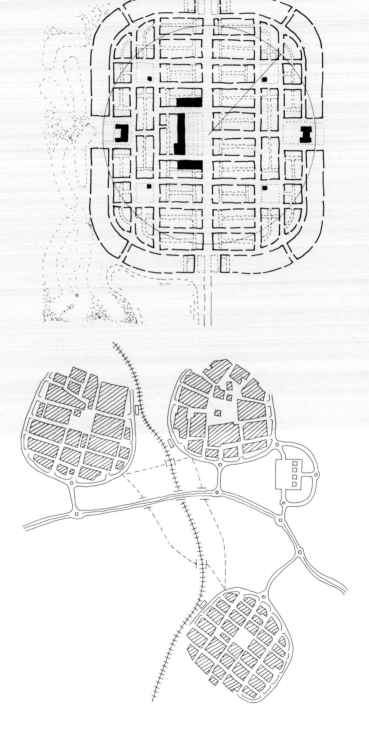

Fig. 5. Duany and Plater-Zyberk's model of traditional neighbourhood development.

Source: Jennings Group Ltd (1992)

Cranbourne Lyndhurst charette, p.7

Fig. 6. A cluster of urban villages.

Source: Aldous (1992) Urban

Villages

But is it possible to combine this type of physical compactness with a 'virtual' compactness? Is there a settlement pattern which will allow local compactness to be complemented by regional compactness - where the connections between development areas are so efficient that they foreshorten the time and distance to travel?

Rickaby *et al.* (in Breheny, 1992b) indicate through their research into land use patterns and transport energy use, that high density linear development is less efficient than 'village dispersal' patterns of growth. They suggest that a light rail rapid transit system between decentralised concentrations of development would increase the attractiveness and energy efficiency of the form. Indeed, many of the compact city proponents have conceded that such a form could provide a very realistic alternative to the compact city.

> The ultimate objective, therefore, is to create a city in which people no longer have a strong desire, nor feel it essential, to make such use of motor vehicles that they constitute a social [and environmental] problem (Thomas, 1978, p.142).

References

Aldous, T. (ed.) (1992) *Urban Villages - A Concept for Creating Mixed-Use Urban Development on a Sustainable Scale*, Urban Villages Group, Morgan Grampian Plc, London.

Audirac, I. and Shermyen, A. H. (1991) *Neo Traditionalism and Return to Town Life: Post Modern Placebo or Remedy for Metropolitan Malaise?* Unpublished paper given in Oxford Polytechnic AESOP Conference July 1991.

Barton, H., Davis, R. and Guise, R. (1995) *Sustainable Settlements. A Guide for Planners, Designers and Developers*, University of the West of England and The Local Government Management Board, Bristol.

Bendixson, T. and Platt, J. (1992) *Milton Keynes. Image and Reality*, Granta Editions, Cambridge.

Blowers, A. (ed.) (1993) *Planning for a Sustainable Environment. A Report by the Town and Country Planning Association.* Chapters 1, 7, 9, Earthscan, London.

Breheny, M. J. (ed.) (1992a) The Compact City. *Built Environment,* **18(4).**

Breheny, M. J. (ed.) (1992b) *Sustainable Development and Urban Form*, Pion, London.

Cadman, D. and Payne, G. (eds)(1990) *The Living City -Towards a Sustainable Future*, Routledge, London.

Calthorpe, P. (1993) *The Next American Metropolis. Ecology, Community, and the American Dream*, Princeton Architectural Press, New York.

Cervero, R. (1991) Congestion relief: the land use alternative. *Journal of Planning Education and Research*, **10 (2)**, pp.119-129.

Commission of the European Communities (1990) *Green Paper on the Urban Environment,* EUR 12902 EN, CEC, Brussels.

Council for the Protection of Rural England (1993) *Sense and Sensibility. Land Use Planning and Environmentally Sustainable Development*, CPRE/CAG Consultants, London.

Debenham Tewson and Chinnocks (1987) *The Geography of Commercial Floorspace 1974-1985*, Debenham Thorpe Zadelhoff, London.

Department of the Environment (1990) *This Common Inheritance. A Summary of the White Paper on the Environment,* Command 1200, HMSO, London.

Department of the Environment (1993a) *Alternative Development Patterns: New Settlements,* M. Breheny, T. Gent, and D. Lock, Planning Research Programme, HMSO, London.

Department of the Environment (1993b) *Migration and Business Relocation: The Case of the South East, Executive Summary,* A. Fielding and Prism Research Limited, Planning and Research Programme, HMSO, London.

Department of the Environment (1995) *Projections of Households in England to 2016,* HMSO, London.

Duany, A. and Plater-Zyberk, E. (1991) *Towns and Town Making Principles,* Harvard University Graduate School of Design/ Rizzoli, New York.

Elkin, T., McLaren, D. and Hillman, M. (1991) *Reviving the City; Towards Sustainable Urban Development,* Friends of the Earth, London.

Engwicht, D. (1992) *Towards an Eco-City: Calming the Traffic,* Envirobook, Sydney.

Fothergill, S., Kitson, M. and Monk, S. (1983) *Changes in Industrial Floorspace and Employment in Cities, Towns and Rural Areas,* Industrial Location Research Project Working Paper 4, University of Cambridge, Dept. of Land Economy, Cambridge.

Gans, H. J. (1991) *People, Plans and Policies. Essays on Poverty, Racism and other National Urban Problems,* Chapters. 1-4, 8, Columbia University Press/ Russell Sage Foundation, New York.

Garreau, J. (1991) *Edge City: Life on the New Frontier,* Doubleday, New York.

Girouard, M. (1985) *Cities and People. A Social and Architectural History,* Yale University Press, New Haven and London.

Gordon, P. and Richardson, H. W. (1989) Gasoline consumption and cities. A Reply. *Journal of the American Planning Association, 55, Summer,* pp.342-46.

Guardian, The (1993) *Shopping Shift that Changed the Townscape,* Various authors, 6 October 1993, p.17.

Jacobs, J. (1961) *The Death and Life of Great American Cities,* Vintage Books/ Random House, New York.

Jennings Group Ltd (1992) *Report of the Cranbourne Lyndhurst Town Planning Charette,* Victoria, Australia.

Jowell, R., Brook, L., Prior G. and Taylor, B. (eds)(1992) *British Social Attitudes: the 9th Report,* Dartmouth, Aldershot.

Katz, I. (1993) Homo shopiens, outlook. *The Guardian,* 30 October 1993, p.25.

Llewelyn-Davies (1994) *Providing More Homes in Urban Areas,* in association with the Joseph Rowntree Foundation and Environmental Trust Associates, SAUS Publications, Bristol.

Macnaghten, P., Grove-White, R., Jacobs, M. and Wynne, B. (1995) *Public Perceptions and Sustainability in Lancashire. Indicators, Institutions and Participation,* Centre for the Study of Environmental Change, Lancaster University.

McLaren, D. (1992) Compact or dispersed? dilution is no solution. *Built Environment,* **18 (4)**, pp.268-84.

McLoughlin, J. (1991) *The Demographic Revolution,* Ch. 1-4, 8, 10, Faber and Faber, London.

Newman, P. W. G. and Kenworthy, J. R. (1989) *Cities and Automobile Dependency. An International Sourcebook,* Gower Technical, Aldershot.

Owens, S. (1986) *Energy Planning and Urban Form,* Pion, London.

Owens, S. and Cope, D. (1992) *Land Use Planning Policy and Climate Change,* HMSO, London.

Pharoah, T. (1992) *Less Traffic, Better Towns,* Friends of the Earth, London.

Royal Society for the Encouragement of Arts, Manufactures and Commerce (1995) *Tomorrow's Company. The Role of Business in a Changing World,* London.

Sherlock, H. (1991) *Cities are Good for Us,* Transport 2000, London.

Sorkin, M. (1993) The politics of propinquity. *Building Design,* 14 May 1993, pp.22-4.

Sudjic, D. (1992) *The 100 Mile City,* Andre Deutsch, London.

Thomas, J. M. in Gakenheimer, R. (ed.)(1978) *The Automobile and the Environment. An International Perspective,* Part III, Chapters 9-14, MIT Press, Cambridge, Mass.

Webb, C. (1995) England: watch this space. *The Times,* August 2 1995, p.16.

Whyte, W. H. (1988) *City: Rediscovering the Centre,* Chapters 20 and 21, Doubleday, New York.

World Commission on Environment and Development (1987) *Our Common Future,* OUP, Oxford.

Worpole, K. (1992) *Towns for People,* Open University Press, Buckingham.

Ernie Scoffham and Brenda Vale

How Compact is Sustainable - How Sustainable is Compact?

Introduction

> ...by-laws which place a limit on the number of houses to the acre, though beloved by the garden-suburb sentimentalists, are the most fatal to the true suburban spirit. It is an essential part of its character that the suburb should constitute a world in itself, susceptible of delimitation. Above all things it needs to be compact. Space as such is not an asset and a low density only dilutes the rich suburban landscape. (Richards, 1946, p.77)

This apparent contradiction in concepts poses the question as to what is meant by compact. Does it mean that buildings, and with them the functions of urban life, should be close together; closer together than is now common? Does it mean, *inter alia*, an increase in density, so that more people and, one might expect, more urban functions are located within a given area? The question sharpens the distinction between density and intensity of development, for they are not the same thing. Density is a quantitative measure of number within a prescribed area, whereas intensity reflects a more subjective measure of built-up-ness or urbanity. Density, in itself, is of little importance unless it is related to built form. Compact is meaningless unless it is related to some facts and figures.

This century bears witness to a vast catalogue of attempts to arrive at a better understanding of the relationship between density and built form, especially in housing and especially in Britain. Some pernicious critics might describe these attempts as crimes and misdemeanours! Therefore, it seems necessary at the outset to place housing densities into some form of perspective against their respective built forms. Ebenezer Howard's 'garden city' reaction to the squalor and overcrowding of the nineteenth century meant 45 houses to the hectare, which at an average four bedspaces per house is 180 bedspaces per hectare (Howard, 1898). Raymond Unwin advised that there was *Nothing Gained by Overcrowding* and his 'town' density, enshrined in the Tudor-Walters report which regulated the four million inter-war dwellings with gardens, and rehoused one third of the population of England and Wales, was 30 houses to the hectare, or 120 bedspaces per hectare (Unwin, 1912). Patrick Abercrombie's three pyramidal, residential density zones for London's postwar reconstruction prescribed 247, 336, and 494 people per hectare (Abercrombie, 1944). For bedspaces read people - both indicate the intended or designed maximum - rather than average density; the latter reflects occupancy rates which, today, are substantially less than actual bedspace potential, whereas in times of overcrowding are substantially more.

By comparison, and to comprehend measures of overcrowding and density in Britain, the planned average residential density of Singapore in the 1970s was 1,000 bedspaces per hectare and the actual density of central Kowloon, Hong Kong, is around 5,000 people to the hectare.

Adequate space

Amid the prevailing mood of postwar optimism for a new society and a fresh urban lifestyle to match its aspirations came Elizabeth Denby's revelation that the densities being achieved by the London County Council's 'mixed development' policy were barely those which already existed in some of the areas the Council was intent on demolishing because they harboured the squalor and overcrowding of the previous century. Her studies of the demolished Paultons Square in Chelsea and Cleaver Square in Lambeth showed that their net residential densities were respectively 40.2 and 42.7 houses to the hectare, and that because these were large three and four storey houses arranged around open squares, their bedspace densities were respectively 321 and 341 to the hectare (Denby, 1956).

Throughout the period of high density, high-rise apartment building which permeated British cities, aided and abetted by cost yardstick and rent subsidy policies to offset the higher cost of high-rise, it was continually necessary for the then Ministry of Housing to remind authorities that high-rise should only be used as a device to achieve higher densities amid predominantly low-rise developments, and to house only those who could reasonably be expected to live in them. But authorities were moved by the available subsidies and by the compliments attached to improved housing statistics. Few of these high-rise developments reached Abercrombie's maximum of 494 people per hectare, and the stories about their social and technical failures are still legion. Their failures remain associated with the confusion of high-rise and high density: housing developments in Singapore and Hong Kong, at twice or three times Abercrombie's inner city density, seem relatively free from these difficulties. Richards rightly observed that 'the real cause of slums is not congestion but poverty' (Richards, 1946, p.77).

The result of ensuring that prescribed sunlight and daylight standards were achieved for all dwellings in mixed developments was that high-rise pushed blocks further apart, leaving increasing amounts of open space between them. The mood of openness, light and air after the claustrophobia of wartime, saw to it that this openness became associated with the openness of suburbia - bringing trees, green and light back into the city. The Centre for Land Use and Built Form Studies at Cambridge brought some statistical clarity to these opposingly similar phenomena. The demonstration that Abercrombie's inner-area density could be achieved by an arrangement of perimeter blocks, which gave everyone immediate access to the ground and a view of the central open space, at last exposed the fallacy that high density meant high-rise and also that it meant compact. It opened up the debate as to what densities could reasonably be achieved by housing on the ground, and posed the yet unresolved question of the interrelationship between land use and built form - between planning and the arrangement of buildings (Martin and March, 1972).

It may be useful to quote some precedents. In an unsuccessful entry for the Golden Lane competition in 1952, David Gregory-Jones answered the brief by an almost too literal interpretation, for he arranged dwelling blocks around the periphery of the site, so achieving a large central square for recreational use. This met the density requirement of 494 people per hectare by buildings which were lower in height than those of any of the prizewinners. Later, the cross-over maisonette block on which he was working at London County Council was demonstrated using a six-storey block surrounding squares of 61m by 55m with a density of 494 people per hectare; but it was never used in this manner: almost all its built versions were in the then conventional mixed developments of a variety of building heights (Scoffham, 1984).

Another similar, unbuilt demonstration came from the Taylor Woodrow Group in a study of Fulham undertaken for the Ministry of Housing. Continuous six-storey blocks were used in comparative layouts at densities of 336, 494 and 618 people per hectare and the built form results were compared favourably with four-storey Georgian terraces in Bloomsbury (Tetlow and Goss, 1965, p.171).

Richard MacCormac came closest to making a breakthrough at Pollards Hill and Eastfields for the London Borough of Merton. Three-storey houses with gardens and integral garages were utilised in continuous, convoluted terrace blocks to achieve densities of 286 and 237 people per hectare, respectively. At Eastfields an exchange of land was attempted so that the adjoining primary school could be located in the centre of the layout, rather than on separate land. If this had been possible the continuous terrace would have achieved the same density with less convolution, giving every house a view of the school playing field. In other words, it would have been less compact, but to the same density (Scoffham, 1984, p.200).

By comparison, the London County Council's Roehampton Estate comprised two-, four-, eight- and eleven- storey blocks and slabs to achieve 247 people per hectare. No dwelling had an integral garage and only the small number of houses in two-storey blocks had private gardens. At the other extreme, that staple of suburbia, the semi-detached house with private garden and attached garage was given attention by William Cowburn in a layout study which demonstrated its potential at densities of up to 193 bedspaces to the hectare (Cowburn, 1968, pp.638-41).

What had been happening for almost thirty years since the start of postwar reconstruction, Lionel March described as the 'intellectual pleasure that is derived from a clever arrangement of inadequate space' (March, 1967). Regrettably, this still continues. While Richards (1946) tells us that space is not an asset to the suburban spirit, it seems quite clear that adequate space is an essence of sustainability.

But what is adequate? It is obvious that prescriptions of residential density are irrelevant, as the same density can conceal a variety of built forms which both psychologically and physically may be either compact or loose, urban or suburban, intense or diffuse. What matters more is the manner in which residential functions are arranged, so as to provide long term flexibility and adaptability. Family composition, life-cycles and lifestyles are constantly shifting; the residential fabric must be capable of sustaining change and be efficiently arranged in relation to immediate residential needs: schools, shops, transportation and, if possible, work. Furthermore, in the wider context of sustainability, the urban fabric must be capable of accommodating activities which permit individual and group autonomy and rely less on unsustainable or unaffordable resources. Density has conventionally been measured within site boundaries without attention being given to the infrastructure and resources needed to maintain that density. For the future, it is no longer possible to think in such a constrained way. A framework is required that acknowledges the provenance of the resources needed to support a settlement within its specific arrangement of buildings.

Flexible frameworks

In 1976, Letchworth Garden City Corporation held an ideas competition about 'places fit to live in and how to create them'. David Dennis' successful entry dealt with urban restructuring by locating central open space corresponding 'to the existing parks and commons that we find throughout London' and grouping around these residential squares each of 426 people, beyond which were employment and shopping, while public transport ran down the centre. Access to employment and public transport fell within five minutes' walk of all the housing. It was the energy crisis provoked by the mid-1970s OPEC oil price review which gave rise to this thinking about optimisation of resources and a search for autonomy. Dennis suggested a framework with which society might identify by familiarity and understanding; it suggested slow change, not of growth, but of optimisation (Rabeneck, 1976, pp.364-5).

Also in 1976, John Seed attempted to model the 'possible spatial characteristics of an urban structure capable of remaining habitable, workable, convenient and attractive, in a context of increased energy constraint'. Using Milton Keynes as a case study he offered a pattern of interactive neighbourhoods - city villages similar in concept to those of Nicholas Taylor (Taylor, 1973) - each being relatively self-contained with a virtually complete spectrum of urban facilities. Seed supported the perimeter concept, for it 'not only has the capacity to accommodate increases in numbers of dwellings in each city square, but each square could also support, in addition to housing, all the necessary local facilities such as schools, recreation space, market garden allotments and other land, including some light industry' (Seed, 1976, pp.564-6).

In similar vein, John Turner advocated a re-evaluation of the Medieval New Town plantation which had encouraged progressive development according to the 'will of autonomously organised people and communities', where individuals were granted freedoms - to dwell and to trade - in return for organised security. Turner advocated 'legislative planning' and argued for a setting out of the limits of what individuals were free to do rather than the imposition of standard procedures to which they must adhere (Turner, 1976).

Such a flexible framework evokes the random nature in which the traditional town or village has grown and mutated over a period of time with a resultant consistency of appearance. A simplicity of approach to built form, density and land use creates arrangements suggesting Georgian streets and squares, collegiate quadrangles and medieval market towns, often of comparable or even higher densities and better land use patterns than many more recent solutions. The nineteenth century terrace eventually came to be appreciated for its advantages, particularly when the 1969 Housing Act found money for its renovation: a house-entrance-road relationship, often a small garden, a flexible arrangement of rooms, a robust construction and a simple shape. Ample size and a simple disposition of space and shape facilitated its adaptation and change. This efficient and flexible disposition of interior space needs to be rediscovered in urban form-making; so many urban spaces are unlet and underused because they have not been arranged to accommodate choice and change.

Prescriptions of sustainability

Twenty years after the mid-1970s oil crisis which, as stated above, prompted the first search for urban forms which conserved resources, the idea of sustainability has re-emerged. Energy consumption, pollution of all kinds and waste are increasingly becoming the legislative measures of urban performance. These intentions, set out in the Commission of the European Communities' (CEC) *Green Paper on the Urban Environment* (1990), are gradually finding their way into UK environmental legislation and are affecting strategies for British cities in the same way that they have brought positive changes to cities in continental Europe. Britain's cities lag some way behind the more enterprising, regionally devolved cities of Germany and France in their infrastructural and environmental changes. But it would be short-sighted to attempt to catch up simply by translating some physical continental solutions to Britain. Their cities are compact in territorial terms, just as central Glasgow and Edinburgh are, because of the twin historical traditions of apartment living and outdoor public activity. The majority of British cities are territorially dispersed and their citizens behave differently. It seems significant, therefore, to question what exactly sustainable living might mean to those who live in them.

Given the pressures upon urban life that are forcing the adoption of some measures of self-sufficiency, investigation seems to be necessary about the way people might want to live, or how they might be induced to change the way they lead their lives in order to encompass a pattern of living that could be described as sustainable. It is not the physical environment that is the bar to using less resources and causing less environmental pollution, but an attitude which says that urban living is somehow such a complex affair that more resources need to be consumed so that individuals can have access to all possible information and activities. The quality of such an instantly accessible lifestyle seems never to be questioned. Whether consumer choice itself is useful to the individual is also never questioned.

The problem seems to be linked to a phenomenon whereby people no longer consume the raw ingredients that they themselves make into the many different items that suit the individual exactly: cooking, knitting, making clothes, all of them activities common in households earlier this century, but which are now increasingly replaced by pre-cooked meals and ready-made clothes. The retail space required to store patterns and materials is considerably less than the retail space required to store ready-made clothes in a whole variety of sizes. Moreover, the journeys between the place of manufacture of the cloth and place of final garment sale are multiplied when people purchase the finished product rather than the raw materials to make the garment. Conversely, the number of different combinations of cloth and pattern when clothes are made at home is considerably greater than will ever be experienced when ready-made garments are purchased, so that paradoxically final choice is in fact more extensive. Earlier this century, for those who did not have the skills or time, others in the immediate locality would make the clothes for them, so that manufacture was kept at a small scale in the local community: a prime attribute of a sustainable approach. Nottingham possesses a skilled female labour force engaged in the international ready-to-wear garment industry which is part of its lace-making heritage; accordingly, there is a significant private trade in purpose-made garment-making for local consumption.

The widespread assumption that nothing is good unless it is supplied from a central source, ignoring what is locally available, applies also to the quest for greater access to information and resources. Thus, people travel to a central library, ignoring the fact that if more contact was made between neighbours, or if locally, people could come together to discover exactly what books each of them owned, many journeys could be made on foot rather than by car. The present assumption seems to be that centrality gives the best access to information. This ignores the fact that information is, in fact, dispersed evenly throughout the population and all that is actually required is access to where and what that information is, and sufficient trust within the community so that this information can be safely accessed. Such trust is more often associated with a local group where everyone knows everyone, than with a large impersonal group. A centralised library now has to have sophisticated surveillance equipment to try to stop books being stolen; a library in a small local school does not.

Just as information might be seen as something that has been handled in a centralised manner rather than realising that it is far more evenly dispersed, so energy generation has been handled centrally for some assumed economy of scale. Energy, as it occurs naturally in the renewable form of sun and wind, is also dispersed, and it may, therefore, be more appropriate to use it locally rather than centrally. What applies to energy also applies to water. Rainwater off a suburban roof in Nottingham meets WHO standards for drinking (Fewkes and Turton, 1994). In an autonomous house in Nottingham, water use has been reduced to 150 litres per day, the same quantity of water that is lost per household per day by Thames Water through leakage within its centralised system (Vale, 1995). A sustainable settlement might reconsider whether centralisation of resource and energy management was appropriate.

Autonomy

It is, of course, transportation which is the culprit for initiating a quest for compactness, in an effort to reduce reliance on the motor car, reduce pollution, limit energy consumption and move more people onto public systems. Unlike most continental European cities, British cities have not sustained their electric trams as primary, clean, unpolluting systems, so in the main they must start from scratch. Without an efficient and clean public transport system which goes where people want it to, they will rely on the motor car which spends the majority of its life parked and will preferably move to where there is an uncongested road and a free car park. Commercial and residential development will follow the same rules. To prevent it means severely punitive taxes, tolls and levies on the use of the car, and planning policies which are able to resist pressure from the commercial interests upon which the city relies. Public transport, especially when operated by private companies, requires customers to sustain it, and to do so it must, in addition to being efficient and clean, be perceived as cheaper than the car for the same journey. None of this seems likely in Britain for some considerable time.

Therefore, it is necessary to look for alternatives that may be more appropriate to Britain's situation. Part of the solution is to reduce the need to travel, part of it is to provide public transport routes which link only those neighbourhoods which make operation financially viable. Another part of the solution might be found in re-examining proposals for structuring neighbourhoods when the car was in its infancy. Radburn, New Jersey, still seems to hold some clues (Stein, 1958). The ten minute maximum safe walking distance from furthest house to community school, and from furthest point to public transport, remains as a reasonable assumption to take; people are not noticeably walking further or faster today. Within this radius local autonomy can be encouraged, and a range of facilities can sustain themselves. As has been shown earlier, net residential densities can reach 500 people per hectare without any sense of overcrowding as long as a proper balance is achieved between land use and built form in order to provide adequate space, so there is a considerable potential population within each walking distance radius.

Progressively autonomous neighbourhoods of this size could each develop their own character based on local skills, topography, education, sport, culture or whatever. Movement between neighbourhoods would be to avail oneself of these interdependent specialisms, the city centre being the largest among them, offering, for the moment, the largest range of centralised facilities which might diminish as local neighbourhoods develop themselves. Public transport would link the neighbourhoods of an increasingly polycentric city (Kurokawa, 1994).

Such a city cannot be prescribed as compact in physical terms. Its neighbourhoods may be dispersed across a considerable distance in order to provide for the inevitably linear nature of a cost effective public transport system. In shape the city might be drawn out in a linear manner along lines of communication, its inter-city rail link being decentralised to a local or regional airport. For Nottingham it is possible, even now, to contemplate a city which stretches along existing rail links from East Midlands airport, to regenerate the now defunct mining areas north of the present city, as well as to serve the leisure and tourism venues of Sherwood Forest. All are part of the city region but are not within the city's administrative boundary. The recent changes in local government administration did very little to perceive, and even less to assist, these kinds of development.

For the city to succeed in these directions it needs to be given more localised power, more autonomy, more ability to make decisions and to secure funds to achieve its own, unique, long term interests - interests which sustain its individuality rather than serve distant global markets. Cities are competing with each other to attract funds, there can be no one universal control for them all; each has its own strengths and peculiarities, each its own character, culture and lifestyle; each needs the freedom to develop its own strategies according to the will of local people; local neighbourhoods need the freedom to be themselves, self-sufficient and independent. Compact in the context of sustainability means increasing independence from those outside forces over which the city and its people have little or no control, and it means greater independent control of those local resources upon which the city depends. This is a compaction of control, not of physical size or form. The better word to describe it might be autonomy.

References

Abercrombie, P. (1944) *Greater London Plan*, HMSO.

Commission of European Communities (1990) *Green Paper on the Urban Environment*, CEC, Brussels.

Cowburn, W. (1968) The context of housing. *Architects' Journal*, **147**, 25 September pp.638-41.

Denby, E. (1956) Oversprawl. *Architectural Review*, **120**, December pp.424-30.

Fewkes, A. and Turton, A. (1994) Recovering rainwater for w.c. flushing. *Environmental Health*, February, pp.42-46.

Howard, E. (1898) *Tomorrow: A Peaceful Path to Real Reform*, Swan Sonnenschein, London; later published as *Garden Cities of Tomorrow*, Faber, London.

Kurokawa, K. (1994) *Intercultural Architecture, the Philosophy of Symbiosis*, Academy Editions, London.

March, L. (1967) Homes beyond the fringe. *Architects' Journal*, **146**, 19 July pp.156-58.

Martin, Sir L. and March, L. (1972) *Urban Space and Structures*, Cambridge University Press, Cambridge.

Rabeneck, A. (1976) Two competitions. *Architectural Design*, **46**, June pp.364-5.

Richards, J. M. (1946) *The Castles on the Ground*, Architectural Press, London.

Scoffham, E. R. (1984) *The Shape of British Housing*, George Godwin, London and New York.

Seed, J. (1976) Sustainable urban structure. *Architectural Design*, **46**, September pp.564-6.

Stein, C. S. (1958) *Towards New Towns for America*, Reinhold, Amsterdam.

Taylor, N. (1973) *The Village in the City*, Temple Smith, London.

Tetlow, J. and Goss, A. (1965) *Homes, Towns and Traffic*, Faber and Faber, London.

Turner, J. F. C. (1976) Principles for housing. *Architectural Design*, **46**, February pp.99-101.

Unwin, R. (1912) *Nothing Gained by Overcrowding*, P. S. King, for Garden Cities and Town Planning Association, London.

Vale, B. (1995) The autonomous house. *Proceedings of the XVth International Home Economics and Consumer Studies Research Conference, Part 1*, September, pp.7-19.

Michael Welbank
The Search for a Sustainable Urban Form

Introduction

As part of the national and international campaign to achieve the goal of 'sustainable development' the search for sustainable urban forms is in full swing. Nearly every facet of the sustainable development movement has its expression in the urban environment, and neither the urban environment, nor the sustainable city, nor the compact city are tidy self-contained packets which can be extracted and studied in a disaggregated manner.

Planners find themselves in the front line of this search, with demands coming from all sides that they take the lead in achieving sustainable development and come forward with sustainable forms for the urban environment, backed by sound research, which are acceptable in social and economic terms. They are being asked to propose solutions to advance a theoretical and complex concept, as yet undefined in its manner of application, in a setting representing the most complex interaction of interests, forces and issues that can ever be imagined - the city. In this amazing imbroglio one easy solution is to call for vision. The danger is that visions, ill-conceived, or with no rationale behind them, could be worse than a 'do nothing' scenario. There is no shortage of advice to planners about the content of the vision, but they are right to be cautious because as professionals they are still being blamed for the results of ill-founded visions of the past.

If they are being asked to lead with vision, then it is at a time when it has become much more difficult - with a 'nimbyesque' public (from NIMBY, Not In My Back Yard), a hyper-critical press, and a consequently nervous political generation in all parties, at all levels - and has made anything other than short term or *ad hoc* planning extremely difficult. And looking at the performance of the planning profession in the postwar years, has the concept of a 'vision' served planning well? Chris Shepley (1995) has identified three distinct periods, each characterised by a different approach:

- The confident but sensitive period (up to about the 1950s)

- The autocratic period (1960s)
- The uncertain and defensive period (1970s/80s)

Period of confidence

This, arguably, stems from the work of Ebenezer Howard and continues with the New Towns, the wartime reconstruction plans and the generation of planners who laid the foundation of the modern profession. It was rooted in the notion of making the world a better place - 'homes fit for heroes', 'new homes for old'; there was a strong element of social conscience in what was done. Howard's writing was not limited to 'land use' but embraced strong overtones of social and economic planning, health and welfare. Moving people out of the East End into leafy new towns in the Home Counties was seen as desirable and healthy. There seems to have been a consensus that these things were being done for the right reasons and that they were the right things to do. Planning, therefore, was visionary and imaginative - confident and effective. But it was sensitive to social pressures and it was operating in a much less hostile atmosphere than today. There was, it seems, less intense political rivalry surrounding planning issues - and less public and press scrutiny of what was going on. The world has changed; and those who demand 'vision' from planners should remember that. It was planning by conviction, yet with sensitivity.

Period of autocracy

In the sixties, thinking on urban issues continued to develop. Regional plans emerged. But, in the cities particularly, planning acquired an apparently autocratic edge. This was equally - perhaps more - associated with other professions as well, notably engineers constructing roads and architects designing tower blocks, often, in both cases, in the face of opposition from the emerging generation of planners. It was planning by conviction with insensitivity.

Period of uncertainty

The more uncertain time which followed for planners was partly a reaction - often unfair but no less potent - to the perceived mistakes of the sixties. There were also wider changes affecting planning, especially after 1979, and there has been increased scrutiny of every move which planners have made since. In parallel with these changes in the status and psychology of planning, it gradually became more bureaucratic. The complexity of the planning system became quite overwhelming; the friends of bureaucracy are not the planners themselves but those few who - by seeking to circumvent, evade, or frustrate the needs and wishes of the wider community - have made it necessary to erect a superstructure of bureaucracy to deal with citizens' rights.

Present day

Planners have moved from confidence to uncertainty, from consensus to hostile scrutiny, and from freedom to bureaucracy. Life has been nearly squeezed out of planning.

And just at this moment in the 1990s the concept of sustainable development sweeps onto the stage, and planners are about to become the heroes in an as yet unwritten play. That would be fine for planners if they only knew their parts. But that is the whole excitement of the present scene. It provides the opportunity to return to a period of planning with confidence and sensitivity, yet based on a set of principles accepted globally and endorsed nationally. Many of these principles relate to the natural realm, but for planners the most important element is to determine urban forms for the future which are sustainable and achievable. Theoretical models need to be tested for robustness by their capability to be implemented in our society today, and for their ability to create sustainable urban environments to last for decades ahead. In the world of planning, however convincing the theory, if the process of implementation produces inequities, economic decline, social injustices and poor 'quality of life', it will fail - society will not stand for it. Thus theory and implementation capability need to go hand in hand.

At present there is a plethora of theories emerging about sustainable urban forms. The purpose of this chapter is to review a number of these, examining both their rationale and their implementation capability, with the aim of advancing the debate and of finding the route to a sustainable urban form. Should it be towards the compact city or not?

The urban environment
The recent interest in the compact city in this country can be traced back to the production of the Commission of the European Communities' (CEC) *Green Paper on the Urban Environment* (1990). This was published before the Rio Conference in 1992, before the *Fifth Environmental Action Programme* in 1992 (Select Committee on the European Communities, 1992), and before the UK Strategy on Sustainable Development in 1994 (HM Government, 1994). Clearly the Paper's author was very much aware of the growing pressures of environmentalism and the emerging concepts of sustainable development. Environmental considerations were within the remit of the EC and always have been. Sustainable development considerations have come to the EC from international agreements and have to be accommodated. At the same time, urban planning issues and the urban enviro.iment were not accepted by member states as being within the purview of the EC.

To a degree this was changed, or perhaps regularised, by the Treaty of European Union 1992. Under Article 2 of the Treaty it is accepted that the promotion of sustainable growth, whilst respecting the environment, is an overarching objective for Europe. Under Article 130 it prescribes that, within all policies, there must be incorporated provisions to achieve a high level of protection of the environment. Article 130 also states that EU environmental policies should contribute to the promotion of measures at international level to deal with regional or global environmental problems. The main theme is to emphasise the need for environmental considerations to become more central in all policies, in all sectors. However, it stops well short of accepting that the urban environment as such could be a proper subject for policies at a European level. Here the principle of 'subsidiarity', as set out in Article 3, applies. It states that decisions should be taken as closely as possible to the citizens affected.

This makes the emergence of the *Green Paper on the Urban Environment* all the more interesting because the subject is an adjunct to EU policy-making and not central to it, nor will it become enshrined in any Directive, nor make its way into national legislation. None the less its impact has been remarkable and it has become one of the base documents in any discussion on the compact city in this country.

The background work to the Green Paper comprised six international conferences on the following themes:

- Disused Industrial Areas (two conferences)
- The Urban Periphery
- The Quality of the Urban Environment, Public Spaces and Green Areas
- Urban Pollution in Northern and Southern Europe (two conferences)

Although these were thematic conferences, it was recognised that dealing with urban problems on a thematic or sectoral basis was failing to deal adequately with the problem of urban areas. For example, however much was being done on a sectoral basis, there was no discernible braking of the flight from older cities of their original population, nor their replacement in these older city areas by new inward migrants, usually the poorer members of society either living in inner city ghettos or low quality housing estates on the periphery.

This process appears inexorable as individuals take their own personal decisions about where to live and work in the knowledge that they have considerable personal mobility and access to technology, enabling them to maintain communications with work, friends, family and institutions wherever they are. Seeking to take remedial action to overcome the most critical of resultant problems whether these be environmental or social has not proved to be the means to the reclamation of the vitality of cities. The Green Paper argues that the city as a whole must be seen as a project in itself:

> Has the spread of 'urban areas' and life styles made the concept of the 'city' irrelevant? True, with a few exceptions, today's cities have little in common with their 18th or 19th century predecessors. Yet the past decades have seen a rediscovery of the value of urban living and a growing appreciation of the importance of quality of life in the cities of Europe. In part this reflects the failure of the periphery: the absence of public life, the paucity of culture, the visual monotony, the time wasted in commuting. By contrast the city offers density and variety: the efficient, time-and-energy saving combination of social and economic functions, the chance to restore the rich architecture inherited from the past. (CEC, 1990, p.19).

Cities, as opposed to the statistical concept of 'urban areas', are projects for a new style of life and work. 'City', with the implication of compactness, is the hypothesis of the Green Paper: it appears early on, the advantages of the concept are set out, and the means to achieve it are identified. However, the paper must be treated with some caution. Attractive as the hypothesis might be to many its validity as the outcome from the thematic conferences must be questioned. Although a sectoral approach to urban area problems can well be demonstrated to fail and from that an argument for an integrated approach sustained, the jump to the compact city concept is more from conviction than from evidence.

In the UK there is precious little evidence to support the idea that the past decades have seen a rediscovery of the value of urban living. In fact there is strong evidence pointing the other way, and there is little change in the general pattern of development established and encouraged in the postwar period to justify any such 'rediscovery'. The exodus from the city - the process of 'extensification' rather than of 'intensification' - has been in evidence for 50 years, and the basic reason for this is that it met people's personal aspirations. In a non-interventionist, market-led society, such aspirations were dominant, and the voluntary exodus from cities over this period far exceeds any planned process.

The validity of the hypothesis of the Green Paper is by no means self-evident to the many millions who had moved out of the cities of the UK in the postwar period. To achieve, in the UK, any widespread acceptance of the city as a place to live and work, the concept will need to be matched to environmental realities and to personal aspirations, and sold as such at a political and social level. It would not be accepted in the UK as an article of conviction, even if it could be demonstrated to be intellectually sound in argument, and attractive in its imagery.

So the ideas of the Green Paper which justify the compact city, as presented to date, have had little impact in the UK. The ideas are presented as concepts of conviction rather than of rationality. While the basic concept of seeking to treat the urban environment as a subject area in its own right is undoubtedly sound, to view it as a justification for the compact city is, as yet, unfounded.

Sustainable development

While the wider European perspective suggests that sustainable development might be related to the compact city, the arguments above indicate that the connection is less clear in the UK. The key document is the Government's report *Sustainable Development: The UK Strategy* (1994). It provides an understanding of how it is proposed the urban environment should be handled in public policy terms, and its relevance to the concept of a compact city. But it leaves many questions unanswered. Does it, for instance, argue for the integration of the consideration of environmental and development issues, and does this lead to any advocacy of a compact city? In fact neither the urban environment nor the compact city are mentioned in the document. It does however refer to the need to enhance the quality of life in urban areas, but it is all in the most general terms and appears more as a 'wish list' than as a co-ordinated strategy. Indeed, it is not a strategy; it is a report, and an excellent report at that. It is comprehensive, and above all has obtained a commitment from all government departments to dedicate their work to the achievement of 'sustainable development', even if we do not yet know what it is. For it to be a strategy there would need to be a cohesive, coherent and co-ordinated set of defined lines of action with targets, resources and policies.

Because of its nature the document does not provide any clear, direct guidance about sustainable urban form. It gives tantalising glimpses of the future of some of the components of urban life. For example, in Chapter 24, Development in Town and Country (HM Govt, 1994), it gives a flavour:

Urban growth should be encouraged in the most sustainable form. The density of form is important. More compact urban development uses less land... (para. 24.20)

Sustainable development within urban areas is closely bound up with the quality of urban life...(para. 24.21)

Building within existing urban areas might improve sustainability by increasing density but there may be a limit to the benefits to be gained... (para. 24.22)

Urban quality depends on the creation and protection of green spaces in cities for amenity and recreation... (para. 24.23)

Quality of life is also materially affected by such factors as the location of homes and work spaces... (para. 24.24)

It is not possible to deny the good intentions of the UK strategy or its comprehensive nature, or indeed its impact in raising awareness and attention to the environmental issues, but when it comes to the urban environment it is of little direct help in providing any specific policies or directions to follow. It acknowledges that urban development and its quality are important in the achievement of sustainable development. The urban environment and the form of future settlements become one of the many aspects of sustainable development which have to be worked out in detail as derivative of a set of general principles. The document states that any advances will be through the planning system, but there it stops. This leaves a lot of unanswered questions, and over the last few years a number of important and interesting lines of investigation have been launched in an attempt to answer them. These are all important in the drive to interpret the concept of sustainable development in the realm of urban areas in general, and the compact city in particular.

Compact city

So where does this leave the search for a sustainable urban form and, in particular, the future for the concept of the compact city? A response to this query very much depends on whether one views a half a pint in a pint glass as half full or half empty.

The most positive and encouraging signs since the publication of the UK Strategy in 1994 are the amount of study, research and debate on the urban environment issue. From Local Agenda 21 work upwards, a great deal of energy and effort has been released on the subject. Three or four years to sort out the application of the principles of sustainable development to the complexity of cities is no time at all - it is the pace and quality of the attack on the problem that is so encouraging. Planners must resist being trapped into taking on board easy superficial solutions under the insistence of single issue pressure groups. It will be a hard task with failures and successes along the way.

The tensions between environmentalists who relate almost entirely to the natural realm, and planners who relate to urban areas, are likely to intensify and even become acrimonious. This tension may force urban planners to look for easy, quick fix answers, and for intellectually attractive theorising to provide apparent solutions to urban problems without any concern for their applicability in practice and for their acceptability to society.

As yet, there is no obvious overarching, simple, theoretical basis to provide the guidance to the achievement of sustainable urban forms. Attempts made through analogy with eco-systems, for example, do not appear to provide such a basis. This was evident following the publication of the *Green Paper on the Urban*

Environment (CEC, 1990), when the European Commission established the Expert Group on the Urban Environment. The Group launched the 'Sustainable Cities Project' in 1993 and published their first report in 1994 (European Commission Expert Group on the Urban Environment, 1994). This project sought to take an holistic approach to the planning and management of cities, and advocated a theoretical basis developed and informed by an eco-system approach; the idea was that the eco-system concept used to provide a basis for the understanding of the phenomena of the natural world could be transferred to cities, which could be viewed as a living organism.

But the reliance on the eco-system concept does not provide any practical approach for the planning of a city. It suggests an intellectual framework, but it does not give a framework for action. And furthermore, the eco-system approach appears unlikely to lead with any certainty to a compact city. The key problem is the multiplicity of eco-systems which make up a living city - all interacting, all changing and all susceptible to unpredictable externalities.

The case for a compact city approach, coming from the Green Paper, arises from conviction and from a dedication to the values of the European cultural tradition. These have attractions: they tend to provide a buzz in historical terms and are visually stimulating. For instance the people of the UK are usually completely won over by the ambience found in the tight cobbled streets of compact cities in Europe, usually remembered as bathed in never ending sunshine.

Another argument set out in the Green Paper for the compact city was social cohesion, which people in general desired and sought. Yet our society is displaying all the characteristics of lack of social cohesion. We may not like this, we may feel it to be lamentable, but until such cohesion is re-established it is unlikely that forcing people into tight physical proximity will help at all - in fact without the pre-existence of such cohesion it could actually be destructive. The enormous voluntary exodus from our cities demonstrates that the desire for social cohesion does not override the desire to live in suburbs and low density urbanised areas, given the benefits of mobility and technology.

Conclusion

The claims for the compact city are neither self-evident nor as yet convincing. The changes presently do not appeal to society, neither are they firm enough to justify any policies to be based on them. The claims may be right, but they remain to date unproved. When, and if, they are substantiated they would form the basis for a new set of policy initiatives which would be difficult to implement.

Sustainable development is often called upon to provide the basis for the argument for the compact city. Interpreted through a concentration on environmental protection, it does not form such a basis. Until the development aspect is taken into the equation this will remain the case, and any mention of development immediately brings in economic and social dimensions. These dimensions, it is often claimed, can be handled by 'demand management', but demand management, however well intentioned, however well motivated, is of no value unless it has social, and thus political, support.

If there is at the moment no general theory available to justify the compact city, what is there available to us in order to achieve the advance towards sustainable development? There is a whole new range of options, ideas and approaches being pursued at the present. As yet it is not clear whether these will lead to a general compact city theory or not, or to some tighter version of Howard's three magnets. We do not know the answers, and it is foolhardy to embrace solutions on the basis of conviction and expect society, as it is today, to accept these. If we do proceed in such a way, it may lead to a slow, step by step advance without any clear picture of the end result at the outset. And on the way there is the need to create a new language, new concepts and new mechanisms of implementation. It can never be fast track, whatever the pressures from lobbyists.

So is it possible that following up sustainable development principles can lead to the compact city? Probably not, but it could result in a move in that direction. All recent UK government Planning Policy Guidance Notes (PPGs) refer to the need to contribute to the achievement of sustainable development without stating precisely how this can be achieved. Even the Environment Agency has been asked to do so but again, the means of achievement are not at all clear. In particular PPG3 on Housing and PPG13 on Transport both stress the need to get the maximum amount of housing within urban areas and to reduce the need for travel. This is totally justifiable on the sole ground of land being regarded as a finite non-renewable resource, that must be husbanded, recycled and reused, let alone for any transport considerations. But achieving maximum amounts of housing cannot be at any price if human and social aspirations are to be met as they should be.

These propositions alone have set up all manner of investigations into, for example, how to measure density more appropriately, how to intensify the utilisation of urban areas acceptably, how to determine capacity limits of urban areas. The results of these investigations and many others to follow will help in the understanding of how to manage urban areas to maximum benefit. This understanding will be unlikely to lead to radical change but may, over time, create a range of new measures influencing urban form, but these may not herald a compact city concept as a norm. All judgements and decisions about urban areas are value driven not technically driven; technical, financial and institutional factors play their part but the final decisions spring from the value system held by the decision makers.

Fast progress will not be made in reversing the spread of the city, which appears to embody social aspirations and meet the economic imperatives of the time. Perhaps the only rational course is to treat the urbanised body as we find it, and not lament that it was not born to be more beautiful in the first place. Logic might indicate what that form might be, but rational thought indicates that all we can do is improve it.

Whilst we do have a number of technical and environmental investigations underway, all of which have relevance to urban areas, the most likely brake on progress will be an under-developed and unsophisticated institutional structure to put them into practice. There is little point in developing technical concepts beyond our capacity to receive and use them through human institutions. The challenge of sustainable development is often portrayed as having to devise institutions to handle the complexities and the range of issues in an integrated way. The same could be said of eco-systems in an urban context, and at present the same can be said for the management of the urban environment.

Many of the issues likely to come forward, such as traffic management and intensification, encompass a wider span than the orthodox remit of land use planning - yet planners are usually saddled with responsibilities for implementing any new initiatives. These need to be handled at a much finer grain than the coarse grain of land use planning. Perhaps the level of urban management is more appropriate. Close management with specific policies being applied will be discretionary. It is here, with complex issues, wide discretion, and the need to balance conflicting claims, that vision combined with sensitivity is needed.

It is possible to put forward a range of measures which cover issues wider than orthodox planning, and would provide benefits if developed and managed on a local discretionary basis. Such measures might include a localised tax base, management systems that evolve differently for different zones, and the encouragement of mixed uses. Experiments with new forms of housing could be undertaken, along with local management schemes, such as street wardens for supervising rubbish, cleaning, parking and maintenance. Further measures could include car- free zones made possible through tax benefits, and residential car-access priority zones.

New management structures and a new vision are needed to achieve such aims in urban areas. It may be that these could be linked to parish councils or to town councils, but unless the means of satisfactorily applying emerging technical solutions for the benefit of the community is on a highly localised basis, then the process of sustainable development is likely to fail. This local approach would, of course, meet the aims of Agenda 21. In this way a step by step approach to the management of our urban areas to achieve sustainable development can take place through urban policies based on good science and good research, implemented through institutions which can meet social, economic, political and cultural aspirations. For planners, it requires vision of some magnitude. But it is perhaps a vision that is unlikely to produce the compact city.

References

Commission of the European Communities (1990) *Green Paper on the Urban Environment*, Commission of the European Communities, Brussels.

European Commission Expert Group on the Urban Environment (1994) *Sustainable Cities Project: First Report*. Brussels.

HM Government (1994) *Sustainable Development: The UK Strategy*, HMSO, London.

Select Committee on the European Communities, House of Lords (1992) *Fifth Environmental Action Programme: Integration of Community Policies*, HMSO, London.

Shepley, C. (1995) *Still Life in Planning*, Address to the Town and Country Planning School.

Katie Williams, Elizabeth Burton and Mike Jenks

Achieving the Compact City through Intensification: *An Acceptable Option?*

Introduction

The compact city is being promoted in the UK and throughout Europe as a component of the strategy formed to tackle the problems of unsustainability. The rationale for its implementation relies heavily on a set of strategic benefits, which are said to be the outcome of more compact urban forms. The arguments are, by now, familiar: in more compact cities travel distances are reduced, thus fuel emissions are lessened, rural land is saved from development, local facilities are supported and local areas become more autonomous. Although the actual effects of many of these claimed benefits are far from certain, for now at least, urban compaction is a policy direction which is being followed.

Herein lies a problem. In academic debate the concepts of sustainable urban forms, and latterly 'compact cities' are often discussed as if they are 'models', which could be built now. The implication is that there are a set of options available for constructing the ideal urban form, and that we can set about creating it. Of course this does not reflect reality. Unless new settlements are built, more compact cities can only be achieved through a process of making existing cities more dense, of encouraging more people to live in urban areas and of building at higher densities: of 'intensifying' cities. Therefore, the strategic benefits suggested at an international, national, regional and even metropolitan level, can only be achieved through maximising the use and form of cities, and this will have local implications, which will be experienced in every neighbourhood, on every street.

The aim of this chapter is to set the compact city debate, and more specifically the 'intensification' debate, in the context of its acceptability to urban residents. Whilst the theory sets out the strategic advantages of compact living, it is crucial that 'intensification' itself delivers the benefits. Most definitions of sustainability emphasise not only environmental criteria, but also issues of social equity and choice, both now and in the future. Therefore any proposed form of development must be agreeable to the urban population. If it is not, those who can will leave the city, and only the most disadvantaged will be left: a scenario which is clearly

83

unsustainable.

It is essential that the strategic objectives deliver some of the local advantages offered in the compact city debate, for example better facilities and services, better public transport, and a more vibrant cultural life. More important still is that, if these benefits do occur, they are not outweighed by the problems of more compact living, such as congestion and overcrowding. In a number of crucial areas of urban life, achieving the balance between 'town cramming' and vibrancy and sustainability will be the key to successful urban development in the future.

The starting point for this investigation must be an understanding of intensification itself. It is a complex process, with many components. This chapter addresses how these parts make up the whole, i.e. the compact city, and investigates whether this 'whole' is acceptable to urban residents, in the current social and political climate.

Urban intensification

The term 'urban intensification' does not have a common definition. It is widely used within discussions of urban form, but generally relates to the range of processes which make an area more compact. Lock suggests that intensification is a process which 'ensure(s) that we make the fullest use of land that is already urbanised, before taking green fields.' (1995, p.173), and Naess has described it as the process of encouraging development to where 'technical encroachments on nature have previously taken place.' (1993, p.309). Roseth, however, describes intensification in terms of urban 'consolidation', which he defines as 'the increase of population and/or dwellings within a defined urban area' (1991, p.30). Roseth's distinction of an increase of both population and built form is useful here, as many of the arguments indicating the link between compact urban living and sustainability rely heavily on higher densities of people, as well as of buildings.

Intensification and consolidation are, therefore, terms used to describe a number of strategies by which an area can become more heavily built-up or used. In Australia consolidation policies have been on the political agenda for over twenty years. Therefore definitions and descriptions of the process are well developed in Australian literature. For example the *National Housing Strategy* (Minnery, 1992) uses 'consolidation' interchangeably with 'densification' and 'compaction' to describe processes such as medium and high density infill housing development, building on larger parcels of land that are currently not built on, and development where there is a greater emphasis on town houses, apartments and terraced houses. In the UK, research into intensification for the DoE has classified the process as encompassing a number of phenomena (Oxford Brookes University and Entec, ongoing). This research defines intensification of both built form and activity. Built form intensification comprises: redevelopment of existing buildings or previously developed sites, at higher densities; sub-division or conversion of buildings; building of additions or extensions to existing structures; and development on previously undeveloped urban land. Activity intensification is defined as: the increased use of existing buildings or sites; changes of use, which lead to an increase in activity; and increases in the numbers of people living in, working in, or travelling through an area.

Local acceptability

The UK Government has recently reaffirmed its commitment to the process of intensification. In the report *Sustainable Development: The UK Strategy* it states that: 'The Government's objective for 2012 is to continue to make the best use of the land resource by maximising the use for development of urban land, especially where it is vacant, derelict or contaminated land, and protecting the open countryside and open land of importance in urban areas.' (HM Govt, 1994, p.43). Planning guidance now also strongly advocates development in existing urban areas; and the recent housing White Paper *Our Future Homes* reiterates this point stating that 'Development within existing towns and cities can be more sustainable than using greenfield sites.' (HM Govt, 1995, p.46).

Urban intensification is, therefore, entrenched in UK strategies for sustainability. But whilst compact city policies must, by definition, advocate a number of the processes outlined above, it must be recognised that the combination of policies, and extent of their implementation should be given attention. As Minnery warns: 'If the current urban form is one which creates difficulties some of these problems are likely to be exacerbated if the form is made more dense.' (1992, p.23). The UK Government is also aware of the potentially problematic nature of intensification. Policy and guidance aimed at promoting consolidation is peppered with notes of caution. For example *Planning Policy Guidance 3: Housing* (DoE, 1992) advises that 'a balance has to be struck between the need for development and the interests of conservation' (para 2), and that 'sensitive planning control is necessary to ensure that the cumulative effects of redevelopment do not damage the character and amenity of established residential areas.' (para 20).

In Australia too, this question of 'balance' and local acceptability has been acknowledged. Minnery (1992) argues that 'The aims of urban consolidation are laudable and broad, but have not always been well received' (p.25), and that 'The local condition and capacity of physical and social infrastructure is a crucial consideration for consolidation policies.' (p.xiv). Furthermore he reiterates the point regarding the local impact of broader policies. He states that consolidation is a 'metropolitan-wide strategy applied locally. Increasing densities can have an impact on a specific locality, associated with a perceived lessening of property values and amenity' (p.25). Finally he concludes that 'Implementation also requires local community support.' (p.xiv).

It is this question of community support that will be discussed further here. In particular the question will be addressed of whether intensification is acceptable in the UK. In his recent paper about the demand for new housing, Lock raises the fundamental question of 'whether higher-density living is attractive in the UK' (1995, p.176). This chapter draws largely on examples from Europe, Australia and the USA to explore issues of acceptability and attractiveness, and to stress the reality of many of the conflicts surrounding the local effects of the compact city. It is not the aim to repeat the theoretical gains and losses, but to highlight common areas of conflict, or of success, from the perspective of urban residents. Of course, adopting this perspective does not suggest that a judgement has been made about whether the views of city dwellers are right or wrong (or sustainable or unsustainable), but it does reflect the importance of local opinion in a system of local democracy. Those implementing policies will be reluctant to do so if the policies themselves are seen to be politically unacceptable at the local level.

There are a number of important arguments within some of the issues affected by intensification that need to be considered. These are: the spatial effects of urban intensification, urban image and vitality, social impacts and service provision, and the effects of intensification on transport.

The spatial effects of urban intensification

Some of the main arguments in favour of a more compact city relate directly to spatial impacts. Primarily it is argued that developing in existing urban areas reduces pressure for development in the countryside and makes the most effective use of urban land, especially if it is derelict, contaminated or vacant. This argument is popular with the rural protection lobby, and those involved in urban regeneration. However, it is unpopular with those who believe that some cities and towns are already developed to capacity, and that any more development would be detrimental to environmental quality in its broadest sense. Collis sums up the worst case scenario when he warns that 'Settlements could consume themselves from within by eating up the private and public greenspace that contributes so much to environmental quality.' (Collis, in Rankin, 1995, p.13).

This perception of over-development has led some local communities to mobilise against what they see as 'town cramming'. They feel that their neighbourhoods are being over-crowded, and are losing amenity. This leads to battles to stave off development, usually on backland sites, or well loved amenity space such as playing fields or sports grounds (*The Times*, 1995; Boyle, 1984). These battles are often fuelled by resentment at the lack of involvement of local people in the development process, and perceived developer greed (Busted, 1980). In most cases arguments focus on the cumulative effect of development and on the value to the community of the land to be built on (Buller, 1985). As Woodward (1988) has argued, derelict urban land may have many informal uses which are of great value, for example as play spaces or wild areas.

In other cities however the situation is reversed; there is a surplus of derelict and vacant land, which can have a downgrading effect on a whole area. Vast sites which are disused, or temporarily given over to car parks, tips or informal play space have a negative effect, both on the visual quality of the city and, psychologically, on local residents. In a recent MORI poll, commissioned by 'Groundwork' (an organisation which attempts to use derelict land for beneficial purposes), it was found that the amount of derelict land was affecting the perceived quality of life of 75% of the population (quoted in Fyson, 1995, p.7). In less prosperous areas urban land has often lain derelict and contaminated for decades, with little or no hope of being developed because of the costs involved. Although the re-use of urban land for housing is strongly advocated in policy, directing development to areas that remain unattractive to the market is difficult.

In places where derelict land is causing blight it is often the residents themselves who attempt to ameliorate the situation, aided or unaided by pressure groups, local businesses or the local authority. Thus there are groups which have actively reclaimed local land for wildlife and other 'soft' uses, and there are many groups campaigning to attract development. For example, in London, where derelict land has risen by 410% between 1974 and 1993 (Wickens *et al.*, 1995), there are groups fighting to bring residential uses back into the city; a group called 'Communities and Homes in Central London' (CHiCL) is a federation of community organisations (including groups from Battersea, Covent Garden and Docklands), which campaigns for retaining the mixed residential and working communities, in and around central London (CHiCL and CRPE, 1995, p.3).

However, whilst some groups have been effective at the local level, the success of local communities in influencing the overall amount of derelict land is questionable. The CPRE has calculated that 39 hectares of urban land becomes derelict each week; and research by Groundwork has concluded that 'it would take 200 years to clear the backlog at current rates' (quoted in Fyson, p.7).

Fig. 1. An example of backland development.

Photograph: Mike Jenks

One way forward in these issues is to involve local residents more fully in planning and development procedures, either to determine which areas are perceived to be causing blight, or conversely to determine which open spaces are seen as particularly valuable. A number of local authorities are now trying to assess local opinion when making judgements of their open space provision. Many are refining purely quantitative measures of land use, and are looking in more depth at the full role and function of urban spaces. The Metropolitan Planning Officers Society Report, *Urban Greenspace Policy Study* (1993), suggests that a far more imaginative approach should be taken to open space provision and that all the functions of greenspace should be considered, such as its role in the urban structure, and its townscape and conservation value. These considerations should be made from a sound basis of complete and up-to-date monitoring of greenspace provision. This includes finding out how local residents perceive open land in their neighbourhoods.

A more considered approach to the spatial effects of intensification by the local authority would represent an important step in overcoming local conflict (Metropolitan Planning Officers Society, 1993). By involving local residents in decision making, open space policies could be legitimised. However, the real problems lie with the development process itself (Evans, 1990). It is extremely difficult for areas in decline to attract development, and it is equally hard for growth areas to resist development on the grounds of its cumulative effects. Whilst local action can affect single sites, the incremental impact of development cycles is far more powerful. Perhaps only higher levels of investment in less prosperous areas (Fyson, 1995), and more sensitive planning controls where towns are 'crammed' (DoE, 1992), can redress the balance.

The image and vitality of the city

Another claimed benefit of compacting cities is that they can upgrade an existing area by offering the best in new design and improving vitality. Infill buildings can contribute to the coherence of the urban fabric, and the reuse and upgrading of existing buildings can have a positive effect on the image of the city. Furthermore, bringing more people into the city can make it more vibrant, and encourage the development of cultural activities and facilities. Thus the image of the city will be enlivened, making it more attractive to both residents and visitors.

Fig. 2. Bringing people back into the city can encourage cultural and community activities.

Photograph: Mike Jenks

However, the public are often critical of the quality and design of modern buildings, especially in historic cities or conservation areas, and in established residential districts. Much of this criticism has been prompted by development in the recent past. The property boom in the 1980s was characterised in many areas by large scale development of poor quality, which added nothing to local identity. Before that, more comprehensive redevelopment had alienated many urban residents in their own home towns. As Barton *et al.* state, 'The functional, aesthetic and social failure of some developments built in the 1960s and 1970s has led to a widespread mistrust of the "experts" responsible for the delivery of built environmental quality.' (1995, p.41). Some commentators believe this mistrust is set to continue. Evans brings the critique up to date, with his analysis of the effects on design of the current planning and development system which - because of increased land prices - he argues, leads to strange new housing layouts, with garages in front of houses and shared driveways, smaller units, and multiple extensions which transform some detached houses into terraced houses (1990, pp.9-11). All these trends, he believes, are reducing the quality of the nation's building stock.

Fortunately, there is another side to this argument. In some of the UK's larger towns and cities, the 1990s have witnessed some popular, high profile development initiatives and schemes. Swanwick has commented that good urban development can and does attract people back into our towns and cities, and gives the examples of recent docklands schemes to illustrate that increases in density do not mean reduction in quality (1995, p.19). Strategies which have deliberately attempted to draw people back into the city have also led to benefits. For example the revitalisation of some areas of London, such as Camden Lock, has led to the mixed use and vitality which is so loved by the advocates of the compact city.

Fig. 3. Increased densities can support local services.

Photograph: Mike Jenks

This bodes well for the quality of urban living which, according to predictions of household formation and size, may be more popular in the future. Research by URBED (Rudlin and Falk, 1995) into the design of 21st century homes revealed that 'the main growing requirement is for childless households', many of whom, they believe, may be 'equally happy with pot plants or balconies as with gardens.' (Falk, 1994, p.352). Thus there is considerable scope for good quality, high density urban housing, as has become fashionable in cities such as Manchester, Glasgow and Leeds. The recent initiative by the Secretary of State for the Environment, *Quality in Town and Country* (DoE, 1994), should also generate means of making our urban areas more attractive to residents.

The success of new urban development hinges largely on its location, design and quality. Therefore it is crucial that those planning and developing urban areas are aware of the type of development that would be popular with existing and prospective urban residents. Punter (1994), and Hubbard (1994) both address this issue. Punter calls for the skills of the 'design controllers' to be questioned, whilst Hubbard compares the public's and planners' views on new development in Birmingham, and argues that planners need to develop a more considered awareness of local needs and wants. Barriers between professionals and the public need to be broken down. By involving the public in initiatives which allow for input, in non-professional language and a relaxed environment, opinions can be freely exchanged, and plans generated.

Encouragingly there are a number of examples of successful initiatives, with those in Birmingham and Leicester attracting deserved publicity. Perhaps only the high levels of public participation which these schemes achieved will give residents what they want, or allow them to understand any compromises that need to be made. As Barton *et al.* argue 'the built environment is not a fixed asset; it constantly evolves, and each increment of development is part of the legacy to succeeding generations.' (1995, p.41). Hopefully the legacy left by the 1990s will be both sustainable and acceptable to city dwellers.

Social impacts and service provision
Intensified urban areas are claimed to lead to more social cohesion and community spirit. It is claimed that they are safer than lower density areas because they are under better surveillance. Most importantly though, they are claimed to be more socially equitable because services and facilities are provided locally, within walking distance of most homes. This provision is enabled by the high densities of people living in the compact city. In turn, access to these services leads to a fairer distribution of the city's resources. As Pacione states, 'The physical accessibility of people to urban services and facilities is a key component of quality of life at the intra-urban level.' (1989, pp.12-18).

Whilst some of these claims may be upheld in some areas, in others, unfortunately, they are not. Intensification has sometimes led to problems of 'bad neighbour effects' - particularly in mixed use areas - and to feelings of overcrowding in the public realm (Building Design Partnership, 1994). Often it has meant influxes of 'new types' of residents, who do not create new communities or merge with the existing ones. In some areas, local services have become overstretched and are unable to cope with incremental increases in population (Light, 1992).

Higher densities also lead to bad neighbour effects in residential areas, where close proximity can lead to conflicts between those with different lifestyles. The example of increased noise pollution provides a clear illustration of such a problem (Planning Week, 1995a). Disturbance has increased dramatically over the last decade or so. This is partly a result of advances in technology, such as car alarms and loud stereo equipment, but it is also a result of the increase in general activity in towns and cities. Dynes (1994) has noted that, between 1980 and 1992, domestic complaints in the UK rose from 31,076 to more than 88,000, and between May 1993 and November 1994 an estimated 17 people were killed, and many more injured, during arguments caused by loud noise late at night, mainly music, revving engines and car and burglar alarms.

Furthermore the arguments about better service provision are yet to be proven conclusively. An article in *Urban Policy Research* (1991) reviewed research investigating the relationship between urban consolidation and service provision and found that: 'To date... there is limited empirical evidence of definite social benefits or costs arising from consolidation'. Pinfield (1995) has also investigated local service provision. He has looked at ways of ensuring that local services meet the needs both of local residents and of sustainability. He highlights the methods generated by the work of the International Council for Local Environmental Initiatives (ICLEI) as being the way forward in solving local environmental problems and conflicts. He suggests that the ICLEI's approach is right, in that local residents should be involved in every stage of the service delivery process, from priority setting through to evaluation and feedback. Approaches such as these are likely to be necessary if the range of local impacts of intensification are to be identified and tackled.

Ensuring that the appropriate local services are provided, and that the social effects of intensification are balanced, will require patience and commitment from urban residents, policy makers and implementers alike. To a certain extent living in urban areas will always require a degree of tolerance by residents; some people are far more accepting of the negative effects of urban living than others. As Davison argues, 'Perhaps we divide naturally into two types: those for whom cities are vibrant and exciting, a focus for human activity; and those for whom they are dirty, noisy and dangerous.' (1995, p3). It may be true that some find city living stimulating and others find it stressful; but that does not mean urban residents should accept excessive pollution, disturbance, crime, poor service provision and unsociable behaviour by others as part of urban life. These are not inevitable consequences of more intensive urban living. Tackling them will require commitment and innovative action, but problems can be ameliorated.

The effects of intensification on transport

Strategic arguments about the proposed benefits to transport of more compact cities are clear, and well documented: compact cities reduce the length of journeys; promote energy efficient modes of travel such as walking and cycling; offer opportunities to reduce private car use; and support public transport. However, whilst some of these benefits may be evident in urban areas, local problems are also very visible. Congestion and dangerous traffic leads to a worse - not better - pedestrian environment (Engwicht, 1992), public transport is often caught up in congested streets, trains and buses are often overcrowded and parking is a serious problem, affecting the character and function of city streets. Far from living in cities connected by good efficient public transport, most urban residents, especially in the UK's larger towns and cities, find themselves battling daily with commuter traffic and heavy vehicles, and not being able to park, even outside their own homes (for example, Davison, 1995).

One solution is, of course, for urban dwellers to give up their cars and attempt more environmentally friendly modes of transport: walking, cycling and public transport. But the indications are that they are unlikely to do that. Research for the DoT states that even in the most heavily parked urban areas people are not planning to relinquish their cars, and are in fact intending to buy more (Balcombe and York, 1993, quoted in Lock, 1995, p.174). Mynors (1995) suggests why this might be the case. He stresses that both market forces and private citizens' views are weighted in favour of the car. Amongst other things, he argues that car travel provides mobility in private and comfort, with a guaranteed seat (and music) from door to door, with shopping or any other baggage, at a marginal cost less than public transport. Furthermore, he suggests that for some the car is a visible status symbol (1995, p.37).

And if the car is the status symbol, then currently, in the UK, public transport is its opposite. It is seen by many as a second rate option, as the *National Travel Survey 1981/91* shows. It states that buses 'could be seen as now mainly used by those who were not able to afford or use rather more convenient and personal forms of transport. The figures... suggest that bus travel is becoming more and more a form of transport of the last resort.' (*National Travel Survey 1989/91*, DoT, 1993, quoted in Mynors, 1995, p.37)

Whilst congestion and parking problems are causing irritation for those who do have cars, the wider implications of mass car ownership are perhaps more problematic for those who are not car owners. For children, the elderly and women (who are proportionately less likely to have access to a car), the situation is poor. The *National Travel Survey 1989/91* has shown that there has been a drop in the number of children walking to school and that cycling has decreased by 18% between 1975/76 and 1981/91 (quoted in Mynors, 1995, p.38). Most of this is attributable to the fact that the volume and speed of traffic has made roads unsafe. Research by Appleyard (in Engwicht, 1992) has looked at the wider influence of traffic in towns. He looked at three similar residential streets in San Francisco, but with very different traffic flows, and found that in the one with the least traffic the residents had three times as many friends as on the street with heavy traffic. He also looked at what people considered to be their 'home territory', and found that people on the 'light' street considered the whole street, whilst people on the 'heavy' street delineated just their own house. This, he reported, was because of the alienating effects of the noise, vibration and fumes which stopped the people of the 'heavy' street from using their road as a social space.

All urban residents are affected by the air pollution caused by increased car use. The DoE's *15th Digest of United Kingdom Environmental Protection and Water Statistics* (DoE, 1993) states that road transport is the biggest culprit for the reduction in air quality, and Hurdle records that, in the UK, 'Deaths rose because of the bad smog episode in December 1991' (1994, p.24). These problems are especially acute in larger towns and cities, and urban residents are becoming increasingly concerned. In Greenwich for example, local residents are campaigning for the closure of a main road because of the resultant poor air quality, and the consequent health implications.

So how does all this affect the prospect of cities becoming even more compact? Is the situation to continue until the point of gridlock? Hopefully not. There are signs that public attitudes to the car may be changing, but only very slowly. Research by MIL Motoring Research (Buck, 1995) showed that almost two thirds of motorists said they would like to see the use of cars actively discouraged, but the problem is that tolls and increased fuel taxes remain unpopular. The majority did, though, endorse stricter parking controls! In some areas urban residents are beginning to weigh up the costs to their neighbourhoods of heavy traffic, and to decide in favour of restraint. For example in Cambridge the council is discussing street closures, and the setting of traffic and pollution reduction targets, aimed at improving conditions in the city centre. These initiatives are being considered because the local authority 'detect a ground swell of public opinion away from the need to give the motor vehicle priority - in order to improve the environment.' (Local Transport Today, 1995, p.4).

Fig. 4. Accommodating the car has a detrimental effect on the character of residential areas.
Photograph: Mike Jenks

One in three English counties has now signed up to some form of travel awareness campaign, the reasoning being that if people understand the damage they are doing to the environment they will use cars less, or more efficiently, for example by car sharing. Other initiatives, such as National Bike Week, Green Transport Week and the 'Don't Choke Britain' campaign have the same aims (Hughes, 1995). In some areas more direct action is proposed. In Edinburgh, for example, there are plans to promote a car-free housing area, where tenants must agree not to own a car (Planning Week, 1995b).

However, whilst these types of strategy may have some success, there are limits to how much people will change their habits, especially if everyone else seems to be carrying on as normal. Many people in the UK have become used to the luxury of owning and using a car and will not give it up lightly. Even if public transport was cheap and efficient, for many people it would still not be perceived as efficient enough to be a substitute for the private car. It seems to be only a matter of time before more direct action is required.

Conclusions

From the examples and arguments presented above it is clear that the local effects of implementing the strategic goals of the compact city are often problematic. There are cases where cities have benefited from intensification, especially where new development has upgraded an area, where an increase in densities has led to a more vibrant and varied way of life, and where high quality urban areas have been created. However, there are also cities, or parts of cities, which are perceived as over-developed, or overcrowded, by their residents, where valuable open space has been lost, traffic is congested, and air, noise and light pollution are having a detrimental effect on the quality of life.

Much of how urban residents perceive their neighbourhood is based on their understanding of the processes which shape it. If these processes are seen as unjust then it is likely that they will remain unacceptable. Currently, whilst sustainability may be high on the political agenda, it is slow to filter through to urban residents themselves. This is worrying, for without an understanding of the aims of intensification, it is unlikely that urban dwellers will accept the compromises they are sometimes being asked to make, and will not relate the local effects with the strategic aims of sustainable development.

Research undertaken by Pinfield (1995) with focus groups in Lancashire highlights this issue. Overall, the groups showed a distrust of public institutions, including government, and were unfamiliar with the term 'sustainable development'. Clearly in such a situation urban intensification is unlikely to be seen positively, unless its outcomes are perceived wholly as urban renewal. However, the same groups showed a strong attachment to local identity and had a sense of community. Perhaps the way forward is to make use of these positive associations by linking them in public perception with the goals of sustainable development.

Making this link may deliver some benefits, but is there any certainty that, even if city dwellers do understand the implications of sustainable development, they will be willing to accept the local implications? Will people curb car use, travel by public transport and accept higher density housing for the sake of future generations? Owens (1995) believes that there is a marked distinction between what people want as citizens and what they want as consumers. As citizens, most people agree with the long term aims of reducing global warming, reducing travel distances and so on; but as consumers, they still want to have access to cars, to not be inconvenienced by public transport, and to carry on consuming goods at the present high rates. As Davison states: 'What is good for us is not necessarily what we want' (1995, p.4). This is clearly illustrated in the transport poll (above) where people endorse restrictions on car use, but only agree on the minimal constraints to their use.

So what options does this leave those attempting to implement the compact city, and to make it attractive to existing and prospective urban residents? First, it is clear that there are benefits to be gained from intensification, and these benefits must be maximised in order to attract those to whom urban living might appeal back into the cities. But there are likely to be conflicts and problems too. Some of these conflicts can be overcome through good local management and community awareness. Local people can become involved in decision making through popular education, citizen participation and involvement in local service development. If some aspects of intensification make urban areas attractive, safe places to live then people will choose to return to the cities. However, whilst education and participation may go some way towards addressing public demands, it may be that *policies* have to address more directly the concept of citizenship (Morrell, 1990). They may have to act more in favour of the citizen than the individual or the market, and lead the way in indicating the importance of sustainability. It is not enough to leave the success or failure of sustainability in the hands of voluntary action, by those residents with the time, resources and ability to become interested in the concept of sustainable development. If we do, this may turn out to be a grossly inadequate response to the actions needed to achieve strategic goals, at the local level, in the compact city.

References

Balcombe, R.J. and York, I.O. (1993) *The Future of Residential Parking*, Transport Research Laboratory, for the DoT, HMSO, London.

Barton, H., Davis, G. and Guise, R. (1995) *Sustainable Settlements: A Guide for Planners, Designers and Developers*, University of the West of England and the Local Government Management Board, Bristol.

Boyle, E. (1984) Guerrilla tactics to keep Dallas out of Dorking. *The Listener*, 11 October, **112(2879),** pp.4-6.

Buck, C. (1995) *MIL Motoring Omnibus*, MIL Motoring Research, (Division of NOP Group), London.

Building Design Partnership (in association with the MVA Consultancy and Donaldsons) (1994) *Chester: The Future of an Historic City*, Cheshire County Council, Chester City Council and English Heritage. Chester.

Buller, H. (1985) *Citizen Action and Urban Renewal: A Case Study*, Oxford Polytechnic, Department of Town Planning, Working Paper no.85.

Busted, M.A. (1980) IBM at Bowden: locational conflict in a suburban area of Greater Manchester. *Manchester Geographer*, Autumn **1(1)** pp.50-70.

Campaign for Homes in Central London and Council for the Protection of Rural England (1995) *Plea for more homes in London*. Press release, 27 July.

Davison, I. (1995) Brave new world? *House Builder*, February pp.3-4.

DoE (1992) *Planning Policy Guidance 3: Housing*, HMSO, London.

DoE (1993) *15th Digest of United Kingdom Environmental Protection and Water Statistics*, HMSO, London.

DoE and DoT (1994) *Planning Policy Guidance 13: Transport*, HMSO, London.

DoE (1994) *Quality in Town and Country, A Discussion Document*, HMSO, London.

DoT (1993) *National Travel Survey 1989/91*, HMSO, London.

Dynes, M. (1994) Ministers plan to pull the plug on noisy neighbours. *The Times,* 21 November.

Engwicht, D. (1992) *Towards an Eco City, Calming the Traffic*, Envirobook, Sydney.

Evans, A. (1990) *Rabbit Hutches on Postage Stamps: Economics, Planning and Development in the 1990s*, The 12th Denman Lecture, Granta Editions, Cambridge.

Falk, N. (1994) Letter to *Town and Country Planning*. December, **Vol. 63, No. 12,** p.352.

Fyson, A. (1995) Don't count on the Lottery. *Planning Week,* 13 April **Vol. 3, No. 15**, p.7.

HM Government (1994) *Sustainable Development: The UK Strategy*, HMSO, London.

HM Government (1995) *Our Future Homes, Opportunity, Choice, Responsibility, The Governments' Policies for England and Wales*, DoE and Welsh Office, HMSO, London.

Hubbard, P. (1994) Professional vs. lay tastes in design control - an empirical investigation. *Planning Practice and Research*, **9 (3)**, pp.271-87.

Hughes, P. (1995) Travel awareness campaigns: taking transport dilemmas onto the doorstep. *Local Transport Today*, 11 May, p.12.

Hurdle, D. (1994) Time for targets for sustainable transport. *Planning,* **1086**, 16 September pp.24-5.

Light, A. (1992) Lack of breathing space. *Surveyor*, 20 August.

Local Transport Today (1995) Street closures and targets planned as Cambridge joint committee tackles traffic. 16 March.

Lock, D. (1995) Room for more within city limits? *Town and Country Planning*, July, **Vol. 64, No. 7**, pp.173-176.

Metropolitan Planning Officers Society (1993) *Urban Greenspace Policy Study*, Metropolitan Planning Officers Society, Oldham.

Minnery, J.R. (1992) *Urban Form and Development Strategies: Equity, Environmental and Economic Implications. The National Housing Strategy*, Australian Government Publishing Service, Canberra.

Morrell, F. (1990) The relevance of citizenship. *Policy Studies,* Winter, **11 (4)**, pp.51-8.

Mynors, P. (1995) Planning policies to reduce transport emissions - will they work? *Report,* February, pp.36-8.

Naess, P. (1993) Can urban development be made environmentally sound? *Journal of Environmental Planning and Management*, **Vol. 36, No. 3**, pp.309-33.

Owens, S. (1995) *I Wouldn't Start from Here, Land Use, Transport and Sustainability*, Linacre Lecture Series, Transport and the Environment, 9 February, Linacre College, Oxford.

Pacione, M. (1989) Access to urban services - the case of secondary schools in Glasgow. *Scottish Geographical Magazine*, **Vol.105, No.1**, pp.12-18.

Pinfield, G. (1995) Indicators, institutions and public perceptions. *Town and Country Planning*. April **Vol. 64, No. 4**, pp.117-9.

Planning Week (1995a) RTPI urges the Government to clarify responsibilities on noise. 31 August, p.22.

Planning Week (1995b) Edinburgh eyes car-free residential zones plan. 30 March **Vol. 3, No. 13**, p.7.

Punter, J. (1994) Design control in England. *Built Environment,* **20 (2)** pp.169-80.

Rankin, R. (1995) Battle of the Greenfield. *Planning Week*, 8 June, **Vol. 3. No. 23**, p.13.

Roseth, J. (1991) The case for urban consolidation. *Architecture Australia*, March pp.30-3.

Rudlin, D. and Falk, N. (1995) *21st Century Homes, Buildings to Last*, URBED, Joseph Rowntree Foundation, York.

Swanwick, C. (1995) All around the houses. *Planning Week*, 3 August, **Vol. 3, No. 1**, p.19.

The Times (1993) Hastings residents opposed to Boots planning application, 7 August.

Urban Policy and Research (1991) Forum special, urban consolidation - an introduction to the debate. **Vol.9, No.1**, p.78-100.

Wickens, D., Rumfitt, A. and Willis, R. (1995) *Survey of Derelict Land in England, 1993. Vol. 1 Report*, HMSO, London.

Woodward, S. (1988) Is Vacant Land Really Vacant? *The Planner*, January, **Vol. 74, No. 1**, p.14.

Part Two
Social and Economic Issues

Part 2
Social and Economic Issues
Introduction

The concept of sustainability is complex, particularly in the urban context; it embraces social, economic and environmental issues, and for urban development to be truly sustainable it must be sustainable on all three counts. Benefits for one issue may result in unacceptable costs for another, as shown starkly by Smyth in his description of the grave consequences of neglecting social and economic concerns in the pursuit of an 'environmentally driven' objective.

General theories surrounding the compact city idea were presented in Part 1; the following two parts of the book dissect some of these theories, and analyse them in more detail. Social and economic issues are examined first. There are two - interrelated - strands to this examination: the first concerns the validity of the claims that in social and economic terms the compact city is the most sustainable urban form; the second concerns the validity of the compact city as a realistic proposition, which is particularly significant in a market-led economy.

Advocates of the compact city claim that intensifying urban areas would lead to safer, more vibrant urban areas, support for local businesses and services, and greater social equity. Many of these arguments were put forward in Part 1, but there is little empirical research to support them. Troy investigates some of the social issues and provides counter-arguments to the commonly claimed benefits. He contends that, in the Australian context, compacting or consolidation would take away from the egalitarian nature of traditional housing, and from the freedoms to pursue family and community life that currently exist. Both Smyth and Troy believe that the less well-off would suffer if the compact city became a reality.

However, it is futile to prove anything about the sustainability of the compact city if the possibility of its realisation is remote. Some of the authors assert that significant proportions of the UK population are still moving out of cities into more rural or suburban areas, and that it is evident that there is a demand for increasing amounts of living space as standards of living rise (Knight; Crookston *et al.*). Since the creation of whole new towns happens infrequently, the compact city is most likely to be brought about by intensifying existing urban areas -

increasing densities, activity and the mix of uses - and by attracting people back into the city. For this to be viable, two conditions need to be satisfied: compacting the city must be a profitable activity for the producers of the built environment (the developers and funding institutions); and, as a key determinant of the first condition, the compact city must be an attractive location for the consumers of the built environment (residents, employers, service suppliers and so on).

Knight and Fulford present their views on the feasibility of the compact city from the point of view of the property market. Fulford gives an optimistic view of developers' attitudes; interviews revealed that, given the removal of certain obstacles, developers would be prepared to entertain the idea of the compact city. Knight is less optimistic than Fulford: he highlights the problems that are often confronted with brownfield development, such as land contamination and fragmented land ownership patterns.

Crookston *et al.* address the viability of the compact city from the consumer's perspective, and assert the importance of quality. They argue that the quality of life in the compact city must be as high as that in the suburbs or country town, or as high as in the non-intensified city, if the proposition is to be attractive. Knight and Green support this assertion. Troy highlights the importance of the cultural context for aspirations and ideas of quality: the compact city concept is more alien to Australian city-dwellers than their European counterparts. There can also be a divergence in opinion between professionals - architects, planners and urban designers - and the general public, in their vision of higher density cities. These differing visions about urban quality influence the feasibility of the compact city. Green believes that a conundrum facing the advocates of sustainable urban form is the possibility that cities may need to be 'thinner' to be attractive.

As Green also points out, there are additional wider influences on the viability of the compact city. The location of housing, employment and services is not dictated simply by the quality of life offered in alternative locations. It is claimed that structural economic and social forces, such as the spatial division of labour, determine urban form. In this case, to reverse decentralisation, it would be necessary to address these wider issues (Green; Troy).

On the whole, the contributors in Part 2 do not dismiss the idea of the compact city, but a common theme running through the chapters is that, for the idea to be successful, social and economic considerations need to be given equal weight to environmental concerns (Smyth), and the compact city needs to be controlled and managed appropriately. There is a belief that urban managers should adopt a realistic, balanced approach (Knight), and that the compact city concept could be extended to include the intensification of a wider variety of settlements, including sub-centres and suburbs, which could be connected by efficient transport links (Troy). A balanced approach may be to aim for the best of the compact city and the best of alternative forms (Knight); and Green argues that, to achieve the benefits of the compact city, a regional approach to the administration of the compact city or compact city-region (Green) should be taken. Attaining a high quality environment in compact centres may first require market incentives (Fulford), high quality service provision, good design of development and transport measures (Crookston *et al.*). Creating socially and economically sustainable cities is difficult and complex. However, the following chapters show the potential of the compact city, and begin to suggest ways in which this potential could be achieved.

Hedley Smyth
Running the Gauntlet: *A Compact City within a Doughnut of Decay*

Introduction

The history of the 'compact city' can be traced back to biblical times when a range of government functions were administered at the city gate, controlling the comings and goings in and out of the city as well as defending it against attack. In Britain, the medieval fortified city gave birth to the suburb outside its walls. The rights conferred upon and economic experience of the 'city' dweller were different, frequently better, than for the 'suburban' counterpart, although there was a strong economic interdependence. Industrialisation and mechanised transportation have created waves of urbanisation which in turn has led to an apparent inability to 'contain' the city. A reappraisal is under way. The theoretical argument for the current interest in the compact city and sustainability is being derived by abstracting from:

- successful development-led inner city regeneration
- the rediscovery of the work of Jane Jacobs (especially 1965, but also 1972)
- a rational 'modern' analysis of urban form by architects (Rogers, 1994)
- an eclectic 'post-modern' application of architecture across the built form
- a social desire for 'spectacle' and vitality (Harvey, 1989)
- a social concern with crime, and the desire to create security through dense development and pedestrianised use of public spaces
- the importance of cities in their regional, national and international contexts both literally and symbolically (Smyth, 1994)
- the need to reduce the local and global environmental impact of urban development

This interest in the compact city follows three main threads - environmental, social and economic. The desire to promote sustainable development, particularly across the range of environmental issues, is the primary focus for current promotion. The concern for security and the stimulation of activity in the city (see for example Comedia, 1991; Poole, 1991) has given rise to questions as to the sort of lifestyle in which people should or can live and work, this being the social thread. A third strand is the competition between cities on regional, national and international levels to capture investment and consumption activities for economic sustainability in a restructuring global economy (Smyth, 1994). While these three threads embrace social, economic and environmental issues, for example cost-benefit analysis is an economic tool applied to environmental issues, the proposals for implementing the compact city are most frequently couched in physical terms. This is because it is tangible, the most easily controllable and in political terms has the fastest impact because it is noticed whether or not the desired social or economic effects are achieved. It also dovetails with the concern for the environment and sustainable development.

The professional advocates of the compact city come in a number of forms. In architecture, the retrospective view is represented by Leon Krier (1984), while the modern approach is exemplified by Sir Richard Rogers (1992; 1994). In planning, the seminal work of Jane Jacobs (1965) has had a great impact since its publication and has been undergoing something of revival in recent years. A number of other professionals from the police through to social analysts have begun to advocate solutions which directly or indirectly feed into this debate upon the compact city (cf. Berman, 1983; Whyte, 1988; Zukin, 1988; Poole, 1991; Comedia, 1991; Coleman, 1990). Some of these solutions are couched in design and development terms. For Krier, Jacobs, Coleman and their respective supporters, the solutions are physical and invoke their own versions of a bygone era or an era that is just passing, which in most cases is a combination of reality and myth (cf. Williams, 1975). Poole is essentially concerned with improving the existing situation by bringing people and activity into the city centre, while Comedia proposes more sensitive design of cities. For Berman the next step is an environmentally and ecologically based form of development, but one that arises out of a new set of social encounters in the city, which challenge the assumptions and social balance within the city.

Berman offers a progressive view. While the entire assumption for his analysis is not shared by this author, the importance of his view is the interrelationship between the physical and the social. There is a momentum building up from these processes that is hard to counteract, nor is there a reward from so doing; indeed the outcome may be a challenge, a new social encounter in the city (Berman, 1983), that helps to usher in sustainable development and the compact city in a dramatic way (cf. Young, 1990; Smyth, 1994).

The aim of this chapter is to explore the potential and dangers of the compact city. The main argument is that the greatest potential can only be achieved where the physical form of the compact city is grounded on a firm social base with identifiable social objectives for the whole city.

The notion of creating a compact city is currently largely driven by environmental considerations. It is a reaction to suburban sprawl and edge city phenomena (see for example Garreau, 1991; Davis, 1990 and Sudjic, 1993), and in particular the inefficiency of these forms, in social and economic costs, and especially in energy consumption and therefore pollution (Rogers and Fisher, 1992). The environmental factors are being seen as the most important and there is a movement towards sustainable development, which has begun to be translated into planning policy and practice. In Britain this is closely coupled with the return to local districts of control over planning policy, and the application of *Planning Policy Guidance 13: Transport,* which advocates land use planning to reduce travel.

It seems inconceivable that anyone would oppose the current tide of opinion towards promoting sustainable development and the compact city in particular. This chapter argues in favour of the compact city, but it is qualified support. The concern is that the theory is being environmentally 'driven' with social and economic issues being effects rather than causal. History generally supports the need for caution. Historically, according to Sudjic (1993), urban theories have failed to realise their objectives and the unintended consequences of implementing them have provoked a backlash after each round of implementation. Sudjic sees these rounds of theory-into-practice in the following way:

> Urban theorists with an architectural bias have put many different glosses on their strategies for shaping the city, but there are two fundamental and sharply opposed recurring themes in their models: the high-density city set against the decentralised, low-density city. At one extreme are those who want to see the existing urban densities maintained, or even intensified, and at the other are the decentralists. Both sides blame each other for all the perceived ills of the modern city. (pp.10-11)

Support is therefore cautioned by historical evidence, which it is suggested may polarise issues into a false debate. The key cautionary matter in this analysis is that the compact city, divorced from social underpinnings, could lurch into a reactionary force for social exclusion and attack. The core may become *a compact city within a doughnut of decay.* The analysis is focused upon the interrelationship of the environmental and social justifications for the compact city. It demonstrates that if clear social objectives are not incorporated into the implemented policies from the start and adhered to throughout, then an environmentally driven policy and practice have the potential to develop into a social backlash, even fascism, based upon environmental determinism and social Darwinism - the theory of determining social and cultural factors through biological processes, namely evolution. Such an outcome would evolve from the unintended consequences of an environmentally based concept of the compact city.

How could this be the case? Is there any certainty of it? The case is derived from evidence that is already available and this is developed in the sections below. There is no certainty about it; indeed it is hoped that we may learn the lessons of the past and address the current evidence in order to avoid such unintended consequences. Therefore this chapter may in some way help to avoid this scenario. As we drive the environmental theory through the entrance to the compact city, let us be sure that we read the warning signs before hoisting the flag on the theoretical palace, and that we administer judgements at the city gate!

Compact city form and constraints

The heart of the city, its historic core, is compact. This is most obvious in the fortified city and walled town. The European model, especially Italian cities and towns, provides examples, but even the modern city of North America has its 'compact centres'. These may be less compact, and are frequently characterised by a series of cores each performing a largely monolithic function, whether the business district or residential area by the docks cited by Jacobs (1965) in New York or the downtown zones in Los Angeles (Davis, 1990). They do not have the mixed use of the traditional European city and as advocated in the compact city concept. They lack the desired social diversity and resulting cohesion, but they are efficient environmentally, as traffic within is minimised, particularly when the monolithic zones are spatially adjacent.

The main physical problem with the compact city is that existing cities are made up of a number of centres which are spread out (Garreau, 1991) within the urban fabric. These are the result of urban sprawl and are the product of achieving economies of scale in retailing or office use, where rents are lower than in the existing core. There are also new compact cores emerging within cities, for example Harbor Place in Baltimore, Canary Wharf in London Docklands or the revitalised area around the International Convention Centre in Birmingham, or those simply in the pipeline such as Spitalfields in London (Harvey, 1989; Sudjic, 1993; Fainstain, 1994; Smyth, 1994). For an enhanced compact city to work, the existing cores will need appropriate infrastructure, and both mixed and diverse uses. Many of the existing areas of sprawl will need to identify centres on which to focus the creation of compaction. In some ways this has already begun; for example in Britain sustainable development policies are endeavouring to focus new development around transport nodes - existing public transport interchanges and possibly massive car parks on city fringes at new terminals to motorways. This in itself is costly and, if requiring relocation, involves considerable energy and financial expenditure as the existing developments are written off and new developments need to be constructed.

These issues are surely resolvable with some creativity. They do not challenge the grounds of the theoretical concept. More pertinent are the economic factors. How can it be achieved? Enhancing the existing core city zones in line with the image of the compact city is achievable. The competition between cities on the world stage will continue to economically drive this process of developing the dense core, albeit supported by central and local government subsidies and policies. The economic tide is in that direction, even though everyone is not yet in agreement:

> Architecture, urban design and town planning have yet to embrace marketing the city as part of the development process; indeed, the public and private sectors have been too concerned with supply-side issues, rather than the nature and extent of demand, competitive advantage, social benefits and what people say they want... (Smyth, 1994, p.260)

Support will also come politically, in order to ensure the economics work for areas of the existing inner city where substantial investment has been made. Continuing to resource and tweak the policy to embrace compact city concepts may not prove too daunting.

Can we therefore conclude that economic issues are underpinning the drive towards the compact city? I think not. The problems really arise when implementing compact development and converting the existing fabric in the more peripheral areas. The political will is absent and economically the areas may be functioning well. The development of Croydon as a satellite centre to the City of London in the 1960s was economically driven and the politics were important but not of national importance (Saunders, 1980). Croydon and its counterparts, the edge city developments, will not be converted to the compact concept in the absence of political will nor from economic motivation, especially when they are functioning well on their own terms. The mediator between the user and the urban form is not primarily the planner but the developer (Smyth, 1985). Sudjic states:

> Developers have the last word in shaping the city, but their room for manoeuvre is severely limited by what the market will bear. They have to work with the current, rather than struggle against it. They are subject to all kinds of pressures, from the changing whims of the banks, to the planners and activists who try to frame legislative means of forcing developers to take the wider urban picture into account. But building a slice of authentic city is a task that is beyond the old-fashioned developer... In its newest incarnation, property development is characterised by what might be called internationalisation and corporatisation. The international nature of development focuses investment on just a few cities where hot money pours in to rebuild skylines. (1993, pp.47-48)

The international developers will not respond to the call for the compact city in peripheral locations, except for massive developments, such as Broadgate in London or Battery Park in New York, where they can largely call the tune.

This section has shown that there are constraints upon creating compact city forms as the dominant or main form. The constraints are largely economic. The compact city theory is not underpinned by economic causal factors: it envisages only positive economic effects.

The only potential solution is to enforce planning policies that are sufficiently draconian to counter the economic forces. These would fly in the face of other concepts, such as empowerment. They would rely on sufficient agreement about the compact city as a solution for a sustainable built form. The seminal work of Ward and Dubos (1972) and the anarchic Girardet (1976) are two early examples of possible solutions favouring regionalisation and decentralisation respectively.

Even if environmental consensus is achievable, this section has demonstrated that business in general, and the developer in particular, are economically driven and will not implement compact city policies unless it is financially beneficial. Draconian planning policies would almost certainly invoke the wrath of developers through the press and lobby groups.

The principal point of this section has been to demonstrate that there are economic problems in enhancing, converting and creating compact city concepts in practice. The conclusion is that the best that can be hoped for is a diversity of built form, which includes the compact city, unless some greater social transformation along the lines suggested by Berman (1983) is experienced. Enhanced and promoted through softer planning policies, the compact city centres will rest alongside existing suburban and edge city phenomena. The result is likely to be a central compact form. It will give rise to the rebirth of the concentric ring model of the city - the compact city in the centre, a transition zone and the suburban outer ring.

Compact city and social inclusion

Two significant steps that can be taken towards facilitating the creation of compact city centres are:

- acceptance of mixed development as a legitimate form of property investment
- the provision of schools with high quality facilities and teaching in central areas

Regarding the first step, financial institutions are highly resistant to mixed uses for property development. This is largely a legal issue, where the length of office leases differs from that of retail. This inhibits opportunities for redevelopment in the long term, and even more severely so when residential development is added to the equation. One solution to address this problem is to create some leasehold standardisation, which may have adverse social consequences for housing legislation and housing security for the occupier, although it may actually stimulate the rented housing sector.

A potential solution is a design and construction one. Buildings could be designed as free-standing frames into which modules are inserted and removed as the balance of uses changes. This is technically feasible: the city would be treated as a racked warehouse; the frames could be extended or demounted and the modules could be recycled, hence offsetting some of the additional capital costs - a case of putting the design approach of 'long life, loose fit' into a framework! The issues concern standardisation of approach, as dictated by frame modules, yet sensitivity and diversity of aesthetic treatment. How acceptable is this approach? It remains to be seen whether it will be tested, but if it is, it will encourage the creation of landmark and trophy buildings that help provide contrast and hence create the 'spectacle' and visual vitality of the city centre (Harvey, 1989; cf. Davis, 1990; Sudjic, 1993; Smyth, 1994).

A common reason given for people moving out of the city centre into the suburban sprawl is that the centre is not a safe and appropriate environment in which to bring up children. Pollution and safety are addressed in the compact city concept. This leaves schooling and school buildings as perhaps the most significant pieces of physical infrastructure and the most important social environment that has to be addressed. School buildings pose major land use issues and the main way of addressing this will be through developer contributions under Section 106 of the Planning and Compensation Act 1991, to both enhance existing schools and create new ones. The cost to the developers will be substantial and the only way of achieving this goal may well be to charge a top-up school fee or encourage private education, which may in turn affect the social environment.

This brings the analysis towards the next issue: for households to choose the urban over the suburban, then the facilities and benefits of the compact living style have to be greater. In attracting households to stay or return to city centres the benefits must be both social and economic. Social gains will be access to a variety of facilities and access that is quick, hence convenient, thus creating vitality and a sense of place. The economic gains will concern the cost of travel and the greater investment value of owner-occupied houses. This raises the issue of income and affordability. To maximise the advantage of many of the social gains of compact city living will require a high income. Therefore those with the higher incomes will be attracted back into the city. They will add a new layer of affluence into the city centre. Indeed, most households will have to have large incomes in order to be able to afford the house purchases, rents and potentially the (top-up) school fees.

Income and affordability will almost certainly mean that those included in the compact city will be amongst the most affluent in society. 'Planning gain' could be used to facilitate a greater social mix within one land use, but this could add to the polarisation between groups, exclusivity being encouraged by developers in order to pay for the social component. In any case the affluent are likely to dominate in terms of new residents within the city. The remainder will be invited to commute in from the suburbs, sustainability prompting a switch from private to public transport (Rogers and Fisher, 1992).

Creating a compact city of high density and mixed use may well induce diversity, except when it comes to social mix. Because social issues are not the central issue of compact city theory, the social consequences are that the whole urban environment is not looked at and certain groups are excluded because geographically they fall outside the remit of the theory. This leads the analysis on to those outside the compact city, to the concentric rings of the transition zone and the suburban sprawl beyond.

Compact city and social exclusion

Those who do not wish to live in the compact city will elect to live in the suburban areas and centres in the outer concentric ring. They will use their income, as is done at present, to live in low density surroundings, relying on speed of access rather than proximity to facilities. For some this will involve long commuter journeys, especially where the workplace is in the city centre. In the latter case, the use of public transport would help to reduce congestion and energy consumption (ironically retaining some of the attraction of decentralised living *vis-à-vis* the city centre).

Therefore, among those whose income permits a choice, some and perhaps many could be attracted to the vitality and benefits of compact city living, while the remainder will continue to live in suburban and rural locations. For those whose incomes inhibit choice, severe social constraints will continue to be experienced. However, the spatial distribution of these social problems will change with the advent of the compact city. Low income households will continue to live in city centres, in suburban and rural areas. However, a very large and significant number will come to live in the transition zone. This will be for a number of reasons:

- continuing displacement as a result of existing inner city urban renewal
- gentrification of the existing city centre fabric, stimulated by compact city policies
- creation of new city development displacing lower income groups, excluded by unaffordable rents and living costs (and possibly exclusion from school places)

In other words, the compact city concept will see a displacement of the socially disadvantaged out of the core and inner city to the transitional zone. It will not of course be a total exclusion, but sufficient to shift the balance and create a different social pattern over the city. The result will be that this zone will become a doughnut of social disadvantage around the compact city.

How can we be reasonably sure that this will occur? There is ample evidence that this is already beginning and that the application of the compact city concept in practice will exacerbate the trend. What is the evidence? There are a number of strands. The first is that gentrification during the 1980s began to accelerate the migration of disadvantaged groups, particularly ethnic groups, out of the inner city to join those who were already inhabiting the transitional zone. In London, Streatham and Norbury are classic examples of this zone, sandwiched as they are between Brixton and Croydon. Similar examples can be found in Birmingham and other major cities in Britain. The process of creating the doughnut is already underway, the compact city therefore comes to give it impetus and a distinctiveness of decay through the resulting intensity and spatial concentration.

The response to this is that urban renewal will simply follow the same pattern. There will be initial attempts to tackle the renewal of the built form in the doughnut ring, but the attempts will be short lived:

> ...each successive concentric ring of development has been developed to serve a shorter period of time. Even if this was not consciously considered, then financing development and construction technology have been geared to the production of buildings with a shorter life cycle. The threat is that whole 'rings' of the city will degenerate simultaneously as each development phase has a shorter life. This poses massive problems because parts of the existing inner cities will be bypassed in favour of development in the next ring. Developments in these outer rings are likely to be of a smaller scale. The land holdings are more fragmented and all the stock will not wear out or fall into disuse simultaneously. (Smyth, 1994, pp.265-6)

A dispersed problem of physical decay will be greater than its inner city forerunner. The fragmentation over space will render it politically more difficult to address. As industrial and other commercial space passes its sell-by date and defies conversion, then it will fall into disuse, and housing, into disrepair. The above passage suggests that the existing core areas may be bypassed and, even if regeneration does occur in the transition zone, the doughnut, then it will still be insufficient to counter the current trends of social and economic disintegration in space. The compact city could exacerbate this scenario further. First, Sudjic (1993, p.53) states, 'developers rely on public subsidy to make their activities profitable', a point echoed by many (for example McGrath, 1982; Barnekov *et al.*, 1988; Boyle, 1989; Harvey, 1989; Brownill, 1990; Davis, 1990; Hambleton, 1990; Fainstain, 1994; Smyth, 1994). The result could be that the resources that might have gone to the transition zone will be retained within the inner city areas in order to help create the compact city. The outcome would be accelerating physical decay of the doughnut and deeper social deprivation. The political point is echoed in that there will be little marketing mileage in the more fragmented and less visible schemes and social projects in the doughnut, although the core may be well be more saleable, especially for world cities, such as London, Paris, Tokyo, Los Angeles and New York.

The doughnut will be the zone in which social problems are concentrated. The characteristics will be poverty, crime, drug abuse and social abuse - an exaggerated form of what is currently seen in inner city and ghetto areas across developed cities of the world. The fragmented nature of the land use and social patterns within the doughnut will make it less visible, and certainly not the image of the city projected through the media (Huggins and Smyth, forthcoming). The social problems may fester and social control will rest in the hands of those members of the population who patrol and control the area: an inverted form of empowerment. The transition zone will socially, as well as environmentally, become a doughnut of deprivation, crime, drugs and all the other symptoms of social decay. Out of the city spotlight in city marketing and politics, off centre stage, the zone will be the gauntlet through which people, goods and infrastructure will have to run to come in and out of the compact city. These arterial routes linking the compact city to the suburban areas will need outside force to impose control over the doughnut, hence alleviating the threat of running the gauntlet.

The doughnut and the gauntlet

The doughnut will be the by-product of a 'modern' architectural analysis of the urban form and the result of an eclectic 'post-modern' application of architecture across the built form. The doughnut will be neither part of the rationale nor a fragment that embraces the right sort of signage for creativity - a threatening ring to live in, punctured by arterial routes across which signs of threat and violence will pervade.

Running the gauntlet invokes some of the images of recent post-modern films, such as the much quoted *Bladerunner*, and brings into being part of the worst scenarios suggested by Harvey (1989). The principal comparison with *Bladerunner* is that affluence is concentrated at the top of the high-rise blocks, in clear weather, the street level being the area of disintegrated life, shrouded in continuous rain. To travel across the city, the elite can fly, the remainder having to enter this street level 'underworld'. The compact city may contain a similar pattern - horizontal rather than vertical in form.

Travelling across the doughnut will carry risks. There are already some low key precedents from which the culture of theft and threat can be extrapolated. The car windscreen cleaning crews who appear in car parks and at traffic lights and the occasional pack of thieves can impose themselves on the stationary motorist. It does not take much imagination nor attendance at many sci-fi films to invoke the insecurity and threat running the gauntlet across the urban doughnut could produce. It certainly would encourage the use of public transport, provided that adequate policing was in place. The threats will come from the disadvantaged trying to survive. Poverty is one issue, yet organised crime, drug abuse and social abuse will all be inextricably linked to it, being fed through theft, hijacking and from dispersed intimidation.

Policing and social control would become a key issue. Policing the arterial routes into the compact city, whether by road, rail or any other form will be the key issue for protecting those crossing the doughnut. This will be necessary to ensure those travelling out of the compact city may do so, while those having to travel into work in the centre may also do so in safety.

The next issue will be to contain the social problems within the zone. Given current trends and results in fighting inner city crime and alleviating poverty, it is likely that the effort will be pure containment rather than solving drugs, crime and other social problems. The third issue will be to protect the edge of the doughnut. Containment therefore is not merely a social issue *per se* but a territorial one too. This will be the most difficult problem for two reasons.

First, and in contrast to the inner city, the perimeter is extensive by virtue of its shape. The resources needed to successfully 'defend' the centre from the social 'dis-ease' will be considerable and there will need to be political justification to muster these. The main border of contention will not be the largest one on the outer edge since this will be more easily managed through the housing market as people relocate to locations further afield. This border will become more graded, especially in times of economic growth. The inner border will pose the main problems. Policing the border will be reminiscent of the biblical and medieval walled city. Development will proceed by turning its back upon the doughnut, and there is evidence of this already occurring through urban regeneration in Los Angeles, Birmingham and elsewhere (see Davis, 1990; Smyth, 1994). In Birmingham the International Convention Centre (ICC), Hyatt Hotel and National Indoor Arena combine to create a wall of development, described as follows:

> The 'wall' symbolically divides the Ladywood district of the city from the centre, which is itself a division between the advantaged and disadvantaged parts of the city. This is only punctuated by Broad Street, which is rather foreboding and windswept and by the footpath through the 'street' of the ICC. (Smyth, 1994, p.156)

The significance of the above quotation is that the three buildings were part of the 1980s urban regeneration partnership development packages to expand the existing city core. In it are contained some of the elements that characterise defending the border:

- the wall
- the developments turning their face to the centre
- the gates in the wall being either uninviting or controlled public space

These design elements will provide the context. It is a context which will discourage further waves of concentric development from expanding the compact city because the wall will tend to cut off those areas.

Policing the wall of the inner border of the doughnut will not be easy. Design has been shown to mitigate some human resource needs for social control, yet the 'street' perception in a compact city, during recession and through media coverage of social decay, may invoke even greater demands for protection from the threat of incursion from the doughnut. There will be both social threats or perceptions of threat - crime, drugs and anti-social behaviour - and threats to property through vandalism, theft and potential property devaluation.

How could those within the confines of the compact city create the climate for justifying the necessary protective resources?

Compact city and social control

Imposing social control will require justification that those living within the doughnut zone are inherently dangerous and that there is no remedy to the situation. The easiest way of achieving this is to state that the social issues are synonymous with the environment. At its extreme this would involve the rebirth of environmental determinism. Such an approach would amount to theoretical reductionism. There is a precedent for this. In the 1920s the Chicago School of sociologists produced a theory of urban ecology. These arguments have been extensively used and criticised, but a reminder of their essence is given below. The main tenet was that the population of the city segregates itself into 'natural areas' (Park, 1915; 1925) in an unplanned way (Alihan, 1964) by race and class (Park, 1925), gender and age (McKenzie, 1925). The individual, living interdependently with others, becomes an organism in a natural process of creating a social equilibrium. The equilibrium is seen as a stable spatial city pattern. This approach has its roots in social Darwinism and environmental determinism. Essentially it takes Darwin's (1950) theoretical assumptions of the survival of the individual for the benefit of the species in its environment and in relation to other species and applies it as competition for survival within one species - the human one (Spencer, 1903). The competition between individuals and their households in space produces the sociologically stable city. It tends to create a concentric pattern in space as identified by the Chicago School. As social Darwinism sees this process as 'natural', therefore the spatial outcome must also be, hence it is environmentally determined - taxes, rents, prices, subsidies, personal preferences and social control all being seen as an expression of this natural law.

This explanation may prove attractive to advocates of the compact city in the future, if it continues to be environmentally driven. It certainly will provide underpinnings to the elite and predominantly more affluent living in the compact city who are fearful about maintaining their security. As it is 'natural' that both sets of population - the advantaged in the compact city and the disadvantaged within the doughnut - are located in their zones, then it becomes natural to defend those territories to maintain the 'equilibrium', even if this means the imposition of social control and force on one group at the instigation of the others. In essence this would usher in some fascist aspects that have been suggested could be on the horizon (Harvey, 1989) and would be in total contradistinction to the guidelines for just urban management (Young, 1990; Smyth, 1994).

What is the evidence that these trends are possible? In general respects, Harvey (1989) offers arguments for serious consideration in an urban context. Specifically on the spatial side there is already a trend in this direction. Herrnstein and Murray (1994) have recently argued that the 'underclass' in American cities are genetically preordained to be disadvantaged, which not only has spatial but strong racist connotations too. This is part of a growing literature, addressing various aspects of life, that draws upon the general literature labelled the 'new socio-biology'. This literature comes from evolutionists in the natural sciences, who have entered the social arena through the back door by assuming that culture is a biological process that is genetically transmitted, or at the very least that is analogous to, and therefore can be modelled through, genetic transmission. Natural science has therefore adopted social Darwinism. The leading proponent is Dawkins, whose work has been popularised from *The Selfish Gene* through to *River Out of Eden*. In one sense it is hard to be critically too harsh on Dawkins. He discounts simplistic approaches to evolution and treats the evolutionary process as one that 'fits' the cultural setting. His assumptions are qualified; however, he works with them and thus follows a long tradition among evolutionary science of building assumption upon assumption. For although it has never been authenticated, the significance of evolution is generally accepted as fact, and certainly there is a growing body of serious science literature that criticises both the general importance lent to evolutionary theory of the traditional strand and its socio-biological mutations (Eldredge, 1995). The very foundations are suspect before anyone might try to build a new urban ecology on top of it.

What this section has shown is that an environmentally driven theory of the compact city could spill over into social concern that may be unacceptable. This is the future which is being addressed. However, in order to avoid social policy arising in a covert way, it would be desirable to have an overt policy today for the compact city.

Conclusion

This chapter has addressed some of the problems that could emerge with the development of the compact city. From a sympathetic starting point, it has stressed the need to have a strong and overt *social* content to compact city concepts. These social policies must address not only the *compact city* itself, but also the *doughnut*, that is the transitional zone surrounding the compact city. It is suggested that this is both important and essential, because economic and political constraints have been identified, and these determine how widespread the compact city concept can be in practice.

We can celebrate the gentle hand of restoration to create a compact city. We must also pay attention to what the other hand is doing, in order that we are not facing a shaking fist within a gauntlet of displaced and growing decay. What the social content of the compact city concept should be for the entire city is a subject for investigation and debate. However, just as there are signposts that have been posted as evidence of the dangers in the compact city concept in this chapter, so there are signposts that can provide base evidence for a social content, some of which have been alluded to within this chapter. A successful compact city will embrace the social and economic considerations on an equal footing with environmental concerns.

References

Alihan, M.A. (1964) *Social Ecology: A Critical Analysis,* Cooper Square Publications, New York.

Barnekov, T., Boyle, R. and Rich, D. (1988) *Privatism and Urban Policy in Britain and the United States,* Oxford University Press, Oxford.

Berman, M. (1983) *All That is Solid Melts into Air,* Verso, London.

Boyle, R. (1989) Partnership in Practice. *Local Government Studies,* March/April, pp.17-28.

Brownill, S. (1990) *Developing London's Docklands: Another Great Planning Disaster,* Paul Chapman, London.

Coleman, A. (1990) *Utopia on Trial: Vision and Reality in Planned Housing,* Hilary Shipman, London.

Comedia (1991) *Out of Hours: A Study of Economic, Social and Cultural Life in Twelve Town Centres in the UK - summary report,* Comedia and Calouste Gulbenkian Foundation, London.

Darwin, C. (1950) *The Origin of the Species by Natural Selection,* Mentor, New York.

Davis, M. (1990) *City of Quartz: Excavating the Future in Los Angeles,* Verso, London.

Dawkins, R. (1976) *The Selfish Gene,* Oxford University Press, Oxford.

Dawkins, R. (1995) *River Out of Eden,* Weidenfield and Nicolson, London.

Eldredge, N. (1995) *Reinventing Darwin,* Weidenfield and Nicolson, London.

Fainstain, S. (1994) *The City Builders: Property, Politics and Planning in London and New York*, Blackwells, Oxford.

Garreau, J. (1991) *Edge City: Life on the New Frontier*, Doubleday, New York.

Girardet, H. (ed.) (1976) *New Towns or New Villages, Land for the People*, Crescent Books, London.

Hambleton, R. (1990) *Urban Government in the 1990s: Lessons from the USA*, Occasional Paper no. 35, School for Advanced urban Studies, University of Bristol.

Harvey, D. (1989) *The Condition of Postmodernity*, Blackwells, Oxford.

Herrnstein, R. and Murray, C. (1994) *The Bell Curve: Reshaping of American Life by Differences in Intelligence*, Free Press, New York.

Huggins, R. and Smyth, H. (forthcoming) *The Media and the City*, Mimeo.

Jacobs, J. (1965) *The Death and Life of Great American Cities: The Failure of Town Planning*, Penguin, Harmondsworth, Middlesex.

Jacobs, J. (1972) *The Economy of Cities*, Penguin, Harmondsworth, Middlesex.

Krier, L. (1984) *Houses, Palaces and Cities* (ed. D. Porphyrios) Architectural Design, London.

McGrath, D. (1982) Who must leave? alternative images of revitalisation. *Journal of the American Planning Association*, **48(2)**, pp.196-203.

McKenzie, R.D. (1925) The Ecological Approach to the Human Community, in *The City* (eds R.E. Park and E.W. Burgess) Free Press, Chicago.

Park, R.E. (1915) *Human Communities*, Free Press, Chicago.

Park, R.E. (1925) The city: suggestions for the investigation of human behaviour in the human environment, in *The City*, (eds R.E. Park and E.W. Burgess), Free Press, Chicago.

Poole, R. with Donovan, K. (1991) *Safer Shopping: The Identification of Opportunities for Crime and Disorder in Covered Shopping Centres*, West Midlands Police, Birmingham and Home Office Police Requirements Support Unit, London.

Rogers, R. (1994) *The Reith Lectures*, BBC, London.

Rogers, R. and Fisher, M. (1992) *A New London*, Penguin, Harmondsworth.

Saunders, P. (1980) *Urban Politics: A Sociological Interpretation*, Penguin, Harmondsworth, Middlesex.

Smyth, H.J. (1985) *Property Companies and the Construction Industry in Britain*, Cambridge University Press, Cambridge.

Smyth, H.J. (1994) *Marketing the City: The Role of Flagship Developments in Urban Regeneration*, E & FN Spon, London.

Spencer, H. (1903) *The Study of Sociology*, Paul, Trench, Trubner and Co., London.

Sudjic, D. (1993) *The 100 Mile City*, Flamingo, London.

Ward, B. and Dubos, R. (1972) *Only One Earth: Care and Maintenance of a Small Planet*, Pelican, Harmondsworth, Middlesex.

Whyte, W.H. (1988) *City: Rediscovering the Center*, Doubleday, New York.

Williams, R. (1975) *The Country and the City*, Paladian, London.

Young, I.M. (1990) *Justice and the Politics of Difference*, Princetown University Press, New Jersey.

Zukin, S. (1988) *Loft Living: Culture and Capital in Urban Change*, Radius, London.

Christopher Knight
Economic and Social Issues

Any city, whether compact or not, is the result of years of development, and such development is an economic activity. However, unlike many less tangible forms of economic activity, its results are long lasting, self-evident and have a direct effect on people's daily lives.

Economic issues

In modern Britain, the vast majority of development is carried out in the private sector. The main reason it is carried out is to create profit. Those carrying it out are many and varied, and each is inclined to march to the beat of a different drum. This variety must be recognised, and included in our thinking, if the compact city is to become a reality. Let us consider a few of those involved. Corporate investors are inclined to take a long term view and own substantial amounts of urban property. For example, in the UK, excluding London, institutional funds own approximately 15% of UK offices (Applied Property Research, 1995). Their goals are to ensure steady, long term and above all secure income. Property is just one source of their investment income, and they will move in and out of the property market as necessary. They are not inclined to change just for the sake of it. Security is all. Therefore, investment fund criteria are defined in great detail and, if a property does not comply, the fund will simply not buy it. New products and new mixes of uses are treated with caution. Convincing the funds to back the compact city in a hurry will be like changing the course of a fully loaded supertanker. It will take a long time and happen only slowly.

Developers on the other hand are true creatures of the market place. They love a fast turnover and a quick profit. Taking risk is an essential part of making that profit. Therefore, so long as they can be objectively assessed, they are more inclined to try out new products in the market place. Developers could thus perhaps prove to be best friends of the compact city.

Private individuals can act as both developers and consumers. For example,

37% of all planning decisions in England during 1994 involved 'householder applications' (Department of the Environment: Planning Statistics Department, 1995). These ranged from house extensions to the construction of new garages. Such developments, albeit on a small scale, clearly have a large cumulative effect on how urban areas look and function. They are undertaken not just for profit, but also for reasons of status, enjoyment and comfort. How do we convince them to do different in the future?

As an alternative to private sector development, public development and many quango projects are nominally less risk conscious since the 'public good' is also a relevant factor. However, controls on public expenditure frequently limit the scope for such pump-priming. It should also not be forgotten that such projects are increasingly accounted for in terms of the market, with the Treasury seeking clear financial returns on new major infrastructure projects.

Each of these actors is likely to perceive their contribution to the compact city differently simply because they have different reasons for being there. If those that develop are many and varied, so are the properties they develop. As an economic product, urban development is heterogeneous. No one building or town is exactly the same as another. They have different histories, pressures, constraints and opportunities. Ultimately, there is not a single property market, there are a multitude of them. The formula for a compact city in one location is not going to be easily transferred to another, without some adjustment. The concept of a compact city must recognise that each town, street and building is unique.

Also, like most markets, the property market is dynamic. It is obvious that in prosperous times there will be a higher demand for sites for such buildings as offices, shops and the like. When the population is increasing or is on the move there will be a larger demand for houses and for an improved standard of housing, both in quality and quantity, particularly when incomes increase. Conversely, recession brings a slowing down of the rate of change. In 1988, 221,700 new houses were built in Great Britain. In 1992, however, just 120,100 new houses were built, only 54% of the 1988 figure (Stewart, 1995). The compact city will have to be robust enough to withstand the continual changes of the property market.

The property market is dynamic in another way too: it is innovative. New products are constantly being created in order to attract customers. Ten years ago the multiplex cinema was in its infancy. Twenty years ago warehouses were modest affairs cheek by jowl with similar-looking factories. Now they are automated monsters next to motorway junctions and the factories are indistinguishable from the offices. The compact city is going to have to be adaptable if it is not to stifle innovation.

Finally, we cannot disregard the competitiveness of our economic system. Companies that find a town too restrictive or expensive often move elsewhere. Locational investment decisions are made by comparing towns, regions and countries. Capital moves internationally. Compact cities will need to be as attractive investment locations as cities that are not compact. Otherwise companies will vote with their feet and the people will follow them.

In summary, as an economic proposition, the compact city must address the following:

- development will be mostly in the private sector

- private sector developers are many and varied, with an equally wide number of reasons for carrying out development
- the properties they develop are heterogeneous so there cannot be just one formula for a compact city

A formula for creating the compact city must:

- be capable of continual adjustment to accommodate the essential dynamics of the property market
- not stifle innovation
- be competitive

Social and practical issues

There are many compact cities in the world already. Any visitor to the central areas of Calcutta, Cairo or Rio will see plenty of examples of high densities of population, mixed land use and multi-mode transport. They will also see the dangers - congestion, increasing pollution, loss of amenity space and reduction in privacy.

These are extremes, but it was not that long ago that we were encouraging people to move out of the cities to avoid just these consequences. Ever since the garden cities movement the trend has been to reduce densities, not increase them. Table 1 illustrates this outward drift. Reversing the process will not be straightforward.

	1961	1971	1981	1991	% change 1961-91
Greater London	7993	7453	6696	6378	-20.2
Birmingham	1183	1098	1007	935	-21.0
Leeds	713	739	705	674	-5.5
Glasgow	1055	897	766	654	-38.0
Sheffield	585	573	537	500	-14.5
Liverpool	746	610	510	448	-39.9
Edinburgh	468	454	437	422	-9.8
Manchester	662	544	449	407	-38.5
Bristol	438	427	388	370	-15.5
Coventry	318	337	314	293	-7.9

Table 1. Population of major cities 1961-91 (thousands).

Source: Census (1991)

The vision of the compact city - its juxtaposition of uses, vitality and efficiency of activity - is easier to paint on a blank canvas than an already full one. The heterogeneous nature of urban areas has already been referred to. Each is a different mosaic of ownerships, land use patterns and infrastructure. Unless assisted by war or wholesale renewal, history shows that our towns and cities have changed incrementally. The step by step approach allows successes and failures to be tested on parts without blighting the whole.

A fundamental ingredient in the success of producing a more compact city will be the attitude and response of existing residents. Save in areas where large blocks of public land can be redeveloped (a diminishing resource), real progress will only be made where individuals are prepared to share a common approach. This will rarely be the case. In the absence of any compulsion, few worthwhile redevelopment schemes seem likely to come forward.

Let us examine for a moment what incentives there could be for land and property owners to become involved. Principally, they would wish to be better off than before. Better off could mean either financial improvement or some other benefit. In reality I see little opportunity for either situation to occur on a widespread basis in already developed areas. Due to the small scale of each pocket of land, the individual would only gain quite marginally, if at all. However, a developer would only be interested in an amalgam of a number of those small pockets to make a scheme worth his or her attention. Persuading numbers of individuals to have a common view in these circumstances is notoriously difficult to achieve. The developer's discount would reduce the individual's margin still further and it is very difficult to see where, even if a group of individuals could be co-ordinated, the financial incentive for any of the parties lies.

Increasingly development is expected to produce the services, facilities and amenities previously provided by the public purse. These benefits can only be funded by the surplus created out of the development itself. Where redevelopment is of land which already has a high value due to previous use, it will be difficult to raise the large sums often needed for new infrastructure. It will be inevitable that the quantity of new development required will often be made up from several small unrelated developments. Each will only produce a small surplus, if any. This demonstrates the real problem even more clearly. Only through the medium of an Urban Development Corporation for example, with large injections of public money, could these problems be resolved.

So, if financial reward is small or non-existent, what other motives would there be? I find it difficult to identify any. Conversely, I can see many reasons why property owners would not wish to see any change at all. It is worth dwelling on these points because I feel they will be a real handicap in progress towards compact city ideals.

Awareness about the environment is as high today as it has ever been. In the context of this debate there are two environments: 'the' environment at large and 'my' environment. The two are not always mutually exclusive. However, concern about 'making the world a better place in which to live' is not always seen as being achieved by individual sacrifices. It is concern for 'my' environment which throws up objections to compact city type development.

Let us look at the likely approach of a typical suburban family group. In the wider environment they are quite content to accept the improvements which follow traffic-calming measures and perhaps even bus priority lanes for example. However, when proposals move onto their own, or immediately neighbouring, territory most will have a less generous response. Most people do not want to live closer to their neighbours as a result of development on either their own or their neighbours' gardens. The theoretical family cannot afford to move away because there is so little profit margin and so they object to the change. Quite apart from not wanting to be physically hemmed in, they also do not want the loss of privacy from closer living and they certainly do not want the pollution, particularly noise, which would follow. It is quite likely that if this family includes an older member there will in addition be sentimental reasons why change would be resisted.

The family already regard their opportunity to access public space as very limited. More homes means more people to use the limited space, and there is likely to be less open space because some will be built upon. Both these factors means a reduction in the family's already limited open space enjoyment.

Current evidence suggests little change in the dominant role of the private car in the next 30 years or so. Even with much improved public transport, car ownership will remain high. Whilst it may be possible in time to change people's attitudes towards greater use of public transport for routine travel, for example to work and school, recreational use of private cars is more likely to increase. It will increase because for many 'the car' and driving are recreational pursuits. A potential adverse consequence of the compact city is the desire of its residents to 'escape' for recreation, thus increasing recreational trips. Certainly there seems to be little evidence of any willingness to give up the freedom and quality of life which individuals' private transport provides, even if there are benefits to be derived from using a better public transport system. Certainly this is the way the theoretical family group view the position and they have no intention of giving up their car or the use of it for unpredictable leisure and recreation trips.

The redevelopment which would be an important component of compact city policy could involve the loss of garage courts and parking areas. There is already congestion on many of the roads due to kerb-side parking. A worsening situation and a handicap to the extension of public transport seems likely to be one consequence of concentrating more housing in the urban area.

It is inevitable, indeed essential, that the approach to development suits the nature and character of not only the city itself, but different parts of the city. Historic areas will continue to need sensitive treatment; the residents of less historic, but attractive, well-designed and planned areas are likely to fiercely resist change even though in theory they have physical capacity to accommodate more houses. It is therefore very likely that attention will be focused on less attractive areas and redevelopment land near to such areas. The potential to create increasing division on a 'them and us' basis is considerable. Our theoretical family group feel threatened. Their way of life is changing. They seem to get all the new development and the problems which follow. They are not at all happy. Division in a community will never produce a balanced and sustainable way forward.

In summary therefore, our family group feel quite threatened: they see a worse future as a result of this compact city idea; a lower standard of living and quality of life; a worsening 'them and us' position; a reduction in their present amenity; and an increase in congestion and pollution, particularly that caused by the motor car.

A pragmatic approach

If sustainability is to mean anything, it means thinking long term. The compact city is a finite resource. If we are to achieve the right balance of quality and quantity there must be a limit to the densities that can be achieved in a compact city. That capacity will vary from place to place, just as our towns and cities vary. But beyond a certain point, it merely becomes town cramming, with all the economic, environmental and social ills that entails. We must seek to reduce the potential for division and conflict within the community.

Also, as explained earlier in this chapter, economically, urban development is a very diverse activity which is difficult to control and difficult to predict. In essence, without compulsion, can the compact city be relied upon to deliver the goods?

In the short term there must be doubts that the compact city can be delivered or that it can be provided with more than only a limited capacity. In the long term, what happens after the compact city? Does the pendulum swing back to urban expansion?

I would like to propose that we need the pragmatic approach of seeking a long term, sustainable balance. The balance should be between the best of compact cities and the best of other forms of development. The pragmatism of this approach is already being recognised in practice. Government policy, provided in *Planning Policy Guidance 3* on Housing, recognises that '...a balance has to be struck between the need for development and the interests of conservation. There can be no question of sacrificing the green spaces which all towns and cities need for recreation and amenity' (Department of the Environment, 1992 pp.1-2).

This need for balance has also been recognised at the local level. Hampshire County Council for example have recognised the limitations of urban areas. Their consultation document, *Hampshire 2011*, published in January 1995, adopts the view that:

> There is a need to establish a new vision of cities and urban life: a commitment to direct investment in Hampshire's urban areas, to the recycling of urban land which is idle or underused and to enhancing the vitality and viability of town and city centres. Improving the quality of urban areas to attract people to live and work in them may require the provision of open space rather than buildings. Greening urban areas is part of maintaining and enhancing their attractiveness. There is, nevertheless, a limit to which urban areas can accommodate development, a limit beyond which the quality of life will not be improved; and beyond which problems of health and safety, congestion and environmental pollution become increasingly acute. (Hampshire County Council, 1995, p.13, paras 33-34)

Likewise, in Bedfordshire, the deposit *Draft Structure Plan 2011* advises that:

> The urban areas cannot absorb all the future growth without conflicting with the aim of improving the attractiveness of urban areas... (Bedfordshire County Council, 1995, p.17, para 1.22)

If the compact city has a finite capacity then it is not on its own a true, long term, sustainable solution. The uncertainty of its ability to deliver must be balanced by other measures to ensure short term delivery as well as long term alternatives. This need not mean continuing with *ad hoc*, peripheral urban growth. There are other strategic options - namely, new settlements. These can be compact towns (if not cities) designed from the start to encourage sustainability, without the constraints imposed in existing urban areas.

A recognition that all new development needs cannot be met in our urban areas is but one step in an important process. The implication is that greenfield sites will be needed - some authorities are even going so far as to nervously suggest new settlements as a possible solution. The new settlement movement of the '80s was ahead of its time. It is probably a good thing that few have been built. Most would have been little more than dormitory housing estates.

Identifying new settlements, variously new villages, urban villages, urban centres and so on is still not sufficient on its own. There has to be clear advice, preferably within a statutory framework, as to what is meant by the term 'new settlement'. A real opportunity exists to evolve the 'plan-led' system and bring forward developments which can make a major contribution to the principles of sustainability. Few of our existing urban areas can be sufficiently adapted to have a real impact on improving the way people live their lives: the existing infrastructure is too rigid and too costly to change. Conversely, with a 'clean' sheet the opportunity is there to create a settlement and community with all the necessary components built-in to enable people to begin to live their lives in a different and better way: better due to environment, ambience, neighbourliness, less pollution, more useful space, less reliance on the car and more on public transport, better health and less social stress. It need be no less compact for being 'new' and providing all these benefits.

The choice of location for these new settlements will be just as critical as the constraints applied to their detailed design. The right location can minimise the need to duplicate expensive resources and can maximise the potential of established resources in neighbouring larger settlements. The balance between on-site provisions of facilities, where justified and economically viable, and reliance on existing facilities will be an important one to strike. In general, day to day needs should be met on site; more exceptional needs can be delivered with greater skill or choice in established facilities elsewhere in larger centres.

In the plan-led system a number of factors are important. One of the most critical is the certainty which new plans are intended to bring. The features which will in the end deliver compact city solutions are complex and there are many uncertainties. Predicting the results with any accuracy will be difficult and perhaps unreliable. The plan-led system provides an admirable framework for compact city ideals to be brought forward. However, there is a very real danger that the system will be discredited if it does not face up to the difficulties and uncertainties involved in compact city development and the time needed to bring individual projects forward. The plan-led system requires a high level of reality, and successful plans will only be implemented where there is a sensible balance between innovation and experience.

Although much of this chapter has been concerned with identifying the problems of the compact city approach, and ends up advocating carefully selected and well defined new settlements, my whole approach is concerned with that over-exercised word 'balance'. I see many pressures to concentrate on urban development strategies, almost at any cost. I hope they will be resisted. Strangely enough, I believe a complementary policy of selective urban regeneration, coupled with even more selective new urban centres or urban villages, will in time deliver yet more opportunities within existing urban areas, as the examples of what is achievable are seen. We cannot force these new ideas on an unwilling audience.

The compact city approach will probably succeed, but with patience, balance and by example. At present I believe we are in danger of expecting too much too soon. Whilst motivated by the need to enhance the general quality of life, the current approach could well do the reverse for a significant proportion of the population - just as was the case with tower blocks.

References

Applied Property Research Ltd (1995) in-house database, London.

Bedfordshire County Council (1995) *Bedfordshire Structure Plan 2011,* Deposit Draft, Bedfordshire County Council, Bedford.

Department of the Environment (1992), *Planning Policy Guidance 3 (Revised): Housing.* HMSO, London.

Department of the Environment: Planning Statistics Department (1995) *General Development Control Returns (PS2 forms).*

Hampshire County Council (1995) *Hampshire 2011, Hampshire County Structure Plan Review,* Hampshire County Council.

Stewart, J. (1995) *Housing Market Report, August 1995,* House-Builders Federation, House-builder Publications Ltd, London.

Charles Fulford

The Compact City and the Market: *The Case of Residential Development*

Introduction

Problems of urban development have often inspired radical and even utopian solutions. The congested towns of the late nineteenth century led Ebenezer Howard to his vision of the garden city, a hybrid form of development which set the advantages of town living in a high quality rural environment. For Frank Lloyd Wright, the advent of mass car-use meant that it was no longer necessary to concentrate activities in cities. Instead, inspired by the independent rural lifestyle of Wisconsin of the 1890s, his ideal urban form was a completely dispersed, low density urban spread - Broadacre City.

Given the squalor which characterised urban life at the turn of the century, it is hardly surprising that many of these solutions involved the abandonment of existing towns and cities. Yet ironically, some of the most pressing problems of contemporary urban development have, in part, been a direct consequence of the visions of the pioneers. Garden cities have left behind both vast tracts of vacant urban land and areas in which the problems of congestion and poverty are as prevalent as ever. Broadacre has become little more than suburban sprawl. This is no coincidence. As Hall (1975, p.80) noted, one of the defining characteristics of the pioneers was their preoccupation with the 'production of blueprints, or statements of the end-state of the city as they desired to see it'. In other words, they ignored the socio-economic processes which determine the feasibility of development.

Today's visionary solution is the compact city. Academics, environmentalists and, more recently, politicians have all been quick to adopt this as an all-embracing panacea for urban ills. Yet this contemporary vision displays the same lack of attention to the crucial question of feasibility. It has simply been assumed that the planning system alone can reverse the counter-urban patterns of development which have predominated over the last 40 or so years. Yet without the co-operation of the development industry, and in particular house-builders, the prospects for realising the long term goal of urban containment are remote.

The purpose of this chapter, therefore, is to examine this question of feasibility from the perspective of the volume house-builder. It is divided into two main sections: the first reviews the principal social and environmental advantages claimed for the compact city; the second presents the findings of an in-depth, semi-structured interview study carried out with 14 major house-builders.

The advantages of the compact city

Support for the compact city has arisen largely in response to concerns about the effects of dispersed patterns of development both on society and the environment. The vitality and diversity of the compact city, it is claimed, will offer a higher quality of life for all its citizens; shorter journey lengths and more sustainable forms of transport will result in reductions in energy consumption and pollution; and containing development within urban areas will prevent further rural land loss. This section provides a brief overview of the validity of the claims made for the compact city. Since these have been well rehearsed, the intention is simply to provide an indication of where the consensus lies (for a fuller discussion of these issues and a more comprehensive bibliography, see Fulford, forthcoming, a).

Social benefits

There is a strong tradition in the UK of equating low density suburban development with a high quality of life. The garden city concept, for example, which dates back to Ebenezer Howard, has been carried forward and promoted enthusiastically by the Town and Country Planning Association (Hall, 1989; Town and Country Planning, 1994). Others too promote decentralised forms of development. March (1974) championed linear, not nuclear developments while Robertson (1990) argued that modern telecommunications allow people to enjoy high quality decentralised lifestyles.

Increasingly, however, there has been growing concern over what Herington (1984) has called 'the outer city'. The European Communities' *Green Paper on the Urban Environment* (CEC, 1990, p.19) heralded a rediscovery of the value of urban living, which it believed 'reflects the failure of the periphery: the absence of public life, the paucity of culture, the visual monotony, the time wasted in commuting'. The compact city, on the other hand, by virtue of its density, is seen as offering a lifestyle which is both varied and culturally enriched.

Jane Jacobs, writing in the 1960s, argued that the city, with its vitality, mix of uses and tradition represents the most desirable form of development for people whilst also encouraging wealth creation and innovation (Jacobs, 1962). For Sherlock (1990, p.53), 'take away the high concentration of people and activities, together with the diversity and vitality which go with them, and there is no longer any point living in a city'.

There are also concerns that dispersal tends to favour the affluent and car-borne members of society. Sociologists, such as David Popenoe (1977) believe that peripheral development has little to offer families who are not self-sufficient (in essence, those who do not have access to private transport). Similarly, while there may be no direct causal link between outer city prosperity and inner city deprivation, a continual outflow of wealth and skilled labour must eventually have an impact on those areas left behind (Herington, 1984; Freeman, 1984). As Elkin *et al.* (1991, p.205) point out, recent structural economic changes have had a disparate impact on different regions and sub-regions, with, for example, most new manufacturing investment occurring in peripheral areas, 'totally divorced from and inaccessible to the poorer inner city population'.

Environmental benefits
Two principal environmental advantages are claimed for the compact city: that it plays a vital role in preventing rural land loss and that it is energy efficient.

Rural land loss
There is little dispute about the strength and ubiquitous nature of the decentralisation process. Over the period 1961-1991, Sinclair (1992) estimated that while the population of England and Wales grew by approximately 5%, the area of land categorised as urban increased by some 25% to 40%. The findings of the Department of the Environment's *Countryside Survey* (1990) were similar. During the period 1984-1990, the built-up area of Britain grew at a rate of approximately 130 sq km per annum, from 16,100 to 16,900 sq km.

This considerable loss of land to development has resulted in an overall decline in the number of species and natural habitats in the British countryside. According to the *Countryside Survey*, between 1978 and 1990, pastures lost 14% and arable landscapes 30% of their species. Woodlands were found to be grassier and to contain fewer varieties of trees. The survey suggests that a large number of species have disappeared because of the destruction of wildlife 'reservoirs' such as roadside verges, river banks and hedgerows. Between 1984 and 1990, 23% - equivalent to 76,000 miles - of the country's hedgerows were lost. While many factors will have contributed to this decline (such as agricultural pollution and intensive farming methods), urban development is identified as a primary factor.

Energy efficiency
Although the prevention of further rural land loss is perhaps the most unequivocal reason for promoting the compact city, much of the debate has focused on the contribution that high density, large urban areas can make to reductions in transport-related energy consumption (see for example, Handy, 1992; Rickaby, 1987; and Owens, 1986).

A useful starting point in relation to density is provided by Newman and Kenworthy (1989). Their analysis of ten cities in the US revealed petrol consumption rates that varied by as much as 40%. In order to explain these differences, they correlated consumption per capita with factors such as income, car ownership and petrol prices, and found largely insignificant correlations. Their analysis of urban density, however, revealed that 'the relative intensity of land use in the ten cities is clearly correlated with gasoline use'. They then suggest that 'urban structure within a city is fundamental to its gasoline consumption' (p.25).

This conclusion has been challenged, most notably by Gordon and Richardson (1989), who, in addition to arguing against public intervention generally, criticised the study for underestimating the importance of non-work trips. However, other studies have produced similar results. Bozeat *et al.* (1992, p.274) found that 'distance travelled to work (is) negatively associated with population density'. Tarry (1992, p.266), in an analysis of accessibility factors at a local level, concluded that 'development to a dispersed and low density pattern is the antithesis of that required to keep journeys short'.

In relation to urban size, most empirical research has found a direct correlation between the scale of urban development and transport-related energy consumption. Again, there have been dissenting voices. Breheny (1995, p.99) for example, in his retrospective analysis of population change over the past thirty years, suggests that 'energy savings from urban containment are likely to be disappointingly low'. Two studies which uphold the consensus view are by Bozeat *et al.* (1992) and ECOTEC (1993). The former used the 1986 National Travel Survey in order to determine total travel by size of urban area. Its findings were broadly that, whereas average weekly travel in urban areas over 250,000 population was 87.7 miles (13.8% by public transport), in rural areas (i.e. less than 3,000 population) the figure was 131 miles (7.9% by public transport).

ECOTEC (1993) provides a detailed breakdown of urban areas by size, giving the distance travelled per person per week by mode in seven different urban size bands. In line with the other studies, Table 1 demonstrates that metropolitan areas (excluding London) appear to induce the least travel, while smaller urban and rural areas are the most fuel inefficient and hence unsustainable.

Urban Area	Car	Bus	Rail	Walk	Other	All modes
Inner London	45.3	12.0	34.1	2.5	16.6	110.5
Outer London	113.3	8.9	23.3	2.6	18.5	166.6
Metropolitan Areas	70.6	16.9	4.7	3.4	17.1	112.7
Other urban over 250,000	93.6	11.2	8.3	4.2	23.9	141.2
100,000 - 250,000	114.8	8.6	11.3	3.2	22.6	160.5
50,000 - 100,000	110.4	7.2	13.0	3.7	20.2	154.5
25,000 - 50,000	110.8	5.7	12.5	3.7	18.2	151.0
3,000 - 25,000	133.4	7.2	8.0	3.0	24.1	175.7
Rural	163.8	5.7	10.9	1.7	28.9	211.0
All areas	113.8	9.3	11.3	3.2	22.0	159.6

Table 1. Distance travelled kilometres per person per week, by mode and urban size.

Source: ECOTEC (1993) (table 9)

The political response

On the basis of this overwhelmingly favourable evidence, the compact city has gained widespread political support in many Western countries. In the UK, the Government has adopted the compact city, making it a central element of its national planning policies and promoting stronger urban containment. *Planning Policy Guidance 13* (PPG13) on Transport (DoE and DoT, 1994) is the most significant recent manifestation of this policy. Its central proposition is that the need to travel can be reduced by influencing the location of development and by encouraging forms of development which promote sustainable modes of transport. Its policies in relation to housing are set out below in Table 2.

Paras 3.2 and 3.3 state that the overall strategy of the planning system in relation to housing should be to:

- [allocate] the maximum amount of housing to existing larger urban areas (market towns and above) where they are or can be easily accessible to facilities... and to a range of transport provision, with particular priority placed on the reuse or conversion of existing sites and properties;
- promote land for housing in locations capable of being well served by rail or

other public transport;

- set standards to maintain existing densities and where appropriate increase them; and
- juxtapose employment and residential uses, where feasible, through mixed use development and by releasing adequate housing land on suitable sites within central areas.

and in relation to development in rural areas,

- promote appropriate development within existing communities.

In addition to this, certain types of development are to be avoided:

- any significant incremental expansion of housing in villages and small towns...
- sporadic housing development in the open countryside
- the development of small new settlements (broadly those unlikely to reach 10,000 dwellings within 20 years)...

Table 2. PPG13 - Proposals for residential development.

Source: PPG13: Transport, DoE and DoT (1994)

As outlined earlier, however, little attention has been given to the viability of these policies from a market perspective. Yet the successful operation of the planning system relies on a certain amount of cooperation from the development industry. Unless planning policy 'goes with the grain', the pressure for the release of sites in unsustainable locations may prove impossible to resist. The likely success of policies for urban compaction will therefore depend on the extent to which they are consistent with the views of the market.

The next section contributes to answering this question by presenting the findings of an interview study of the viability of the compact city from the perspective of the residential developer (the interview study is reported in more detail in Fulford, forthcoming, b).

The interview study

The Credit Lyonnais Laing listing of house-builders (by unit completions, 1992 financial year order) was used as the basis for identifying potential interviewees. Initial reactions were favourable, with 14 of the 17 contacted agreeing to an interview. For the purposes of the research, they were divided into three broad categories: six 'mainly greenfield', three 'mainly urban' and five 'mixed'.

The interviews covered a range of topics, including the house-builders' current patterns of development activity, their general awareness of sustainability and their views on the viability of the compact city proposals. To enhance the relevance of the interviews to UK developers, the questions were constructed loosely around the proposals contained in PPG13, focusing in particular on the viability of directing development into existing urban and rural settlements as well as on the prospects for promoting high density, mixed use developments.

The main overall finding of the study was that most of the house-builders, although aware of the problems with the compact city, were generally positive about the need to redirect more development back onto urban sites. This is a surprising result, given volume house-builders' traditional preference for greenfield development (a fact borne out in the initial section on current patterns of development activity). It is also an encouraging result, since most of those involved in the development process, especially planners, assume that residential developers are profoundly suspicious of urban sites.

The house-building industry, however, is by nature conservative, succinctly summarised by one house-builder's comment that 'pioneers get arrows in their backs', and given that current patterns of development are well established, the move away from decentralised development will require more than the imposition of a new policy framework. It must also be economically viable. To this extent, it will be conditional upon the removal of the many constraints identified by the house-builders. These, together with strategies for change (many of which were identified by the developers) are outlined below.

Urban development

The house-builders felt that attempting to allocate 'the maximum amount of housing to existing larger urban areas' (PPG13, para 3.2) should not be achieved at the expense of quality open spaces, or as one house-builder put it, 'urban lungs'. Despite this, there is a considerable amount of derelict and under-utilised land which should be brought back into effective use. The principal difficulty, therefore, is not with the total quantity of urban land, but with the constraints on development which often characterise urban sites.

Contaminated land

Although land contamination was seen as a barrier to urban development, the interviewees stressed that, whilst requiring specialist knowledge, the costs of decontamination could normally be recouped in the land value. The major concern for the house-builders was underestimating the extent of the contamination in the site valuation. This situation is further aggravated by the complex array of regulators, and hence the possibility of receiving conflicting advice and guidance.

In order to encourage house-builders onto inner urban sites, agreed standards of decontamination are required. Furthermore, these should be graded, so that a site targeted for redevelopment as industrial warehousing, for example, does not require the same amount of investment as a site destined for use as a school (this 'suitable for use' approach has been adopted in the recent Environment Act 1995). Equally, there is a need for some form of 'decontamination certificate', issued by a nominated regulatory authority, to indemnify developers against future liability claims.

Where it is not profitable, or indeed possible, for private sector developers to tackle contaminated sites, public sector agencies should take the lead in assembling sites and overcoming their constraints. Given that this process in itself 'adds value', some of the costs would be passed on to the purchaser through the higher value achievable upon resale (see Dixon and Richards, 1995, for a discussion of the problems of valuing contaminated land).

Problems of land acquisition

Many vacant urban sites cannot be made available for development because they are subject to multiple ownership and conflicting interests. Acquiring suitable quantities of land, a perennial concern of any large house-builder, can therefore be more problematic in an urban context. A number of developers referred to the difficulties of obtaining sites large enough to achieve the economies of scale available on greenfield sites.

The developers also noted that local authorities are often reluctant to release urban sites for residential development. No less than nine out of fourteen developers felt that local authorities unnecessarily withhold urban land from development because it is earmarked for one particular use. Redundant manufacturing land, for example, may not be released for a housing scheme, even though the original use no longer represents a commercially attractive proposition.

A number of ideas were put forward by developers for overcoming the problems of land-banking in an urban context: additional powers could be granted to public sector agencies (such as an English equivalent of the Welsh Development Agency) to facilitate the compulsory purchase of land held in passive ownership; owners of vacant sites should be required to put forward practical proposals for development, or risk becoming liable to financial penalties; equally, the establishment of much closer working relationships between developers and local planning authorities would enable sites to be targeted for redevelopment and their constraints identified so they could pass more easily into active ownership.

Company structure

Most volume house-builders are geared primarily towards the acquisition and development of greenfield sites and use a factory style 'box building' approach to development. While this may work on greenfield sites, it is clearly not suited to the more idiosyncratic urban sites. A shift to predominantly urban development will involve the house-builders in fairly substantial company restructuring and will require the acquisition of specialist knowledge, including, for example, a greater emphasis on refurbishment. Apart from one developer, however, refurbishment was only undertaken in the context of large new-build schemes, and often it was a consequence of a planning obligation (for example, the retention and restoration of a listed building).

Although not insurmountable, such fundamental change can take time, especially given that most large house-builders will have a large land-bank of greenfield sites. The problems of diversifying into a new market can be overcome through the recruitment of urban development specialists, a greater reliance on consultants or through merging with other firms.

Development in rural areas

Where housing needs 'cannot be met in central locations in larger urban areas', PPG13 recommends 'appropriate development within existing [rural] communities'. It therefore extends the philosophy of containment into the rural context, advocating infill and at the same time identifying three types of rural development which should be avoided: incremental expansion of housing in villages and small towns; sporadic housing development in the countryside; and small new settlements (which are set out in para 3.2 of PPG13 as 'those unlikely to reach 10,000 dwellings within 20 years').

The majority of developers believed that, even where local opposition could be overcome, the infrastructure and services found in many smaller settlements would be unable to cope with the burden of additional development. The consensus was that some 'unsustainable' rural development would be inevitable.

Incremental expansion of housing in villages and small towns

This was seen to be particularly difficult to prevent, since it fulfils people's aspirations for more space while allowing them to remain in areas they are familiar with. It is also popular with developers (the facilities are usually there to support new development and infrastructure can be easily extended). Furthermore, local authorities are often more than willing to release peripheral (and even green belt) land for development in order to meet the housing quotas imposed on them through structure plans.

Sporadic housing development in the open countryside

Sporadic development in the open countryside was generally acknowledged to be environmentally unacceptable (although popular with house buyers). Four developers stated explicitly that it should be avoided. Given the strong bias against this kind of development and the high costs of providing infrastructure to isolated developments, it would not be difficult to deter sporadic housing development.

Small new settlements

In addition to the myriad planning restrictions, new settlements were generally seen as problematic. The huge servicing costs involved in building new settlements mean that a site only becomes viable if it is sufficiently large to be able to absorb these costs. The minimum number of dwellings was said to be in the region of 750 (the level at which a primary school could be sustained). There is thus a considerable gulf between the size of site which is viable from a developer's perspective and the minimum size in terms of sustainability. This may in turn lead to pressure for the release of sites for small new settlements.

High density development

Another key precondition of the compact city is that development should be high density. This is reflected in PPG13, which states that local authorities should 'set standards to maintain existing densities and where appropriate increase them...' (PPG13, para 3.3).

High density development, particularly within a central urban context, is often the most profitable option for house-builders. The main obstacle identified by the house-builders was the disparity that currently exists between the focus of national planning policy guidance and its application at a local level. So while it is generally accepted (by organisations such as Friends of the Earth) that a net residential density of about 300 people per hectare (pph) is sustainable, new residential development in England tends to be in the region of 50-90 pph. Even supposedly high density Inner London local authorities, such as the London Borough of Haringey, impose maximum densities in the region of 125 pph. Table 3 illustrates the considerable discrepancy between existing and optimal density levels.

Approximately half the developers believed that high density schemes are often rejected because planners take the view that developers are only interested in trying to extract the maximum level of profit from a site. A second contributory factor is the high level of car parking required on new developments. Despite recent improvements, the planning system still pivots around the requirements of the car, with road capacity influencing development location, and parking provision dictating density. As a consequence of this, many proposals put forward for urban infill developments are rejected because they are unable to provide the high levels of car parking deemed necessary by local authorities. As one house-builder commented, the results are 'vast tracts of land covered in tarmac, monotonous suburban housing estates and unimaginative cul-de-sacs'.

Existing	GRD	NRD	Source
London	56	168	Newman & Kenworthy (1989)
Hong Kong	293	879	Newman & Kenworthy (1989)
Los Angeles	20	60	Newman & Kenworthy (1989)
Melbourne	16.4	49.2	Newman & Kenworthy (1989)
Paris	48.3	144.9	Newman & Kenworthy (1989)
Tokyo	105.4	316.2	Newman & Kenworthy (1989)
Toronto	39.6	118.8	Newman & Kenworthy (1989)
Camden (London Borough)	56	168	Camden UDP
Haringey (London Borough)	66	198	Haringey UDP
(max. permitted for dev't)		125	
Islington (London Borough in 1965)		740	Milner-Holland (1965)
England - new residential		47-94	Bibby & Shepherd (1990)
Milton Keynes		67.5	Sherlock (1990)

Optimal	GRD	NRD	Source
Public Transport	30-40	90-120	Newman & Kenworthy (1989)
Walking	100	300	Newman & Kenworthy (1989)
Sustainable Urban		225-300	Friends of the Earth
Central/Accessible Urban		up to 370	Friends of the Earth

Table 3. Existing and optimal urban densities.

Note: all figures are in people/hectare
GRD (Gross Residential Density): population divided by geographical area
NRD (Net Residential Density): excludes open spaces and non-residential land

Although there are potential infrastructure and resource problems associated with higher densities (see for example, Lock, 1995; and Knight, 1995), there is clearly scope for a substantial upward revision of permitted development density. There was a generally acknowledged need among the developers for planning guidance which ensures that development plans do not set maximum densities at levels which are undesirably low.

Mixed use development
Another key requirement of the compact city proposals is that residential, employment and leisure uses should be brought together 'where feasible through mixed use development' (PPG13, para 3.3). Although aware of the advantages, the house-builders were not particularly receptive to the concept of mixed use development and identified a number of fundamental problems.

First, there is the difficulty of recreating the atmosphere generated by existing, successful mixed use areas, such as central Oxford. New developments cannot act as magnets for goods, services and people in the same way as areas which have grown 'organically'. In addition, where a relatively affluent local population does not exist, it is difficult to support such an intensity of local services.

Second, decades of functionalist land use planning policies have fixed into the psyche of the house buyer the belief that his immediate environment should be predominantly residential. Although the idea of walking to work is appealing in principle, 'no one', as one house-builder commented, 'wants a factory at the bottom of their garden'.

The third problem stems from the simple economic reality that a landowner will usually seek to maximise profits on the sale of land. The user who can offer the highest price will, planning permitting, secure the site. Although some token mixed use can then be extracted by means of a Section 106 agreement, this generally does not create successful mixed use schemes.

A final problem arises from investors' current attitudes towards mixed use developments. As one interviewee put it, 'the financial equation becomes blurred'. A number of factors contribute to this, including: the problems associated with the increased restrictions on working practices in urban areas; the preference for industrial or commercial sites which have good access to motorways; and the continuing use of traditional methods of valuation which rely on comparables derived from historic data, and which are not geared towards specialist transactions.

Radical changes are thus required if mixed use development is to compete on a level playing field. The over-specialisation of urban areas could be avoided through the creation of a separate, or revised, Use Classes Order. Similarly, specific mixed land use designations in the local plan would ensure that it is not necessarily the highest bid which secures the site for development. Furthermore, efforts need to be directed at changing the public's and investors' perceptions of mixed use development. Clever design, incorporating, for example, landscape buffers, can mitigate the effects of commercial or light-industrial uses on residential areas.

Clearly not all areas will be suited to all types of use. Integrating commercial activities into the urban residential fabric could result in less efficient use of land since, within densely populated urban areas, the existing requirement for low-rise industrial buildings would have to be reversed. Equally, some uses will always require peripheral sites with high land-consumption.

Summary of main findings

The principal findings of the interview study can be drawn together as follows:

- The house-builders were generally positive about the need for a more sustainable pattern of urban development.
- They identified a considerable number of obstacles to the successful implementation of the compact city, notably land contamination, restrictive planning policies, and the difficulty of creating successful mixed use development.
- A number of strategies for change were identified, including: a 'decontamination certificate'; a market oriented public sector agency to tackle problematic sites; an upward revision of acceptable development densities; and the creation of a new Use Classes Order to promote mixed use development.

Conclusions

There is a widespread belief among those involved in the development process that, although the compact city has clear environmental and social advantages, it would be unworkable from a market perspective. However, this was not what was found in the interview study. Despite the great number of obstacles identified by the house-builders, they were positive both about the need for containment and the prospects for implementing compact city proposals. Indeed, far from rejecting the compact city as an unattainable planning blueprint, some of the interviewees suggested that the policy framework should be tightened further still. It is, after all, uncertainty that leads to costly, misplaced planning applications.

The pioneers of the past, as noted in the introduction to this chapter, believed that all that was required for a good policy was a good blueprint. Yet what this study has shown is that however carefully plans for urban development are thought through in principle, they have always to be tested out in practice. In this study, the generally positive attitude among the interviewees to the need for a more sustainable pattern of urban development was contrary to expectation. Recognition of this could make a significant difference to policy and planning in this area. If practical proposals for overcoming the constraints to the implementation of the compact city are devised, this research has illustrated that the house-builder could be persuaded to play a full role in the process of urban containment.

A new vision is today more essential than ever if urban development is to become more sustainable. The compact city could be that vision, but on-going research into its practical application is essential if the blueprint is to become a reality.

References and further reading

Bibby, P. and Shepherd, J. (1990) *Rates of Urbanisation in England 1981-2001*, Pion, London.

Bozeat, N., Barrett, G. and Jones, G. (1992) The potential contribution of planning to reducing travel demand, PTRC, 20th Summer Annual Meeting, *Environmental Issues: Proceedings of Seminar B*, PTRC, London.

Breheny, M. (1995) The compact city and transport energy consumption. *Transactions of the Institute of British Geographers NS*, **20**, pp.81-101.

Commission of the European Communities (1990) *Green Paper on the Urban Environment*, CEC, Brussels.

Department of the Environment (1990) *The Countryside Survey*, HMSO, London.

Department of the Environment (1994) *Planning Policy Guidance 13: Transport*, HMSO, London.

Dixon, T. and Richards, T. (1995) Valuation lessons from America. *The Estates Gazette*, **9529**, pp.110-112.

ECOTEC (1993) *Reducing Transport Emissions Through Planning*, HMSO, London.

Editorial (1994) City or Surburbia. *Town and Country Planning*, **63 (9)**, p.226

Elkin, T., McLaren, D. and Hillman, M. (1991) *Reviving the City: Towards Sustainable Urban Development*, Friends of the Earth, London.

Freeman, H. (1984) *Mental Health and the Environment*, Churchill Livingstone, London.

Fulford, C.M., (1994) *Sustainable Urban Form and the Residential Developer*. Unpublished MPhil Dissertation, University of Reading.

Fulford, C.M., forthcoming (a): *The Compact City and the Residential Developer*, - I. Occasional Papers, University of Reading.

Fulford, C.M., forthcoming (b): *The Compact City and the Residential Developer*, - II. Occasional Papers, University of Reading.

Gordon, P. and Richardson, H.W. (1989) Gasoline consumption and cities - a reply, *Journal of the American Planning Association*, **55**, pp.342-345.

Hall, D. (1989) The case for new settlements. *Town and Country Planning*, April, **58(4)**, pp.111-114.

Hall, P. (1975) *Urban and Regional Planning*, Unwin and Hyman, London.

Handy, S.L. (1992) Regional versus local accessibility. *Built Environment*, **18(4)**, pp.253-267.

Herington, J. (1984) *The Outer City*, Harper and Row, London.

Jacobs, J. (1962) *The Death and Life of Great American Cities*, Cape, London.

Knight, C. (1995) The pitfalls of 'town cramming'. *Planning Week*, 8 June.

Lock, D. (1995) Room for more within city limits? *Town and Country Planning*, July, pp.173-176.

March, L. (1974) Homes beyond the fringe, in *The Future of Cities* (eds A. Blowers, C. Hamnett, and P. Sarre) The Open University Press, London.

Milner-Holland, E. (1965) *Report of the Committee on Housing in Greater London*, Cmnd 2605, HMSO, London.

Newman, P. and Kenworthy, J. (1989) *Cities and Automobile Dependence: An International Sourcebook*, Gower Technical, Aldershot.

Owens, S. (1986) *Energy, Planning and Urban Form*, Pion, London.

Popenoe, D. (1977) *The Suburban Environment: Sweden and the United States*, University of Chicago Press, Chicago.

Rickaby, P. (1987) Six settlement patterns compared. *Environment and Planning B, Planning and Design*, **14,** pp.193-223.

Robertson, J. (1990) Alternative futures for cities, in *The Living City: Towards a Sustainable Future* (eds D. Cadman and G. Payne) Routledge, London.

Sherlock, H. (1990) *Cities Are Good For Us,* Transport 2000, London.

Sinclair, G. (1992) *The Lost Land,* Council for the Protection of Rural England, London.

Tarry, S. (1992) Accessibility factors at the neighbourhood level. PTRC, 20th Summer Annual Meeting, *Environmental Issues: Proceedings of Seminar B*, pp.257-270, PTRC, London.

Martin Crookston, Patrick Clarke and Joanna Averley

The Compact City and the Quality of Life

Urban regeneration and the compact city are right in line with the policy of most Western governments. They are, however, a long way adrift from the record and reality of the postwar West. If idea and reality are to be reconciled, it is vital that our towns and cities can offer a quality of life - a 'vision' of the liveable city - which can compete with the rural dream in many people's minds. This vision is not an ideal form. It is made up of practical elements which need money, attention and time, to produce better-managed and cared-for urban places.

Policies and trends

The compact city concept has much to commend it in terms of sustainable development. The benefits of concentrating new development within existing urban areas are widely recognised, notably in the European Communities' *Green Paper on the Urban Environment* (Commission of the European Communities, 1990). In summary, these benefits include: assisting the process of urban regeneration; capitalising on existing investment in infrastructure and community facilities; bringing back into productive use derelict and contaminated land; and improving the range and quality of facilities available to local residents. For the environment, benefits would be in terms of promoting the use of public transport; reducing the need to travel, and journey lengths, particularly by private car; and reducing pressure on the countryside.

The concept fits well, too, with the principles set out in *Sustainable Development: The UK Strategy* (UK Government, 1994), and in emerging planning policies. The UK Strategy advocates making the most efficient use of existing urban areas, making them more attractive as places to live and work and bringing derelict and contaminated land back into productive use. Government planning advice in PPG13 recommends 'allocating the maximum amount of housing to existing larger urban areas' (Department of the Environment and Department of Transport, 1994, para 3.2) while the recent White Paper, *Our Future Homes,* sets a target of accommodating at least half of future housing within existing urban areas (UK Government, 1995).

So far so good, in policy terms. In reality though, the prognosis is not good. There are two main concerns. First, our urban areas have been in decline for several decades now, with the better off and more mobile moving out, precisely because they perceive a decline in the quality of urban life, and better quality in suburban and ex-urban locations. If, for example, we look at the OPCS (Office of Population Censuses and Surveys) analysis of population change for different urban types, we can see that between 1981 and 1991 more than 580,000 people moved away from principal urban settlement categories; the most significant gains were in the following categories:

- resort and retirement (+416,000)
- mixed and accessible (+228,000)
- remote largely rural (+444,000)

If we look at the example of the West Midlands region, we can see that the metropolitan authorities are losing around 10,000 people per year, mainly to the surrounding shire counties.

These trends are well established, and many people with a choice continue to vote with their feet. Clearly, it will take a great deal more than a few well chosen words in the UK Strategy for Sustainable Development and in regional planning guidance to slow down, let alone reverse, these trends (Government Office for the West Midlands, 1994).

A second reason for concern is that in thinking about the compact city we have failed to look properly at the relationships between urban concentration, sustainable development and quality of life. Instead we have been drawn into a debate about housing numbers, density and housing form. This may be the nitty-gritty of urban planning, but if the compact city is to be a success we must raise our sights and think at a higher level about the quality of the compact city as a place to live. The failure to articulate the vision is demonstrated by comments in the planning press, such as, 'imposing high-density living to save the countryside is to be deplored', and 'sustainability of high-density compact cities runs counter to the aspirations of the great majority of the public to have a house on the ground with a garden' (Fyson, 1995, p.19).

Idea and reality

So if the city is to be a place where people want to live, it has to be both attractive as an idea and attractive in reality. There needs to be a positive, environmentally-led vision of what urban life can be: an image which can compete with the powerful anti-urban ethos and trends that are predominant.

The problem with the compact city label is twofold: it combines the threat of town cramming ('compact', as in car sales and estate agency speak, meaning cramped and poky), with a somewhat irrelevant-seeming continental European notion of a densely-packed bustling little market town, all piazzas, courtyards, apartments with balconies, and street festivals. It makes the English uneasy, as though someone is trying to create Siena or San Gimignano in Walsall or Kettering. The English (much more than the Scots and the Welsh) and the North Americans seem much less at ease with urban life than the French, Germans or Swiss, all of whom seem to be quite happy to know that the countryside is out there if they happen to want to use it, but are much less driven by a burning desire to live in it or something like it.

So we need an ideal, or a vision, but one that is relevant to British circumstances and ideologies. Thomas Sharp, one of the inter-war generation of town planning proponents, and an anti-suburbanite of some venom, regarded the move to the suburbs as an escape by 'an unorganised band of prisoners breaking gaol, with no very definite plans for what lies before them...'. He believed this stemmed from their being 'sick of the wretched towns they have to live in...', so cities and towns should be changed, 'adjusting, adapting, exploiting them to our changed circumstances' (Sharp, 1940, pp.40-45). This at least contained an understanding of the dynamics of cities, and a relevant prescription for change; his contemporaries in Le Corbusier's CIAM Group confined themselves to invective: 'the suburb is an urbanistic folly...carried to its extreme consequences in America...one of the greatest evils of the twentieth century...' (Le Corbusier, 1943, quoted in Oliver *et al.*, 1981, p.40).

To be relevant, the vision cannot be anti-suburban. By any measure, most British people live in suburbia: London outside the half-dozen innermost boroughs; the conurbations outside the Victorian core; and the rest of the country other than the former market towns and extensive but lightly-populated areas which are still genuinely rural and not outer-outer suburbs. The vision has to relate not just to the urban core areas, which we are trying to re-popularise and repopulate; the suburbs too have to be addressed. They must become more compact, more liveable in a sustainable way.

Perhaps two challenges emerge. First, how can we make our towns and cities - in the familiar 'central place' sense - a location of choice for more people? This is sometimes seen as a gentrifiers' charter. And it is true that we have a model of the virtuous circle whereby an inner area (Kentish Town, Battersea, the Merchant City) recovers from decline because it has become acceptable or even fashionable as a middle-class place to live. But this process is not simply confined to colonisation by middle-class incomers. London's East End, deserted since before the war by generation after generation of its children, now holds them; not just the City dealers, but upholsterers and cabbies too, who would formerly have moved 'down the line' to Barking or Billericay as soon as they could, only coming back on Saturdays to do Roman Road Market and visit the grandparents. Of course, many do move out still, but not all of them; and that is an important point: all we need is for ordinary people to consider the city an acceptable option, and not as Sharp's 'gaol' from which escape must be engineered unless you are a student or a pensioner (Sharp, 1940).

And the second challenge is: how can we make the whole city, including and especially the suburbs, offer a quality of life that will be urban and sustainable, and yet still be attractive to a people who are fundamentally most at ease with the suburbs and their strange but often successful interpenetration of the natural and the man-made, the individual and the social?

Provisional steps to a liveable city

How should we think about liveability, attractiveness and urban quality, whilst trying to fit them into a policy framework which stresses sustainability and compactness? The thinking needs to cover several - interrelated - aspects of the urban planning context:

- housing density: not wasting space, not cramming either
- transport: playing to the city's strengths
- parks, schools, leisure: quality services and facilities
- urban management and safety
- the housing market: offering range and choice

Housing density

> To say that cities need higher dwelling densities and high net ground coverages, as I am saying they do, is conventionally regarded as lower than taking sides with the man-eating shark. (Jacobs, 1961, p.231).

Housing density is contentious. Previous research by the authors for the Joseph Rowntree Foundation showed that for three case study urban areas (Newcastle, Cheltenham, and Lewisham in Greater London), housing densities could be increased by as much as 25% before resulting in significant changes in urban form, such as traditional street patterns giving way to house forms, and this could increase housing capacity by about 19%. With less demanding parking standards this increased capacity could be achieved without any serious impacts at all (Llewelyn-Davies, 1994a).

Subsequent work for the London Planning Advisory Committee (LPAC) explored this potential further, and concluded that maximum density standards and car-parking requirements (notably one off-street space per new dwelling) could be relaxed quite markedly; even in the London Boroughs. Much housing potential could be released, without damaging environmental quality, if planners switched from rigid density limits to careful control of design, pragmatic use of on-street spaces to meet parking demand, and retention of street trees, planting and public open space (Llewelyn-Davies, 1994b).

Critics argue that dropping the parking requirement is unrealistic and a recipe for impossible congestion, and that the maximum density controls should be kept because they avoid the risk that developers will cram every site with ultimately sub-standard and undersized dwellings. The authors' view is that the second danger can be avoided by local planning control officers doing their job properly in terms of site briefing and urban design guidance. On the first point, it seems that parking requirements are simply a waste of time, effort and living space, given the impossibility of keeping up with the rate of increase of both car ownership and use.

Transport

Transport is closely bound up with the arguments for achieving quality high density environments. An important potential strength of towns and cities is their ability to provide for the movement needs of people with reasonably full lives, without the car being essential, which it is, realistically, in the outer suburbs and the countryside. The effect of this can be seen (though not overwhelmingly) in the Census of Population car ownership patterns in London: whereas car ownership rates elsewhere generally track household income and socio-economic groups very closely, this is less the case in the inner areas, where some households at least are clearly choosing not to have a car even where they can afford it. This is partly because of the difficulties in parking and garaging cars, no doubt. But it is also partly because public transport meets many more of the daily movement needs (which will, in any case, be on average easier to meet because of the very density of jobs and other opportunities that the city provides). Tim Pharaoh (1991) makes the interesting point that London's outer suburbs were built to work like this too. 'Metroland' was focused round the station; cycle, bus and walk trips met almost all other needs. Can we edge more of the city back towards this balance? Well, it may be possible, but it is unlikely to be effected by making people feel guilty about owning and using their cars or by dire threats about the ozone layer (technology will surely produce a non-polluting car before much longer). Much more relevant is a strategy aimed at making the places themselves more compact, busy, convenient and attractive, and supporting and improving the public transport which serves them.

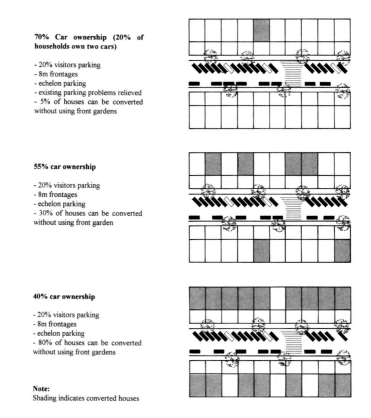

70% Car ownership (20% of households own two cars)

- 20% visitors parking
- 8m frontages
- echelon parking
- existing parking problems relieved
- 5% of houses can be converted without using front gardens

55% car ownership

- 20% visitors parking
- 8m frontages
- echelon parking
- 30% of houses can be converted without using front garden

40% car ownership

- 20% visitors parking
- 8m frontages
- echelon parking
- 80% of houses can be converted without using front gardens

Note:
Shading indicates converted houses

Fig. 1. Capacity for conversions: remodelling the street.

Good quality services and facilities: parks, schools, leisure and fun

One advantage of cities is that they can support the provision of high quality cultural and recreational facilities and services. In general the larger the population the better the range, choice and quality. Culture and entertainment are singled out by the UK Sustainable Development Strategy as the distinguishing advantages of cities which 'should encourage people to want to live and work' in them (UK Government, 1994, p.161).

The down side is that leisure and fun uses have to compete with other urban uses and this tends to make leisure activities expensive. Pressure on municipal budgets means that public provision has given way to private, and many municipal facilities are now operated by the private sector, with a much more commercial ethos than was formerly the case. Worse still, as demand tends to exceed supply - especially in the evenings and weekends - many people, and particularly the less well-off, are squeezed out.

But there are other issues too. As demands become increasingly sophisticated and economies of provision greater, the pattern of provision becomes coarser. While facilities become more sophisticated they tend to become more expensive and less convenient to visit, involving journeys along congested streets, or multiple bus trips. All this acts contrary to the objectives of a compact city with convenient, high quality, local facilities.

In our compact city we must also be much better at providing and managing open space. The Victorians recognised the value of good quality local open space and of park keepers and groundsmen. In a recent guide to the city of the future, the *Independent* (Spackman, 1995) identified the premium people will increasingly pay for proximity to green space because, they say, 'we don't make it anymore'. True; but what is worse is that we do not maintain and capitalise on the investment that previous generations have made on our behalf. The downward pressure on local authority spending has meant that open space has lost out to more critical local services - education, 'meals on wheels' and the like - and maintenance budgets have been cut, facilities and equipment run down, and park keepers sacked. Fortunately there are signs that this process is about to turn full circle. For one thing, the DoE are researching whether better supervision of parks (i.e. park keepers) could reduce vandalism!

Yet there are many examples of parks and open spaces which do fulfil their potential - where local authorities have been prepared to invest in improvements, supervision and maintenance, and in encouraging private sector initiatives. Crystal Palace Park in South East London is one such example. The value people attach to such good quality provision is there for all to see. Go any Saturday or Sunday and you will find hundreds, even thousands, of people enjoying themselves, certainly people from Sydenham, Penge, Norwood and Dulwich, and indeed from much further afield where there is no equivalent local provision.

Open space is a crucial component in our vision of the compact city. We must recognise the direct link between good quality open space and the quality of urban life. Again the UK Sustainable Development Strategy makes this link: it states quite clearly that 'urban quality depends on the creation and protection of green space in cities for amenity and recreation' (para 24.23); but we must follow this through into official planning guidance and into resource decisions. We must, for example, begin to take a more rounded (and more accurate) view of investment in open space. This might include increased productivity of a de-stressed and relaxed workforce, as well as its contribution to a wider strategy which is concerned with making better use of existing urban infrastructure and reducing expenditure on meeting 'relocated demand' elsewhere. This is hardly new thinking. The Cadburys, Salts and Rowntrees all recognised the economic benefits that flow from investment in social and community facilities.

This logic applies across the full range of services which cities provide: health, education, social services and so on. Our vision of the compact city is founded on a commitment to provide its citizens with the first class services they demand and deserve; facilities and services which will genuinely encourage people to want to live and work in urban areas. This is almost the opposite of what is happening at present - instead of urban dwellers suffering poor, run down and overstretched public services, and the inconvenience and danger of car-borne commuter traffic through their living environment, they would see government spending programmes being bent in their favour, and decisions about traffic and transport starting with a concern for their convenience and quality of life rather than that of through-commuters. This demands a wholly new way of thinking about how we resource cities, but it also demands a much greater commitment to quality - to people and places - on the part of those who manage our cities.

Urban management and safety

As well as being exciting and fun, cities are dangerous - or so the image goes. Certainly, a component of the drift to the suburbs is the wish to trade insecurity for security, noise for tranquillity, and dirt and disorder for cleanliness and order. Whatever the actual incidence of violence, if people feel unsafe in the area, they will want to leave it if they can; if a street feels unsafe, fewer people will use it, and it will become even less safe. Better policing practice can help, but it cannot solve the problem; as Jane Jacobs (1961) observed 35 years ago, 'The first thing to understand is that the public peace...of cities is not kept primarily by the police, necessary as police are. It is kept primarily by an intricate, almost unconscious, network of voluntary controls and standards among people themselves, and enforced by the people themselves'. Jack Straw MP attracted much criticism for pointing out that one of the effects of government policies on homelessness, benefits and unemployment had been to degrade the street environment and the very people who (are forced to) use it (1995, speech at Lewisham Town Hall, 4 September: *Reclaiming the Streets*).

Our cities and towns, particularly the central and inner areas, often convey exactly the worrying mixture of neglect, danger and unreliability that reinforce the spiral of decay, and encourage anyone who can leave to do so. Not all of this is the product of national government penny-pinching and short sightedness - though a lot is. Some of it can be avoided by good urban management: Islington is better run than Hackney (both inner city, both Labour, similar histories); Sheffield is better run than Liverpool; everywhere is better run than Lambeth; the Scottish towns and cities are generally cleaner and more cared-for than their English counterparts. This is an issue of competence, and of commitment; and it extends beyond local government, to visible on-street services, reliable public transport and to the cleanliness and state of repair of parks, playgrounds, schools and shopping precincts. Running urban local authorities well is difficult, but it is not impossible. A vision which mends cracked paving-stones and keeps dog excrement out of children's playgrounds is more important than one made up of Olympic bids, new concert halls, and shiny new community workspaces, because it relates more to people living there, enjoying the place, feeling safe and at ease.

Working with the market

No doubt much of what we have said so far sounds like a simple plea for more resources to be spent in the towns and cities. That is, in the authors' view, an inevitable component of a rational strategy for liveable, compact, sustainable cities. There is, nevertheless, more to it than that: we can work with the market as well.

At present, there is a vicious circle at work in how the housing market operates, to discourage compactness and urban living. Developers interviewed in the study for the Joseph Rowntree Foundation by no means ruled out inner city development - indeed, one or two specialised in it - but the general picture was that the perceived demand was for conventional suburban and ex-urban housing, because it was 'what people wanted'. On average, urban sites were more likely to be more complicated, physically more constrained and more costly (in a range £1,850 to £12,500 per home on the sites surveyed). So both supply and demand were working to deflect developer interest. And in some areas, only housing with some sort of subsidy, generally for the 'affordable housing' market or to house people primarily on benefit, was being completed (Llewelyn-Davies, 1994a).

This suggests two interesting conclusions. First, developers are not, as some commentators suggest, just following the herd instinct and building the sorts of schemes that everyone else is, simply because everyone else is. They are perfectly prepared to entertain development on urban sites, if the return is seen to be worth the extra hassle. And second, it ought to be possible to devise mechanisms which do close that gap, and which do tilt the market more towards in-town development (including rehabilitation), in a way which broadens the choice of housing rather than restricting it to the social housing sector. The Joseph Rowntree study suggests alterations to the VAT regime, a better-organised and more predictable grant regime, and tighter restraints on greenfield sites in order to focus interest on the brownfield opportunities (Llewelyn-Davies, 1994a).

Other sorts of incentive are worthy of consideration. The Irish government gives sizeable tax breaks to encourage investment in targeted areas of Dublin and other towns. This seems to have produced some urban renewal in areas, notably Temple Bar on the south side, that might otherwise have struggled to reach a critical mass of mutual support and reinforcement. However, other districts on the north side have shown much slower response to such incentives. Understanding the differences between the scenarios might help illuminate where incentives would be useful. And rather than the middleman getting the incentive, what about the end-user? Is it possible to envisage targeted government support for mortgages, down payments or shared-ownership deals, where they have an urban regeneration pay-off ? If we want to get the most out of the places where society has invested so much physical and social capital over a hundred years or more, it seems well worthwhile exploring how the power of the market can be nudged in the direction of helping rather than hindering.

Belief in the city
The twentieth century, particularly in Britain and America, has witnessed a double-edged attitude to cities. We do not like cities so we are not very good at running them, and because we are not very good at it, we do not like them. This seems to stem partly from a widespread, if not universal, Arcadian vision in people's minds. It has to be recognised that we are not going to change the hearts and minds of hundreds of millions of people: we can appeal to environmental guilt, we can try to make every town centre a sort of Covent Garden, we can stop new out-of-town superstores (now that there are eight hundred of them); but it still will not stop most people in Britain aspiring to a dream cottage, nestling below the Downs, for when they win the Lottery, get promotion, or sell the flat in Kilburn. But it does not need to. What we do need to do is provide more people with a quality of life in towns and cities which is a reasonable and enjoyable

alternative to their idyllic rural pipedream.

This means practicalities - the density, transport, parkland and urban management actions that are sketched out above. And it also means something more holistic: a positive belief, at both local and national government levels, that cities and towns can absorb more activities and more people; that they can do this in their centres, in their inner areas and in the much-maligned suburbs; and that policy, intelligently and consistently applied, can nudge our cities slowly but surely in the direction of greater liveability, attractiveness and compactness.

So the vision we are talking about is not in any way an unachievable aspiration, or an idealised return to the market town and Athenian agora of the past. Grenoble's transport system, Stirling's management of its old town, Islington's turn-around of its dustbin collection, Almere's sustainable new settlement planning, all exist as present-day virtues. They are aspects of the vision, examples that can demonstrate to people that urban living does not have to mean inferior quality. All the elements need bringing together in our towns and cities. Then people (investors, potential residents, and planners) can have confidence that the city has a future that they might choose to share.

References

Commission of the European Communities (1990) *Green Paper on the Urban Environment, COM(90)* 218, CEC, Brussels.

Department of the Environment and Department of Transport (1994) *Planning Policy Guidance 13: Transport,* HMSO, London.

Fyson, A. (1995) Route to good practice. *Planning Week,* **Vol. 3 No. 33,** pp.18-19.

Government Office for the West Midlands (1994) D*raft Regional Planning Guidance for the West Midlands,* Government Office for the West Midlands, Birmingham.

Jacobs, J. (1961) *The Death and Life of Great American Cities,* Random House, New York.

Le Corbusier (1943) (Edouard Jeanneret-Gris, dit) *Le Charte d'Athenes,* Plon, Paris.

Llewelyn-Davies (1994a) *Providing More Homes in Urban Areas,* School for Advanced Urban Studies, Bristol, in association with the Joseph Rowntree Foundation, York.

Llewelyn-Davies (1994b) *London's Residential Environmental Quality,* London Planning Advisory Committee (LPAC), London.

Oliver, P., Davies, I. and Bentley, I. (1981) *Dunroamin: The Suburban Semi and its Enemies,* Barrie and Jenkins, London.

Pharaoh, T.M. (1991) Transport: how much can London take? in *London - A New Metropolitan Geography* (eds K. Hoggart and D.R. Green) Edward Arnold, London.

Sharp, T. (1940) *Town Planning,* Penguin, Harmondsworth.

Spackman, A. (1995) House or flat? Town or country? Big or small? Rent or buy? *The Independent on Sunday,* 26 March, p.12.

UK Government (1994) *Sustainable Development: The UK Strategy,* Cm 2426, HMSO, London.

UK Government (1995) *Our Future Homes, Opportunity, Choice, Responsibility,* Cm 2901, HMSO, London.

Ray Green

Not Compact Cities but Sustainable Regions

Introduction

At the turn of the last century, cities were densely populated, overcrowded and unhealthy. Dispersal was a remedy advanced by the garden city movement, adopted in the building of the New Towns and continued on a massive scale by the unplanned migration of millions of people from major cities to country towns and villages. At the turn of this century, dispersal is castigated as wasteful of land and resources, and the compact city is being promoted as the most sustainable of urban forms. The case has been made for the supply of housing land to be increased in metropolitan areas but high levels of demand persist in small towns and villages throughout rural Britain. A vast potential for growth has been built into the economic and demographic structure of the Shires, particularly in southern and central England. New manufacturing and service industries, a highly skilled and well educated labour force, high levels of prosperity, expanding services and improved accessibility will induce further growth outside the metropolitan areas. This is recognised by recent projections of employment and population and in regional planning guidance issued by the Government. Any significant shift in housing and industry towards metropolitan locations would require a level of economic and planning intervention far greater than is proposed by any political party. Yet to accept the projected development of the Shires would be to leave many metropolitan areas bereft of development and would seriously inhibit progress towards the major compact city.

The restructuring of industry and the redistribution of the population

At the end of the Second World War, in 1945, the majority of people still lived in fairly compact cities in high density housing close to factories, shops, schools, churches, hospitals and cinemas. Public transport was cheap and frequent, car ownership was low and only a minority travelled far to work. Many facilities were within walking distance of home. Communities remained close knit, but outside the largely middle-class suburbs standards of accommodation and service were poor. Over half the labour force worked in mining, iron and steel manufacture, heavy engineering, shipbuilding, and textiles, within the distinctive industrial conurbations of Clydeside, Tyneside, Teeside, Merseyside, South Lancashire and South and West Yorkshire, South Wales, Birmingham and the Black Country, and East London. Light industry had spread west of London and was worthy of particular note in the Team Valley estate on Tyneside; it would become a feature of the New Towns and would spread throughout the land, but in 1945 it made only a minor contribution to the economy.

In 1943 the Royal Commission on the Distribution of the Industrial Population (Barlow, 1943) proposed measures by which industry could be guided to areas of surplus labour; the purpose was to maintain full employment in all localities. The policy was maintained for some 25 years until structural changes in industry rendered it ineffective. The decline of our traditional heavy industries, the shift in employment to services and the increased number of part-time jobs, mostly for women, are well documented; so is the devastating effect on industrial towns and on many inner city areas. The expansion of some manufacturing sectors and the rapid growth of many small new industries in the shires of central and southern England seems less well appreciated. By 1992 these 26 counties (Fig. 1) contributed over one third of the value added by manufacturing industry to the national economy, and their output was greater than in the combined areas of neighbouring London, South Wales and Avon, and the metropolitan West Midlands; and it exceeded that of any other region of Britain (Table 1).

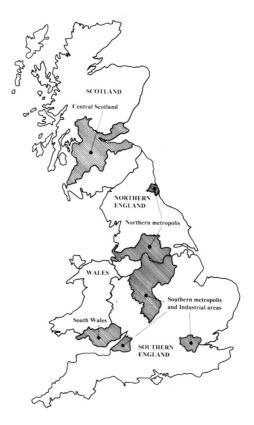

Fig. 1. The lands of Britain.

Regions of Britain	Net value added	
	£m	%
Central Scotland	6,579	6.2
Rest of Scotland	2,220	2.1
Metropolitan North of England	16,173	15.3
Rest of North of England	13,379	12.6
South Wales	3,673	3.5
Rest of Wales	1,685	1.6
Metropolitan South of England	26,713	25.2
Southern and central shires	35,379	33.5
Great Britain	105,801	100.0

Table 1. Manufacturing industrial output 1992.

The growth of the southern and central shires was in services, as well as in manufacturing. Gross Domestic Product had also reached about one third of the national total (Great Britain Central Statistical Office, 1995) and while agriculture remained important, employment roughly matched the national pattern (Office of Population Censuses and Surveys, 1991). Taken together, the shires of central and southern England may now form the most important industrial region of Britain. Industry and population in the southern and central shires have grown in tandem. Between 1971 and 1991 their population increased by over two and a quarter million to reach a total of eighteen and a half million, rising from 30% to 34% of the national total. During the same two decades the adjoining southern 'metropolitan and industrial' areas decreased in population by over one million and in the rest of Britain the population decreased by nearly another million (Office of Population Censuses and Surveys, 1991). Net migration accounted for 70% of the increase in the central and southern shires.

Since 1945 three significant shifts in population have been discernible. First, people spread out within expanding cities as the postwar housing programme gained momentum, the numbers of families sharing accommodation were reduced and occupancy rates fell. Large new estates spread cities outwards at a far greater rate than could be offset by the rebuilding of war damage or inner area slums. Second, people were offered homes and jobs in new and expanded towns, in a planned dispersal which was later continued by the private sector, but in a less co-ordinated pattern. People from metropolitan and older industrial areas sought work in dispersed locations, and new industry was established to take advantage of the expanding labour force. Third, people began to commute longer distances to work, especially along the motorways, dispersing housing demand and indirectly adding to both the local labour force and local entrepreneurial skills.

The processes of growth are cumulative and persistent. Once set in motion, they are difficult to deflect and even more difficult to reverse. Even recession may boost dispersal by encouraging district councils to establish business parks. There are few country towns without an industrial or commercial estate and there are many villages in which small business developments are encouraged. Access to the motorway system is easy from most of lowland England and any disadvantage arising from a dispersed location is likely to be offset by the greener environment. New industry has been more than matched by new housing, and other facilities have followed. Research sponsored by the Department of the Environment (Bibby and Shepherd, 1990) shows how widely dispersed development was in England during the mid-1980s, and how great the land take was. Between 1985 and 1988 the number of residential hereditaments (properties that can be inherited) increased by an estimated 726,760, and 29,995 hectares changed from rural to urban use. In most counties the housing increase was between 1% and 3% of the total. A lower share was recorded only in the northern counties of Northumberland, Durham, Tyne and Wear, Cumbria, Cleveland and Merseyside. A higher share was recorded only in Greater London, Essex, Kent, Hampshire and Devon (Fig. 2).

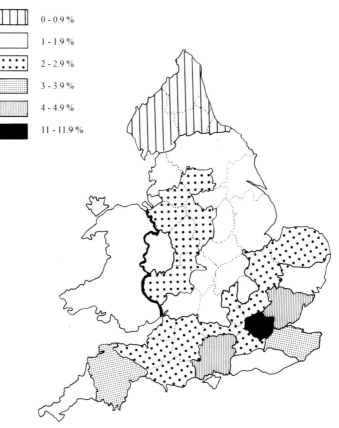

Fig. 2. Increase in hereditament in England 1985-1988. Proportion of total of each county.
100% = 726,760
Source: Bibby and Shepherd (1990)

The greater part of this housing provision doubtless followed the dictates of structure and local plans but as these tend to allocate land roughly in proportion to the existing size of settlements, the pattern is not so much changed as enlarged. From the development of housing and industry follows a related expansion of schools, health centres, hospitals and superstores in the larger centres (the provincial cities and country towns) to which people are expected to travel from surrounding villages. The overall pattern of settlement remains much as when serving a predominantly agricultural population except that the town has added the function of the village to its own. The country town now offers a quality of living able to satisfy a wide range of interests, material and cultural. The overall result is that in the shires of central and southern England there are hundreds of small but expanding villages, towns and cities, served by a comprehensive system of motorways and inter-city railways, easily accessible to airfields and ferry terminals. developing their own cultural life and together comprising a market of over 18 million people. Their politics have shifted perceptibly left and they will probably determine the political composition of the next Government. To thwart their will could be to court political suicide.

Future prospects: supply and demand

The Government has set a target for 50% of new homes to be built on re-used urban land. Most derelict urban land lies within Greater London, the metropolitan counties, and the old industrial and mining towns of central Scotland, northern England and South Wales. This policy for the supply of housing land goes some way towards satisfying the advocates of the compact city and the environmental lobby, but it conflicts to a significant degree with the pattern of demand and with the allocations for housing made in the Government's regional guidance. The demand for new housing tends to follow shifts in employment, the preferences of the retired and the wealthy and, to a less extent, the policies being followed for the satisfaction of social need. In this section the conclusion is drawn that so strong are the social and economic forces of dispersal, the outcome of present planning policies is likely to be a combination of sprawl outside the major cities and metropolitan rehabilitation, in a form dictated by the Government's promise to reuse derelict land.

The demand for development land

The Cambridge Regional Economic Review of 1990 (Cameron *et al.*, 1990, p.7) projected UK growth in output and found that in the four southern and eastern regions the rate of growth up to the end of the century would be higher than the national norm, whereas it would be lower than the norm in all other regions. The North-South divide would continue to widen. Employment prospects were expected to follow the same pattern. When assessed for individual counties (and regions in Scotland) the prospects were found to be better in non-metropolitan than metropolitan areas and even brighter in the shires of southern and central England (p.38), (see Table 2).

By these projections the metropolitan and older industrial and mining areas are set to lose over three quarters of a million jobs in ten years while the southern and central shires will gain half a million. The reality may differ considerably from the projection but the message is clear that the potential lies with continued dispersal.

Regions of Britain	jobs (thousands)
Central Scotland	- 91,000
Remainder of Scotland	+ 14,000
Northern metropolitan counties	- 230,000
Remainder of North	+ 21,000
South Wales	- 33,000
Remainder of Wales	+ 12,000
Metropolitan and industrial South	- 409,000
Southern and central shires	+ 567,000
Great Britain	- 149,000

Table 2. Employment Prospects (1990-2000).

The Office of Population Censuses and Surveys (OPCS), the General Register Office in Scotland and the Welsh Office make projections of population by age. They indicate a labour force increasing by nearly 900,000 in the 15 years 1996-2011. Projections are also made for each county, and these include assumptions for migration. The results are shown in Table 3 (Government Statistical Service, 1994a, 1994b; Scottish Office, 1995).

Table 3. Projected changes in the population of working age (1996-2011).

Regions of Britain	population change (thousands)
Scotland	- 106.7
Northern metropolitan areas	+ 10.3
Remainder of North	+ 46.6
South Wales	+ 31.7
Remainder of Wales	+ 1.7
Metropolitan and industrial South	+ 247.7
Southern and central shires	+ 647.7
Great Britain	+ 879.0

Comparison of Tables 2 and 3 suggests that if the Cambridge economists have assessed employment prospects correctly there will be an even greater than anticipated movement of workers southwards and outwards from the major cities. In other words, employment stimulus to housing demand is likely to be far greater in non-metropolitan areas and at its greatest in the central and southern shires of England. Prospects elsewhere seem to range from fairly to extremely bleak unless growth patterns are changed dramatically by Government intervention. The failure of the postwar attempt to guide industry to areas of labour shortage suggests that political parties will be wary of this form of intervention.

The retired population is also projected to increase, from greater longevity and as a bulge in the now middle-aged population moves on. The south coast is well established as a retirement area, as are some rural districts. In these areas there is a large turnover of houses, and a considerable industry is engaged in providing homes and services for the elderly. Whether a greater proportion of the retired can be induced to remain in the major cities will depend on success in improving safety and convenience. The prognosis is poor. It may prove easier to convince younger people of the attractions of city life: the continuing expansion of further education, the desire by many young people to leave home and the failure to provide campus accommodation for students has created a demand for small units of accommodation for short period occupation. The need is difficult to assess but projections of the 16-24 age range and trends in education suggest that young persons' housing could be a significant factor in compacting the city.

The increasing numbers of elderly and young people wishing to live alone, greater birth control, and changing social attitudes have led to vast increases in the number of small households. An extra 3.3 million single adult households are anticipated over the next 20 years in projections made by the DoE in England and by the Welsh and Scottish Offices (DoE, 1995; Government Statistical Service, 1994a, 1994b). In contrast the increase in households with two or more adults will only be just over half a million (Table 4).

| Regions of Britain | Total no. thousands | Household increase | | | |
| | | Single adult | | Two or more adults | |
		no. thousands	%	no. thousands	%
Central Scotland	199	207	104	-8	-4
Remainder of Scotland	125	97	78	+28	+22
Northern met. areas	428	440	103	-12	-3
Remainder of North	326	309	95	+17	+5
South Wales	100	89	89	+11	+11
Remainder of Wales	58	58	100	0	0
Met. and ind. South	872	906	105	-34	-4
Southern and central shires	2047	1422	69	+625	+31
Great Britain	4155	3528	85	+627	+15

Table 4. Household projections (1996-2016).

Additional single adult households will be concentrated in the metropolitan areas while the extra larger households will form - or move to - 'rural' Britain. Half the new households are expected to be in the southern and central shires and of these, about one third will contain two or more adults (with or without children).

New building provides the main opportunity to compact cities but at any one time new dwellings are only a small proportion of the owner-occupation market. The prosperous set the demand for new owner-occupied housing, either those with capital or those who can afford mortgage repayments. For the most part the building industry has supplied low density 2-3 bedroom houses in dispersed locations. Provision for first-time buyers has not changed this preference. The less well off are left to purchase whatever is available at the lower end of the market or to seek rented accommodation through councils and housing associations, whose total stock is falling. Thus while the need for housing will be substantially increased by the formation of single adult households, predominantly in the cities, the supply of houses by the private sector will be directed towards the more prosperous larger households in the shires.

Recent regional planning guidance for housing generally spans the 15 years from 1991-2006 and is expressed in terms of additional dwellings to be provided in each county per annum. Comparing that provision with the average annual increase in households from 1996 to 2016 (Table 5) it would seem that planning allocations in Scotland, Wales and the North of England are likely to be generous, but less sufficient in the South of England where development pressures are greater. It would be possible to make up the southern shortfall in metropolitan areas but such a policy would need to be supported by strong measures to deflect demand from the shires.

Within the southern and central shires of England, regional planning guidance accepts continued dispersal, as indicated in Table 6. With the exception of the Home Counties, where green belt and other restrictions apply, allocations are roughly in proportion to population.

The significance of these figures is that for at least the next ten years half the new housing will be spread over the southern and central shires of England unless present plans are modified. Should the full 20-year housing requirement of the shires be met, and should there be no increase in building densities and should the total land requirement for housing, factories, superstores, hospitals, schools and open spaces be similar to that for the period 1985-88 (Bibby and Shepherd, 1990), the transfer of land to urban uses could be as much as 270 square miles. With the political importance attached to achieving more sustainable forms of development it is likely that the land take will be reduced, but unless new planning policies are introduced nationally and regionally, development will still be dispersed. Within the shires there is little reusable urban land and most development would fall on greenfield sites. It follows that the Government policy to locate 50% of new housing on reused urban land can be achieved only if almost all the housing allocations in metropolitan and industrial areas are met on derelict or disused land. Present policies raise the spectre both of sprawl in the countryside and urban renewal dictated by dereliction. Neither would create sustainable forms of development.

Regions of Britain	Average no. of households forming p.a. in 1996-2016 (thousands)	Average no. of dwellings to be provided in development plans p.a. 1991-2006 (thousands)
Central Scotland	10	not available from
Remainder of Scotland	6	the Scottish Office
Northern met. areas	21	20
Remainder of North	16	18
South Wales	5	5
Remainder of Wales	3	4
Met. & ind. South	44	37
South & central shires	102	84

Table 5. Household projections and regional planning guidance.

% share of total allocation	No. of counties
0 - 1.9	1
2.0 - 3.9	14
4.0 - 5.9	8
6.0 - 7.9	3

Table 6. Distribution of housing allocations between the shires of southern and central England.

Towards the sustainable region
This analysis of trends and projections makes clear the difficulties likely to be faced if more compact cities are to be created. It will not be sufficient to address the location of housing without also considering how to arrest the dispersed growth of industry and commerce. Nor will the housing market be attracted to city development on a significant scale unless the demand leaders can be persuaded that city living offers more than living in a small town in the country. Growth outside metropolitan areas is a cumulative process by which housing creates a labour supply which in turn attracts commerce and industry which again attracts more housing and the facilities demanded by the successful and prosperous. Modifying this process requires a qualitative rehabilitation of cities, an aim which has eluded decades of politicians and professionals. There is also the underlying suspicion that the more civilised city will be 'thinner' (Ward, 1989) and that one consequence of effective rehabilitation will be greater dispersal. The compact city presents a planning conundrum.

The compact city can be achieved only if statutory planning policies are supported by economic and social measures. If the object is to bring people and activity back to the major cities, massive financial incentives and a high degree of social control seem inevitable. One is economically suspect, the other is probably unacceptable politically. If the purpose is to achieve a greater degree of compaction in a wider range of settlements the prospects are better, although intervention in the location of industry and in the workings of the land market may still be necessary. Planning policy throughout Britain still seeks containment, tempered by some selectivity in the expansion of country towns and villages. The results do not greatly encourage the conservation of resources although it is excessive to lay the blame for rising energy use entirely at the door of dispersal. Higher standards of living are as much the cause of rising demand as is low density of development, and there are many other factors. However, there remains the belief that higher densities and more efficient public transport will encourage sustainable lifestyles; thus the case for shifting from policies of containment to policies of compaction.

City planners and politicians tend to see the city as the core of a region of concentric rings of lessening intensity. These range from central and inner areas through suburbs and green belt to more or less accessible rural areas. From this viewpoint the compact city might be achieved through higher density building in the city, related to fast and efficient public transport.

However, success implies a sufficient rate of new building to intensify activity in selected locations within inner green belt boundaries or some other city limit. The indications are that the greater amount of land development will be outside metropolitan boundaries (Table 7) unless there is massive intervention in the housing and industrial land market. Tight high density living in major cities, admired by many architects and advocated by the environmental lobby, has no place in most people's vision of 21st century Britain. The popular model derives from the country town, adapted to provide a wide range of services and facilities. Easy access to main road and rail brings metropolitan facilities also within its orbit. The shires of southern and central England offer the widest choice of such country towns, combined with the best economic prospects in Britain.

Region of Britain	Area (sq km)	Area Urban area (sq km)	Inc. in households	Land take sq km	% increase
Central Scotland	19,230	*	199,000	*	
Remainder of Scotland	51,937	*	125,000	*	
Northern met. areas	6,078 1,942	428,000	30	4.6	
Remainder of North	32,073 2,098	326,000	206	9.8	
South Wales	3,627	*	10,000	*	
Remainder of Wales	17,141 *	58,00	*		
Metropolitan and industrial South	13,316	3,179	872,000	144	4.5
Southern and central shires	78,972	7,247	2,047,000	723	10.0

Table 7. Land take 1996-2016 based on household projections and the rates of urbanisation 1985-88.

* not available

From within, the shires of central and southern England may be seen as a developing region with an expanding industrial base, its own commercial infrastructure and markets, a developing transport system, and decreasingly dependent upon the neighbouring metropolitan centres for the essentials of everyday life. Fig. 3 illustrates this view of the Shires. Other accessible rural areas may be developing in the same way. Even at higher densities, the continued incremental growth of the many small towns and villages would promote dispersal and encourage the greater use of private transport. Present plans perpetuate a settlement pattern designed to serve farming and forestry, not to support the sustainable development of a major industrial growth area. The criteria of sustainable development point towards greater self-containment of larger towns, linked by a public transport system capable of competing successfully with the car. One attempt to apply these criteria to a real situation was made by the Town and Country Planning Association (TCPA) in South Devon (Green and Holliday, 1991) and is illustrated in Fig. 4. More theoretical models are suggested by Breheny and Rookwood (Blowers, 1993) but far more work is needed to apply theory to practical situations.

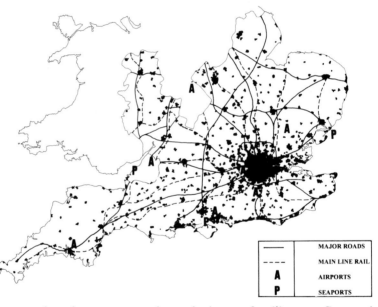

Fig. 3. The southern and central shires as a separate region: settlements, major roads, ports and airports.

——	MAJOR ROADS
- - - -	MAIN LINE RAIL
A	AIRPORTS
P	SEAPORTS

It seems clear that we are caught on the horns of a dilemma. Compaction would be most effective in the major cities where the demand for new building is too low, and more difficult to achieve in the countryside where the demand is high. Politicians accept that people are unlikely to forego willingly the freedom they have gained to reside and work where they choose when they can afford to do so. Planners working within the statutory system will find it difficult to introduce policies for compact development while the major growth area of Britain is still treated as a series of outer zones, enduring undue pressures from metropolitan centres. The shires of southern and central England fall within five planning regions administered from London, Birmingham and Bristol. It is a political recipe for another major planning disaster. The present regional planning framework seriously inhibits the promotion of sustainable development in the areas where policies for compact urban growth are most urgently needed. To become a reality, the concept of the compact city must be modified to fit the evolving pattern of industry and population. The North-South divide is a spatial fact of economic life; the separate administration of Scotland and Wales is a fact of political life. If these facts of economic and political life are brought together, the arrangements now in place for Scotland and Wales could be extended to northern and to central and southern England. Each of these 'lands' could then develop social, economic and political institutions suited to its particular circumstances and culture. The pattern of settlement and transportation and the overall management of land and energy resources would be amongst the primary responsibilities of the lands' administrations.

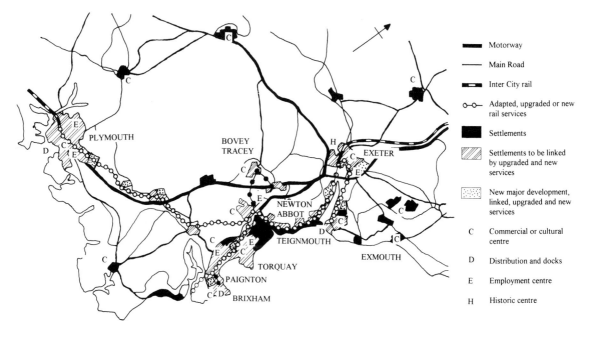

Fig. 4. The social city in South Devon.

Source: Nick Matthews TCPA

The present statutory system of structure and local plans would continue but within a more robust social and economic framework. The local authorities would become responsible for co-ordinating the developments of the increasing number of local trusts and companies providing health, education and other local services and infrastructure. These planning provisions would facilitate more compact building in towns and cities but the impetus must come from the community at all levels. Without a real political will there is no practical way forward. The planning dilemma between dispersal and concentration is reflected in the political conflict between centre and locality. Major planning policies are by character national and regional, but local communities seek greater control over their futures. The compact city might be better conceived as the compact community, offering a more sustainable lifestyle in city and countryside. There will be many forms of compact development and there should be great scope for the involvement of people of all ages in many places. It will be the responsibility of architects, planners and politicians to ensure that communities are fully involved in the sustainable development of all regions - assuming that the economic growth of the shires is globally sustainable, but that is another story.

References

Barlow (Chairman) (1943) *Royal Commission on the Distribution of the Industrial Population*, HMSO, London.

Bibby, P.R. and Shepherd, J.M. (1990) *Rates of Urbanisation in England 1981-2001,* for the DoE, HMSO London.

Blowers, A. (ed.) (1993) *Planning for a Sustainable Environment,* Earthscan, London.

Cameron, G., Moore, B., Nicholls, D., Rhodes, J. and Tyler, P. (eds)(1990) *Cambridge Regional Economic Review,* Department of Land Economy, University of Cambridge.

Department of the Environment (1995) *Projections of Households in England to 2016,* HMSO, London.

Green, R.J. and Holliday, J.C. (1991) *Country Planning - A Time for Action,* TCPA, London.

Government Statistical Service (1994a) *Household Projections for Scotland,* Scottish Office, Edinburgh.

Government Statistical Service (1994b) *Population and Projections for Wales,* Welsh Office, Cardiff.

Great Britain Central Statistical Office (1995) *Regional Trends No. 30,* HMSO London.

Office of Population Censuses and Surveys (1991) *Census Key Statistics for Local Authorities.* HMSO, London.

Scottish Office (1995) *Subnational Population Projections,* Scottish Office, Edinburgh.

Ward, C. (1989) *Welcome Thinner City,* Bedford Square Press. London.

Patrick N. Troy

Urban Consolidation and the Family

The Australian Government has recently adopted a policy of urban consolidation in an attempt to curb environmental stress in cities. The policy has been justified on social grounds, and it is claimed that a more compact city would result in social as well as environmental benefits. This chapter critically assesses the turn-around in Australian urban policy and its implications for the family and community: it discusses the advantages, in social terms, of the traditional Australian city; the reasons and justifications for a shift in policy; and the likely effect on urban social issues as such a policy is pursued.

Traditional Australian housing
One of the central features of the history of economic growth in the developed world is that as living standards have risen households have wanted more space - private as well as public - in which they can pursue an increasingly rich variety of activities. The history of the dwellings we occupy reveals an evolution from simple shelters, to houses in which sleeping rooms were separated from cooking and eating, to those in which parents had bedrooms separate from children and where there was space for recreation other than in the kitchen or bedroom. In modern times the demand for specialised space within the home and recognition of the need for privacy have also fuelled the demand for increased enclosed space.

Simultaneously, we have seen households demand external space in the form of gardens, and part of the attraction of the suburb was that it offered houses in gardens. The garden space allowed households the freedom to extend their houses when they could afford to, and to improve their standard of living by their own domestic production. It gave them safe spaces in which their children could grow up and a private setting for many family activities. In short, the gardens gave them a degree of independence and freedom of expression no other form of housing could offer. It gave them a form of housing which met most of their needs for the greater period of their lives.

When allied with the desire for home ownership (which was used as a major element of family policy), the house in its own garden became the distinguishing feature of Australian cities. Moreover, the high level of owner-occupation, 50% at the turn of the century, was mostly of separate houses in their own gardens. The later increase to 70% by 1960, which gave Australia the highest level of owner-occupation in the developed world, meant that this form of housing and tenure was a significant feature of the egalitarian nature of Australian society. The commitment of governments in the post World War II period to improve the standard of housing of all Australians, including the poor, was largely to build houses with their own gardens.

As living standards have risen, in addition to more private outdoor space, people have also wanted greater public space in the form of parks, playing fields, golf courses, public arenas and promenades. The early town planning movements were energised by people wanting both more private and public open space and more felicitous relationships between the activities pursued in the city. The ideals which drove the reformers were built around notions of health, equity, amenity and efficiency. But the way these objectives would be realised was by developing an environment where the family could flourish: where it could retreat and find strength and solace; where children could be raised in healthy, safe environments; but where the family could also engage with the rest of the community in the pursuit of its cultural and recreational interests and in the celebration of local and national events.

The family was the linchpin of the postwar reformist agenda. Strengthening it was seen as the way to secure the future of the society, as a way of inculcating or transmitting desired social values, and as a way of ameliorating the excesses of the economic system. Enabling families to have a house and garden gave them the opportunity to improve their standard of living by their own efforts. This connection between the family and urban form has been central to the development of the Australian city. The notion of community was also a central element of postwar housing policies and planning reform as it was assumed that continuity and stability fostered civic virtues. Community was central to the planning for, and provision of, primary schools, shopping and recreation facilities.

The advent of urban consolidation policy

Over the past 30 years state governments have increasingly faced serious problems in meeting the demand for urban services resulting from the growth of urban populations and their rising expectations of service standards. By the mid-1980s the declining population and especially the fall in school enrolments in the inner areas began to cause concern. Governments were facing a situation where new fringe developments needed schools yet there appeared to be surplus capacity in the existing areas. The situation was compounded by the fact that declining family sizes meant that a given area of housing produced lower school enrolments than had occurred only a generation earlier when the primary school catchment areas had been developed.

Faced with this situation governments and their advisors looked for a solution which would reduce the pressure on public funds for investment in infrastructure. Their solution was to introduce a consolidation policy. Under this policy it was thought that consolidation, also called urban containment or the development of compact cities, would reduce the demand on governments for infrastructure capital in several ways:

- by increasing density in the inner areas, where it was argued there was excess capacity in the full range of services, governments hoped to defer construction of additional infrastructure
- as a result of reducing the size of new housing allotments and increasing the proportion of medium and high density dwellings in new development, governments expected that the length of pipes, wires and roads needed to service the new areas of expansion would be reduced
- by increasing density governments expected more people to use public transport (especially fixed rail modes), reducing the need for roads, and reducing air pollution
- with a more compact city personal and freight delivery trips would be shorter

To justify their decisions governments first drew attention to the costs of urban services. They then focused on the alleged environmental consequences of the traditional form of development. Finally, in all states, governments and their advisors advanced quasi-demographic arguments in favour of changing urban form. They drew attention to the changes in household size and the ageing of the population which had occurred over the previous 20 years, and argued that traditional suburban expansion of houses on separate allotments did not meet the rapidly growing needs of the smaller households. It was also claimed that consolidation policies would result in cheaper housing and greater choice in both housing and lifestyle.

The 'cost of urban services' argument cannot be explored here; suffice it to say that it is almost without foundation. The alleged savings in service investment because of spare capacity in older areas is largely illusory, and the savings on high density over traditional density developments is so small that its costs may well outweigh any benefits. The environmental issues will be reviewed in the chapter entitled *Environmental Stress and Urban Policy,* in Part 3. The issues are more complex than have been presented and the traditional form of development may well be the most effective form for minimising environmental stress. The demographic argument used to rationalise the policy of consolidation will now be analysed.

The validity and likely social consequences of consolidation policy
The fact that the various Australian censuses show that the proportion of one or two person households has increased has excited much interest. This increase is a natural consequence of the fall in the birth rate, older age at marriage, increasing freedom and economic independence of women, and general increase in living standards. It is argued, from an 'efficiency' point of view, that this has resulted in many households living in dwellings 'too large' for them. From this it is implied that many would prefer to shift to smaller dwellings if they were available.

Size of dwelling
The censuses reveal that a significant proportion of one and two person households already live in smaller dwellings and have done so since 1947. About half the one and two person households in Australia in 1991 lived in smaller housing (that is, in dwellings with one or two bedrooms). Another point laboured in the debates is

that, while the average household size has fallen, the average size of dwelling is said to have increased. But, in terms of rooms designated as bedrooms, the housing stock has been remarkably stable over the recent period with approximately half of all dwellings having three bedrooms and another quarter having two.

However, the reason for the excitement is the reported increase in the average size of *new houses* in Australia which is claimed to have risen from 130 to 187 square metres between 1970 and 1989. There are several aspects of the data which are ignored. First, the increase in construction of very large houses was for a small proportion of the market yet it had a marked effect on the average. Second, while on average new houses may have increased in size it cannot simply be asserted that the average size of the *stock of dwellings* has increased. The data relate to the flows of new houses, not to the flow of new dwellings. Over the period, the proportion of dwellings described as flats increased significantly. This was due to an increase in the proportion of new dwellings built as flats, and the conversion of other buildings, such as warehouses, to flats. Many of these flats were substitutes for the smaller houses. This would have had the effect of reducing the demand for new smaller houses and thereby reducing the 'average' for new houses. But the average size of new dwellings would have risen less than that of new houses.

It could be argued that the issue of dwelling size is irrelevant. Or perhaps the increase simply represented an increase in living standards and was evidence of the strength and progress of the Australian economy.

Block size

It is frequently argued that block sizes in urban housing subdivisions are 'too large'. The claim is usually in some undefined absolute sense but is meant to imply that the size of residential blocks has led to increased costs in the provision of services. Reference is made to the 'quarter acre block' (approximately 1,000 square metres or one tenth of a hectare) as though that was the standard or average size. Net residential density in terms of dwellings per hectare of new residential development has risen substantially over the postwar period. The average block size is now about 700 square metres which is about two thirds the size claimed. (The median-sized new block in Sydney for example is now around 550 square metres). The fall in average block size has occurred as a result of the measures adopted by planning authorities, local governments and service agencies in order to eliminate sprawl.

The density of residential development has little impact on the density of the city as a whole. If all other space standards were reduced there would be some reduction in the overall land used in a city and therefore in infrastructure costs. But this effectively means, in an economy which responds to market pressures, that the main options are to reduce the space standards for low income housing (because this form of housing is most directly affected by government policy) and for public circulation and recreation. Unless amenity is to be reduced, less private open space should be compensated for by more public open space. The present policy has had the perverse result of increasing density of dwellings at the fringe, which is leading to a concentration of low income households at the fringe. It also has the effect of producing block sizes so small that it is impossible to plant even medium-sized trees in most of them, thus reducing the amenity of development.

Relocation and transaction costs

The proposal that households should move to housing 'more appropriate to their needs' (meaning smaller dwellings) takes no account of the costs of moving from one dwelling to another. There are two kinds of cost. The first cost is financial. In the case of owner-occupied dwellings this includes transaction costs, public taxes, and estate agents' and lawyers' fees, which amount to between 7% and 11% of the value of the property being sold. There are also costs of acquisition - lawyers' fees, mortgage establishment costs where necessary, building inspection fees and so on. Renters also have relocation costs which include moving and establishment expenses.

The second kind of cost relates to social dislocation and re-establishment; this cost is no less real than the financial cost and may be even more important to the individuals affected and to their communities. The costs may include the wrench from familiar surroundings that the residents themselves have developed using much creative effort and energy. No less significant is the social dislocation which breaks friendships of long standing and mutual support among neighbours. These are often specially important for the elderly who live in many of the allegedly 'under-occupied' dwellings.

Efficiency arguments about the need to encourage people to relocate to smaller dwellings as their household size falls ignore the distribution of benefits and costs of the moves. The benefits from the policy of relocation derive from the alleged public gains from an imagined increase in efficiency in the provision of housing. The costs, however, are borne by the individuals affected. The communities, in which the households which are allegedly 'over consuming' housing live, are destabilised when its older members move out.

The prices of the 'more appropriate' dwellings are frequently no less than the dwellings vacated so that the 'efficiency gain' is at the cost to the mover of earlier payment of transaction costs and taxes. Although the policy is aimed significantly at older people, most medium density dwellings are not designed with older, less agile or frailer occupants in mind, or they are for the upper end of that market. Moreover, moves to 'more appropriate housing' in the form of retirement villages frequently require a considerable entrance premium and a progressive loss of equity in their unit in the village. These latter points often worry older people because they fear a loss of independence and see their capacity to 'leave something for their children and grandchildren' reduced. Some even worry that if they live long enough they may not have the resources to remain in the 'village'.

Housing 'need'

The typical family life-cycle is seen as one in which a couple sets up a home together, often in rented, multi-dwelling accommodation, until the first child is born when they move out to a house which they have usually bought in the suburbs. Although the household might move within the house market before the children leave home, it is assumed that once the children leave, the household is occupying a house which is too large for it. The further assumption is made that when household members retire they will have a reduced need for housing and that when one partner dies the need will again be reduced.

There are a number of problems with this argument. Instead of a life-cycle approach, life courses should be considered in terms of trajectories and transitions.

Although the housing career of an individual is usually an 'upward' progression it may also be 'lateral' or 'downward'. Indeed, an individual may experience a series of transitions which take them 'up', 'down' or 'sideways' at different stages in their life. An individual may leave the parental home but return to it, enter owner-occupation but then move to rental accommodation, establish a home with another person, leave, then establish a home with the same or another person at a later period. The permutations and combinations are as varied as the people concerned. Increasingly children are returning to live with their parents after even quite long periods away.

The sequential life-cycle approach employed takes no account of the historical fact that individuals have tended to consume more, rather than less, housing to make themselves more comfortable as their discretionary income and wealth has risen and their children have become financially independent. It also takes little account of how individuals use the space in and around their dwellings. The simple assumption that because the children have left home the remaining household does not need the space 'freed' ignores the way households actually use the space for return visits by the children and their households, by grandchildren and other relatives, by friends and for a rich miscellany of activities, hobbies and pursuits.

The assumption that when people retire they will have a reduced need for housing is also inconsistent with the actual behaviour of households. If the policy analysts had their way, individuals would be forced to occupy smaller dwellings precisely at the point when they begin to spend a greater proportion of their time in and around their homes and need the extra space. The increasing incidence of individuals retiring at younger ages will tend to increase the numbers of households which spend the greater part of their life in and around the home. The increased numbers living to old age will probably mean an increase in the demand for housing and garden space rather than a decrease. Exercise in the garden is an aid to the health of households, especially of older citizens. It is extremely important for their continued psychological health that they have contact with a type of environment with which they have already established a relationship. Moving them to dwellings without gardens may not be beneficial to their continued health.

Health

The research into earlier attempts to introduce high density housing both in Australia and overseas found evidence that it had a detrimental effect on household life and particularly on the health of children. Much of this research was into high-rise high density housing but the central points were that high density housing had low levels of privacy and provision of community facilities and services, that the high density housing militated against households exercising appropriate supervision of children, and that high density housing gave households little choice or flexibility in their home-based activities.

The attempts early in the twentieth century to provide more parks and gardens in cities grew out of a strong conviction that developments which had more open space in the form of private and public gardens were healthier. The cleaning effect that trees have on air pollution both in taking up carbon dioxide and in removing particulates is a major reason private and public garden space should be preserved. That is, on grounds of improved public health and increased amenity, the policy should be to preserve traditional density development rather than destroy it by reducing public open space and lot sizes for some perceived short term gain.

Choice

A major argument in the policy debate has been that households have too narrow a choice among different kinds of housing. Much of the argument rests on the claim that households would move to smaller dwellings or different types of dwelling if there was a 'better' choice. It implies that developers have failed to supply appropriate housing. But there is no evidence of such a gap.

Apart from the general statement that people should have more choice, the arguments surrounding it seem to reduce to five questions: issues of dwelling size, dwelling type, design, location and housing tenure.

Dwelling size, type and design

The argument about increased choice in dwelling size rests on the claim that there is too little variation in the size of dwellings. It is argued that the conventional house which has three bedrooms, or flat which has two bedrooms, offers limited choices to the public. There seems little recognition in this argument that this size of dwelling is the market response to demand, and that, in any event, it provides most of their occupants with the flexibility in living arrangements and activities they desire.

One of the reasons households prefer traditional houses is that they meet their desire for a separate front and back door and for some private outdoor space. The space available to households enables them to invest in their own symbolism; they can determine how they will show their public face and they can maintain a more intimate private face at the back door. Some hold the view that with better design the demands for privacy and outdoor space can be met on smaller lots. Frequently the critics of the design of suburbs of Australian cities imply that higher density development would be of a higher aesthetic standard with a greater level of amenity. No analysis is presented to support the assertion and the aesthetic poverty of much of the higher density development does not support it. There seems to be an overweening desire on the part of proponents of consolidation to 'educate' people, to change their preferences, to 'lead' the unwilling into higher densities. It is hard to escape the conclusion that many of the medium density developments that professionals decide are 'good' design are not so regarded by the general public.

Issues of location

People choose where to live because, within their means, the dwelling and its location best meets their needs. Much of the policy debate, however, assumes that people seek or should seek good access to the centre of the city, and that they are frustrated from living closer to the centre by the present form of the city. The choices people make of where to live, work, shop and pursue their cultural and recreational interests suggest that the city they experience is not highly centralised: their location choices are influenced by considerations of urban structure rather than form.

Housing tenure

The argument that present housing policy offers people little choice in their tenure raises interesting questions. Approximately 92% of people own a dwelling at some stage in their life and almost 85% continue to own until near the end of their lives. At any time over the last 30 years approximately 70% of households

161

owned or were purchasing their own dwelling. There is substantial historical evidence that home ownership is regarded as one of the distinguishing features of Australian society and that it is a state to which the 'ordinary working man' (or woman) can reasonably aspire. Post World War II policies fostering home ownership gave low income households a chance to share in the bounty of the nation.

The weight of this evidence suggests that the economic as well as non-economic benefits of owner-occupation are substantial, that people understand this and that their aspirations in this direction are likely to remain strong over the foreseeable future. In this case notions of increasing 'tenure choice', if it means reducing owner-occupation, do not appear to be consistent with community expectations and desires. The owner-occupancy rate of flat dwellers is lower than that of house dwellers, but introducing policies to increase the supply of flats in the belief that this will reduce owner-occupancy rates and thereby increase the tenure choice is misguided. Forms of tenure other than owner-occupation will only prove attractive if they can provide similar security to residents.

It is hard to escape the conclusion that much of the contemporary argument about the lack of choice in Australian housing is manufactured controversy and much of it is an implied criticism of people's choice of houses over flats. Both the survey evidence and the choices people make reveal a strong preference for single family houses in their own gardens, for owner-occupation over renting or other forms of tenure, and for a decentralised structure of cities over the highly centralised structure implicit in current housing and urban policy. People have been giving clear indications of their choices, yet government policy is designed to pursue directions diametrically opposed to them. The paradox is that the vigorous enforcement of consolidation policies is actually leading to reduction of choice.

Lifestyle

The comment that the traditional form of housing does not offer a sufficient variety of lifestyles is one of those curious propositions which gain currency but which are little explored. At its heart commentators seem to be saying that living at a high density is in some way more enriching; that high density living is more cultured and relaxed. The model seems to be related to an elitist urban lifestyle in which individuals eat out, engage in the pursuits of a romanticised cafe society, have the time to enjoy morning coffee over the newspaper, and explore the antique shops, bookshops and art galleries.

Enjoyable as these activities are, they are not the daily options or desires of the overwhelming majority of the population. The proliferation of coffee shops, bistros, restaurants and sidewalk cafes in most parts of most of our cities over recent years is a response to changing social behaviour, increasing affluence, the commodification of leisure, and to the needs of tourists (both domestic and international), but most of us use them only on special occasions or as part of our recreation. Whether people eat out or visit art galleries and antique shops is more closely related to their disposable income and their range of cultural interests than to the form of the city. For all the yearning by some commentators and policy advisors to return to some halcyon past, such urban lifestyles were never the daily life experience of more than a small minority. Indeed, a vibrant street life has not always been regarded as an attractive feature of Australian cities. The street gangs (and their associated territorial disputes) now evident in some North

American cities mostly come from high density environments, but proponents of high densities presumably do not wish to argue that they are a result of density.

None of the proponents of this imagined urban lifestyle provide an analysis of who actually lives in the manner they yearn for, or any historical explanation of the social and cultural processes which produce it. Nor is there much evidence to support the proposition that higher density living leads to greater creativity or higher levels of cultural expression. We would be hard pressed to explain the success of the majority of Australian writers, painters, singers, musicians, intellectuals or even political leaders were that the case.

There are those who complain that the suburbs provide few opportunities for the social life of teenagers. It is undoubtedly true that some people, young and old, find that some of the suburbs are limited in their range of opportunities for the pursuit of their cultural and social interests, but the response should be to explore cultural policy and the way facilities and services are provided rather than simply assume that a change in the form of the city will rectify the perceived shortcomings.

By and large the suburbs, especially those developed in the '50s, '60s and '70s, but not the newer ones, have sufficient playing fields for a wide range of organised sports. But any parent who has heard teenagers complain that 'there is nothing to do' in their free time quickly realises that they do not mean sport. Nor do they mean there are not enough opportunities to engage in art and craft or other hobby groups. Teenagers may simply mean that they have not enough pocket money left to attend a film, disco, band or spectator sport such as basketball, or to visit some favoured cafe or milk bar to 'hang out' where their parents are not in control. They may be making an observation about the alienating nature of modern society, the commodification of cultural activities, the passivity of film and television and the homogenised pap those media project, their need to express their independence or simply their need to make contact with others of the same generation. One explanation of the occupation of city streets at night by groups of young people, who may be perceived to be threatening to others and a danger to themselves, is that the dwellings they come from have insufficient space for them to have privacy.

Complaints about social opportunities and activities should not be interpreted solely or even significantly as related to the form of development. Propinquity may increase the likelihood of social contact but we also know that at a high density people act to preserve their personal space and privacy; that is, they withdraw from contact with others or try to limit interactions. We simply do not know whether higher density will eliminate the complaint of lack of choice of activities. The notion that the form of development can make up for all the other aspects of Australian urban society which lead to people feeling unfulfilled in some way is expecting too much of the urban environment.

Education infrastructure
The issue of 'spare capacity' in government schools deserves separate comment because it looms so large in the calculations over alleged spare capacity in infrastructure in the inner areas and in the calculations for the cost of infrastructure provision on the fringe. It is also the only service for which a claim that it has surplus capacity could credibly be made.

The 'common sense' solution of seeking to minimise investment in schools by trying to focus that part of the population having children into areas where there were apparent surpluses in school capacity was powerfully attractive. Superficial analysis indicated that all that had to be done was to encourage the younger growing population into the inner areas. One problem was that the apparent surplus capacity was in schools which were no longer regarded as adequate for modern teaching. Another was the assumption that simply encouraging people back to the areas in which the alleged surplus capacity existed would result in the same 'crop' of children being accommodated in inner areas as was attracted to outer areas. On average, the households who live in the higher density areas do not have as many children as those in lower density areas. Focusing redevelopment in an area because of the claimed surplus capacity in the schools may have the perverse effect of reducing the numbers of school children in that area.

To some extent the apparent surplus capacity in government schools arose because of the policy of using school buildings and facilities as single-use facilities, that is, using them only for a limited range of educational activities. If the schools, especially primary schools, were used as accommodation for a range of educational, cultural and recreational activities and services, including child care services, the issue of over- investment in educational infrastructure would be placed in perspective. For example, if school provision was better planned in relation to the surrounding area, its construction could be phased so that its assembly halls, libraries and recreation facilities could be used for community uses. The alleged surplus capacity would thus be used for other desirable activities.

The future of Australian housing

The crude physical determinism implicit in the romantic image projected by proponents of higher density housing, that it will produce a stronger sense of community and that people will discover the virtues of neighbourliness and become more caring and sharing, is inconsistent with the realities of urban living. Paradoxically, people are expected to 'keep themselves to themselves' - to have a high degree of independence yet maintain a sense of social or communal engagement. It is easier to achieve both independence and engagement with one's neighbours in conventional housing. High density housing is more likely to provide the conditions for anonymity and withdrawal as people act to preserve their privacy and personal space. In a society which has fostered individualism, reduced emphasis on collective consumption, and supports separatism, the idea that increasing densities will cause people to be more concerned with, and benevolent toward, their fellow citizens is fanciful. The sense of community is more deeply a function of the way we value the unity, integrity and equality of the development of our culture than of propinquity or geographical boundaries.

The implications of contemporary urban policy for the household are:

- the household should move to a new dwelling each time it increases or reduces in size
- the household should occupy less space
- the household should make greater use of public space and less of private outdoor space
- the household should make more use of public transport to get to, and participate in, its diverse range of activities - in the modern city this inevitably means reducing its range of activities

The net impact of the policy on family-households is that it would convert them into peripatetic units with little sense of stability or engagement in their own history. The stability and continuity of the household is partly achieved by its continued location in a particular place - one to which its members know they can return to reconnect with their own past, where they can find the bric-a-brac of their childhood, where the memories by association can be revitalised, where the comforting familiarity can be valuable for the subsequent partners and children of household members in gleaning some understanding of their partners and parents. The mechanistic notions of household life and its life course implicit in current policy are fundamentally inimical to the structure and operation of family life as we know it. It also means the sense of obligation and commitment to other households - the sense of community - is weakened to the ultimate disadvantage of households themselves.

The implications of the consolidation policy for family and society are in stark contrast to the egalitarian picture painted at the beginning of the chapter. The validity of the arguments in support of this new policy is highly questionable; a change in the traditional form of housing would be a serious loss to the Australian family.

Part Three
Environment and Resources

Part 3

Environment and Resources

Introduction

The compact city debate has been driven largely by environmental arguments: for example, that it is the most energy efficient urban form, it reduces the need to travel and hence transport emissions; and that it conserves the countryside. The previous section investigated the importance of social and economic arguments to the general debate; this section now examines the environmental issues in more depth. First, the environmental claims made in support of the compact city need to be tested, and supported by empirical research, if they are to form the basis for urban policy. Secondly, as well as contradictions with other issues, there may be internal contradictions to the environmental arguments in support of the compact city; there may be counter-claims that reveal ways in which the compact city is *not* environmentally sustainable. The following chapters address both these problems.

Transport is arguably the single biggest issue for environmental arguments relating to urban form, as reflected by the large number of chapters devoted to this topic. It is claimed that the compact city reduces travel demand, increases the propensity for walking and cycling, and supports public transport. But is this actually the case? Barrett investigates the effect of density on travel demand, particularly for work-related travel. Farthing *et al.* investigate the effect of increased accessibility to local services and facilities on non-work-related travel behaviour, and Nijkamp and Rienstra analyse the public transport dimension. From this work it is not at all clear that the compact city would yield the advantages it is claimed. The authors tend to agree that local journey lengths may be reduced, but this may not be significant in comparison with the longer trips associated with recreation. They are also united in their belief that a modal shift away from the private car is unlikely.

With rising car ownership, transport issues may continue to control and influence urban form in the way they have done in the past - a case of the tail wagging the dog - in which case a re-emergence of the more traditional compact urban form would remain an elusive goal. Barrett and Nijkamp and Rienstra point to the wider structural influences on travel behaviour, such as current employment and leisure patterns. Perhaps there is little that a change in urban form, if it could be brought about in the first place, could achieve - or perhaps decentralisation has already gone too far. The contributors also highlight other contradictions inherent within the claimed transport benefits of the compact city, such as the potential *negative* transport effects, including congestion and parking difficulties, and their detrimental impact on local businesses.

As the antithesis of compact city theory, there is a school of thought amongst environmentalists that the most sustainable way to live would be to return to rural areas and local self-sufficiency, to reduce the importing of goods and services from far-off lands, and to commune more closely with nature. The arguments are based on the assertion that cities are the most unsustainable form of settlement - they consume the most and waste the most - and this theory forms the basis of the counter-arguments to the environmental arguments in favour of the compact city. Troy represents one such alternative view. He identifies the environmental benefits of the low density form of traditional Australian cities and argues that the implementation of compact city through so-called consolidation would result in increased environmental stress.

There is some consensus amongst the authors of Part 3 that there may be more effective ways of reducing environmental unsustainability than trying to change urban form. Barrett and Troy suggest that changing people's behaviour, introducing environmentally friendly technologies, and developing renewable energy could all have a major part to play. In general they believe that the compact city has some potential if the counter-arguments are addressed. None the less, a comprehensive approach is required: an approach which addresses urban form alone is not enough.

George Barrett
The Transport Dimension

Introduction

The form of our cities to a large extent reflects the transport technologies which were dominant at different stages of their development. The traditional dense European city can be viewed as a product of the external economies of agglomeration in an era of slow and costly transportation. The coming of the railways permitted increased residential decentralisation - in particular to areas within walking distance of the new stations - and marked the start of the trend towards lower residential densities in central areas of cities such as London. Bus transport brought greater flexibility to the suburbanisation process. The era of the motor car added a further dimension, producing fundamental changes in the character of many European cities and allowing the creation of the low density, weak-centred cities of North America.

Increasing concern about the implications - especially for environmental quality - of the seemingly inexorable growth in car usage has generated particular interest in how planning policies might utilise the apparently greater transport efficiency of traditional urban forms to at least moderate the pressures for growth in travel demand. This interest was given particular impetus by the work of Kenworthy and Newman (1989) and it has been taken up in particular in the national land use policy frameworks of the Netherlands (Huut, 1991) and, more recently, the United Kingdom (Departments of the Environment and Transport, 1994). The low prospective rates of population growth in western Europe mean however that here at least the prime interest has to be in the implications of alternative options for accommodating incremental growth, rather than in the possible form of entirely new major settlements.

A range of cross-sectional evidence is available on how density and urban size influence travel behaviour, some of which is reviewed later in this chapter. However, the economic and social interactions, and potential market responses, to new policies made possible by modern transport technology mean that land use policies and their implications need to be considered at the level of the city region, rather than just in relation to the city itself. Here the research evidence is much more limited but the chapter summarises some of the key findings of recent research (ECOTEC, forthcoming), undertaken to inform the debate on new draft regional policy guidance for the UK West Midlands.

Judgements about the appropriateness of new policy directions need, of course, to be made in the light of both their likely effectiveness - in this case in relation to objectives to limit growth in travel demand - and their prospective wider consequences for economic efficiency and other policy objectives. The transport aspects of these issues are considered at the end of the chapter, before some brief overall conclusions.

Residential densities, city size and travel behaviour

Residential densities emerge from a range of studies as the single most important land use related influence on personal travel behaviour. International comparisons of gasoline usage per head in different cities (Kenworthy and Newman, 1989) suggest that consumption rises at an increasing rate as densities fall. The lowest density US cities, such as Houston, apparently have levels of consumption per head up to ten times those of high density Asian counterparts such as Hong Kong, Singapore and Tokyo.

Table 1 presents some summary evidence on the relationship between density and travel behaviour in the UK. Higher densities appear to be strongly associated with lower levels of total travel and with the increased use of modes other than the car.

Density (persons per hectare)	All Modes	Car	Local Bus	Rail	Walk	Other[1]
Under 1	206.3	159.3	5.2	8.9	4.0	28.8
1 - 4.99	190.5	146.7	7.7	9.1	4.9	21.9
5 - 14.99	176.2	131.7	8.6	12.3	4.3	18.2
15 - 29.99	152.6	105.4	9.6	10.2	6.6	20.6
30 - 49.99	143.2	100.4	9.9	10.8	6.4	15.5
50 and over[2]	129.2	79.9	11.9	15.2	6.7	15.4
All Areas[3]	159.6	113.8	9.3	11.3	5.9	19.1

Table 1. Density and distance travelled per person per week by mode (km): UK 1985/1986.

Source: National Travel Survey. 1986

Notes:
1. Other refers to two-wheeled motor vehicles, taxis, domestic air travel, other public transport and other types of bus (school, hire, express and works).
2. Data exclude all trips less than 1.6km and only refer to the main mode used for a trip. It therefore excludes the walking element of all non walk trips.
3. Population density figures were taken from the OPCS sampling frame which is based on the Postcode Address File. Population figures are from the 1981 Census.

Such evidence should be treated with a degree of caution. The highest density neighbourhoods are typically located near to town and city centre facilities; frequently they are disproportionately occupied by households with below average incomes and relatively low rates of car ownership. However, studies which have attempted to control for such influences (for example, ECOTEC, 1992) suggest that density still exerts a significant effect on travel behaviour, independent of these factors.

The mechanisms through which higher densities suppress travel - in particular, car travel - are less well understood but are potentially important from a policy perspective. They are likely to include effects associated with:

- increases in the range of opportunities of different sorts which can be accessed within a given travel distance - and in particular within convenient walking time;
- increases in the scale and range of services which can be supported within particular localities and thus reductions in the need to travel elsewhere;
- the creation of densities of 'trip ends' that are high enough to support public transport;
- the imposition of a range of constraints on the ownership and use of private vehicles.

Turning to the question of urban size, it is clear in general terms that the residents of large urban areas tend to travel less and make more use of public transport than do those who live in small towns - and especially rural areas. This is not solely a reflection of the effects of density. Again however, it is likely to reflect factors associated with the range of opportunities and facilities which areas can provide, as well as their capacity to support public transport or car use.

Table 2 presents summary evidence on the relationship between urban size and different aspects of travel behaviour in the UK. This confirms that there is a clear contrast in overall levels of travel between the major urban areas, urban areas with between 25,000 and 250,000 population, small towns and rural areas. Residents of the major conurbations also make notably greater use of buses.

The relationship between settlement size and travel behaviour is fairly complex. More detailed analysis suggests that there is no significant relationship between urban size and travel in the largest urban areas, particularly once factors such as car ownership and socio-economic composition are taken into account (ECOTEC, 1992). The high levels of car travel in Outer London are also to some extent anomalous.

Detailed analysis also points to differences in the relationships between urban size and work and non-work travel. Work-related travel starts to rise sharply as the population size of an area falls below 50,000; in the case of non-work travel the threshold appears to be lower - at around 25,000 people (Barrett, 1995). This indicates that, whilst relatively small urban areas can support a reasonably wide range of leisure and shopping facilities, only larger urban areas can offer a full spectrum of job opportunities. The research discussed later, for example, indicates that, whilst Telford has developed as a strong comparison and convenience shopping centre, it still sees substantial out-commuting to centres such as Birmingham, particularly by those seeking higher-order service sector jobs.

In the UK there is insufficient data to allow systematic overall comparisons between levels of travel in individual settlements. However, the evidence which is available suggests that relatively dense cities - preferably with a population in excess of 250,000 - are likely to be the most efficient form of development from the viewpoint of minimisation of travel, especially car travel. This tends to be supported by the evidence for the one element of travel - travel-to-work - where good data are available. In the West Midlands case study discussed below, for example, Coventry - a fairly compact city with some 300,000 inhabitants - emerges as having notably short average journey-to-work lengths, combined with high usage of public transport.

Area	All Modes km (%)	Car km (%)	Local Bus km (%)	Rail km (%)	Walking km (%)	Other[2] km (%)
Inner London	141.3	76.2 (54.0)	12.0 (8.5)	34.1 (24.1)	2.5 (1.8)	16.6 (11.6)
Outer London	166.6	113.3 (68.0)	8.9 (5.3)	23.3 (14.0)	2.6 (1.6)	18.5 (11.1)
West Midlands urban area	121.2	83.8 (69.2)	14.8 (12.2)	5.5 (4.5)	3.2 (2.6)	13.9 (11.5)
Greater Manchester urban area	128.8	87.2 (67.7)	15.7 (12.2)	5.4 (4.2)	3.7 (2.8)	16.8 (13.1)
West Yorkshire urban area	136.4	85.5 (62.7)	17.7 (13.0)	3.2 (2.3)	3.6 (2.7)	26.4 (19.3)
Glasgow urban area	91.2	49.5 (54.3)	16.4 (18.0)	4.9 (5.3)	4.4 (4.9)	16.0 (17.5)
Liverpool urban area	89.3	54.0 (60.4)	17.1 (19.1)	6.1 (6.8)	2.6 (3.0)	9.5 (10.7)
Tyneside urban area	109.3	63.7 (58.2)	19.8 (18.1)	2.9 (2.7)	2.7 (2.5)	20.2 (18.5)
Other urban areas over 250,000	141.2	93.6 (66.3)	11.2 (7.9)	8.3 (5.9)	4.2 (3.0)	23.9 (15.9)
Urban areas population 100,000 to 250,000	160.5	114.8 (71.5)	8.6 (5.4)	11.3 (7.0)	3.2 (2.0)	22.6 (14.1)
Urban areas population 50,000 to 100,000	154.5	110.4 (71.5)	7.2 (4.7)	13.0 (8.4)	3.7 (2.4)	20.2 (13.0)
Urban areas population 25,000 to 50,000	151.0	110.8 (73.5)	5.7 (3.8)	12.5 (8.3)	3.7 (2.5)	18.2 (12.1)
Urban areas population 3,000 to 25,000	175.7	133.4 (75.9)	7.2 (4.1)	8.0 (4.6)	3.0 (1.7)	24.1 (13.7)
Rural areas	211.0	163.8 (77.6)	5.7 (2.7)	10.9 (5.2)	1.7 (0.8)	28.9 (13.7)
All Areas	159.6	113.8 (71.3)	9.3 (5.8)	11.3 (2.1)	3.2 (2.0)	22.0 (13.8)

Table 2. Settlement size and total distance travelled per person per week by mode (km): UK 1985/86.[1]

Source: National Travel Survey Data. 1986

Notes:
1. Excludes trips under 1.6 km.
2. 'Other' refers to two wheeled motor vehicles, taxis, domestic air travel, other public transport and other types of bus.

It would be wrong to create an impression that the density and size of the urban area are its only land use characteristics which influence travel behaviour. It has long been known (for example, Thompson, 1977) that centralisation of facilities can be a powerful factor promoting the use of public transport - though it may produce long journey lengths. Suburban workplaces appear to benefit from relatively short journey lengths though they are more car-dependent. In contrast, peripheral business park locations appear to combine both long journey lengths and high levels of car dependency (ECOTEC, forthcoming).

The wider city region: the case of the UK West Midlands

The scale of the process of residential decentralisation from UK cities which has taken place in recent decades, and the potential opportunities for decentralisation created by a modern transport infrastructure and the car, mean that the effects of new land use planning and transport policies have to be viewed at the regional level.

Many of the issues involved are well illustrated by the West Midlands, a metropolitan area with a population of some 2.6 million[1] people within a wider region of mainly freestanding towns and rural areas of broadly similar population size. Although still the centre of the UK motor industry, the region has seen substantial restructuring. It lost 4.2% of its total jobs between 1971 and 1991, with rapidly growing service employment (+43%) being insufficient to offset fully the shake-out in manufacturing employment which has occurred, especially during the 1979-1981 recession.

The region has seen a very marked process of decentralisation of both population and employment. Between 1971 and 1991 the population of the metropolitan area declined by 213,000 or 7.7%, principally as a result of migration to the surrounding shire counties and especially the so-called 'middle ring' towns around the metropolitan area. While much of the migration in earlier decades was a product of active planning policies, the more recent movement seems to have been to a greater extent market led.

Employment decentralisation has also been extensive and, to a large extent, market driven in recent years. Between 1981 and 1991 employment in the metropolitan area fell by 6.5% whilst that in the shire counties grew by 8.8%. As well as the drift of employment to areas in and around the shire towns, there has been a tendency for employment to shift from the core of the metropolitan area to its periphery, with the development of locations around the M42 and the outskirts of Coventry as important new office sites.

The composition of travel by journey purpose in the region is fairly similar to the national average. Total travel is however somewhat below average, primarily because of the relatively low levels of car travel in the metropolitan area. There are significant - two-way - travel flows between the metropolitan area and the surrounding shire county towns, as shown in relation to travel-to-work in Fig. 1, but because of problems with the data it is not possible to say what proportion of total travel in the region such flows constitute. Nevertheless, it is clear that the flows broadly correspond to gravity model principles, being positively related to the size of the areas concerned and negatively related to the distance between them.

As elsewhere, almost all of the major trends in travel behaviour conflict with objectives of sustainable development and a range of other policy concerns. Although rates of growth in travel in the region in recent years have been slightly below average, they have still been substantial. For example, between 1985/86 and 1989/91 car travel grew by 23%. There has been a particularly marked increase in the use of the car for travel to work; bus travel generally has shown a substantial decline.

A range of factors have no doubt contributed to these trends, including:

increases in incomes and car ownership; demographic changes - particularly the growth of the young retired; and economic and social changes which have tended to widen the areas over which people and businesses conduct their interactions. However, the growing interlinkages between the metropolitan area and the rest of the region have clearly played their part.

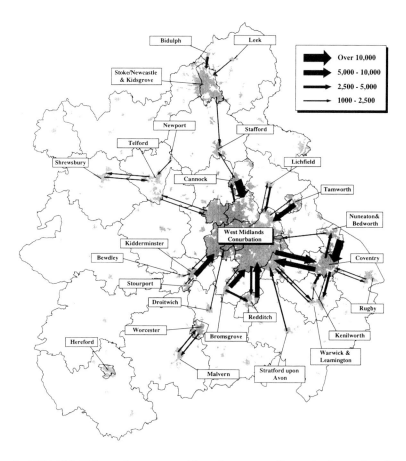

Fig.1. Main commuting flows between urban areas in the West Midlands region 1991.

In 1971 135,600 people commuted into the metropolitan area from elsewhere in the West Midlands, whilst 41,000 metropolitan area residents commuted to jobs in other parts of the region. By 1991 these figures had risen to 160,000 and 55,000 respectively. The commuting is focused in particular on the range of some 20 towns located in a 25km ring around the metropolitan area. Commuting flows again closely follow the gravity model pattern, with the expression Percentage commuting $= 2000/d^2$ (where d is distance from the metropolitan area) predicting flows to within two percentage points, for 21 out of the 31 areas considered.

Travel in the course of work has also grown sharply - by some 21% between 1985/86 and 1989/91 - although here again the rate of growth has actually been below the national average. A high proportion of such travel is very localised, but much of the growth is clearly linked to the wider process of economic integration and what has been termed the growth of global value chains (Porter,

1990). The available data, which for technical reasons probably understate inter-regional travel, indicate that around 30% of such trips which cross the metropolitan area boundary have origins or destinations outside the region altogether.

Convenience shopping patterns in the region remain relatively localised and the metropolitan area has a strong network of local centres. Data provided by a major food retailer indicate that, excluding one store located within a regional centre, journeys undertaken by over 65% of the customers to 11 stores are of a duration of under 10 minutes. However, distances travelled for comparison shopping have grown rapidly, partly as a result of factors such as the development of the Merry Hill regional centre and the apparently increasing attraction to metropolitan area residents of some centres elsewhere in the region, such as Telford.

Leisure-related travel raises special problems because of its domination by the car, its relative importance and its strong long term growth. Whilst little is known about trip patterns it is noteworthy in the context of the discussion of policy issues that over a quarter of all such trips in the region are now of more than 50 miles (Department of National Heritage, 1993).

The structural changes discussed at the beginning of this section have in many ways been unhelpful in their effects on travel behaviour. The shift from manufacturing to service employment is likely to have increased overall levels of both travel and car dependency. Overlaying maps of patterns of residence and employment (ECOTEC, forthcoming) indicates the much greater typical separation of places of residence and work of service industry workers, than of manual workers. Many service activities also, by their nature, demand personal contact in the course of work. Occupational composition emerges as an important influence on most aspects of travel behaviour (ECOTEC, forthcoming).[2] The development of Birmingham as a national and international service centre will also have contributed to the growth of inter-regional travel.

The decentralisation of population and probably that of employment too will also have contributed to growth. Comparisons of patterns of migration and commuting flows strongly suggest an association between migration and increased commuting journey lengths. Migrants tend to a large extent to move out from the metropolitan area in a radial pattern from their original place of residence, presumably trading increased commuting costs for greater residential space at lower cost (Barrett, 1995).

The cross-sectional evidence on urban and non-urban travel behaviour discussed earlier would itself suggest that this process of population decentralisation is likely to add to travel. In practice its actual effect appears to be substantially greater than implied in such comparisons because people moving into new developments seem on average to adopt much more car-dependent lifestyles than those of established shire county residents (ECOTEC, forthcoming).

The effects of employment decentralisation are more difficult to assess. The movement of economic activity out to the areas of population growth creates the potential for shorter journey-to-work trips. It may however in practice generate long distance, diffuse, orbital trip patterns which cannot be served effectively by public transport. It is certainly true that many of the new peripheral office developments are associated with high levels of car dependency and long journey lengths, although they may not, of course, be representative of other types of new development in the areas concerned. Equally, the dispersion of manufacturing plants may add to other forms of travel - notably freight movements - particularly with the growing adoption of just-in-time production systems.

The trends discussed here are probably not untypical of what is happening across much of the UK and indeed much of the Western world. In the author's view they reflect, to a large extent, the role of improved road infrastructure and lower real transport costs in reducing the external economies of agglomeration which underpinned the traditional dense European city, and, indeed, the emergence in many cases of new congestion-related diseconomies.

Such trends, of course, sit uneasily with the very notion of a self-contained, compact and travel efficient city. The typical land use policy response being adopted in the UK appears to involve an attempt to combine some degree of move back in the direction of - or at least slowing of the movement away from - the compact city, with an attempt to focus the decentralisation that does occur in ways which support public transport. The key questions for current purposes - to which we now turn - are how far the sorts of changes identified here can realistically be arrested, and what are the likely consequences of the attempt to try?

The emerging policy issues

There seems little doubt that policies to encourage a focusing of development on urban areas, and to increase residential and employment densities, have some potential to reduce overall levels of travel and secure a mode shift in favour of public transport. However, simulation exercises (ECOTEC, 1992) suggest that, at least under current conditions, this potential is not very great. The major rationale of such policies, in transport terms, is probably therefore to help create - or preserve - land use patterns which, unlike those, for example, of much of North America, are not inherently car-dependent. This will also have potential benefits in helping to preserve flexibility for future transport policy options.

In practice a range of factors will constrain the capacity of governments to pursue such a policy direction or constrain its likely effectiveness, including: the relatively limited scale of new development in relation to the existing building stock in most Western economies; the legacy of existing policy commitments and development permissions; physical and political constraints on densification, and the inevitable competition between areas for development, particularly in an era of high unemployment. The latter is a particular issue in the UK because of the weaknesses of its strategic policy framework.

The effects and the effectiveness of the policy will also be influenced by the adaptive responses of those affected. Higher income groups will inevitably be able to continue to migrate to areas of existing development outside the cities and to commute back. The effects of new controls on urban and rural housing development are likely to include the shifting of development pressures to beyond the area of control, and a bidding-up of rural house prices to the detriment of their existing communities. There is evidence that existing green belt controls have effects of this type (ECOTEC, 1992).

Lower income groups will not, of course, have this option to the same extent, although some may still commute very long distances, as was seen amongst people squeezed out of the South East housing market in the boom conditions of the late 1980s. It seems inevitable that those who remain will not only have reduced residential space but will also face higher relative housing costs.

The approach will also involve some real economic costs. There is evidence (for example, Keeble and PACEC, 1992) both that rural firms are on average more efficient than their urban counterparts and that the greater availability of space which they enjoy plays an important part in this advantage.

Clearly, higher densities are likely to result in increased congestion. This raises three concerns. First, it is clear that congestion itself has significant costs (for example, CBI, 1991; and Newbery, 1990). Second, the simulation evidence (ECOTEC, 1992) suggests that many - or in some cases all - of the benefits from the reduced potential for travel created by this type of policy could in practice be lost through the adverse effects of congestion on vehicle routing and operating conditions. Third, even if the policy does reduce vehicle emissions, its effects may be to concentrate them to a greater extent in the precise areas where they cause most damage and adversely affect most people. This raises some basic questions about whether the underlying policy objective is to reduce travel or to limit its adverse consequences.

The policy could be made more effective, and its adverse effects reduced, through complementary policies to raise the real costs of travel. Arguably, this could help to re-establish some of the traditional private benefits from location in a dense urban area. The problem is that the scale of the price increases needed to bring this about may need to be very large. It is noteworthy that other European countries, such as Italy, which have long had much higher fuel prices than the UK, have comparable levels of car travel. Much of the consumer response to higher fuel prices in practice takes the form of the purchase of more fuel efficient cars rather than lower levels of travel. Again this raises some basic questions about the underlying objectives of policy.

Many of the problems involved would be resolved if, through environmental improvements, public transport investment and other measures, more of the population could be persuaded of the benefits of traditional urban lifestyles. In the English-speaking world, at least, such a conversion seems to have so far proved elusive.

Conclusion

The compact city, with its potential transport efficiency, inevitably represents an attractive model to those who view with concern the growth in travel and its environmental consequences. In practice it seems clear that improvements in transport systems have led to both a fairly rapid process of decentralisation from our existing urban areas, and a reduction in the extent of aspects of their self-containment. Efforts to create or preserve traditional urban forms have some short-run potential to reduce travel but they are probably best seen mainly as a form of contingency planning. It would be wrong however to see them as either an easy or a totally costless policy option.

Notes

1. Except where otherwise stated all employment data are derived from the Census of Employment; migration and commuting data are drawn from the Census of Population; travel data for 1989/91 were provided directly by the Department of Transport and are drawn from the National Travel Survey.

2. Some 77% of the average distance to work by car of residents in different areas can be explained by just four variables; occupational composition (measured as the proportion of the population in social classes A and B); whether the area is rural; whether it falls within the metropolitan area; and - in other cases - distance from the metropolitan area.

References

Barrett, G. (1995) Transport emissions and travel behaviour: a critical review of recent European Union and UK policy initiatives. *Transportation*, January.

CBI (1991) *Trade Routes to the Future*, CBI, London.

Department of National Heritage (1993) *Day Visits in Great Britain 1991/92*, HMSO, London.

Departments of the Environment and Transport (1994) *Planning Policy Guidance 13: Transport*, HMSO, London.

ECOTEC Research and Consulting Ltd (1992) *Reducing Transport Emissions Through Planning*, HMSO, London.

ECOTEC Research and Consulting Ltd (forthcoming) *Travel Patterns in the West Midlands: Implications for Sustainable Development Policies*, Department of the Environment.

Huut, R. Van (1991) *The Right Business in the Right Place*, PTRC Conference Papers, London.

Keeble, D. and PACEC (1992) *Business Success in the Countryside: Performance of Rural Enterprises*, HMSO, London.

Kenworthy, J. and Newman, P. (1989) *Cities and Automobile Dependence*, Gower Technical, Aldershot.

Newbery, D. (1990) Pricing and congestion: economic principles relevant to pricing roads. *Oxford Review of Economic Policy*, **Vol. 6 No. 2.**

Porter, M. (1990) *The Competitive Advantage of Nations*, MacMillan, London.

Thompson, M. J. (1977) *Great Cities and their Traffic*, Penguin, Middlesex.

Stuart Farthing, John Winter and Tessa Coombes

Travel Behaviour and Local Accessibility to Services and Facilities

Introduction

The debate over the importance of land use planning measures in reducing transport emissions and energy use (see Newman and Kenworthy, 1989; Gordon *et al.*, 1991; Newman and Kenworthy, 1992) has highlighted a good deal of uncertainty about the characteristics of intra-urban travel behaviour and of its determinants, and also a relative lack of empirical research into the issue. This chapter assesses the importance to intra-urban travel behaviour of accessibility and focuses on accessibility to local facilities and services. Such a focus has been given recent importance by the endorsement in *Planning Policy Guidance 13: Transport* (Departments of the Environment and Transport, 1994) of neighbourhood planning, integrating both housing and service provision, as a way of reducing the demand for travel and of encourging environmentally friendly forms of travel. The issue is also important because accessibility is likely to be particularly important for the sorts of discretionary (non-work) trips made to such facilities. After a review of the existing literature on the topic, the chapter reports the results of some empirical research based on new urban developments in Avon.

The importance of accessibilty to intra-urban travel

As part of measures to reduce fuel use and emissions of greenhouse gases, the debate about local facilities and services highlights the importance of two aspects of travel behaviour. First, there is the mode of transport used for journeys. In particular there is an interest in encouraging trips on foot or by cycle rather than by car since the former are more energy efficient than the latter (Banister, 1992; Banister *et al.*, 1994). Second, there is the length of journeys themselves, particularly of course by car. Most journeys seem to use little fuel (Banister, 1994), but the shortening of car journeys can contribute to energy saving even though car engines do not work most efficiently on short trips.

What does the literature say about the importance of accessibility in affecting these aspects of travel behaviour? There appear to be two stances on the importance of accessibility to discretionary intra-urban travel, reflecting the wider debate about the compact city. First, some commentators place considerable emphasis on the importance of accessibility. In reviewing a range of studies Hanson and Schwab (1987, p.735), for example, talk about the significance of 'the individual's location *vis-à-vis* the distribution of potential accessibility sites', as the 'conventional wisdom' of transport planning. Commentators have pointed to a steady decline in the accessibility of services, schools and shops to the majority of the population (Elkin *et al.*, 1991). This has been linked to the growth in the number and length of journeys by car, revealed by statistics from the *National Travel Survey* (Department of Transport, 1993). Other research, whilst stressing the importance of walking trips for shopping, has shown the relatively poorer accessibility to shops for residents of new peripheral housing areas (Guy and Wrigley, 1987).

Perhaps the strongest evidence for the importance of accessibility in determining travel behaviour for non-work purposes comes from Hillman *et al.* (1976). They identified a range of local facilities and services and made a study of the travel behaviour of young women with children in a number of survey areas in the outer metropolitan area of South East England. They found that the local provision of facilities (measured in terms of a ten minute walk) was associated with a higher likelihood of walking to that type of facility, though optional car use reduced the likelihood of walking. Local provision also led to more frequent use of that type of facility. The implication of this (although it was not directly measured in the research) is that because the facilities are local, young women will walk to them. They also suggested that within the general area of discretionary (i.e. non-work) travel, there were greater or lesser extents of discretion for this group of women. Some facilities (they picked out post offices and chemists) were always visited wherever they were provided; others (such as playgrounds, parks and laundrettes) were visited much more frequently when they were provided locally. Accessibility therefore has a differential impact on the mode of travel, distance of travel and frequency of use for different facilities.

Other commentators have taken a more sceptical line on the importance of accessibiltity. Breheny (1992), for example, questions the concept of facilities that meet the everyday needs of all households. He suggests that this neglects the growing importance of specialist goods and services, in particular recreational facilities, where local provision is impossible. It is possible to point here, too, to the growing diversity of households and household structures, and the growth in the importance of 'consumption' in the meaning and significance of people's lives.

The notion of discretion in trip-making behaviour raises questions about the importance of accessibility to local facilities and services. Adler and Ben-Akiva (1979) stress that households accumulate needs for goods and services and that these needs can be met by scheduling trips to activities and locations away from the home. Some trips can be deferred, and possibly combined with other activities. Other trips, however, are obligatory and cannot be deferred and these are more likely to take the form of single purpose trips. The combining of purposes in one trip, it is suggested, may be more important for households in areas where general accessibility is poor, allowing them to reduce total travel time and thus reduce the disadvantages. The local provision of facilities will therefore only be significant to households and those undertaking trips in the context of total household activities and the scheduling of trips to meet multiple needs.

Empirical work also seems to suggest more ambivalent results as far as the importance of local accessibility is concerned. The work of Hanson and Schwab (1987) using data from Sweden concluded that though there is some relationship between travel characteristics of individuals and accessibility it is not as strong as expected in the literature and that personal and household characteristics are more important. Travel behaviour is strongly related to role differences of individuals within households. Gender and employment status are two (linked) factors of considerable importance in defining these roles (see also Hanson and Hanson, 1981; Pas, 1984). Access to a car is also important in explaining aspects of travel behaviour. Despite these general conclusions, Hanson and Schwab (1987) found that individuals with many opportunities close to home made a higher proportion of their trips on foot or cycle. And contrary to the results of Hillman *et al.* (1976), Hanson and Schwab found that this did not hold for non-working women with access to a car. A study by Handy (1992) in California also showed that there are more walking trips in areas of high local accessibility, but in terms of reducing travel the results were ambiguous.

The research conducted for the UK government (Tarry, 1992; ECOTEC, 1992) was rather inconclusive on the importance of accessibility to the encouragement of walking and cycling. It looked at 'centres' rather than facilities (and concentrated on shopping), and reported wide variations between study areas in the use of different modes of transport, but found that 'surprisingly distance does not appear to be a major factor explaining these differences. It is difficult to discern clear influences on modal choice at the local level due to the number of factors involved and their inter-relationships'. (ECOTEC, 1992, p.47).

Evidence from Hanson and Schwab (1987) on the impact of accessibility on the distance of journeys suggests that accessibility is weakly related to the overall amount of discretionary (non-work) travel, but is strongly related to travel distances associated with shopping and personal business. This was true for all groups and revealed that higher home-based accessibility levels mean lower travel distances for these purposes.

Three conclusions can be drawn from this review of the literature. First, further research is needed that takes account of the discretionary nature of facility use. If a particular facility (a post office, say) is always visited by someone in the household wherever it is located in relation to home, then it is this type of facility on which the advocates of local facility provision should concentrate attention. Trips that have to be made will potentially be reduced in length and may thus encourage travellers to walk. Moreover, if these trips are frequent then the potential impact on total travel could be considerable. Second, in undertaking research in this area it is important to recognise that the scheduling of trips to meet a range of accumulated household needs does not guarantee that a facility that is provided locally will necessarily be the one that is visited and, if it is visited, it may be visited as part of a longer multi-purpose trip and therefore, perhaps, by car. Third, the importance of the different roles of individuals within a household needs to be acknowledged and these factors need to be controlled in any research. The following sections describe the method, and results, of the empirical research carried out by the authors.

Research methods
The data on which this chapter is based were collected as part of a study of the planning and implementation of facilities on new large-scale housing developments in Avon. Five developments with different levels of local facility provision were selected for detailed study (see Fig. 1). They range from large-scale urban extensions (Bradley Stoke North, Bradley Stoke South, Worle) to infill development on the periphery of the Bristol and Kingswood urban area (Longwell Green) and a substantial village expansion (Peasedown St John) some miles from Bath. The advantage of selecting new developments that were being developed over essentially the same time period was that the socio-economic and demographic characteristics of the population would be similar (young owner-occupiers) though, of course, there would be variation between individuals and households.

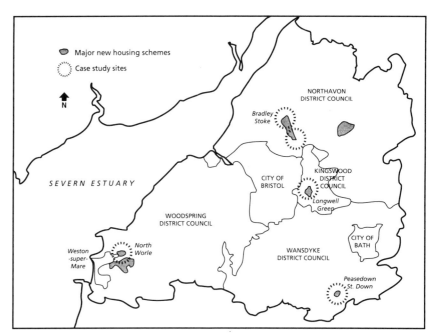

Fig. 1. The location of the five case study developments.

Local facilities
The first stage of the research was to undertake a survey of the facilities available on each of the developments. The survey covered a range of nineteen facilities, using the lists produced by Hillman *et al.* (1973; 1976) and Hillman and Whalley (1983), and revealed that there were different levels of availability of these facilities on the developments and therefore different levels of accessibility to such facilities for the residents. In order to focus on facilities for which local availability would have maximum potential impact on mode use and journey lengths, a smaller group of seven facilities was selected for detailed investigation. These were selected because their use appears, from the existing literature, to be the least discretionary and because they were likely to be used frequently. The seven were: open space, a food shop, a newsagent, a post office, a primary school, a public house, a supermarket, and a secondary school. In practice some preliminary analysis of use patterns, from our travel behaviour survey described below, revealed that they were used frequently.

Travel behaviour

The data on travel behaviour, and personal and household characteristics of residents, were collected by means of postal questionnaires sent to a sample of addresses selected from the electoral register on each development. The personal questionnaire asked about the last trip that the person completing the questionnaire had made to each of the facilities listed, while resident on the development. This therefore allowed the collection of data about even infrequent trips by different household members. The questionnaire requested details of the location of the facility visited, the timing of the visit, the starting point for the trip (home or work), the mode of travel, reason for mode of travel, time spent on the journey, and availability of alternative means of travel to make the journey. Two personal questionnaires were delivered to each address and, where the household consisted of more than two persons, the covering letter asked for the questionnaires to be completed by the two persons whose birthdays were closest to the date of the letter. Children aged five or over were to be included in the survey and an adult was requested to complete the questionnaire on behalf of each child. A household questionnaire was also enclosed, requesting information on household composition, car ownership and socio-economic status. A response was received from 25% of addresses. There was some bias towards older residents in the response and a particular under-representation of children, suggesting that the request to include children's travel behaviour was not heeded.

After responses were received from each household, the location of each facility visited was marked on a map, and a grid reference was noted for the home address and the location of the facility visited, in order to calculate distances travelled.

For the purpose of the research a trip was defined as a journey which originated at home and which included a visit to the facility in question. In addition to journeys which were single purpose, involving travel to the facility and then a return journey home, there could be more complex trips, involving stops at one or more facilities, or journeys involving a visit to a facility on the way to work. However, facilities visited on trips originating from the workplace are excluded from the results presented here because the interest in the research is in the impact of the provision of facilities near the home.

Results

Mode of travel

The interesting variables in this analysis are either binary (or categorical) or can be treated as such. Logistic regression can analyse situations where there is a binary dependent variable - in this case a walking trip, as opposed to a trip by any other mode. It computes an equation that fits the the best 'observed' to 'predicted' pattern for the dependent variable, and it measures the statistical significance of each independent variable in explaining the dependent variable. In this case the null hypothesis is that there is no association between mode of travel used (for a trip to a particular facility) and each of the variables measuring local provision, car availability, presence of children in the household, age, gender and employment status of the trip maker.

The results of this analysis are shown in Table 1. These would seem to indicate that the provision of a facility on a development does not in itself encourage enough use of that facility and enough walking trips to that facility to significantly alter the balance of trips between walking and driving. The two exceptions are secondary schools and public houses. Since most journeys on foot are short, in order for local provision to have a significant impact on the mode used for travel, the local facilities must both provide the services that people want and fit in with the general activity and trip-scheduling patterns discussed above (Williams, 1988). For example, the trip to the local pub is probably more likely to be a single purpose trip for social reasons and, because of the drink-driving laws, is sensibly undertaken on foot.

Table 1. Significant relationships between trip to facility on foot and personal, household and facility provision variables.

	Super market (n=417)	Food shop (n=210)	News-agent (n=344)	Post office (n=293)	Primary school (n=117)	Secondary school (n=57)	Public house (n=277)
Age, under 16							
Age, 16 - 44							
Gender (male/female)			*				
Full-time Worker							
Part-time Worker							
Retired							
1 car household	**	**					
2 or more car household	**	**	**	**			**
Children <16yrs. household	*	*					
Local facility						**	**
Constant	**						

Correlations: * 95% significance level ** 99% significance level, n = number of trips in the sample.

The choice of secondary schools is an important issue for parents. Recent emphasis on parental choice in education policy would indicate a great sensitivity to the quality of education provided at different schools, and statistics from the *National Travel Survey* suggest that there has been a considerable growth in the length of journeys to school in recent years (Department of Transport, 1993). Nevertheless there are capacity limits and admissions policies in schools which mean that parental choice is constrained. All of this suggests that the outcome of local provision will not be easy to assess in the case of schools. The fact that the provision of a secondary school encourages walking indicates that the school is perceived by local parents to be satisfactory (on new developments they will be new and well equipped); that local children can gain admission to that school; and that they are allowed to travel on foot, and without a parental escort. In the case of primary schools local provision alone does not encourage walking (although the Wald statistic is nearly significant at the 5% level), indicating that parents tend to drive their children to primary school wherever it is located.

There is, as would be expected (since non car owning households do not have the option of using the car), a strong negative impact from car ownership for a number of facilities. Persons in households with one car or two or more cars were much less likely to walk than persons in non car owning households. This applies to trips to supermarkets, food shops, and newsagents. Persons from households with two or more cars are also less likely to walk to the post office and the pub. Not surprisingly, the research suggests that quite different activity patterns exist for men and women (related to women's role in terms of child care and other domestic responsibilities). The presence of children in the household is also likely to lead to walking trips rather than other modes, in particular for food shopping at the supermarket and at smaller convenience food shops. Also, men seem to be more likely than women to walk to the convenience food shop.

Distance of travel

If local accessibility does not encourage walking, does it reduce the distance that people travel by car to access facilities? Multiple regression analysis was undertaken to measure the impact of local provision of facilities on trip lengths by car, controlling for the same range of personal, household and car ownership variables that we have considered before. For five out of the seven facilities, local facility provision reduces the length of car-based trips (see Table 2). It does not influence the length of car-based trips to either primary or secondary schools, though the signs of the variables are negative and the coefficient is almost statistically significant for trips to primary school. The explanation here is that a substantial number of the local trips are on foot in any case, the car-based journeys being the longer ones.

Other factors, controlling for local facility provision, also play a part in reducing journey lengths. Households with one car travel less far than those with two or more, for trips to the post office. People in households with children travel less far to the post office and also to the primary school; in the first case it is probably due to the payment of child benefit at local post offices, and in the latter case it is likely that trips by children to schools are locally oriented but trips by adults for other leisure purposes may be to schools in a number of locations.

	Super market (n=354)	Food shop (n=118)	News-agent (n=166)	Post office (n=174)	Primary school (n=77)	Secondary school (n=39)	Public house (n=165)
Age, under 16							
Age, 16 - 44							
Gender (male/female)							
Full-time Worker		*					
Part-time Worker							
Retired							
1 car household							
2 or more car household							
Children <16yrs. household	*				**		
Local facility	**	**	**	**			**
Constant	**	**	**	**	**	*	

Table 2. Significant relationships between distance travelled by car and personal, household and facility provision variables.

Multiple regression: * 95% significance level, ** 99% significance level, n = number of trips in the sample.

For open space visits, employment status seems to play a part in local use. Full-time and part-time workers are more likely to use closer facilities than those who are economically inactive, or unemployed or in full-time education. Males seem to use more distant facilities than females.

The conclusion of this analysis is therefore that facility provision stands out as a variable which can reduce trip lengths by car. Though this research has not assessed the impact of this reduction on the total journey length, taken together with the findings of Hanson and Schwab (1987), it suggests that it will also reduce journey lengths.

Conclusions

The evidence from the research described here does not support the assumption in recent policy advice that increasing the local availability of facilities (and therefore their accessibility) *per se* will have a significant impact in encouraging walking to those facilities. Amongst a list of seven facilities which were used frequently by residents (wherever they were located), only two - a secondary school and a public house - resulted in a shift away from car trips towards walking trips. However, local accessibility does help to reduce the length of car journeys to those facilities, though whether this reduces the total amount of travel by car for these households cannot be determined. In general, personal and household characteristics, including in particular car ownership, appear to be more significant than accessibility in affecting mode use. The findings of this study suggest that measures to discourage car use directly (such as taxation) as well as measures concerning land use will be needed in order to bring about a reduction in car use.

References

Adler, T.J. and Ben-Akiva, M. (1979) A theoretical and empirical model of trip chaining behaviour, *Transportation Research B*, **Vol. 13** pp.243-57.

Banister, D. (1992) Energy use, transport and settlement patterns, in *Sustainable Development and Urban Form*, (ed. M. Breheny), Pion, London, pp.160-81.

Banister, D. (1994) Research evidence: overview, in *Reducing the Need to Travel - The Planning Contribution Conference Paper*, Oxford Brookes University, December.

Banister, D., Watson S. and Wood, C. (1994) *The Relationship Between Energy Use in Transport and Urban Form,* Working Paper 12, Bartlett School of Planning, UCL, London.

Breheny, M. (1992) The contradictions of the compact city, in *Sustainable Development and Urban Form* (ed. M. Breheny) Pion, London, pp.138-59.

Department of the Environment and Department of Transport (1994) *Planning Policy Guidance 13: Transport,* HMSO, London.

Department of Transport (1993) *National Travel Survey 1989/91*, HMSO, London.

ECOTEC (1992) *Reducing Transport Emissions Through Planning*, HMSO, London.

Elkin, T., McLaren, D. and Hillman M. (1991) *Reviving the City: Towards Sustainable Urban Development*, Friends of the Earth, London.

Gordon, P., Richardson, H.W. and Jun, M.J. (1991) The commuting paradox: evidence from the top twenty. *Journal of the American Planning Association*, **47(4)**, pp.138-49.

Guy, C. and Wrigley, N. (1987) Walking trips to shops in British cties: a empirical review and policy re-examination. *Town Planning Review*, **58(1)**, pp.63-79.

Handy, S. (1992) Regional versus local accessibility: neo-traditional development and its implications for non-work travel. *Built Environment,* **18(4),** pp.253-67.

Hanson, S. and Hanson, P. (1981) Travel activity patterns of urban residents:

dimensions and relationships to socio-demographic characteristics. *Economic Geography*, **57,** pp.332-47.

Hanson, S. and Schwab, M. (1987) Accessibility and intra-urban travel. *Environment and Planning A,* **Vol.19,** pp.735-48.

Hillman, M. and Whalley, A. (1983) *Energy and Personal Travel: Obstacles to Conservation*, PSI, London.

Hillman, M., Henderson, I. and Whalley, A. (1973) *Personal Mobility and Transport Policy*, PEP, London.

Hillman, M., Henderson, I. and Whalley, A. (1976) *Transport Realities and Planning Policy: Studies of Friction and Freedom in Daily Travel*, PEP, London.

Newman, P. and Kenworthy, J. (1989) Gasoline consumption and cities - a comparison of US cities with a global survey. *Journal of the American Planning Association*, **Vol.55**, pp.24-37.

Newman, P. and Kenworthy, J. (1992) Is there a role for physical planners? *Journal of the American Planning Association,* **58(3)** pp.353-61.

Pas, E. (1984) The effect of selected socio-demographic characteristics on daily travel-activity behavior. *Environment and Planning A*, **16,** pp.571-81.

Tarry, S. (1992) Accessibility factors at the neighbourhood level, in *PTRC 20th Summer Annual Meeting, Environmental Issues: Proceedings of Seminar B*, London, PTRC, pp.257-70.

Williams, P.A. (1988) A recursive model of intra-urban trip-making. *Environment and Planning A*, **20**, pp.535-46.

Peter Nijkamp and Sytze A. Rienstra

Sustainable Transport in a Compact City

Introduction

A general phenomenon experienced by almost all cities in the world has been the emergence of green and diffuse suburbs around the city centres. As a result, the population density in cities has decreased significantly. The private car has brought low density living within the reach of large groups of upper and lower middle-class families. In fact, suburbanisation of living is a consequence of various broad changes in society, such as income increase, smaller households, more leisure time, and changing housing preferences. However, suburbanisation is also usually associated with negative socio-economic and environmental impacts, including longer working and shopping trips, increased energy consumption, pollution, accidents, and problematic public transport provision (Masser *et al.*, 1992).

Suburbanisation of living was followed in subsequent years by a second wave of suburbanisation of employment. Thus, dwellings as well as jobs tended to disperse further from urban centres into wider metropolitan areas, a process which may be called extended suburbanisation or counter-urbanisation (Breheny, forthcoming).

The development of decentralised cities, as well as other trends in the economy and society, have caused an enormous increase in car use, even in urban areas. At the same time, the length of commuting trips has increased greatly. Consequently, the external costs of transport have risen drastically; according to recent calculations these may account for some 3% of Gross National Product (Verhoef, 1994).

Development in most large cities of the Western world seems to be following a more diffuse spatial pattern. In spatial planning however, a contrasting concept is gaining much popularity. This concept is embodied in the 'compact city', where housing is provided in a relatively high density form, and where jobs are concentrated in the central city and in a limited number of sub-centres. The compact city has become a leading principle in Dutch physical planning in recent years, and is currently being adopted in Europe as an objective of urban planning (Breheny, forthcoming).

Such a compact urban spatial organisation could have major impacts on the future of transport (level of mobility, modal split). Current transport policies in many countries (especially north-western Europe) focus on stimulating public transport, and on reducing car use and travel demand, so as to reduce environmental externalities and congestion. The compact city could be successful in supporting collective modes of transport and reducing urban travel demand. At the same time however, it should be noted that the compact city concept has some intrinsic limitations in terms of quality of life, land use and prices, and congestion; and furthermore, many other factors (level of well-being, telecommunications) impinge on the future of transport and the introduction of new transport technologies.

In this chapter we will investigate how far a compact city might contribute to the achievement of more environmentally sustainable transport by the so-called collectivisation of the transport system. Another advantage of the compact city could be the reduction of travel distances (Organisation for Economic Co-operation and Development, 1995); however, we will not discuss this possibility explicitly here.

The structure of the chapter is as follows: first, we will analyse the extent to which collectivisation of transport could contribute to a reduction in externalities; next, the theoretical relationship between transport and urban form will be discussed; we will then identify other strategic factors which influence the collectivisation of urban transport; from this we will turn to some empirical research on the compact city, by presenting the results of a questionnaire survey of Dutch transportation experts on the feasibility of new transport systems; and finally, we will draw some conclusions.

Sustainability and the collectivisation of transport

As discussed above, transport policy in many countries is focusing on the reduction of the external costs of transport by stimulating a modal shift from the private car to public transport (see for example, ECMT and OECD, 1995). It seems to be a legitimate question to ask how far collective modes are more sustainable. One of the main advantages of public modes is that they are more energy efficient than the private car, which results in lower emissions of harmful gases, like CO_2, and also of gases which cause smog (see Table 1).

Passenger train	Car	Tram metro	Bus
71	201	100	159

Table 1. Modal comparison of CO_2 emissions in grams/ pass.km. (index).

Source: Netherlands Railways (NS)

Note: These figures should be used with care, as the uncertainty margin may be up to 25% or more, depending on the assumptions regarding seat occupancy, technology used, vehicle use etc.

Most collective transport modes are powered by electricity. For future emission reductions therefore, the way electricity is produced in the next decades is important. For example, when coal is used, CO_2 emissions may not be reduced significantly, but when solar or wind energy, biofuel, or nuclear generation is used, the emissions may be reduced much further (the latter, of course, has other negative impacts on the environment).

But there are also other advantages from a modal shift (Vleugel, 1995):

- the use of space is more efficient (or the capacity of the infrastructure is larger), which may be especially important in a compact city in which there is little space
- collective modes produce a smaller amount of solid waste, partly because of the long lifetime of vehicles
- collective modes are safer and have fewer social costs
- there is less noise and air pollution because of the use of electricity instead of fossil fuels - this advantage is especially important in urban areas

It may be concluded that the collectivisation of transport could offer an important contribution to the achievement of sustainability goals. However, policies to encourage this are fraught with a variety of problems, which may emerge in several fields. Firstly, therefore, we will discuss the relationship between urban form and transport, and then we will investigate other factors which are important in influencing transport sustainability.

Transport and urban form
Existing locations (of residences, industries, public services, recreational areas and so on) determine transport needs in the short term. Consequently, land use planning, territorial planning or physical planning are important policy intervention measures in coping with transportation issues. There are some fundamental principles related to land use (Owens, 1992).

First, the quantity of space and land is limited. The use of land can to some extent be intensified by using the 'third dimension' - air and subterranean space; this option may be especially important for the compact city concept.

Second, various types of land use are not compatible with one another at short distances from each other, either because of negative external effects, or possibly because the high market price for certain specific categories of land excludes land uses with a low rate of return on investment.

And third, land use is significantly influenced by institutional measures imposed by spatial planning. In this respect European countries have different traditions. For example, the Netherlands and the United Kingdom have a relatively well-developed planning system on various spatial scales, whereas, for example, Italy and Greece have systems that enable many 'degrees of freedom'.

Regarding the objectives of spatial planning for the collectivisation of transport and reduction of transport needs, much research has focused on the relationship between urban form and passenger transport. Urban form in this context means size and density, i.e. where the interdependent workplaces and dwellings are located within the metropolitan area (see for example Banister and Watson, 1994; ECMT and OECD, 1995; Wegener, forthcoming). One of the major conclusions so far is that several higher density cities are associated with a high use of public transport and with low gasoline consumption (Newman and Kenworthy, 1989), but it should be noted that these findings cannot easily be generalised. The environmental and energy benefits of compact cities depend to a large extent on the size and structure of incoming and outgoing commuting flows, as well as on the location of workplaces; also, from an economic perspective, changes in land prices ought to be considered: therefore an unambiguous answer is often impossible.

A powerful barrier to the adoption of a new transport technology appears to be the spatial inertia of the built environment and of infrastructure networks. Artefacts following from land use, such as housing blocks, industrial estates and transport infrastructure, have a long life-cycle in relation to the capital investment involved. As a result, different types of land use are fixed for a number of decades. So, once the infrastructure is built, it will be there for a long period (especially in historical city areas). As a consequence, technologies which imply step by step (incremental) or small-scale change may have a better chance of adoption in the urban territory than technologies implying radical change of infrastructure and land use.

Other factors influencing urban transport

Although the intricate relationship between transport and spatial organisation is widely recognised, other driving factors that are critical for the future of the urban transport system may also be distinguished (Rienstra *et al.*, forthcoming). In this section we will briefly outline such factors.

Economic and institutional factors

In recent years a marked shift in emphasis towards economic principles can be observed for combined transportation, environment and spatial policy. In spatial planning a trend in favour of abolishing planning systems can be found, because government intervention is considered to be less effective and less acceptable in society (Fokkema and Nijkamp, 1994). Due to the trends discussed earlier however, it is questionable whether the compact city could come into existence without a strict governmental planning policy.

In transport policy various user charge principles are increasingly being discussed and implemented; these include road pricing, toll principles, parking fees and perhaps, in the long term, even tradable permits. These measures mainly affect car transport, and may stimulate the use of public transport.

However, there is also a trend to abolish unjustified and unnecessary protectionist or privileged regulations in order to increase the efficiency of transport operations. In this respect there is increasing focus on the efficiency and profitability of, for example, public urban transport companies (Nijkamp and Rienstra, 1995); in many UK cities the public bus companies have been privatised, which has had an enormous impact on the way the bus network is operated. In this way the profitability of links and of the total network - and as a result, spatial threshold factors - of public transport modes have become more important. These factors are concerned with the minimum volume of passengers, between given points, that are necessary for a collective transport mode to be in operation and for it to be feasible from an economic perspective. In this respect, barriers to adoption arise when spatial threshold (minimum) levels of demand for collective modes are not reached, for example, due to a low population density. Spatial upper level factors are different, in that they are associated with a particular type of vehicle and the maximum distance it can bridge. Barriers may arise when the transport distance needed exceeds the critical upper level of the spatial range of the transport mode in question.

A major disadvantage of public transport in urban areas is the waiting time; because of the short distances involved, travelling time is largely dependent on waiting times. The poor competitive position of public transport *vis-à-vis* the private car may be shown for example by figures in the Netherlands: 40% of all car trips are for distances below 5km, while this figure is only 16% for all public transport trips (calculations based on Central Bureau of Statistics, 1994). Consequently, the frequency (and reliability) of vehicles is very important to make the system competitive with the car, but for this again a high level of demand is necessary for profitability.

Another way in which collective systems may be distinguished from individual ones concerns their dependence on supplementary transport systems. Travelling by collective modes is inter-modal by nature, while individual modes offer door-to-door transport. This makes the functioning of collective modes dependent on the level of connectivity with other transport systems (including walking and cycling) that offer transport to and from the nodes. Co-ordination problems between different modes therefore may be an important factor in the failure of collective transport.

The compact city, in which voluminous transport flows occur between the compact city centre and its sub-centres, could therefore be a vital precondition if public transport modes are to be successful. However, socio-psychological factors also play an important role.

Socio-psychological factors

The private car appears to be psychologically very important, because of the pleasure, privacy, personal control and representativeness it can offer (Vlek and Michon, 1992). People may perceive the same benefits for diffuse life patterns; living conditions in compact urban areas may be considered to be worse than in more diffuse cities.

Another problem for collectivisation of transport is that the behaviour of individuals is hard to change, particularly while the disbenefits of other transport options are difficult to perceive, and while there is community resistance to the construction of large-scale infrastructure in cities with little space. Subterranean construction may be an (expensive) solution to the latter obstruction. Large-scale measures to reduce car traffic in cities may not be socially acceptable. On this point it should be added that, in democratic countries, governments will not introduce measures which contrast greatly with public opinion (Rietveld, 1995). Therefore, a change in attitude would first have to occur before the policies discussed above could successfully be introduced.

It may be concluded that a more compact city would be preferable for the collectivisation of urban transport, but that it is questionable whether such a policy could succeed, because of other factors. Therefore, it is of interest to investigate the views of transportation experts on the future of urban spatial organisation and the transport system. This will be the subject of the next section.

Expert opinions on the compact city and the future of urban transport

To investigate the future of urban transport a postal questionnaire survey was sent to Dutch transportation experts. For a detailed description and account of the questionnaire we refer to Nijkamp *et al.* (forthcoming); here we note only that the response rate was 36% (271 questionnaires), and that the response gave a representative picture of the sample. The main subject of the survey was the future of urban transport in relation to spatial organisation. In the questionnaire, respondents were asked to indicate both expected and desired future developments in transport; this was in order to analyse the discrepancy between reality and desire, and to give the descriptive and normative opinion on future developments.

Expected and desired spatial and modal split developments

Expected spatial developments at the urban scale

At the urban level it is expected, by 44% of the respondents, that there will be moderately compact urban development, or, in other words, that the policy to achieve more compact cities will largely succeed (see Fig. 1). As a result, the trend towards 'green suburbs' will generally be halted. It is striking that only 14% expect a more diffuse spatial organisation, a proportion which is surprisingly small in view of recent trends.

Next, it is of interest to assess how the expected spatial developments are related to the modal split. Most respondents expect the modal split to change in favour of the private car, while about one third think that it will change in favour of public transport, or that no increase in car use will occur. A cross-tabulation analysis shows that only the segment which expects a development towards a compact city also thinks a shift in the modal share may occur in favour of collective modes. However, the majority expect the modal split to change in favour of the private car.

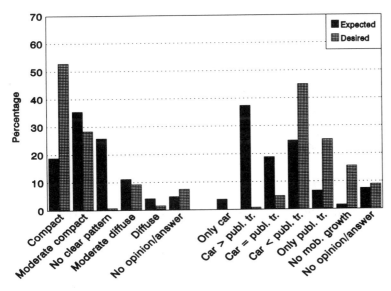

Fig. 1. The expected and desired urban spatial organisation and the resulting change in the modal split (n=271).

Desired developments at the urban scale

When the desired changes are analysed, a majority of the experts are in favour of a compact urban structure, while a large minority would wish to see a moderately compact organisation. Only a small group think that a (moderate) diffuse spatial organisation is desirable. Concerning the resulting changes in the modal split, it appears that 94% of respondents favour a shift towards public transport. Many respondents are also in support of a growth in car mobility, but a large group wish there to be no mobility growth and only growth in public transport. Cross tabulations reveal that in general the same trends as found for expected developments can be identified.

The resulting transport system

The experts were asked to give scores for expected and desired changes, on a 1 to 10 scale (a rating system which is common in the Netherlands) for policy measures, existing transport modes and the potential for new modes. The results are outlined below.

Expected and desired policy measures

The expert views on future urban transport are depicted in Fig. 2. The highest score for expected policy measures is for an increase in parking levies which may make the use of private cars less attractive. The second highest score is for a reduction of the number of parking spaces, which is expected to be introduced to a smaller extent than an increase in parking levies. Road pricing is not expected to be introduced on a large scale.

The scores for desired measures are all higher than for expected ones, although for parking levies this score is just a little higher. It is still the highest score however, with a reduction of the number of parking spaces in second place. The new technology of road pricing also gets a much higher score, so it may be concluded that experts believe this option should be introduced on a reasonable scale. As expected, the standard deviation of this measure is the highest, which means that the experts disagree most on this measure. Other policy measures which are mentioned by the respondents are: changing the spatial organisation, park and ride systems, and car sharing ('call a car').

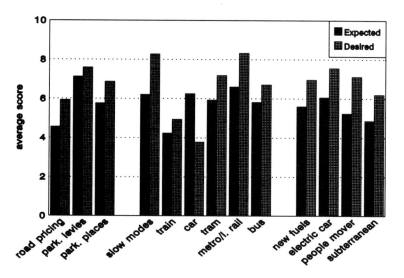

Fig. 2. The average scores on measures and modes in the urban transport system. Score 1 - 10; 1 is lowest, 10 is highest (n = 254-266).

Expected and desired use of conventional modes

The scores given by the experts on the expected use of conventional modes of transport all (except for the train) fluctuate around 6. The highest score is assigned to metro and light rail systems, which are expected to be introduced on a larger scale than is the case now. This situation is fairly likely, since for example in several Dutch cities (Amsterdam, Rotterdam) new links are under construction. For the remainder, the car and slow modes (cycling, walking) are given the next highest scores, while the bus and tram get somewhat lower scores. It seems plausible that the score for the train is somewhat lower since this mode is not primarily used for urban transport, although it is sometimes used as an urban mass transit system.

When the scores for desired changes are analysed, all modes are given higher scores, except the private car, which is plausible because of the strongly negative external effects of this mode. The slow modes and metro or light rail in particular receive very high scores of above 8, implying that the modal split in urban traffic should change in favour of these modes. Also the tram and bus receive relatively high scores, while the score for the private car is below 4; a much lower modal share is regarded as desirable for the conventional car.

Expected and desired use of new modes and technologies

Respondents were also asked to assign scores for several new technologies and modes which might be introduced before the year 2030. The highest score for expected change is found for electric cars, although this score is only about 6, which means that large-scale introduction is not expected. The second highest score is for new fuels (for example, liquid hydrogen), which implies again an improvement in the position of the private car. The people mover has a fairly low score, while subterranean transport is only expected to be introduced on a small scale. So, in summary, improvements of the private car are likely to be introduced, while other developments have far less chance of success, in the opinion of experts.

The scores for desired changes are all higher than for expected changes. Thus, the experts do not expect the introduction of new modes and technologies to happen to the extent they would like. The electric car is again awarded the highest score, followed by the people mover. In addition, somewhat higher - but nevertheless low - scores are given to the introduction of new fuels and subterranean transport by car and train. Other modes mentioned by the experts are passenger transport by water, improved human-powered vehicles and the electric bicycle.

Conclusions

From the results discussed above, it may be concluded that the private car and its improved versions are still expected to dominate the urban transport system in the future (although various policy measures may be introduced to make the car less attractive). It appears that the experts expect this to occur even though they believe that the urban spatial organisation will become more compact.

In the desired situation however, there would be a greater emphasis on collective modes, while more and severe measures would be introduced to make the car less attractive as the dominant mode. These developments would be favoured in a situation where the organisation of urban space is more compact.

Conclusions

In theory there is a clear positive relationship between concentrated spatial form and collectivisation of the transport system. In practice however, problems may occur in achieving both a more compact spatial urban pattern and a modal shift towards collective modes. For both possibilities, it is clear that current trends - like the abolition of spatial planning and the deregulation and privatisation of the public transport sector - will have to change drastically. Also, socio-psychological factors may have to change, or else it will not be feasible to introduce such changes, due to lack of support from the public.

In this respect it is interesting that most Dutch transportation experts expect compact city policies to be fairly successful. Apparently, they think the trade-off between preferable environmental conditions and living conditions will be in favour of the former. However, at the same time it is not expected that a modal shift in the urban transport system will occur to a great extent. The experts believe that only the introduction of metro or light rail systems will be significant, while the only new technology will be the electric car. If these expectations become reality, congestion in urban areas may increase greatly and most externalities will not be reduced.

In the desirable world of the Dutch transportation experts however, the compact city would be introduced, accompanied by a large-scale modal shift towards collective modes and new transport technologies. It is clear, however, that for this to happen, many current trends would have to be modified and turned in a more environmentally sustainable direction.

It is evident that a clear and consistent policy package is a *sine qua non* for collectivising urban transport. Such a package may consist of strict land use and development control policies; an increase in fuel prices; the introduction of telematics; stimulating integrated commuting strategies by employers; large-scale investment in public transport; improvements in the efficiency and attractiveness of public transport; and the stimulation of walking and cycling (see also ECMT and OECD, 1995). Such a policy package, however, may meet a lot of resistance in society and it will therefore be difficult to implement in any consistent way.

It may be concluded that policies aimed at achieving a compact city together with collectivisation of transport - which may lead to the fulfilment of sustainability criteria - are possible and even desirable. The introduction of such policies, however, will be faced with severe difficulties from all sides.

References

Banister, D. and Watson, S. (1994) *Energy Use in Transport and City Structure*, Planning and Development Research Centre, University College, London.

Breheny, M. (forthcoming) Counter-urbanisation and Sustainable Urban Forms, in *Cities in Competition: The Emergence of Productive and Sustainable Cities for the 21st Century* (eds Brotchie, J., Batty, M., Hall, P. and Newton, P.) Longman Cheshire, Melbourne.

Central Bureau of Statistics (1994) *De Mobiliteit van de Nederlandse Bevolking 1993*, CBS-no. N8, Voorburg/Heerlen.

European Conference of Ministers of Transport and Organisation for Economic Co-operation and Development (1995) *Urban Travel and Sustainable Development*, Paris.

Fokkema, T. and Nijkamp, P. (1994) The changing role of governments: the end of planning history? *International Journal of Transport Economics*, **21 (2)**, pp.127-45.

Masser, I., Svidén, O. and Wegener, M. (1992) *The Geography of Europe's Futures*, Belhaven Press, London.

Newman, P.W.G. and Kenworthy, J.F. (1989) Gasoline consumption and cities; a comparison of US cities with a global survey. *Journal of the American Planning Association*, **55 (1)**, pp.24-37.

Nijkamp, P. and Rienstra, S.A. (1995) Private sector involvement in financing and operating transport infrastructure. *Annals of Regional Science*, **29 (2)**, pp.221-235.

Nijkamp, P., Rienstra, S.A. and Vleugel, J.M. (forthcoming) *Sustainable Transport; an Expert Based Scenario Approach*, Kluwer, Boston.

Organisation for Economic Co-operation and Development (1995) *Urban Energy Handbook; Good Local Practice, OECD,* Paris.

Owens, S. (1992) Energy, environmental sustainability and land use planning, in *Sustainable Development and Urban Form* (ed. M. Breheny, M.) pp.79-105, Pion, London.

Rienstra, S.A., Vleugel, J.M. and Nijkamp, P. (forthcoming) Options for Sustainable Passenger Transport; an Assessment of Policy Choices. *Transportation Planning and Technology.*

Rietveld, P. (1995) Political economy issues of environmentally friendly transport policies, paper presented at the VSB-Symposium on *Transport and the Global Environment,* February 9 and 10, Amsterdam.

Verhoef, E.T. (1994) External and social costs of road transport. *Transportation Research,* **28A (4),** pp.273-287.

Vlek, C. and Michon, J.A. (1992) Why we should and how we could decrease the use of motor vehicles in the near future. *IATTS-Research,* **15 (2),** pp.82-93.

Vleugel, J.M. (1995) *Milieugebruiksruimte voor Duurzaam Verkeer en Vervoer; een Analyse van de Toepasbaarheid voor Beleid,* ITL-publication no. 21, Delft University Press, Delft.

Wegener, M. (forthcoming) Reduction of CO_2 emissions of transport by reorganisation of urban activities, in *Transport, Land Use and the Environment,* (eds Hayashi, Y. and Roy, J.R.) Kluwer, Dordrecht.

Patrick N. Troy
Environmental Stress and Urban Policy

Introduction

Modern cities are inherently ecologically unsustainable because they need to import food, energy and raw materials; they produce more waste than they can cope with within their boundaries; and they radically change the ecology of their sites. The larger the concentration of population the less sustainable it is. Even if we extend the boundary of the city to include its hinterland we cannot usefully describe it as potentially ecologically sustainable. The more the city becomes part of the international economic order the less it can be seen as 'ecologically sustainable' in any operational sense.

The low density form of traditional Australian cities has recently come under attack as the antithesis of the sustainable urban form promoted by the compact city advocates. As a response to increasing environmental stress and concern about the profligate waste and consumption of urban sprawl, 'consolidation policies' are being introduced. These policies are in effect the realisation of the compact city concept.

This chapter examines the sustainability of Australian cities in terms of environmental issues. It critically assesses proposals to change city form as a way of reducing urban environmental stress, and discusses how policy options might be better considered. Environmental stress in Australian cities is made up of a variety of components. For each component, the following will be discussed:

- the issues, problems and concerns for sustainability
- potential solutions to the problems, particularly in terms of urban policy
- the significance of consolidation policies, or urban density, in ameliorating or exacerbating the problems

Water consumption and drainage

The growth of the major cities and the increase in per capita consumption of water has reached the point where there is a crisis in the capacity to meet the demand. The high variability of rainfall in Australia has led urban water authorities to build dams and water storages capable of holding enough water to sustain urban areas for long periods.

The profligate attitude to water consumption has had the effect of creating a serious problem of drainage in urban areas. As areas become more built-up, the volume of water draining off can cause acute local flooding and can also cause massive pollution in the receiving waterways because of the material transported by the surface water. Sewage from residential areas is relatively benign but, when mixed with water-borne wastes from industry and commerce, produces a waste stream which can be difficult to process. The volume of sewage produced in large cities and discharged to the ocean through a small number of outfalls may also lead to high point sources of pollution which exceed the local capacity of the ocean to receive the wastes, leading to local destruction of the ecosystem. The high volumes discharged may also lead to wastes being washed up on local beaches, destroying their amenity and presenting local health hazards.

The compact city concentrates the population in one area, which has the effect of concentrating demand for water supply and drainage; local problems may therefore be more acute. With more impervious surfaces and hard standing, drainage is more difficult, and increased development begins to preclude the operation of natural drainage.

An important key to improving sustainability would be to reduce consumption through education and consequent moderation of the behaviour of present residential, industrial and commercial water-users. This could be aided through pricing strategies, particularly for industrial users. Education programmes have proved to be successful with residential users, but less so for industrial and commercial users; for this group a combination of enforcement of regulations and pricing signals is more effective. Pricing water and sewerage appropriately has led to a dramatic reduction in water consumption for industry and commerce.

In addition consumption could be reduced further through on-site recycling. Residents can be encouraged to install tanks to store rain for domestic consumption. New housing can be constructed to harvest rain water for domestic uses and to make better use of recycled water for toilet flushing and so on. The gardens and dwellings are then designed to reduce water use. The sewerage system could be redeveloped to encourage the use of 'dry' sewage systems or local treatment plants using new technologies in such a way that most of the treated effluent could be recycled for use in the same area.

Drainage demands can be minimised by adopting the principle of natural drainage. This new approach to design requires a new approach to paving and hard standing. Roads and footpaths would be designed to be less impervious so that they shed less of the water which falls on them, or shed it in such a way that it is directed into public and private gardens and ponds, and its run-off is slowed. The major benefit of the alternative approach would flow both from the reduced need for large scale investment in dams, trunk mains and pumping systems, and from a reduction in the load on the existing systems.

Because of the concentrated demand and lack of impervious surfaces, higher densities hinder rather than help the sustainability of water supply and drainage. Space is crucial in order to recycle and store water on-site and to install local treatment systems. Green space in the city would be particularly important for the integration of drainage channels and ponds. The traditional low density form of Australian cities favours sustainable drainage systems.

Gardening practices and food production

Gardening practices such as composting and mulching and home production of food could play a part in relieving environmental stress in cities. The potential of gardens has largely been ignored in arguments for consolidation.

Food production should be encouraged in order to make cities more sustainable and to reduce pressure for monocultural developments in agriculture and slow the clearance of more natural bushland. Incentives might include removing regulatory barriers and creating, encouraging or promoting local seed exchanges, and the local exchange, marketing or bartering of surplus production. Encouraging better husbandry and gardening practices, including the use on site of mulch and composted household and garden wastes, would save water and reduce drainage.

Tree and shrub planting, especially of 'natives', would help cool the environment in summer, help cope with air pollution and provide habitats for birds and other fauna. Urban plantations might also be developed to provide fuel for space heating. Although this would increase air pollution in the short run, the fact that it is a renewable resource opens the possibility of a fuel demand and supply equilibrium which is closer to neutral in its impact on the environment than the present reliance on fossil fuels. In any event, the use of new efficient combustion chambers for wood-burning space heaters rather than open fires will reduce air pollution.

The application of natural drainage principles to the design of residential estates and the adoption of grouped housing development practices in which much of the private garden space is developed as communal garden space opens opportunities for new approaches to gardening and tree planting, including trees for fuel. Residential development can be designed to facilitate mulching, composting, recycling of water and reduced run-off while creating high quality space.

Consolidation, or intensification, of urban areas would inevitably lead to a reduction in garden sizes and an increase in the number of dwellings without gardens. The potential benefits from both private and communal gardening call into question the advisability of these new policies. Conversely, the traditional form of Australian cities is well suited to a renewed emphasis on the role of gardening and food production.

Waste management

Local authorities have developed community collection and disposal systems based on the use of landfill sites. The cost of coping with wastes using the traditional landfill processes will become increasingly expensive as sites become more difficult to find and higher standards are set to minimise the impact of waste disposal on the water table or on natural drainage catchments.

Analysis of the stream of domestic wastes suggests that recycling and composting can reduce the amount going to landfill sites by as much as 70%, greatly prolonging the life of current sites. A major benefit of this approach is that aerobic composting of this waste results in less environmental stress than disposal via landfill because the latter, after it is covered, occurs in anaerobic conditions resulting in the production of methane which is twenty-one times more damaging as a greenhouse gas than carbon dioxide. The significance of this is that landfill generation of methane has a greenhouse effect equivalent to approximately 40% of the carbon dioxide production of all transport. As the major portion of the source of methane from landfill sites is domestic and garden waste, the policy should be to encourage developments in which the private garden spaces are large enough to compost wastes on site. This would enable reduction in methane with the equivalent of up to, say, 20% of the carbon dioxide production of transport energy consumption which on current estimates exceeds the alleged energy savings resulting from increasing urban density. It should be noted that the carbon dioxide equivalent of agricultural production of methane, mostly from cattle and sheep, actually exceeds that from transport. Few proponents of consolidation consider a major change in our diet as a way of reducing urban environmental stress.

The streams of waste from commercial and industrial processes are more readily modified and reduced by redesign of the processes themselves. In many cases the establishments can more easily cope with their own wastes if they have space near their plant. The wastes from one industrial process may be the material inputs for another. Again, consolidation policies would not help.

The stream of wastes from the construction industry is a significant proportion of the wastes disposed of by landfill. Increasing proportions of materials from demolition of old buildings are now being recovered and recycled, but much more could be. Greater consideration of the energy costs of construction would lead to greater reuse of existing buildings, the construction of new buildings from less energy expensive materials, and the more efficient use of materials to reduce the flow of wastes.

The introduction of charges related to the volume and type of wastes collected from different types of development would make the population more aware of the costs of waste disposal and of its impact on the environment. Residents would be encouraged to separate out wastes which can be recovered and recycled, or composted and used for mulch on site, thus reducing the volume to be transported to tips. Therefore housing forms which allow residents to minimise the wastes transported from their property should be encouraged. Commercial and shopping centres can be developed with facilities which make it easier to separate and recycle materials. Industrial plant can be developed to reduce the waste stream by treating more of it on site.

Most areas of traditional residential development can cope with their own kitchen and garden wastes by composting but this is not a viable option for the great proportion of higher density housing. In a compact city industrial and commercial undertakings may find their sites too cramped to redesign their processes to reduce waste production or process it on site.

Noise pollution

Most urban activities result in noise: whether it be the busy hum of a factory; the hubbub of music and conversation from a cafe; the incessant driving beat of a disco; or, most commonly, the pervasively intrusive sounds of traffic. The amenity of an area may be affected by its ambient noise level, which is frequently that of the traffic passing through. Excessive noise levels may injuriously affect the health of residents.

There is little data relating to the ambient noise levels of different forms of development although it is clear that noise is one of the sources of friction among residents of higher density housing. Noise can reduce the privacy of an area. An area regarded as quiet, peaceful or tranquil is a positive feature. This condition is more likely to be found in traditional residential areas than in the compact city. The denser the development the more likely it is that the sounds of traffic, police sirens, fire engines and trains will be reflected and reverberate, producing the familiar noise of the city. Lower density development allows the sounds from the individual sources to attenuate without being intrusive.

Air pollution

One reason factories were and remain separated from residential areas is that many processes resulted in the release of particulates and gases which are offensive or toxic or both, even if they are not greenhouse gases. The dust and grit deposited on households from factory emissions may not be injurious to health, although some are, and some contribute to the greenhouse effect, but they add to the discomfort of life and the cost of cleanliness for those nearby. Higher density development, in which industrial or commercial processes are allowed in residential areas, increases the risk of such exposure.

A second source of air pollution is that which comes from the conscription of residents in the olfactory delights of neighbours' meals or activities. Invasions of privacy may be experienced by households living at higher densities when they can tell from the breeze that their neighbours are about to feast on some aromatic dish. Living near a restaurant or even a sidewalk cafe can result in exposure to aromas which all do not find pleasing all the time. These experiences are rare in traditional Australian housing but would be common in the type of high density, mixed use development promoted by the proponents of the compact city.

Energy consumption

Energy consumption is an important source of stress to the environment because it exacerbates the greenhouse effect. The greater proportion of the energy is consumed at fixed-point sites in the production or creation of the urban environment, in the operation of the city, and in mobile sources of consumption as its inhabitants pursue their interests and activities. About 36% of energy consumed is in the form of petroleum products. Although other important greenhouse gases are generated by energy consumption, this discussion is confined to consideration of carbon dioxide, which is taken as the indicator of total greenhouse gas emission. Renewable energy accounts for only 6% of Australian energy consumption, all of which is used at fixed points of consumption. The greater part of the 94% of non-renewable energy sources is consumed at fixed points.

A significant proportion of energy is used in the manufacture of building materials, their fabrication into components and fittings, and in the construction of buildings. The activity in the construction sectors is one of the main contributors to energy consumption and carbon dioxide emissions nationally (Tucker and Treloar, 1994). In addition to the embodied energy of a building a significant proportion of energy consumed in the construction phase is in the waste generated during construction.

Holland and Holland (1994) report that weatherboard houses embody one sixth the energy of brick veneer houses of the same thermal resistance and that timber framed houses 'store' 7.5 tonnes of carbon whereas steel framed houses release 2.9 tonnes to the atmosphere. That is, timber houses produce less environmental stress than houses using significant amounts of steel or bricks. Multi-storey housing is usually built from materials which are more energy expensive. Structural requirements and considerations of fire safety and privacy generally dictate the use of bricks, reinforced concrete and steel in buildings over two storeys. For buildings over three storeys only bricks, reinforced concrete or steel may be used, and their embodied energy may be higher than the energy required to operate them for their life. The embodied energy of high-rise housing is also likely to be very high relative to its operation because of the higher level of investment in fixtures and fittings. There are no ways to reduce the embodied energy of existing buildings so the focus of energy efficiency policy must be on new development and on the refurbishment of existing buildings.

More off-site fabrication of components and building elements can reduce wastage from off-cuts but the wastage is still significant. The strategy should be to encourage low embodied energy forms of housing and commercial buildings and to encourage methods of construction which minimise waste production. Pursuit of this suggests that clearing low-rise development to replace it with high density or high-rise buildings, which is implicit in consolidation policy, is not a policy directed at the reduction of environmental stress. Demolition of buildings which have not outlived their physical life should be regarded as an 'environmentally unfriendly' activity in the context of embodied energy and resultant carbon dioxide emissions (Tucker and Treloar, 1994). One environmentally friendly approach would be to return to more labour intensive methods of construction, including the use of stone. Traditional forms of low density housing are usually built from wood and clay bricks, or concrete blocks. They may be built from natural materials such as stone, rammed earth or wood which are relatively inexpensive in terms of embodied energy.

Energy is also consumed in the operation of the built environment, for space heating and cooling, lighting and water heating. Due to rising living standards energy consumption is constantly increasing. Buildings can be designed to take better account of the local climate for their space heating, cooling and lighting. In some regions this will require that they be designed to ensure maximum protection from the sun in summer, and to minimise the use of materials which increase the heat load on the building. They can also be designed to make maximum use of natural cooling and ventilation. In other regions where buildings must be heated in winter they can be oriented to trap as much solar energy as possible. Appropriate design and siting as well as the use of appropriate materials in their construction can result in significant gains in efficiency through the passive heating of buildings. In some regions all the space heating needs of buildings can be met in this way.

In larger buildings, especially offices and larger apartment blocks, better energy management programs for the building as a whole can lead to significant energy savings. Similarly, better energy management and the redesign of manufacturing processes can result in savings.

Claims are made that the energy costs of the traditional form of housing are too high and that alternative higher density development would lead to great energy savings in the operation of dwellings. The implicit argument is that the form of housing affects the level of energy consumption. The validity of the claim depends on the way the occupants of different forms of housing use their dwellings and whether the demolition of the existing housing and its replacement with higher embodied energy dwellings is energy efficient. Household expenditure surveys reveal that expenditure on energy is greater for conventional houses than for high- or low-rise flats. When these figures are adjusted for household size, the relative order of expense changes, with the higher density housing being the more expensive per capita. Households with higher income and wealth spend more on energy.

Separate houses consume more reticulated energy than medium density housing or flats but it is more likely to come from a wider variety of forms than in flats. High-rise flats are more likely to use electricity for all their energy needs whereas houses are more likely to use renewable sources such as wood and solar power for a significant proportion of their needs. Households in semi-detached housing (including terrace houses and town houses) spend nearly as much on energy as those in separate houses and it is again more likely to be as electricity or natural gas. But the fact that households spend so little of their income on fuel and power, 2.6% compared with 3.4% on alcoholic beverages and 15.1% on transport, suggests that they would be loath to spend large sums on altering their dwellings to achieve greater energy efficiency. This could change if energy prices were increased.

Offices cannot function without the continuous consumption of large amounts of energy for heating, cooling and air-conditioning. Moreover, they need a lot of energy to operate lifts. For a variety of reasons, including safety, high-rise buildings whether for offices or residences can use only the more expensive forms of energy for their operation. Safety, convenience and local air pollution considerations mean that the major energy source in the form of electricity rather than say, coal, oil or gas may be used in their operation, but this form of energy is the most expensive in terms of its global environmental impact.

It is clear that lower density development is more likely to be able to meet its energy needs using renewable sources such as wood and solar energy than higher density development. Furthermore lower density development is more likely to be able to maximise advantages from orientation and design, and from energy reductions due to garden space.

Transport and communication

The second major use of energy in cities is in transport. The use of the motor car has become the major environmental consideration in the debate over urban form and, in particular, the compact city. The focus of urban policy has been to try to moderate demand for travel by changing the form of urban areas. The central problem on which commentators, activists and politicians should focus is the pollution resulting from the operation of internal combustion engines. Of the petroleum products used in Australia about 61% are consumed in the road transport sector; this is about 22% of total energy consumption. About 60% of all road travel in Victoria is in the Melbourne metropolitan area. One third of all road travel in Australia is for business and approximately one half of this is by car. About 23% of all travel by road is for journeys to or from work, that is, commuter travel, with more than a quarter of all car travel being for that purpose. In all, about 57% of road travel could be regarded as consumption potentially influenced by urban form.

Assuming that the distribution of road travel is similar in the city to that in the way urban systems are developed and managed. The issue is more complex and problematic than contemporary urban policy appears to recognise. A full accounting of the social and environmental consequences of the form and structure of Australian cities and the way they are serviced would suggest a change in policy over the directions which have been taken. Increasing housing density:

- decreases capacity to cope with domestic wastes and reduces opportunities for recycling
- reduces capacity to harvest or otherwise cope with the rainfall on urban areas and reduce run-off
- makes it harder for urban residents to produce much of their own food
- increases air pollution because it reduces space for growth of trees and shrubs that purify the air and cool the urban area
- reduces chances of growth of wood for fuel, and reduces habitats for birds and other native fauna
- increases congestion, which increases accidents and energy losses

In addition, the reduction in energy consumption in housing thought to be associated with increased residential density is more apparent than real. The paradox is that even if increased density leads to reduced energy consumption, which is an environmental benefit, it is offset by the environmental deterioration experienced in other parts or elements of the urban system.

Australian cities are faced with some significant problems not the least of which are the environmental stresses to which they are subjected. The primary cause of environmental stress is the number of people behaving in a way that undervalues the external environmental costs of their actions. The strategic objective must be to reduce the number of people behaving in this way. The question is: which mechanism is likely to most readily achieve it? A tactical response would be to develop policy which is based on an assessment of its likely effect on achieving the objective. Changes in behaviour are notoriously slow but can be speeded up by the adoption of new technology.

Changes in approaches to the design, construction and use of buildings are slow whereas changes in technology used in production of equipment such as cars can be much faster. Even if all new dwellings were built to reflect the current concern over energy consumption it would take a long time to obtain substantial reductions in stress because the rate of change in the housing stock is very slow (additions to the stock are about 1.5% per annum); furthermore, houses have very long lives. Modifications to existing houses could slightly speed up the rate of change and therefore savings of energy and water consumption. Changes to other dwelling types are harder to make and result in smaller savings. Changes to the sources of power of cars can have greater effect. New technology can be quickly introduced and lead to a significant reduction in energy consumption, though it takes at least a decade to replace the fleet of cars.

Energy reductions due to changes in city form are even harder to achieve and slower to introduce because they are directed at the physical outcomes of a complex set of economic and social processes but not the processes themselves. Moreover, reductions are hard to relate to urban form because the energy intensity of urban living is falling, that is the gross domestic product per unit of energy consumed in urban areas has been increasing over time. Total energy consumption may be

Australia as a whole and that the greenhouse gases generated per kilometre of travel are the same for all vehicle types (trucks and buses generate more than cars, and motor cycles less), journeys to and from work in the cities by road are estimated to be responsible for about 3.4% of total carbon dioxide production. This gives an upper estimate of the reduction in greenhouse gas (carbon dioxide) emission which theoretically could be obtained by transferring all journeys to or from work in the city by road transport to some alternative form of transport. This is a crude estimate because, even if it was desirable and could be achieved, the alternative modes of transport other than walking or cycling would also consume energy - usually leading to the production of greenhouse gases.

What would be the attitude to the car if it was powered by a non-polluting form of power? Few would argue against its undeniable attractions although some might still hold that for reasons of community its use for private travel should be discouraged. The recent history of the car indicates that it has improved in efficiency dramatically over the last 20 years. As car ownership levels off and as the vehicle fleet continues to become more efficient with present technology, Australia will experience a fall in its greenhouse gas emissions from cars. New forms of motive power can be expected to produce even lower emissions.

Communities should endeavour to find ways of pursuing their interests and activities in ways which minimise environmental stress. Stress from the kinds of technologies employed in transport should not be ignored in this endeavour. The question is: how can a community pursue its interests and retain the freedom to travel when and where its members wish without creating environmental stress? Trying to limit choices of when and where to travel cannot be successful. Some technologies such as tele-commuting can reduce work travel but because people are social creatures they have a strong need for a high level of interaction with others, to 'know' their environment and develop a familiarity with their cities. To the extent that tele-commuting becomes more widespread and people spend more time working in and from their homes, they will want more space both in and around their homes to make themselves more comfortable. An increase in tele-commuting would weaken the argument for consolidation because it would tend to reduce the need to commute to city centres.

The author is not proposing a technologically determined solution to the problem of environmental stress associated with the present form of motive power in cars. But with the right kinds of social pressures allied with appropriate market responses greenhouse gases can be reduced without changing the form of Australian cities.

One response to the amount of energy consumed by transport would be to try to reshape the demand by relocating destinations. The first and most obvious initiative would be to try to harness the processes which are already occurring in urban areas, and develop them as 'sets' of connected centres. Ideally, these centres would be connected by a well developed, public transport system (not necessarily fixed rail). The decentralisation of retailing, commerce and public administration would also need to be accompanied by a cultural development policy which ensured that investment in cultural and recreational facilities were developed in and as part of each of the centres.

Another way to encourage the development of sub-centres would be to introduce pricing and regulatory policies designed to shorten trips or to discourage them from the central business district and focus them on suburban centres. Prices would be set by the communities which bear the costs of congestion and the responsibility for investing in roads, and could be expected to result in changes to the location decisions of individuals and firms. Areas within cities and regions which had low levels of use and congestion would have lower road prices, which would tend to attract development away from areas and regions with high levels of cost and congestion and therefore higher prices.

If households can satisfy their needs for mobility by organising the distribution of their destinations so that they have wide choices in employment, commercial, cultural and recreational activities close to where they live they would have less need to travel. But this is the paradox which many policy-makers fail to recognise. Enhanced mobility gives people greater access to a wider range of interests and activities and allows them a higher degree of engagement with other like-minded members of the various communities to which they belong, thus enriching their lives and contributing to social and economic vitality. The notion that people will be prepared to accept a circumscription in their range of interests by confining their travel to public transport or only to those activities they can reach close to their homes is a fundamental misunderstanding of their desires and their willingness to bear the cost of satisfying those desires, reflected in the fact that they spend such a high proportion of their income on transport. But it is still worth providing opportunities close to where people live and charging them for the full cost of their travel. Both will have some impact on the volume of travel.

The policy of consolidation is often justified on the grounds that it reduces the journey to work and, by implication, air pollution. It is also predicated on the assumption that more of these journeys would be transferred from private cars to public transport. None of the proponents of the policy make any estimate of the reduction in the length of journey to or from work which they claim would follow from consolidation nor do they provide any estimate of the reduction in greenhouse gases which they claim would follow from transfer from cars to public transport. That is, they provide no estimate of the reductions in 'essential' transport energy consumption which they claim would arise from a change in urban form.

In reviewing the plethora of studies designed to show how increasing the density of urban areas would reduce travel, Breheny (1992) came to the conclusion that it would not.

Attempts to limit the use of the car would seriously affect the way business is conducted. It would seriously affect the way goods and materials are transported and services provided. Further developments in information technology will lead to more business being conducted or arranged without personal meetings but it is inconceivable that modern business can be conducted without some form of private transport. The organisation of production, the close connection between production and retailing together with the organisation of the entry and distribution of imports and the collection and assembly of exports now relies to a large extent on the transport by road of goods and services. It is inconceivable that Australian cities can now be operated without a major and efficient road transport system.

A high proportion of local employment is by local people so that we cannot expect a great reduction of work trips without a massive change in the distribution of jobs. There is no indication that we can expect such a rearrangement of employment, nor, given the benefits of separating industrial and much commercial activity from residential areas, should policy be directed to achieve it. Increasing

density is unlikely to affect the employment distribution or the propensity of people to travel to work by public transport. Furthermore, most of the debate over travel focuses on journeys to and from work yet more than half of all travel by cars is for 'private' trips - for cultural, recreational and shopping activities.

Proponents of consolidation argue that people should be encouraged to live at higher densities so that their transport needs can be more efficiently met by public transport. They argue that trips by public transport use less energy than by cars. When the comparisons are adjusted to account for system energy consumption and occupancy rates, the differences are minimal. Public transport services have been of reducing significance in the operation of the Australian city, meeting the trip needs of fewer people. Fixed track services are radially oriented and as the proportion of jobs in central areas continues to fall they cater for a smaller proportion of trips. Publicly provided transport is heavily subsidised yet serves only a small proportion of the population. The environmental argument for public transport is weak and those who interpret a commitment for it in terms of fixed rail systems ignore both the way the cities operate and the wants of their citizens.

In summary, the arguments that consolidation would reduce environmental stress from transport, through a reduction in travel demand and increased public transport use, have been shown to be weak and in some cases, misconstrued. Moreover, the compact city would increase congestion, and increased fuel inefficiency, energy losses and transport accidents would ensue.

Energy production

Much of the debate over energy has focused on its consumption in urban areas but we should also be concerned about the environmental impact of its production. The most significant sources of energy in terms of their increase in stress on the environment are: coal, which is mostly converted to electrical energy; gas, which is mostly used for heating; and petroleum products, a high proportion of which is used for transport. Although its consumption occurs largely in urban areas, electrical energy is usually produced at distant locations on or near the coal fields. The conversion of coal into electrical energy occurs at a relatively low level of efficiency: the process of winning the coal, burning it, converting water to steam, steam to mechanical energy and mechanical energy to electricity is very inefficient. More losses occur in transmitting electricity from the point of generation to its point of use. The overall system has a very low level of efficiency, which means that electricity generated in coal-fired power stations is costly in terms of environmental stress.

The extraction of gas and its transportation to the point of consumption incurs little loss of energy and therefore results in little environmental stress. The production of petroleum products involves the refining of crude petroleum and results in significant energy loss, which almost invariably occurs in or close to the major urban areas in which the products are consumed. Denser forms of urban development rely on greater consumption of electrical energy, which is not only more expensive in money terms but because of the low efficiency in its production and distribution is more expensive in terms of total energy consumption and therefore in its contribution to greenhouse gas production.

Summary

The focus on ecologically sustainable development raises serious questions about increasing but it is being used more efficiently.

While the strategy must be the modification of private and public behaviour of people, the tactics should be to focus on those elements which are most amenable to change and on those elements which have a high rate of depreciation. The strategy should be to ensure the provision of more and better information and the encouragement of a more open debate on urban issues. It should also be to introduce more appropriate pricing of a variety of urban services as a means of changing behaviour. Physically determinist policies such as the present consolidation policy are least likely to achieve the tactical response desired by the politicians or the strategic objective of more equitable, efficient and environmentally least stressed urban areas.

The Australian city has inherited a form which reflects its cultural and political values and which, it turns out, offers the best chance of meeting equity, efficiency and newly recognised environmental targets. The form may well be the accidental or felicitous outcome of historical processes but the policy should now be to intentionally preserve and develop it.

References

Breheny, M. (ed.) (1992) *Sustainable Development and Urban Form*, Pion, London.

Holland, G. and Holland, I. (1994) *Difficult Decisions About Ordinary Things: Being Ecologically Responsible About Timber Framing*, paper presented to Urban Research Program Seminar, Research School of Social Sciences, Australian National University, Canberra.

Tucker, S. N. and Treloar, G. J. (1994) Energy embodied in construction and refurbishment of buildings. *Buildings and Environment*, Proceedings of the First International Conference, Building Research Establishment, Watford, UK.

increasing but it is being used more efficiently.

While the strategy must be the modification of private and public behaviour of people, the tactics should be to focus on those elements which are most amenable to change and on those elements which have a high rate of depreciation. The strategy should be to ensure the provision of more and better information and the encouragement of a more open debate on urban issues. It should also be to introduce more appropriate pricing of a variety of urban services as a means of changing behaviour. Physically determinist policies such as the present consolidation policy are least likely to achieve the tactical response desired by the politicians or the strategic objective of more equitable, efficient and environmentally least stressed urban areas.

The Australian city has inherited a form which reflects its cultural and political values and which, it turns out, offers the best chance of meeting equity, efficiency and newly recognised environmental targets. The form may well be the accidental or felicitous outcome of historical processes but the policy should now be to intentionally preserve and develop it.

References

Breheny, M. (ed.) (1992) *Sustainable Development and Urban Form*, Pion, London.

Holland, G. and Holland, I. (1994) *Difficult Decisions About Ordinary Things: Being Ecologically Responsible About Timber Framing*, paper presented to Urban Research Program Seminar, Research School of Social Sciences, Australian National University, Canberra.

Tucker, S. N. and Treloar, G. J. (1994) Energy embodied in construction and refurbishment of buildings. *Buildings and Environment*, Proceedings of the First International Conference, Building Research Establishment, Watford, UK.

Australia as a whole and that the greenhouse gases generated per kilometre of travel are the same for all vehicle types (trucks and buses generate more than cars, and motor cycles less), journeys to and from work in the cities by road are estimated to be responsible for about 3.4% of total carbon dioxide production. This gives an upper estimate of the reduction in greenhouse gas (carbon dioxide) emission which theoretically could be obtained by transferring all journeys to or from work in the city by road transport to some alternative form of transport. This is a crude estimate because, even if it was desirable and could be achieved, the alternative modes of transport other than walking or cycling would also consume energy - usually leading to the production of greenhouse gases.

What would be the attitude to the car if it was powered by a non-polluting form of power? Few would argue against its undeniable attractions although some might still hold that for reasons of community its use for private travel should be discouraged. The recent history of the car indicates that it has improved in efficiency dramatically over the last 20 years. As car ownership levels off and as the vehicle fleet continues to become more efficient with present technology, Australia will experience a fall in its greenhouse gas emissions from cars. New forms of motive power can be expected to produce even lower emissions.

Communities should endeavour to find ways of pursuing their interests and activities in ways which minimise environmental stress. Stress from the kinds of technologies employed in transport should not be ignored in this endeavour. The question is: how can a community pursue its interests and retain the freedom to travel when and where its members wish without creating environmental stress? Trying to limit choices of when and where to travel cannot be successful. Some technologies such as tele-commuting can reduce work travel but because people are social creatures they have a strong need for a high level of interaction with others, to 'know' their environment and develop a familiarity with their cities. To the extent that tele-commuting becomes more widespread and people spend more time working in and from their homes, they will want more space both in and around their homes to make themselves more comfortable. An increase in tele-commuting would weaken the argument for consolidation because it would tend to reduce the need to commute to city centres.

The author is not proposing a technologically determined solution to the problem of environmental stress associated with the present form of motive power in cars. But with the right kinds of social pressures allied with appropriate market responses greenhouse gases can be reduced without changing the form of Australian cities.

One response to the amount of energy consumed by transport would be to try to reshape the demand by relocating destinations. The first and most obvious initiative would be to try to harness the processes which are already occurring in urban areas, and develop them as 'sets' of connected centres. Ideally, these centres would be connected by a well developed, public transport system (not necessarily fixed rail). The decentralisation of retailing, commerce and public administration would also need to be accompanied by a cultural development policy which ensured that investment in cultural and recreational facilities were developed in and as part of each of the centres.

Another way to encourage the development of sub-centres would be to introduce pricing and regulatory policies designed to shorten trips or to discourage them from the central business district and focus them on suburban centres. Prices would be set by the communities which bear the costs of congestion and the responsibility for investing in roads, and could be expected to result in changes to the location decisions of individuals and firms. Areas within cities and regions which had low levels of use and congestion would have lower road prices, which would tend to attract development away from areas and regions with high levels of cost and congestion and therefore higher prices.

If households can satisfy their needs for mobility by organising the distribution of their destinations so that they have wide choices in employment, commercial, cultural and recreational activities close to where they live they would have less need to travel. But this is the paradox which many policy-makers fail to recognise. Enhanced mobility gives people greater access to a wider range of interests and activities and allows them a higher degree of engagement with other like-minded members of the various communities to which they belong, thus enriching their lives and contributing to social and economic vitality. The notion that people will be prepared to accept a circumscription in their range of interests by confining their travel to public transport or only to those activities they can reach close to their homes is a fundamental misunderstanding of their desires and their willingness to bear the cost of satisfying those desires, reflected in the fact that they spend such a high proportion of their income on transport. But it is still worth providing opportunities close to where people live and charging them for the full cost of their travel. Both will have some impact on the volume of travel.

The policy of consolidation is often justified on the grounds that it reduces the journey to work and, by implication, air pollution. It is also predicated on the assumption that more of these journeys would be transferred from private cars to public transport. None of the proponents of the policy make any estimate of the reduction in the length of journey to or from work which they claim would follow from consolidation nor do they provide any estimate of the reduction in greenhouse gases which they claim would follow from transfer from cars to public transport. That is, they provide no estimate of the reductions in 'essential' transport energy consumption which they claim would arise from a change in urban form.

In reviewing the plethora of studies designed to show how increasing the density of urban areas would reduce travel, Breheny (1992) came to the conclusion that it would not.

Attempts to limit the use of the car would seriously affect the way business is conducted. It would seriously affect the way goods and materials are transported and services provided. Further developments in information technology will lead to more business being conducted or arranged without personal meetings but it is inconceivable that modern business can be conducted without some form of private transport. The organisation of production, the close connection between production and retailing together with the organisation of the entry and distribution of imports and the collection and assembly of exports now relies to a large extent on the transport by road of goods and services. It is inconceivable that Australian cities can now be operated without a major and efficient road transport system.

A high proportion of local employment is by local people so that we cannot expect a great reduction of work trips without a massive change in the distribution of jobs. There is no indication that we can expect such a rearrangement of employment, nor, given the benefits of separating industrial and much commercial activity from residential areas, should policy be directed to achieve it. Increasing density is unlikely to affect the employment distribution or the propensity of people to travel to work by public transport. Furthermore, most of the debate over travel focuses on journeys to and from work yet more than half of all travel by cars is for 'private' trips - for cultural, recreational and shopping activities.

Proponents of consolidation argue that people should be encouraged to live at higher densities so that their transport needs can be more efficiently met by public transport. They argue that trips by public transport use less energy than by cars. When the comparisons are adjusted to account for system energy consumption and occupancy rates, the differences are minimal. Public transport services have been of reducing significance in the operation of the Australian city, meeting the trip needs of fewer people. Fixed track services are radially oriented and as the proportion of jobs in central areas continues to fall they cater for a smaller proportion of trips. Publicly provided transport is heavily subsidised yet serves only a small proportion of the population. The environmental argument for public transport is weak and those who interpret a commitment for it in terms of fixed rail systems ignore both the way the cities operate and the wants of their citizens.

In summary, the arguments that consolidation would reduce environmental stress from transport, through a reduction in travel demand and increased public transport use, have been shown to be weak and in some cases, misconstrued. Moreover, the compact city would increase congestion, and increased fuel inefficiency, energy losses and transport accidents would ensue.

Energy production

Much of the debate over energy has focused on its consumption in urban areas but we should also be concerned about the environmental impact of its production. The most significant sources of energy in terms of their increase in stress on the environment are: coal, which is mostly converted to electrical energy; gas, which is mostly used for heating; and petroleum products, a high proportion of which is used for transport. Although its consumption occurs largely in urban areas, electrical energy is usually produced at distant locations on or near the coal fields. The conversion of coal into electrical energy occurs at a relatively low level of efficiency: the process of winning the coal, burning it, converting water to steam, steam to mechanical energy and mechanical energy to electricity is very inefficient. More losses occur in transmitting electricity from the point of generation to its point of use. The overall system has a very low level of efficiency, which means that electricity generated in coal-fired power stations is costly in terms of environmental stress.

The extraction of gas and its transportation to the point of consumption incurs little loss of energy and therefore results in little environmental stress. The production of petroleum products involves the refining of crude petroleum and results in significant energy loss, which almost invariably occurs in or close to the major urban areas in which the products are consumed. Denser forms of urban development rely on greater consumption of electrical energy, which is not only more expensive in money terms but because of the low efficiency in its production and distribution is more expensive in terms of total energy consumption and therefore in its contribution to greenhouse gas production.

Summary

The focus on ecologically sustainable development raises serious questions about the way urban systems are developed and managed. The issue is more complex and problematic than contemporary urban policy appears to recognise. A full accounting of the social and environmental consequences of the form and structure of Australian cities and the way they are serviced would suggest a change in policy over the directions which have been taken. Increasing housing density:

- decreases capacity to cope with domestic wastes and reduces opportunities for recycling
- reduces capacity to harvest or otherwise cope with the rainfall on urban areas and reduce run-off
- makes it harder for urban residents to produce much of their own food
- increases air pollution because it reduces space for growth of trees and shrubs that purify the air and cool the urban area
- reduces chances of growth of wood for fuel, and reduces habitats for birds and other native fauna
- increases congestion, which increases accidents and energy losses

In addition, the reduction in energy consumption in housing thought to be associated with increased residential density is more apparent than real. The paradox is that even if increased density leads to reduced energy consumption, which is an environmental benefit, it is offset by the environmental deterioration experienced in other parts or elements of the urban system.

Australian cities are faced with some significant problems not the least of which are the environmental stresses to which they are subjected. The primary cause of environmental stress is the number of people behaving in a way that undervalues the external environmental costs of their actions. The strategic objective must be to reduce the number of people behaving in this way. The question is: which mechanism is likely to most readily achieve it? A tactical response would be to develop policy which is based on an assessment of its likely effect on achieving the objective. Changes in behaviour are notoriously slow but can be speeded up by the adoption of new technology.

Changes in approaches to the design, construction and use of buildings are slow whereas changes in technology used in production of equipment such as cars can be much faster. Even if all new dwellings were built to reflect the current concern over energy consumption it would take a long time to obtain substantial reductions in stress because the rate of change in the housing stock is very slow (additions to the stock are about 1.5% per annum); furthermore, houses have very long lives. Modifications to existing houses could slightly speed up the rate of change and therefore savings of energy and water consumption. Changes to other dwelling types are harder to make and result in smaller savings. Changes to the sources of power of cars can have greater effect. New technology can be quickly introduced and lead to a significant reduction in energy consumption, though it takes at least a decade to replace the fleet of cars.

Energy reductions due to changes in city form are even harder to achieve and slower to introduce because they are directed at the physical outcomes of a complex set of economic and social processes but not the processes themselves. Moreover, reductions are hard to relate to urban form because the energy intensity of urban living is falling, that is the gross domestic product per unit of energy consumed in urban areas has been increasing over time. Total energy consumption may be

Part Four
Measuring and Monitoring

Part 4
Measuring and Monitoring
Introduction

The case for the compact city remains largely unresolved. The debate in previous chapters has indicated a range of issues in which there is a degree of uncertainty. Competing and conflicting claims, which of necessity are argued from an incomplete knowledge base, exist in theory, in the concept of sustainability, and in relation to environmental, economic and social issues. However, there is an imperative to gain a deeper understanding of the compact city. This is particularly important as policy is promoting new compact forms, while at the same time the results of implementation are largely unknown and hard to predict. Yet the very complexity of cities means that such knowledge is hard to gain.

Many attempts have been made to increase the knowledge base. The UK government, for example, has funded a number of significant programmes of research stemming from its 'Sustainable Development' strategy. Work has been carried out on the quality of development in cities, towns and country, research into the intensification of development and activity in urban areas, land use studies on brownfield sites, and research will soon be commissioned into density and environmental capacity. Government funding has also been earmarked through the Research Councils with special programmes about global environmental change and sustainable cities. In addition to government funding, a whole range of research into sustainability and energy efficiency is being undertaken in universities and industry. It is impressive, but is it enough?

The city, whether compact or not, is a holistic system and the relationships between the parts are complex, and the effects not easy to predict. The need for more scientific and objective knowledge has led to measurement and monitoring at the local scale and the strategic level. But the ability to cope with very large and complex systems gives rise to a dilemma, as the larger the scale, the more indicative and uncertain the outcomes are likely to be. Many methodologies tend to separate out issues into discrete and researchable parts to reduce that uncertainty. Well founded knowledge about the parts is valid, but for many problems associated with urban development and the city, more sophistication is needed. For the compact city, it may be that the only certainty is uncertainty itself.

The four chapters in this part of the book consider some of these issues, ranging from overall policy to the site specific local scale. When policies for more dense urban form are proposed, this has to be made without full knowledge or the ability to predict the consequences. While some methods drawing on environmental and risk analysis may be useful, Wilson draws attention to the precautionary principal and suggests that not only should uncertainty be recognised, but it should be accommodated within the decision making process at the settlement and individual project scale. Research might help to increase certainty, and Burton *et al.* review the wide range of research that has been undertaken in this field and point to a number of shortcomings. They argue that the complexity of the compact city should be faced, and that research should be better structured and integrated.

Even when there are clear objectives to achieve more compact development within existing urban areas through the intensification of development and activity, difficulties arise. The result in theory might be a strategic benefit, but the impacts may be negative for those living locally. How acceptable, and therefore, how sustainable intensification in existing areas might be is shown to involve many interrelating factors that need to be taken into account. Burton *et al.* suggest a predictive method to help assess and promote beneficial outcomes. However, the addition of new development and intensification cannot proceed unless there is the physical space to accommodate it. A city, town or urban area will have a certain capacity threshold beyond which it is likely to degrade. This is particularly so in historically and environmentally sensitive locations. The extent to which an area might accommodate development has been measured by an environmental capacity approach (Drummond and Swain), which provides a method for local authorities to assess urban areas. Even at the local scale, complex and interrelated problems exist. The compact city may reduce the number of journeys by private car, yet dense urban forms affect traffic volume and flow, and also the associated pollution. Such an issue cannot be seen in isolation, and Riain *et al.* show the complexities of the modelling required to understand the ways in which pollution is dispersed, and the interacting effects of street networks and urban form.

As advances in knowledge are made, such as those in the following chapters, there still remains an overarching need to understand the relative significance of the research in the context of the compact city as a whole. Much of the work concentrates on a single sector, or has dealt with individual elements in the urban equation, but has not attempted to address the multiplicity of interacting systems which make up the urban environment. Research that enables single-sector, empirical work to be located within the complexities of the city, and that helps understand the trade-offs and contradictions that are inevitable remains a priority for the future.

Elizabeth Wilson

The Precautionary Principle and the Compact City

Introduction

The precautionary principle, often cited as one of the principles of sustainability, implies that decisions by governments, institutions and individuals need to allow for and recognize conditions of uncertainty, particularly with respect to the potential effect on the environment of policies and projects proposing physical development. The principle has been adopted in the Rio Declaration, in the EU's Environmental Action Plan, and in the UK in the government's Environmental Strategy and Sustainable Development Strategy.

However, there has been very little discussion of its application to such important policy areas as the future form of urban settlements, including the arguments around the compact city. There is, as yet, insufficient understanding of what is meant by the adoption of a precautionary stance, and how this is to be integrated into decision-making on development policies and projects. Various standards for risk assessment for nuclear facilities and for major accidents have been developed, but these may not be appropriate to other types of projects or policy areas, and in particular for the selection of alternative development or settlement patterns, or urban forms such as the compact city.

Moreover, there is evidence that there is considerable difference of opinion over the meaning of precaution between scientists, regulators, elected representatives and the general public. The furore caused by Greenpeace's opposition to Shell UK's proposed deep sea disposal of the Brent Spar North Sea oil platform confirms that scientific judgements of risk and uncertainty need to recognise the political dimension (in this case both international and national).

Major decisions need to be taken over the next few years, for example by the UK government for the accommodation of new households, in the light of household forecasts, and we therefore need to pay attention to what acting in a precautionary way might mean, and the different perceptions of decision-makers and potential residents. How far can we reach agreement over the risks associated with future forms of urban development?

Such agreement requires a recognition of the judgments made about the nature of environmental risks at a global and local level, which in turn requires an understanding of the influences on scientific knowledge, and on the perceptions of contemporary societies, as well as discussion of the means of taking into account the interests of future generations.

This chapter raises some of the issues which need to be addressed in this neglected area of public policy, and proposes ways of adopting a precautionary approach through developing methodologies for dealing with the communication of risk and uncertainty in the policy appraisal process.

Precaution and the compact city

Some of the recent writings on the future of the city have used the language of crisis and potential catastrophe to frame the debate: Richard Rogers, for instance, introduced his Reith Lectures of 1995 with 'the shocking revelation - to me as an architect - that the world's environmental crisis is being driven by our cities...the scale, and the rate of increase, of our consumption of resources, and the pollution it inflicts, is catastrophic' (Rogers, 1995).

While allowing that this may be an understandable use of hyperbole to attract an audience's attention, it nevertheless represents a valid perception about the plight of the planet and our urban areas. Cities have long been associated with particular environmental problems - with efforts to resolve some of the human health issues of overcrowding and unsanitary conditions giving rise to locally poorer environmental conditions - but overlaying this is now a wider concern about the global consequences of the resource consumption and waste flows generated by their activities (Haughton and Hunter, 1994). The commitment to sustainability has extended the terms of debate over the problem of cities across both space and time, with at the least an acceptance of the need to take the interests of other contemporary peoples and of future generations into account. For instance, the possible consequences of energy consumption (particularly carbon-intensive patterns of fuel consumption in the developed and developing world, strongly related to certain urban forms), have prompted international research on climate change and international agreements on targets for reducing carbon emissions (UNCED, 1993; HMG, 1994a). How much are the concerns about the future of urban settlements, their form and function, and some of the arguments put forward for the compact city a reflection of different judgements about the global and local risks we face?

The formative EC *Green Paper on the Urban Environment* argued the case for cities as 'projects for a new style of life and work' (CEC, 1990, p.19). The Green Paper warned of the problems associated with the urban environment - of pollution, of the townscape, and of the treatment of open or natural spaces - and argued in particular for the compact city with spatially mixed uses, on the grounds of the untenability of the risks of the alternatives. These risks were not articulated, but it is clear from the language of the report that the authors saw the problems of derelict land and urban sprawl laying 'siege to the more structured parts of the city' (CEC, 1990, p.13) as risks of social and political breakdown.

The UK Government in its Sustainable Development Strategy identifies other risks related to the concept of sustainability. It refers to the need to improve the quality of urban life primarily in land resource terms, in order to avoid the risks of continuing the current trend for people to move from urban to rural areas and of creating further development pressure on the countryside. However, the Strategy recognises that 'building within existing urban areas might improve sustainability by increasing density, but there may be a limit to the benefits to be gained. Careful design will be needed to avoid loss of open space and environmental quality within urban areas' (HMG, 1994b, p.161). The Strategy referred to the research on urban intensification reported elsewhere in this book as 'looking at whether there is a clear limit to which built-up areas can be developed without resulting in loss of urban quality' (p.161).

Such concerns are the focus of many of the campaigns of environmental groups in the UK, such as that waged by the Council for the Protection of Rural England in its Urban Footprints Campaign, which publicised a view that 'the vital resource which our countryside represents for us all risks being lost forever while our cities increasingly stand as monuments to neglect' (CPRE, 1994, p.2). The Secretary of State for the Environment, in his speech at the launch of the campaign, alluded to the sense of urgency in the assessment of the risks of allowing cities to decay in hoping 'that in thirty or forty years' time people will look back on today and say, they realized the danger, they realized it quickly enough to avoid it' (Gummer, 1994).

At the same time, there is increasing evidence of the risks to human health associated with the current dependence on particular travel patterns. The Dobris report for the European Environment Agency (EEA) on Europe's environment reported that 'urban areas in Europe show increasing signs of environmental stress, notably in the form of poor air quality, excessive noise and traffic congestion', while 'on the other hand cities absorb increasing amounts of resources and produce increasing amounts of emissions and wastes' (EEA, 1994, p.16). The Sustainable Cities Project was a response to the wishes of the European Parliament and the Commission to recognise 'the need to give more recognition at European Union level to the problems of cities' (EU Expert Group, 1994, p.21)., Their first report went beyond the concerns of the Green paper with urban form and land use to examine examples of the management of urban society.

The report examined three groups of tools for sustainable urban management, including those for developing environmental polices, for building collaboration and partnership, and for developing environmental indicators. It was based on an assumption that the problems of the city exemplified the interaction between urbanization and economic change and environmental conditions, and that policy towards delivering more sustainable urban futures needed, despite the principle of subsidiarity, resolution at the European scale.

Urban air quality has been identified as one of the most serious threats, particularly acute in the light of forecasts that the rise in vehicle numbers might offset any measures aimed at reducing emission levels (HMG, 1994b). The significant policy shift, for instance, towards developing an air quality policy, and giving local authorities enabling powers to draw up air quality management strategies, illustrates the judgements being made at political and scientific levels about the effect to human health of emissions, particularly from our forms of urban transport (DoE, 1995a; Williams, 1995). Many other commentators on the future of cities (for example, Evans, 1990 and Breheny, 1992) have cited other risks to the quality of life of intensifying cities.

It is clear that the language in which much of the debate about the future of cities is being conducted represents significant judgments and perceptions by policy-makers, individual actors and the public, about the relative risks of both action and inaction. In these circumstances, therefore, we might expect the adoption of the precautionary principle to have real impact on the expression of policy choices on urban areas, and the decisions on those choices. In order to be prepared to act in a precautionary fashion, to determine policy in the absence of firm scientific evidence, we need to acknowledge the range of uncertainties prevalent in this scale of decision-making, and the influences on the judgements of those involved in shaping the decisions.

The following section outlines the origins of the precautionary principle and its current status as a key element of sustainable development, before considering its applicability in policy for settlement and urban form planning.

The status of the precautionary principle

At both international and national levels, governments have committed themselves to the adoption of the precautionary principle. The Rio Declaration from the UNCED Summit of 1992, for instance, proclaimed that 'in order to protect the environment, the precautionary approach shall be widely applied by states according to their capabilities. Where there are threats of serious or irreversible damage, lack of full scientific certainty shall not be used as a reason for postponing cost-effective measures to prevent environmental degradation' (UNCED, 1993, Principle 15). The European Union's Fifth Environmental Action Programme *Towards Sustainability* also explicitly states that one of 'the guiding principles for policy decisions under this Programme' derives from the precautionary approach (CEC, 1992, chapter 2).

O'Riordan and Cameron (1994), in the introduction to their book on the precautionary principle, argue that the well documented global environmental stresses have stimulated the development of the principle in three ways: in requiring collective action to safeguard critical life-support processes such as the assimilative capacity of natural systems; in requiring the burden of environmental responsibility to be shared; and in prompting global citizenship, whereby individuals and households should adopt an attitude of care across time and space. They go on to suggest that the way the precautionary principle is evolving is further shaped by a recognition that the nature of scientific knowledge is changing, in the face of possibly unpredictable and indeterminate global environmental change, and yet, the momentum of international global agreements requires significant changes in national economies ahead of conventional scientific proof. The recent focus of the European Union on the future of urban areas, discussed above, illustrates very well the evolution of the principle through the commissioning of further research on the environmental health of Europe (such as the Dobris report), while also arguing for European-wide policies on cities to be debated and promulgated. In the sphere of domestic and international law, O'Riordan and Cameron argue that practice is also shifting the burden of proof to those who propose development from those who suffer development.

But what do these factors mean in practice for those nations, such as the UK, which are trying to implement the provisions of both Rio and the EU's environmental policy while maintaining a commitment to establishing a firm scientific basis for decisions (as well as a degree of national sovereignty in land use policy areas such as urban form)?

The genesis of the precautionary principle in the legalistic tradition of Germany

(Boehmer-Christiansen, 1994) might be thought to sit uneasily with the UK's more pragmatic approach to environmental policy. Nevertheless, the UK government's first expression of an environmental strategy, the White Paper *This Common Inheritance*, made a formal commitment to precautionary action:

> Where there are significant risks of damage to the environment, the Government will be prepared to take precautionary action to limit the use of potentially dangerous materials or the spread of potentially dangerous pollutants, even where scientific knowledge is not conclusive, if the balance of costs and benefits justifies it. This precautionary principle applies particularly where there are good grounds for judging either that action taken promptly at comparatively low cost may avoid more costly damage later, or that irreversible effects may follow if action is delayed. (HMG, 1990, p.11)

This principle was taken further in the UK's Sustainable Development Strategy, which it produced in response to Rio: it promotes precaution as one of the specific principles to pursue sustainable development, arguing that:

> ... the government remains committed to basing action on fact, not fantasy, using the best scientific information available; precipitate action on the basis of inadequate evidence is the wrong response. However, when potential damage to the environment is both uncertain and significant, it is necessary to act on the basis of the precautionary principle. (HMG, 1994b, p.32)

The Strategy also points out that the Rio wording 'is a useful reminder that the principle can be applicable to all forms of environmental damage that might arise; nor should it apply only to actions of government' (HMG, 1994b, p.33).

This commitment represents a major extension of the principle from the relatively confined policy worlds of the approval of new processes and the release of genetic material into the wider sphere of urban and land use policy. Such transfers of ideas from one disciplinary tradition to another are a feature of the efforts being made to give greater weight to environmental considerations in all public and private economic decisions. But what guidance is available for applying the principle of precaution to these wider spheres?

Some light can be thrown on the scope for applying the principle by examining the concepts of risk and uncertainty in the context of assessing the environmental effects of certain development actions - indeed, recognition of the nature of risk and uncertainty is a key part of fleshing out the precautionary approach. The UK's Sustainable Development Strategy states that 'Risk assessment is one of the great challenges in sustainable development policy; the best available science is required to identify the hazards and their potential consequences, and to weigh up the degree of uncertainty' (HMG, 1994b, p.198), and referred to further guidance on risk assessment.

Risk and uncertainty
The subject of risk and uncertainty has seen a lively debate in recent years across a number of disciplines, with the rise of interest in environmental liability for

firms and corporations, and with the development of a cultural theory of the way in which society constructs the concept of risk (Beck, 1992; Wynne, 1994; O'Riordan and Cameron, 1994; ESRC, 1994; Adams, 1995). The risk assessment paradigm, which assumes that risks can be quantitatively measured, and that risk management is the province of risk experts able to take an informed and objective view of risk assessment, has been challenged by these critical perspectives in ways which might help inform the extension of the precautionary principle to urban settlement and urban form policy-making.

The Royal Society's report on *Risk: Analysis, Perception and Management*, for instance, discussed many of the conceptual problems related to risk assessment. Risk assessment, according to the report, is conventionally defined as risk estimation (the identification of outcomes, the estimation of the magnitude of the consequences of those outcomes, and the estimation of the probability of these outcomes) and risk evaluation (the process of determining the significance of these risks) (Royal Society, 1992).

An evident clash was brought out in the report between those who promoted a view of risk as amenable to quantitative calculation, and a social science perspective which emphasises that neither risk assessment nor risk perception is a one-dimensional concept, but that both are conditioned by 'social and institutional assumptions and processes' (Royal Society, 1992, p.7). The perceptions vary between different groups and individuals, depending on their interests, and on social, psychological and cultural factors.

Many of these arguments are referred to in the Department of Environment guide on risk assessment (DoE, 1995b), which attempts to address the integration of such concepts into governmental decision-making. It elaborates on the relationship between the precautionary principle and risk, and on the nature of conclusive evidence. While arguing that 'scientific evidence is seldom likely to be conclusive with respect to environment and health', it maintains the White Paper's reliance on developing a sound scientific basis for decisions, and advocates a cautious approach: 'the precautionary principle is not a license to invent hypothetical consequences' (DoE, 1995c, pp.44-45).

It can be argued, of course, that uncertainty is 'a characteristic of any dynamic, natural system...and of all decision-making', and that 'dealing with decision uncertainty is largely an issue of seeking to clarify and understand different perceptions, values and concerns' (Petts and Eduljee, 1994, p.123), but there is a tension between the Government's need for firm science on which to base its decisions, and the nature of scientific evidence, which may be particularly acute in the context of environmental decision-making. Brian Wynne has referred not only to the way in which scientific knowledge is likely to reinforce dominant interests, but also to the proposal that 'the form in which scientific knowledge is practically articulated prescribes important aspects of [...] social relations and identities' (Wynne, 1994, p.176). He uses the example of global environmental policy to argue that the construction, authority and credibility of scientific knowledge needs examining through the sociological concepts of social and cultural identification.

An illustration of the divergence between the views of experts and of other groups in society is found in research commissioned by the UK Department of the Environment from Oxford Brookes University on the relationship between land use planning and pollution control. The research found that elected local authorities, democratically accountable to the local electorate, had broader perceptions of environmental risk than those of the pollution regulatory authorities (DoE, 1992a). Indeed, subsequent to this research, most commentators have concluded that there remains 'serious ambiguity' over the issue of environmental risk assessment in planning (Weston and Hudson, 1995, p.189; Weatherhead, 1994). An understanding of the different interests at play - the need of the Government to have clearly defined regulatory spheres of influence, for instance, and the conflict between central and local government - should lead no one to be surprised at this ambiguity as a way of obscuring possible conflicts.

Individuals' perceptions of risks have also been shown to be significantly influenced by cultural factors such as the prominence of an environmental issue, itself the result of complex processes of 'claims-making activity' by pressure groups in the media (Rose, 1993; Hansen, 1993). We know also that perceptions are influenced by people's level of trust in the operators of a process or policy; for example: the degree of sense of personal control over the activity; the way in which the risks or benefits of an action are distributed and shared; familiarity with the actions; proximity in time and space; and sensitivity to bad news (Royal Society, 1992; DoE, 1995c). These factors clearly influence the way in which individuals and societies judge the outcomes of policy, and their input to opportunities to participate in that policy-making. However, we know very little systematically about the formative influences on land use planners' perceptions of risk or their response to the precautionary principle, nor about the attitudes of the public to balancing conflicting risks, such as those involved in arguments about future urban form.

Most of the literature on the perception of risk in physical development projects has concerned the siting of major hazardous installations such as nuclear waste reprocessing facilities (Kemp, 1992), petro-chemical plants, and other waste facilities (Petts, 1992). This is understandable, when risk assessment in the Anglo-American tradition has its roots largely in the assessment of 'technological and major accident hazards where the effects may be immediate or acute', or where there are chronic health risks (Petts and Eduljee, 1994, p.116). However, concerns about threats to the global environment, such as through climate change or the loss of major environmental assets, such as biodiversity, are prompting the application of the precautionary principle to a far wider range of actions, including, for instance, policy towards settlement patterns and urban form.

We may therefore expect to see an extension of some of the concepts for dealing with risk and uncertainty in conventional risk analysis to much broader areas of decision-making. These will also need to take into account the broader constituency (of experts, professionals, elected representatives and members of the public) involved in making decisions on this range of development. Despite the evident difficulties in reconciling different judgments about the risks which urban areas face in the future, and which they pose at present, some means is needed for building-in the widest spectrum of judgments, from all sectors of society, about the validity and the weight to be given to these risks in making decisions on forms of development such as the compact city.

The rest of this chapter discusses one possible approach, that of the environmental appraisal of polices and plans.

Uncertainty in environmental appraisal

Since 1988, in the European Union, there has been a requirement for the environmental effects of a small number of major development projects to be assessed, and it is being suggested that some of the techniques of environmental assessment (EA) be extended to the strategic level of policies, plans and programmes. The arguments for undertaking these appraisals at plan-making stage are strong, relating both to the need to integrate environmental considerations more fully into decision-making, and to the perceived inadequacies of the system of project EA. Project EAs tend to react to, rather than anticipate, development proposals; to fail to consider the need and justification for the project, and alternative sites or processes; and to ignore cumulative impacts (such as those from a series of separate projects over space or time) (Therivel *et al.*, 1992). Support for environmental appraisal at the earlier, more strategic level of decision-making has, therefore, been growing at European, national and local government level.

The Commission of the European Union is considering again a possible directive requiring member states to undertake EA at the strategic level (CEU, 1995), and in the meantime strategic assessment is beginning to be undertaken for a number of European Union initiatives, such as applications for funds under the Structural Fund instruments (Wilson, 1993), and programmes being developed under the Trans-European networks programmes, such as the development of a High-Speed Rail network (Mens en Ruimte, 1993).

The UK government first committed itself to appraising the environmental effects of policies, plans and programmes in the Environment White Paper of 1990, as part of the greening of government initiative (HMG, 1990): a guide advocating certain techniques for such appraisals (DoE, 1991) was followed by a report giving examples of where such appraisal has been applied within government (DoE, 1994). The government's stance in these publications has been seen as a means of proving that systems of environmental appraisal were in place in the UK in order to ward off further efforts by the EU to draft a directive requiring strategic environmental assessment (Wilson, 1993). Nevertheless, the government has issued guidance to all local planning authorities (LPAs), requiring them to undertake environmental appraisals of their development plans as part of their plan formulation process (DoE, 1992b), and LPAs have been perhaps surprisingly quick to adapt to this new requirement, with some 180 environmental appraisals of structure, local or unitary development plans underway or completed by the end of 1994 (Therivel, 1995a).

Many of these appraisals employ a matrix method for assessing policies against key environmental indicators, following advice on good practice from the Department of the Environment (DoE, 1993). This advice suggests appraising the policies and proposals of the plan against a number of criteria characterized at three levels: global sustainability (criteria such as rate of CO_2 fixing and transport energy-efficiency); natural resources (such as air and soil quality); and local environmental quality (such as landscape, open space and building quality).

Although some of the environmental appraisals acknowledge areas of uncertainty in that, for instance, the cells of the appraisal matrices are allocated neither positive nor negative scores (Therivel, 1995b), many issues of uncertainty remain: there are difficulties of both process and content.

For instance, there are problems of method in aggregating appraisals against different criteria (Merrett, 1994); there are uncertainties over how the environment is defined (whether it should include the natural, social and economic environments); and there is wide variation over the involvement of the non-specialist public in undertaking the appraisals (Wilson, 1994). Some of the appraisals are undertaken in-house by professional staff, and others involve external environmental consultants, but while all entail consultation with statutory and non-statutory agencies, there is less consistency over whether, or how, to involve the public.

Confirmation that the public's views on environmental criteria may differ from those of professionals is offered by the recent Lancaster study on public perceptions of sustainablity, which concluded that, while 'sustainability' for many people may approximate to their notions of the long term, their interpretation of it differs from the local authority's model, and their attitudes are influenced by their sense of empowerment (Lancaster University, 1995).

Environmental appraisals, understandably, face a dilemma of the reliability of predictions: plans relate to a time scale of 5-15 years, and there is uncertainty over fundamental factors affecting the distribution of development and population, such as household forecasts, the price of fuel, and the global economy. Some of these factors might explain why alternative strategies and polices, such as alternative development patterns and urban forms, are 'addressed in a haphazard fashion' (Therivel, 1995b, p.25).

Alternative development options are evaluated in different ways in these appraisals. While Bedfordshire, for instance, adopted a target of '80% of all new built development to be situated within urban areas and sites within the growth corridors', and examined the role of structure plan policies and other action in helping to achieve that target, it did not explicitly build in any allowance for predictive or institutional uncertainty (Bedfordshire County Council, 1995). Oxfordshire, on the other hand, which appraised four development options, not including an option of concentration on the urban area of Oxford, attempted to identify positive and negative impacts in the short and long term, and to indicate their relative significance (Oxfordshire County Council, 1995).

Hertfordshire's approach has been to extend the environmental appraisal into what they term a sustainability appraisal, incorporating economic, social and cultural issues in a process which related the land use strategy to a broader community vision for the future of the County. They tested that vision with the public through a highly resource-intensive 'soundings' consultation. From this process, they assessed three options - new settlements, peripheral expansion of towns, and urban regeneration - and selected the latter as the preferred option. While the County believes this option 'is possible and can be carried out sustainably', it recognizes that there is not complete agreement (Rumble, 1995, p.35).

Hertfordshire's experience was that, despite having the benefit of a State of the Environment report, an environmental strategy, a public consultation exercise involving focus groups, and being one of the pilot counties for the Local Government Management Board's exercise on developing environmental indicators (LGMB, 1994), a surprising number of uncertainties were revealed during the appraisal (Rumble, 1995).

Some of the techniques examined elsewhere in this book, such as environmental capacity studies, and the more consistent use of agreed indicators, should improve our knowledge, and hence the basis on which decisions about urban form are made, although questions have also been raised about their validity (Grigson, 1995). However, extending the scope of such appraisals to the regional tier, through regional planning guidance, as a way of better integrating socio-economic development and the bio-physical environment (Glasson, 1995) - potentially the most appropriate level for resolving some of the contradictions of the compact city (Breheny, 1992) - will not necessarily resolve the uncertainties which relate to the very nature of complex systems and differing judgements of risk.

It is difficult to see, therefore, how the precautionary principle can be introduced into development planning at this scale without a more systematic treatment of the issues of uncertainty or risk which arise in these appraisals, or a methodology for consistent understanding of these areas.

A possible method for handling uncertainty

What seems to be needed is some way of systematically debating the global, regional and local environmental risks associated with particular forms of urban development, in the context of spatial planning systems. This will need to recognize, and allow for, different perceptions of risk and uncertainty in ways unfamiliar to our present system of forward planning. The early heady days of strategic planning in the 1960s and early 1970s paid some attention to measures of robustness and flexibility in plan formulation and plan appraisal, but these were interpreted in the context of the systems approach to strategy, with little recognition of the nature of the environmental uncertainties which characterise contemporary decision-making.

An initial approach to improving the systematic treatment of uncertainty as a means of adopting the precautionary principle in spatial planning might involve:

- identification of the different bases for assessing, perceiving and communicating uncertainty and risk in spatial planning;
- identification of the groups - experts from different disciplines of ecology, risk assessment, environmental health, land use planning, elected members, pressure groups, individual members of the public - engaging in the decision-making process;
- the development of a methodology sensitive to the different groups, planning systems and natural systems of different urban regions.

The EU has published a report on methodologies for environmental assessment at the strategic level (SEA) of policies, plans and programmes (CEU, 1994) which usefully documents recent experiences with SEA and gives an overview of methodologies, including methods employed for dealing with uncertainties. The report argues that uncertainties in appraisal, at this level, derive from uncertainties over both impact prediction and decision-making. The former might include uncertainty over the scope of the project or plan, especially where the proposal is separated into different elements for the purposes of obtaining separate consents (such as from the pollution regulatory agencies and from the land use authorities); baseline information may be lacking or inconsistent, and models for predicting impacts, particularly at the strategic level of plans and programmes, may be inappropriate. Uncertainties in decision-making arise where choices have been made in the development of the policy or proposal, such as the selection of options, the justification for that choice, and the selection of different indicators to comply with different regulatory regimes. It is also likely that a weighting system for evaluating significance will have been used, which may be implicit rather than explicit. Those involved in decision-making may employ different tolerances of uncertainty than members of the public, for instance, over the consideration of the worst-case scenario.

Possible methods for dealing with these uncertainties, identified in the CEU report, include: the use of extreme scenarios to demonstrate a range of uncertainty; sensitivity analysis to indicate responsiveness to changing variables; or decision analysis to estimate the likelihood of the significance of impacts. The report also suggests the value of clearly showing different points of view on the choices in the appraisal, or even - a case of the precautionary principle in practice - postponing decisions until uncertainties are resolved.

Conclusions

The precautionary principle requires that uncertainty be recognised in general spatial planning decisions as well as at individual project level. In the current policy climate, where competing claims are being made about the risks associated with different population and household projections, about the most appropriate urban forms for meeting these projections, and about the implications these have for global and local environmental resources, a systematic understanding of the adoption of a precautionary approach is essential.

In this chapter I have tried to show that those involved in plan-making - central government, regional and local government, the statutory bodies responsible for nature conservation, environmental health, air quality, water resources and soil, pressure groups and the public - may have very different interpretations of what the precautionary principle might mean in practice. As more expectations are placed - or dumped - on the land use planning system to further sustainable development, we need to be alert to these differences, and the possibility that the call for 'firmer science' on which to base our decisions will not resolve the essentially political nature of the decisions.

The House of Lords Select Committee on Sustainable Development expressed a similar view: 'At root, decisions about the precautionary principle are political and ethical, and as values change so will the basis of decisions' (House of Lords, 1995, p.13).

It seems likely that as we involve the public and elected members in environmental appraisal, they will take a more cautious view of policies and the development to which they give rise. The great virtue of environmental appraisal is that it should make explicit the judgements we make about the state of the environment, and the values we bring to bear in estimating the significance of predicted impacts, and enable these to be systematically taken into account in decision-making. The debate about the compact city should benefit from this.

References

Adams, J. (1995) *Risk*, UCL Press, London.

Beck, U. (1992) *Risk Society*, Sage, London.

Bedfordshire County Council (1995) *Bedfordshire Structure Plan 2011: Technical Report 6, Environmental Appraisal*, Bedfordshire County Council, Bedford.

Boehmer-Christiansen, S. (1994) The precautionary principle in Germany:

enabling government, in *Interpreting the Precautionary Principle* (eds T. O'Riordan and J. Cameron) Earthscan, London, pp.31-60.

Breheny, M. (1992) The contradictions of the compact city form: a review, in *Sustainable Development and Urban Form* (ed. M. Breheny) Pion, London.

Commission of the European Communities (1990) *Green Paper on the Urban Environment*, EUR 12902 EN, CEC, Brussels.

Commission of the European Communities (1992) *Towards Sustainability: A European Community Programme of Policy and Action in Relation to the Environment and Sustainable Development*, COM (92)23 final, CEC, Brussels.

Commission of the European Union (1994) *Strategic Environmental Assessment: Existing Methodology*, DGXl, Brussels.

Commission of the European Union (1995) *Draft Proposal for a Council Directive on Strategic Environmental Assessment*, DGXI, Brussels.

Council for the Protection of Rural England (1994) *Urban Footprints*, CPRE, London.

Department of the Environment (1991) *Policy Appraisal and the Environment*, HMSO, London.

Department of the Environment (1992a) *Planning, Pollution and Waste Management*, HMSO, London.

Department of the Environment (1992b) *Planning Policy Guidance 12: Development Plans and Regional Planning Guidance*, HMSO, London.

Department of the Environment (1993) *East Thames Corridor: A Study of Development Capacity and Potential*, HMSO, London.

Department of the Environment (1994) *Environmental Appraisal in Government Departments*, HMSO, London.

Department of the Environment (1995a) *Air Quality: Meeting the Challenge - the Government's Strategic Policies for Air Quality Management*, HMSO, London.

Department of the Environment (1995b) *A Guide to Risk Assessment and Management for Environmental Protection*, HMSO, London.

Economic and Social Research Council (1994) Risky Business, in *ESRC Newsletter*, ESRC, Swindon.

European Environment Agency (1994) *Europe's Environment - The Dobris Assessment: An Overview*, EEA, Copenhagen.

European Union Expert Group on the Urban Environment (1994) *European Sustainable Cities: First Report of the EU Expert Group on the Urban Environment Sustainable Cities Project* XI/822/94-EN, Brussels.

Evans, A. (1990) Rabbit hutches on postage stamps, in *Planning and Development in the 1990s*, The 12th Denman Lecture, Department of Land Economy, University of Cambridge, Cambridge.

Glasson, J. (1995) Regional planning and the environment: time for a SEA change. *Urban Studies*, **32(4-5)**, pp.713-731.

Grigson, W.S. (1995) *The Limits of Environmental Capacity*, Barton Willmore Partnership and House Builders' Federation, London.

Gummer, J. (1994) *Address by Secretary of State for the Environment to Urban Footprints: the Launch of CPRE's Urban Initiative*, 15 November, CPRE, London.

Hansen, A. (ed.)(1993) *The Mass Media and Environmental Issues*, Leicester University Press, Leicester.

Haughton, G. and Hunter, C. (1994) *Sustainable Cities*, Jessica Kingsley

Publishers, London.

Her Majesty's Government (1990) *This Common Inheritance: Britain's Environmental Strategy* Cm.1200, HMSO, London.

Her Majesty's Government (1994a) *Climate Change: The UK Programme* Cm.2427, HMSO, London.

Her Majesty's Government (1994b) *Sustainable Development: The UK Strategy*, Cm.2426, HMSO, London.

House of Lords Select Committee on Sustainable Development (1995) *Report from the Select Committee on Sustainable Development* Vol.1 (HL Paper 72), HMSO, London.

Kemp, R. (1992) *The Politics of Radioactive Waste Disposal*, Manchester University Press, Manchester.

Lancaster University Centre for the Study of Environmental Change (1995) *Public Perceptions and Sustainablity in Lancashire: Indicators, Institutions, Participation*, Lancashire County Council, Preston.

Local Government Management Board (1994) *Sustainablity Indicators Research Project: Report of Phase One*, LGMB, Luton.

Mens en Ruimte (1993) *The European High Speed Train Network: Environmental Impact Assessment*, CEC DGVII Transport, Brussels.

Merrett, S. (1994) Ticks and crosses: strategic environmental assessment and the Kent structure plan. *Planning Practice and Research*, **9(2)** pp.147-150.

O'Riordan, T. and Cameron, J. (1994) *Interpreting the Precautionary Principle*, Earthscan, London.

Oxfordshire County Council (1995) *Oxfordshire Structure Plan 2011: Environmental Appraisal of the Consultation Draft*, Oxfordshire County Council, Oxford.

Petts, J. (1992) Incineration risk perceptions and public concern: experience in the UK, in *Waste Management and Research*, **10.**

Petts, J. and Eduljee, G. (1994) *Environmental Impact Assessment for Waste Treatment and Disposal Facilities*, Wiley, Chichester.

Rogers, R. (1995) The Reith lectures: learning to live with the city. *The Independent*, 13 February.

Rose, C. (1993) Beyond the struggle for proof: factors affecting the environmental movement. *Environmental Values*, **2(4),** pp.285-298.

Royal Society (1992) *Risk: Analysis, Perception and Management*, The Royal Society, London.

Rumble, J. (1995) Environmental appraisal of Hertfordshire County Council's Structure Plan, in *Environmental Appraisal of Development Plans 2: 1992-1995* (ed. R.Therivel op. cit.).

Therivel, R. (1995a) Environmental appraisal of development plans in practice. *Built Environment*, **20 (4)**, pp.321-331.

Therivel, R. (ed) (1995b) *Environmental Appraisal of Development Plans 2: 1992-1995*, School of Planning Working Paper 160, Oxford Brookes University, Oxford.

Therivel, R., Wilson, E., Thompson, S., Heaney, D. and Pritchard, D. (1992) *Strategic Environmental Assessment*, Earthscan, London.

United Nations Conference on Environment and Development (1993) *Earth Summit Agenda 21: the United Nations Programme of Action from Rio*, United Nations Department of Public Information, New York.

Weatherhead, P. (1994) Burning issues in a policy vacuum. *Planning Week*, **2(14)**, pp.12-13.

Weston, J. and Hudson, M. (1995) Planning and risk assessment. *Environmental Policy and Practice,* **4 (4),** pp.189-192.

Williams, C. (1995) Planning practice rises to air quality challenge. *Planning*, **1126,** pp.28-29.

Wilson, E. (1993) Strategic environmental assessment: evaluating the impacts of European policies, plans and programmes. *European Environment,* **3 (2)**, pp.2-6.

Wilson, E. (ed.) (1994) *Issues in the Environmental Appraisal of Development Plans*, School of Planning Working Paper 153, Oxford Brookes University, Oxford.

Wynne, B. (1994) Scientific knowledge and the global environment, in *Social Theory and the Global Environment* (eds M. Redclift and T. Benton) Routledge, London pp.169-189.

Elizabeth Burton, Katie Williams and Mike Jenks

The Compact City and Urban Sustainability: *Conflicts and Complexities*

If we can really understand the problem, the answer will come out of it, because the answer is not separate from the problem (Krishnamurti)

Introduction - the problem

At the 1992 UN Conference on Environment and Development in Rio de Janeiro, the Rio Declaration, signed by over 150 countries, set out principles for achieving sustainable development. To support the declaration, the summit adopted Agenda 21, an action plan for the pursuit of sustainable development into the next century, addressed to international agencies, national and local governments and non-government organisations (United Nations, 1993).

Policies have already been formulated in partial fulfilment of the commitments made at Rio (UK Government, 1994; DoE and DoT, 1995). The Government regards the land use planning system as being at the heart of the UK Strategy for Sustainable Development. Sustainability is now a material consideration in terms of planning law. At the city level, local planning authorities are obliged to have regard to the objectives of sustainability in formulating development plans and considering individual applications for development. They are advised that sustainability can be achieved through directing development to existing urban areas rather than peripheral or greenfield locations, and through encouraging higher densities and mixed uses - that is, through encouraging the process of urban 'intensification'.

The compact city has been advocated by many as the most sustainable form of development. However, much of the theory has not been validated by empirical research and the arguments in support of the compact city remain contentious. To many of the claims there are either counter-arguments or conflicts at the local level. For example, it is claimed that the compact city protects the countryside, and lowers the level of emissions into the environment by reducing vehicle use. The counter-arguments are that there is increased traffic congestion which leads to greater local air pollution in urban areas; noise pollution is greater; and ecologically important urban green spaces are lost. Also it is claimed that the compact city can improve the economic attractiveness of an area, thereby encouraging small-business start-ups and support for local businesses. But it could be argued that the compact city generates higher land prices, making housing and business premises prohibitively expensive. Or it is claimed that the compact city fosters social and cultural diversity and activity, and provides a livelier, safer and socially equitable environment. The counter-arguments are that higher densities lead to more crime; the disadvantaged suffer most from the resulting high land prices, noise and pollution; and that the compact city is not socially acceptable due to perceptions of overcrowding and loss of privacy.

There are many other examples of claims and counter-claims within compact city theory (Breheny, 1992). Furthermore, there are difficulties in the implementation of the compact city because of implications for lifestyles, and the mismatch between strategic benefits and perceived disadvantages at the local level (Kenworthy, 1992). In certain respects, current social and cultural aspirations run counter to the concept.

Local planning authorities are only too aware of local resistance to the idea of intensification as shown by the rise in so-called 'NIMBY' (Not In My Back Yard) pressure groups who are opposed to what they see as 'town cramming' (Cheshire, 1992). How do local authorities know that intensification will yield benefits for sustainability in their local areas? And, if they are certain that benefits are possible, how can the consequent negative effects and local resistance be overcome? Urban managers need a way of assessing, measuring and predicting with some certainty the effects, or the sustainability, of intensification in their localities; they need tools for reconciling the competing concerns of the compact city.

The problems presented in the compact city debate are threefold:

- the claims about the sustainability of the compact city have not been proved
- the feasibility, or social acceptability, of the compact city remains questionable
- tools to ensure successful implementation of the compact city are required

Further research is essential if each of these problems is to be solved. But before the problems can be solved, they must first be understood. This chapter attempts to pinpoint the major challenges of the research problems generated by the compact city debate. It examines the issues that need to be addressed in terms of the complexity of urban sustainability and the complexity of the compact city concept itself. Then the scope, contribution and shortcomings of research to date are discussed. Finally the authors present the research approach of their current project for the Department of the Environment, which is looking at the intensification of development in urban areas (Oxford Brookes University and Entec, ongoing).

The complexity of urban sustainability
According to Church, 'It has become a truism to say that there is an urgent need to tackle the 'urban agenda' and to attempt to sketch out the working reality of 'sustainable cities'. Yet there is little consensus as to the nature of a sustainable city, or indeed whether such a thing is actually possible.' (1995, p.13). Assessing the sustainability of an industrial process or a method of energy production is

relatively simple in comparison with the sustainability of a city. Cities are complex; they are made up of layer upon layer of physical, historical, economic and social systems. To make assessments of urban sustainability, the complexities need to be unravelled. The following issues are arguably the most significant complexities facing urban sustainability researchers today.

Differing definitions of sustainability

The most common definition of sustainable development is that used at the Rio Earth Summit - development which meets present needs without compromising the ability of future generations to achieve their needs and aspirations - but Winter claims there are currently over 200 definitions in operation (Winter, 1994). At the moment the concept is 'so amorphous and open to such wide interpretation that it is degenerating into a bargaining device or marketing tool used by sectional interests in pursuit of their own goals... The absence of a firm and generally accepted philosophical and theoretical framework underpins the current malaise' (Tate, 1994, p.367-8).

The wide range of issues

Sustainable development concerns the current depletion of resources, but it is not only natural resources that are at stake but other qualities such as 'landscape quality, our heritage, tranquillity and the ability of urban areas to provide for safe, healthy and enjoyable living' (Connell, 1995, p.177). The objective must be to maintain the overall character and quality of the environment. Social and economic issues, as well as environmental issues, need to be considered; socially unsustainable conditions can ultimately lead to environmental unsustainability. Nijkamp and Perrels claim that a non-sustainable city would be recognised by 'population decline, environmental degradation, inefficient energy systems, loss of employment, emigration of industry and services, and an unbalanced social-demographic composition' (1994). And according to Levett, 'There are limits to the amounts of (for example) poverty, inequality, loss of opportunity, indignity, uncertainty, stress and disruption which the people in a city... can cope with before basic norms of decent behaviour, tolerance, compassion and collective identification... break down' (1995, p.164). The International Council of Local Environmental Initiatives (ICLEI) have developed a new definition of sustainable development for local government purposes: 'Sustainable development is development that delivers basic environmental, social and economic services to all without threatening the viability of the natural, built and social systems upon which these services depend.' (quoted in Pinfield, 1995).

Interacting issues

Not only do cities contain a wide range of issues, but the issues are interacting; these interactions also influence whether or not the city is sustainable. There are competing claims and internal and external contradictions for nearly every action designed to promote sustainable development. For example, it may be environmentally sustainable to ban all vehicles from the city centre in order to reduce pollution, but this may have a detrimental effect on economic sustainability as local businesses may suffer; or it may be socially unsustainable because pedestrians feel unsafe at night. Levett criticises the compartmentalisation of issues in the Government's *RPG3 Strategic Guidance for London 1995* as it represents a 'failure to try to understand the interaction of economic, social and environmental processes in the city as an integrated system' (Levett, 1995, p.166). To assess urban sustainability, the city must be viewed as a whole and all issues need to be taken into account.

Local acceptability

Even if a measure is deemed to be sustainable, it may not be acceptable to the local population. This is particularly significant in the present political climate which gives primacy to the market. The compact city will not be sustainable unless it offers a high quality of living for all its inhabitants. Along these lines, the United Nations Environmental Programme defines sustainable development as 'improving the quality of life within the capacity of supporting ecosystems'. Recent trends do not offer great hope for the acceptability of the compact city. A survey conducted in Norway by Naess revealed that concentrated urban development with area-conserving dwellings and restrictions on car traffic would be perceived by many as an unacceptable curtailment of the freedom of the individual (Naess, 1993). Advocates of the compact city argue that the increased numbers of single person households has created a demand for small, high density dwellings within easy access of the leisure and cultural facilities of the city centre. However, latest trends in the UK indicate that the proportion of detached houses granted mortgages by all lenders increased from 38% in 1992 to 44% by the end of 1993; at the same time the proportion of new flats fell from 13-14% of all mortgages on new homes in 1992 to 7% at the end of 1993 (Stewart, 1994). The question of local acceptability is complicated further by the constant change in living standards and expectations. This dynamic element must also be taken into account.

Social equity

Just as development may be sustainable in terms of one issue but not another, so development may be sustainable for one sector of the population but not for others. For example, the effect of a new out-of-town shopping centre, as shown by Rees (1988), can lead to the advantaged being better off, at the expense of the transport disadvantaged (those without access to cars). The resulting decline in the local shopping centre and the inaccessibility of the new shopping opportunities can lead to increased prices and limited choice for those without cars (usually the least well off). Stretton warns that urban consolidation would end the present egalitarian nature of Australian cities where land allocation for the rich and poor is relatively equal. He asserts that 'if governments do succeed in imposing some higher density on Australian cities, there is not much doubt that the rich and middle classes will hang onto their houses and gardens, and it will mostly be the poorest households who lose their private space' (Stretton, 1994, p.134).

Friends of the Earth pinpoint social equity as one of the four tenets of sustainable development (Elkin *et al.*, 1991), and many others support this view (Blowers, 1993; Sherlock, 1990). There is much discussion about the definition of social equity but the general consensus is that it refers to distributive policy or courses of action which lead to an equalising of the conditions of the naturally advantaged and disadvantaged in society (Laws, 1994; Smith, 1994). Social equity is also important because a widening gap between the advantaged and disadvantaged can have detrimental consequences for environmental sustainability; deprivation and poverty have been shown to be a major root of environmental degradation and resource depletion (Holmberg *et al.*, 1991).

Fig. 1. Many people still aspire to owning a detached house in the suburbs.

Photograph: Mike Jenks

Differing levels of sustainable development

The sustainability of a city can be considered at many levels, from the individual street to the neighbourhood and to the city as a whole; and according to Naess, 'Not only do the resource consumption and emissions of the city influence its neighbouring countryside, but the metabolism of cities has important environmental impacts at a global level.' (Naess, 1993). There may be conflicts between sustainability at the different levels, or between strategic and local goals. In assessing city wildlife in Cambridge, Lewins argues that '...sites should not be judged by their absolute characteristics, for example by comparison with national criteria, but by their importance within the context of the city, its wildlife and their accessibility for local populations' (Lewins, 1995). Furthermore, a 'sustainable' measure imposed in one place can lead to negative effects elsewhere. Assessing urban sustainability must therefore consider the effects on the city as a whole and at the more strategic level, regionally and globally.

The complexity of the compact city concept

The implementation of the compact city concept, through intensification, is one example of action proposed to achieve sustainable cities. The previous section discussed the complexities of urban sustainability; this section outlines the complexities of the compact city concept itself. In assessing whether or not intensification achieves sustainability, the following aspects need to be considered.

The many faces of the compact city

The compact city can be defined in many ways; it is not a homogeneous phenomenon. Creating the compact city can involve the intensification of built form or the intensification of activity, and within each of these processes there

235

are an infinite number of permutations: development intensification can take the form of redevelopment, new development on previously open land, extensions or conversions; activity intensification can be the result of increased numbers of people living, working or visiting an area, increased traffic on the roads, or an increase in the use of existing land and buildings. Furthermore, each of these types of intensification has a unique character; the form of intensification is influenced by its use, design and scale. The time-scale of intensification can also vary, from large, one-off developments to small, incremental developments over a longer period of time (Oxford Brookes University and Entec, ongoing).

Fig. 2. Two contrasting types of intensification: backland development and increased town centre activity.

Photographs: Mike Jenks

236

All these factors create the heterogeneity of the compact city. The concept can be realised in many different guises and each one will be different in terms of the sustainability criteria outlined in the previous section. For example, activity intensification is often considered to have worse effects than development intensification, particularly when associated with non-local traffic; development on previously derelict land is generally seen positively; redevelopment which replaces unattractive older buildings is frequently popular; and reactions are less adverse with small-scale, incremental, unobtrusive development (Oxford Brookes University and Entec, 1994, quoted in Lock, 1995). The diversity of the compact city must be acknowledged.

The characteristics of intensified areas

Another influence on the sustainability of intensification is the nature of the areas in which the process occurs. The character of an area is made up of both social and environmental features. For example, development in areas where the land is of special environmental significance could be seen as environmentally unsustainable. Conversely, intensification in areas where there is a large amount of derelict land could have the effect of upgrading the area and improving social and economic sustainability.

High status areas with a lot to lose from development (through reduced property prices and amenity) tend to be the most resistant to intensification. Yiftachel and Betham conducted a survey of residents in Perth to examine attitudes towards higher densities. They found that approval for higher density development increased the closer the residents lived to the centre. In addition, younger residents tended to be more positive about higher density development. In other words attitudes were not uniformly spread. They concluded that in suitable locations and amongst certain groups there is a definite receptivity to a higher degree of consolidated development (Yiftachel and Betham, 1992).

Fig. 3. Conversions and subdivisions in a high density residential area can lead to severe parking difficulties.

Photograph: Mike Jenks

237

Differing combinations of types of intensification and types of area

It would be impossible to assert that a certain type of intensification, or intensification in a certain type of area, is always sustainable; it depends on the relationship between the two. For example, residential development in a predominantly residential area may be acceptable where non-residential development would not. Conversely, additional residential development in an area where facilities such as schools and surgeries are already overstretched could aggravate the problem and compound unsustainability. Understanding the relationships between intensification types and areas is crucial in solving urban sustainability problems.

The extent of intensification

A particular form of development may be shown to be sustainable in its particular setting, but there are limits to this state. The UK Strategy for Sustainable Development warns of the need to establish limits to which built-up areas can be developed before loss of urban amenity is incurred (UK Government, 1994). Development may be sustainable up to certain limits but not beyond. Measures can be introduced which have the effect of raising the threshold of acceptability or sustainability so that more development can be absorbed. For example, an increased amount of new housing in an area may eventually lead to unacceptable pressure on utility provision (water supply and drainage, electricity, gas, and so on), but if new technology is installed to increase the capacity of the existing systems then further development may be possible. Intensification is a dynamic process, but the limits and thresholds must be understood for the compact city to be sustainable.

Fig. 4. There may be a limit to the no. of extensions and loft conversions that can be tolerated before there is a perceived deterioration in the quality of the street.
Photograph: Mike Jenks

External factors

There are external influences on the sustainability of the compact city; these influences are 'external' because they operate across a wider range of issues than urban sustainability and the compact city. For example, the policies and management practices in an area can affect the manifestation of the compact city. Management systems may be able to reconcile the conflicts inherent in a mixed use development when it would otherwise be unsustainable. Or local authorities may improve the quality and accessibility of existing open space so that the development of other open spaces is acceptable. There are wider forces which influence both the feasibility and sustainability of the compact city. Kivell (1993) identifies these processes currently as:

- decline of manufacturing
- suburbanisation versus decentralisation
- new economic activities and locations
- technological change
- social and lifestyle trends

If wider trends preclude a sustainable urban form, then these trends must first be addressed. In assessing the sustainability of the compact city it is necessary to understand the significant external factors.

Compact city research

Research is needed for three different elements of the compact city debate, as identified in the introduction. There is a need to test the claims about the sustainability of the compact city; to test the feasibility, or social acceptability of the concept; and to generate tools to ensure successful implementation. A broad range of research is now being, or has been, carried out in all three fields. This cannot be described in any detail here, but a summary of the scope of the work will be outlined; ultimately the complexities outlined above must be addressed before pronouncements can be made with any degree of certainty.

Testing the claims of the compact city

There is a vast amount of interest in sustainable development, spanning many different disciplines - and emanating from academic institutions, national and local governments, international political institutions, worldwide organisations, local pressure groups, research bodies, and local communities. Much of the research is not related directly to the compact city debate, but may have important implications for it. The topics are varied, and include: Third World or global sustainability issues; ecology; the greening of the economy and businesses; sustainable agriculture and forestry; sustainable tourism; political economy issues; the greening of environmental law; the role of institutions in achieving sustainability; sustainability in the energy industries; feminist perspectives; and sustainable regeneration. Although links with the compact city may sometimes be remote, this research deserves attention because urban form may impinge on these other important issues; the research may inform or illuminate the compact city debate.

Some of the sustainable development topics under investigation are more directly related to cities. These include: sustainable development through land use planning; reviving the city; sustainable buildings; energy and urban form; sustainable transport; pollution dispersal and urban form; and, of course, the role of density in achieving sustainability. Some of the research remains in the realm of theory and this needs to be supported by further empirical research. Of the empirical research, much is single issue; that is, it investigates one particular claim about the compact city, such as the reduction in travel demand (Newman and Kenworthy, 1989) or the efficient use of energy (Owens, 1992). The problem with this type of research is that it takes no account of conflicts with other issues. Where research does examine a range of issues, it may provide information on sustainability for many or even all of the issues that need to be addressed, but lacks a method for making an overall judgement on urban sustainability; the overall effects need to be considered and weighed together, and the relative importance of different issues needs to be taken into account. Another problem with research into the sustainability of the compact city concerns the testing of claims that it is more socially sustainable: this often examines the overall effect rather than the differential experience or social equity effects.

There are still opposing views on the claims about the compact city, and as there is no common agreement on the meanings and definitions of the terms used in the research, it is difficult to compare the different studies. For instance, there is no professional or technical agreement on how to measure density. The Government is now calling for research proposals to address this issue. As Lock states, 'Without a common language it is difficult for us to draw out the components of successful intensification and identify what should be avoided' (Lock, 1995, p.173). Often studies are carried out by interested parties in pursuit of their own agendas. There is a need for a structured, comprehensive approach to assessing the disparate studies, in order to arrive at a balanced, fully informed view of the sustainability of the compact city. The evidence from empirical research is so far inconclusive; the battle between those in favour of the compact city and those against still rages. This suggests that further work is essential.

Testing the feasibility of the compact city

There is a body of sustainable development research which is investigating the feasibility of incorporating sustainability objectives. This includes studies of: public perceptions and values; the potential of community participation and democracy in bringing about change; the potential for institutions to implement proposals; the significance and viability of lifestyle changes; and the role of environmental education. Research into the role of grassroots environmental action has been stimulated partly by the local implementation of Agenda 21. All these strands of work are applicable to the compact city concept, which is just one of a whole range of sustainable development propositions.

Research is also being undertaken to investigate the feasibility of the compact city specifically. Some of this is focused on the *physical* feasibility of increasing densities in cities. For example, work for the DoE is being carried out (Halcrow Fox, ongoing) to investigate the main obstacles to the development of urban sites, and to investigate how more housing can be accommodated in existing urban areas (Falk and Rudlin, 1995). Studies have been made of the impact of local authority density policies which show that, through the reduction of parking expectations, density could increase without detracting from environmental amenity (Llewelyn-Davies, 1994). Much of this research is positive because it makes practical suggestions for the implementation of the compact city idea. However, the evidence for the social acceptability of the proposals is more contradictory. For example, it has been suggested that high density housing with minimal parking provision would be acceptable because the development would simply attract those without cars, or discourage residents from owning them. However, work for the Department of Transport by the Transport Research Laboratory has an entirely different perspective (Balcombe and York, 1993) and claims that difficulties in parking do not deter people from car ownership.

In some cases a converse problem occurs; social acceptability is used as the sole measure of feasibility without taking on board the malleability of market preferences or the non-uniform attitudes across the social spectrum. In looking at whether intensification would be acceptable in one particular area, the effects in alternative areas, and the opinions of potential new residents, also need to be included. More sophisticated methods of analysing social viability are required.

Studies have also been carried out to examine the economic feasibility of the compact city, in particular from the developer's point of view. This work is generating practical suggestions, such as the removal of certain obstacles and creation of incentives, which would increase economic viability.

Generating tools for the compact city

Local planning authorities need to be able to assess whether development would be sustainable and to determine which policies would lead to the most sustainable urban form; they need to know what type of intensification would be most sustainable in a particular location, and which policies would minimise the possible negative effects of otherwise positive development. They also need to know the limits to development; to have a method for determining capacity. General research testing the claims about the compact city may provide some indications of what type of intensification works best in given locations, but it is not specific enough to be applicable to individual circumstances. An area by area assessment, and regular measuring and monitoring, are required.

Again, there are many studies that address this element of the compact city debate. To be relevant they do not have to be related directly to urban form because they may concern the assessment in general of actions designed to improve sustainability. The following topics are covered: environmental impact assessment; policy evaluation techniques; monitoring technology; environmental threshold methods; forecasting; modelling; capacity evaluation methods; sustainable management; and, perhaps most importantly, sustainability 'indicators'.

Not surprisingly, much of the research is being instigated by those responsible for managing the environment (natural and built) at the local level, particularly local authorities. Local Agenda 21 (LA21) and development plan formulation both require local authorities to implement sustainable development principles. Localised research can yield useful information, particularly about environmental assets and public perceptions. However, assessments need constant updating, and measurement and evaluation techniques for local authorities must be based on data which are easily available and relatively quick to collect, as resources are generally limited; thus the rise in interest in 'indicators'. Indicators allow assessments to be made using limited, representative information; they are measures, often numeric, aimed at charting progress towards sustainability.

At the Rio Earth Summit it was agreed that 'indicators of sustainable development need to be developed to provide solid bases for decision-making at all levels and to contribute to self-regulating sustainability of integrated environmental and development systems.' (United Nations, 1993). The United

Nations Environment Programme, the OECD and the EU are all working on indicators (OECD, 1991, 1993; EU, 1994), and the DoE is developing national environmental indicators (due 1996). A group of environmental organisations in the UK has set up the 'Green Gauge' to monitor environmental quality (Environmental Challenge Group, 1994; English Nature, 1994). The UK LA21 Steering Group recognised that indicators would be a valuable tool in the LA21 process, and established the Sustainability Indicators Research Project to chart new territory; and the Local Government Management Board (Barton *et al.*, 1995; LGMB, 1995) has developed and tested sustainable development indicators for use by UK local authorities.

A survey undertaken by Nathaniel Lichfield and Partners to contribute to the UK's Report to the United Nations Commission on Sustainable Development, highlighted the difficulties local authorities are facing in implementing sustainable development, even if they know what it is in the first place (Morgan *et al.*, 1993). However, some authorities, such as Lancashire, Leicester and Nottingham are pioneering the field. Leicester claims to be the first city in the UK to produce a report on local measures of quality of life and environmental sustainability; they use 14 key indicators (Leicester City Council and Environ, 1995). The London Planning Advisory Committe (LPAC) suggests targets for achieving sustainable development in London (LPAC, 1995), and for their Structure Plan review West Sussex County Council (Connell, 1995) adopt an environmental capacity approach.

The advantage of the indicators approach is that it can accommodate the whole range of issues, including subjective criteria. Stewart describes the work on indicators by the Local Government Management Board as a 'quantum leap' (1995, p.12). He asserts that it allows better judgements to be made at the local level through a comprehensive, structured framework. However, it has several drawbacks. One is that it does not resolve the problem of the relative weight of each indicator and the interrelationships between them. As Milne says '. . . a 'nest' of interrelated indicators may be necessary' (Milne, 1994, p.17). Furthermore, '...if there are different levels of application of the concept of sustainable development - such as global, regional and local - how do indicators link across the spectrum, if at all?' (Stewart, 1995, p.12). There needs to be co-ordination between national and local level initiatives, and between the different national initiatives being taken by a variety of bodies (including the National Rivers Authority, English Nature and the Countryside Commission).

There are doubts about the ability of local authorities to deliver sustainable development (Winter, 1994). A weakness of local authority approaches is that they look at the predicted development effects, but sustainability is influenced by many other factors - over which planning has relatively little jurisdiction. Moreover, local research may not be applicable generally.

Another area of particular interest to compact city research is that of 'capacity'. Capacity studies confront the question of the degree or extent of intensification which would be sustainable. As Connell states, 'Revealing environmental limits is important. It requires 'state of the environment' reporting and leads to setting of targets and indicators which suggest thresholds and limits beyond which environmental damage becomes serious.' (1995, p.177). Arup Economics and Planning, in their work on environmental capacity in the historic city of Chester (funded by the DoE, English Heritage, Chester City Council and Cheshire County

Council) have produced a conceptual model for establishing the environmental capacity of an historic city and its hinterland (Arup Economics and Planning and Building Design Partnership, 1995). As for indicators, capacity methods are a positive development since they provide a more informed basis for judgement. The shortcomings, however, are identified by Grigson (1995) and Packer (1995). They argue that the method developed in Chester requires an over-ambitious amount of data, and requires a fair amount of subjective judgement and professional decision-making in analysing it, i.e. it lacks objective authority.

It is evident that tools are being developed by a wide variety of interested groups. But there needs to be integration between the different approaches and at different levels for the tools to be effective. A fundamental problem is that, for all studies designed to monitor progress towards sustainability, there is no consensus on the definition of sustainable development in practice; this leads to an absence of specific targets. Research has at its heart the objective of sustainable development, but what this means in reality is unknown, or varies according to the predilections of particular groups. Whatever the quality of monitoring and modelling, it is of little use unless linked to appropriate action, but how can this be determined without an explicit understanding of the goal?

Intensification research as a potential model

This research currently being undertaken by the authors for the DoE represents an attempt to overcome some of the problems outlined in the previous sections. It is limited to the subject of intensification which, although broad, does not cover the whole range of compact city issues. However, it is a new approach to urban sustainability research, in which some of the complexities and conflicts are addressed (Oxford Brookes University and Entec, 1994). The work comprises elements of all three of the compact city research aspects listed above. The compact city claims have been tested through detailed case studies of the effects of intensification in 12 areas; the feasibility of the compact city has been tested through surveys of local attitudes to intensification and interviews with developers; and the ultimate aim of the research is to provide a method for local planning authorities to assess intensification in their own areas and to predict the likely outcome of further development. The research is intended to represent a new way of producing guidance:

- For the first time an objective base from which to formulate policy will be developed;
- Instead of addressing single issues, the research examines the many inter-relating elements within the urban equation and intends to provide guidance for the totality;
- The intensification assessment method takes into account the divergence between levels of acceptability in different localities. Local judgement is built into the assessment. Absolutes and national standards are considered to be inappropriate when intensification that is acceptable in one area is not in another;
- The research has indicated that there appear to be no fixed capacities for development in urban areas but that there are thresholds, which can be overcome through ameliorative action. However in assessing the acceptability of intensification within an area, it is impossible to investigate thresholds for

single issues such as traffic or open space because it is the way that the different issues interact and balance each other that seem to be more crucial. The research aims to provide a way of taking all the issues into account and assessing them in their totality;

- Although the assessment method for LPAs is based on objective measures and statistical analyses, it is not intended to be narrowly prescriptive. It aims to provide flexibility and to allow local planners to formulate policy based on both strategic goals as well as local acceptability.

The research is not yet complete, and it will not provide all the answers to the conundrums of the compact city, but it may make some steps towards overcoming some of the problems.

Conclusions

The chapter began by suggesting that to solve a problem it is necessary first to understand it. The problem at hand is a momentous one: how to achieve urban sustainability through the implementation of the compact city idea. The problem of urban sustainability has been partially unravelled and shown to be made up of a wide range of interacting issues which operate at different levels and on different sectors of the population. The compact city must be feasible as well as theoretically beneficial. The problem of how the compact city can deliver sustainability is also complex; it depends on the relationship between the form and location of intensification, the extent of intensification, and the policy, management and wider socio-political and economic context. The chapter has also shown the immense range and scope of current research, and some of the limitations in terms of the complexities involved.

There are many strands to compact city research, and even more to sustainable development research in general. The compact city debate does not stand in isolation; it is important that it is located within the wider context of research which covers the comprehensive range of issues. For example, to determine whether or not the compact city is a significant and viable option for achieving sustainability, it is necessary to compare it with the alternatives. Other options may appear to be potentially more effective. Education, discussion and debate will be central to improving this understanding. Creating a more sustainable future for the planet will require co-operation and global partnerships. It will require the sharing and integration of knowledge across disciplines. The contemporary emphasis on reductionism and individualism in post-modern life should be over-ridden.

Steps have already been made in this direction. Research bodies are beginning to organise research around sustainability themes. The Engineering and Physical Sciences Research Council in the UK is implementing a targeted programme of research entitled, *Towards Sustainable Cities*. This initiative has links with the Economic and Social Research Council and the Natural Environment Research Council, and the objective is to promote multidisciplinary research which will be beneficial to central and local government, transport operators, utilities, industry and commerce. It addresses some of the complexities of the subject through an emphasis on the link between technology, citizens' aspirations and political choices.

Many conferences on the theme of sustainable cities have been organised in order to contribute to the dissemination of knowledge across subject boundaries, and the journal, *Sustainable Development,* has similar aims. The International Sustainable Development Research Network has recently been established, with the aims of bringing together research from a range of disciplines and disseminating best practice. There needs to be an increased amount of dialogue at all levels. For this to be effective, there should be a common language; common definitions of sustainability goals. Unless there is consensus on the objective, it will be difficult to arrive at a common solution. Lastly, if compact city research is to be integrated, then action should be too. Policies at different levels and across different policy areas need to be co-ordinated.

It is often said that there is no easy solution to complex problems. The conclusions are that research has begun to address the complexity but further work is required, and - perhaps more importantly - the work needs to be better co-ordinated, integrated and structured. The problem cannot be simplified and it certainly will not go away. But if research is carried out with a full understanding of the problem, then the goal of achieving urban sustainability may be nearer. After all, 'If politics is the art of the possible, research is surely the art of the soluble.' (Sir Peter Medawar).

References

Arup Economics and Planning and Building Design Partnership, in association with Breheny, M. (1995) *Environmental Capacity: A Methodology for Historic Cities,* English Heritage, Northampton.

Balcombe, R.J. and York, I.O. (1993) *The Future of Residential Parking,* Transport Research Laboratory, for the Department of Transport, HMSO, London.

Barton, H., Davies, E. and Guise, R. (1995) *Sustainable Settlements: Guide for Planners, Designers and Developers,* University of the West of England and Local Government Management Board, Luton.

Blowers, A. (1993) Environmental policy: the quest for sustainable development, *Urban Studies,* **30(4/5),** pp.775-796.

Breheny, M. (ed.) (1992) *Sustainable Development and Urban Form,* Pion, London.

Cheshire, P. (1992) Why Nimbyism has sent British planners bananas, the *Guardian,* 3 August 1992.

Church, C. (1995) Sustainable cities, *International Report,* February 1995, pp.13-14.

Connell, B. (1995) Development pressures, environmental limits, *Town and Country Planning,* July 1995, pp.177-179.

Department of the Environment and Department of Transport (1995) *Planning Policy Guidance 13: Transport,* HMSO, London.

Elkin, T., McLaren, D. and Hillman, M. (1991) *Reviving the City: Towards Sustainable Urban Development,* Friends of the Earth, London.

English Nature (1994) *Sustainability in Practice,* English Nature, Peterborough.

Environment Challenge Group (1994) *Green Gauge: Indicators for the State of the UK Environment,* Environment Challenge Group, London.

European Union Expert Group on the Urban Environment (1994) *European Sustainable Cities,* First Report, EU, Brussels.

Falk, N. and Rudlin, D. (1995) *Building to Last: A 21st Century Homes Report,* URBED, London (in association with the Joseph Rowntree Foundation, York).

Grigson, S. (1995) *The Limits of Environmental Capacity,* House-Builders Federation in association with the Barton Willmore Planning Partnership, London.

Halcrow Fox (ongoing) *Planning and Housing Land,* for the Department of the Environment.

Holmberg, J., Bass, S. and Timberlake, L. (1991) *Defending the Future: A Guide to Sustainable Development,* Earthscan Publications Ltd and the International Institute for Environment and Development, London.

Kenworthy, J (1992) Urban consolidation: an introduction to the debate, *Urban Policy and Research,* **9(1)**, pp.78-99.

Kivell, P. (1993) *Land and the City: Patterns and Processes of Urban Change,* Routledge, London.

Laws, G. (1994) Social justice and urban politics: an introduction. *Urban Geography,* **15(7)**, pp.603-611.

Leicester City Council and Environ (1995) *Indicators of Sustainable Development in Leicester,* Environ, Leicester.

Levett, R. (1995) Sustainable London? Unequivocally not. *Town and Country Planning,* July 1995, pp.164-166.

Lewins, R. (1995) Cambridge sets rules to defend city wildlife. *Planning,* 4 August 1995, p.1130.

Llewelyn-Davies (1994) *Providing More Homes in Urban Areas,* School for Advanced Urban Studies, Bristol (in association with the Joseph Rowntree Foundation, York).

Local Government Management Board (1995) *Sustainability Indicators,* Consultants' Report of the Pilot Phase, LGMB, Luton.

Lock, D. (1995) Room for more within city limits? *Town and Country Planning,* July 1995, pp.173-176.

London Planning Advisory Committee (1995) *State of the Environment for London,* LPAC, London.

Milne, R. (1994) Land is the problem for green indicators. *Planning,* **1099,** p.17.

Morgan, G., Fennell, J. and Farrer, J. (1993) Authorities struggling to deliver sustainable plans. *Planning,* **1047,** p.20-21.

Naess, P. (1993) Can urban development be made environmentally sound? *Journal of Environmental Planning and Management,* **36(3)**, pp.309-333.

Newman, P. and Kenworthy, J. (1989) *Cities and Automobile Dependence,* Gower, Aldershot.

Nijkamp, P. and Perrels, A. (1994) *Sustainable Cities in Europe: A Comparative Analysis of Urban Energy-Environmental Policies,* Earthscan Publications Ltd, London.

OECD (1991) *Environmental Indicators,* OECD, Paris.

OECD (1993) *Indicators for the Integration of Environmental Concerns into Transport Policies,* Environmental Monograph 80, OECD, Paris.

Owens, S. (1992) Energy, environmental sustainability and land-use planning, in Breheny, M. (ed.) *Sustainable Development and Urban Form,* Pion, London.

Oxford Brookes University and Entec Shankland Cox (ongoing) *The Intensification of Development within Existing Urban Areas,* research for the DoE.

Packer, N. (1995) Conundrums of critical capacity. *Planning Week,* 1 June 1995, p.15.

Pinfield, G. (1995) Sustainable services for local communities. *Town and Country Planning,* July 1995, pp.180-181.

Rees, J. (1988) Social polarisation in shopping patterns: an example from Swansea. *Planning Practice and Research,* **6**, Winter 1988, pp.5-12.

Sherlock, H. (1990) *Cities are Good for Us: The Case for High Densities, Friendly Streets, Local Shops and Public Transport,* Transport 2000, London.

Smith, D. (1994) Social justice and the post-socialist city. *Urban Geography,* **15(7)**, pp.612-627.

Stewart, J. (1994) *Housing Market Report 23,* House-Builders Federation, March 1994, London.

Stewart, R. (1995) Indicating the possible. *Planning Week,* 9 February 1995, pp.12-13.

Stretton, H. (1994) Transport and the structure of Australian cities. *Australian Planner,* **31(3)**, pp.131-136.

Tate, J. (1994) Sustainability: a case of back to basics? *Planning Practice and Research,* **9(4)**, pp.367-379.

UK Government (1994) *Sustainable Development: The UK Strategy,* HMSO, London.

United Nations (1993) *Earth Summit Agenda 21: The UN Programme of Action from Rio,* United Nations, New York.

Winter, P. (1994) Planning and sustainability: an examination of the role of the planning system as an instrument for the delivery of sustainable development. *Journal of Planning and Environment Law,* October 1994, pp.883-900.

Yiftachel, O. and Betham, M. (1992) Urban consolidation: beyond the stereotypes. *Urban Policy and Research,* **9(1)**, pp.92-95.

Peter Drummond and Corinne Swain

Environmental Capacity of a Historic City: *The Chester Experience*

Introduction

Historic cities in England represent perhaps the epitome of the compact city. They are free-standing settlements with strong local identities. They have well defined city centres, often physically delineated by former city walls, and high quality townscape with mixed land uses. Peripheral development has generally been controlled either by green belt policies or local restrictions, so that there is often no more than two miles between the nearest countryside and the centre.

With the premium now put on a good quality environment, historic cities are increasingly under pressure to expand. Continued outward growth from greenfield business parks and residential development leads to the risk of eroding the setting of cities and hence their special character. The increase in development of new forms of out-of-town retailing and leisure provision tends to weaken the viability and vitality of the historic core. Within the historic core, pressure to accommodate large developments can destroy the intricate urban grain, where narrow lanes and intimate spaces have previously given a human scale, and extra development within the city risks the loss of green areas, and raises the spectre of town cramming.

It is not just pressure of development, but also of increased activity that may cause problems. Ever increasing levels of car ownership and usage often result in antagonisms between pedestrians and vehicles, parking problems in narrow streets and squares, and difficulties in servicing shops and businesses. Large numbers of visitors can also lead to potential conflicts with residents, and wear-and-tear on the fabric of the very place they come to see. Pressures such as these are being experienced in many medium sized towns and cities, but they are more extreme in historic cities because of their simultaneous attraction to different types of activity.

However, historic cities are also real places facing problems such as unemployment, social stress, dereliction, and the lack of affordable housing. There is often a facade of prosperity which hides real problems. Historic cities cannot be frozen in time.

The Chester context

It was against this background that a study programme was initiated in 1992 by English Heritage, the Department of the Environment, and the local authorities responsible for Chester. Its aim was to investigate:

- whether it was possible to identify the environmental capacity of a historic city and, if so, how?
- whether is was useful to apply the outcome of such a study to Chester, as at the time there were opposing views about the city's future.

Three phases of work were subsequently undertaken, led by the consultancies represented by the two authors: the aim of the first phase was to set out a possible methodology for identifying environmental capacity (Ove Arup, 1993); the second phase applied this methodology to Chester and made specific recommendations for the city (Building Design Partnership, 1994); and the third phase refined the methodology in the light of the Chester study (Ove Arup and Building Design Partnership, 1995).

The concept of environmental capacity

Environmental capacity is an important concept which needs to be explored if development is to be sustainable. To make progress in moving towards the goal of sustainable development, it is necessary to translate the concept into practical working methods. The research proposed a working definition of environmental capacity as a level which maintains the ability of the environment to perform its various functions. This recognises that there are limits beyond which the environment cannot adapt. The concept is most developed in relation to the natural environment and can be applied at different spatial scales, from the global to the local. When applied to the human and built environment, environmental capacity is dependent on *subjective* expectations of the local character. Hence the enjoyment of a reflective setting, such as a monastery, would be impaired by too many people, whereas the enjoyment of an urban event, such as a street festival, is enhanced by crowds (Fig. 1).

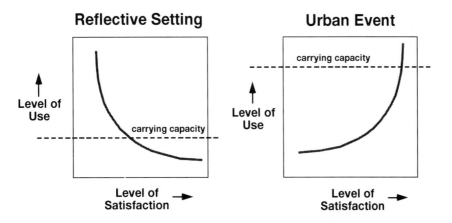

Fig. 1. Contrasting carrying capacities.

In applying the concept of environmental capacity to historic cities, the aim was to define the *size* of the city beyond which its fundamental character might change. But how should this size be defined? Any notion of an optimum population was quickly dismissed as too simplistic. The limiting factors must be related to the specific elements of the locality. Three forms of limiting factors were defined:

- constraints to outward expansion, for example in Bath the city sits in a bowl surrounded by wooded valley sides
- constraining characteristics of the historic core, for example in Canterbury the centre is tightly defined by the remains of Roman walls and the area around the medieval cathedral
- constraints on the rate of growth that it is possible for a city to assimilate, without prejudicing its character.

In reality the environmental capacity of a city is likely to be defined by a combination of these limiting factors. But the difficulty when dealing with human resources is the lack of definable thresholds. If it is possible to define a set of limiting factors at the present time, is this a limit for all time or can it be raised through better management?

A number of guiding principles were used to refine the environmental capacity concept. Four main sources have been drawn upon in seeking a theoretical underpinning for a methodology to establish the environmental capacity of a historic city. These included components from financial sources, recreational carrying capacity studies, ecological monitoring studies and scientific method. Analogies were drawn from financial sources, for example the concept of *critical capital*, which refers to resources which must be retained for future generations (Jacobs, 1991), and *constant assets*, which are assets of a lower value, the loss or alteration of which can be traded off against compensatory assets (English Nature, 1992). The study sought to extend the use of these principles, which have previously been applied to natural resources. The notion derived from recreational carrying capacity studies was that capacity is a function of both the characteristics of a place, and the perception of its users. Tensions arise from the interaction of these two elements; management strategies then seek to resolve them (see Fig. 2).

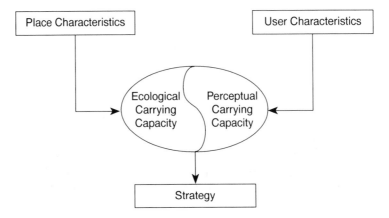

Fig. 2. Interrelationships of carrying capacities.
(adapted from Clark, R. and Stankey, G. 1979)

250

The use of *indicators* has been taken from ecological monitoring studies. Indicators can be used to provide warning signals. They are of most use where there are easily identifiable thresholds. The study sought to extend their use from the physical environment to the historic and cultural environment. Finally, general scientific method suggested the need to incorporate *predictive ability*. The study method therefore includes the generation and testing of scenarios, which can identify capacity constraints in advance, and prevent the making of critical mistakes. Scenarios are identified in terms of changing activity levels in different sectors. The implications are then tested in terms of the tensions previously identified.

An environmental capacity method

The method incorporated the components described above in the form of twelve tasks brought together into a structured framework. The first part of the method examined the tensions arising from the interaction between physical characteristics and economic activities. The method used both technical and perception studies. The output from this is an initial *capacity framework*. The second part tested the initial conclusions through the use of scenarios. It looked at the impacts of these scenarios on a defined set of indicators. These analyses lead ultimately to the production of guidelines to be used to inform management plans, and to act as a precursor to development plan preparation. A simplified version of the methodology is shown in Fig. 3. Having defined the concept of environmental capacity and devised a methodology, this was then applied to the city of Chester.

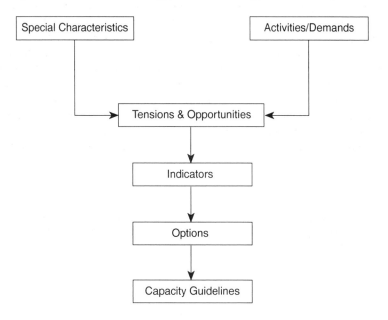

Fig. 3. Identifying environmental capacity.

The Chester study

The aim of the Chester study was to try to define the environmental capacity of the city. The starting point was to identify the elements of Chester's natural and built environment that are fundamental to its special character. These are the elements that should not be lost or damaged, because they are irreplaceable. The study focused on seven elements:

- well defined edges of the urban area
- the compact nature of the city
- environmental features
- historic buildings and monuments
- townscape
- archaeology
- shopping

In considering the future of Chester, the consultancy team identified the main pressures that were acting upon the city's special characteristics, investigated a number of key issues, and devised indicators to assess whether pressures were increasing or easing. These related to development pressures on the city edge, and to the impact of tall buildings on the historic setting. Within the city core there were pressures on green spaces, and large developments threatened the townscape, urban grain and areas of archaeological interest. There were also threats to historic buildings through adaptations or under-use, and pressures from increased tourism, traffic congestion and parking (Fig. 4). For many of these key issues, a 'capacity guideline' was proposed, setting out a level at which capacity may be reached and should not be exceeded. Taken together these guidelines formed a framework for measuring the environmental capacity of Chester.

Fig. 4. Pedestrian and vehicular conflict in Eastgate street, Chester.
Photograph: Building Design Partnership

Options

Planning for the future of a city involves a complex series of choices and decisions, which can only be taken over a period of time. The Chester study simplified the process by devising a set of broad directions (or scenarios) that the city could take over the next 20 years. The effects of these scenarios were then assessed with particular attention to Chester's special characteristics and the pressures already identified. These assessments were carried out in two stages. Firstly, it was necessary to identify where the city could accommodate growth without damaging Chester's special character. The study termed this the identification of 'land capacity'. Secondly, it was necessary to identify what effect the different scenarios might have on the capacity framework of issues already identified, such as the protection of the historic building fabric, or the transport network.

Five scenarios for the future of Chester were evaluated in this way. These were:

- minimal change - implementing only those developments that already have planning permission, followed by a policy of restraint in the city
- trend change - maintaining Chester's existing role as a sub-regional centre for employment, shopping and housing
- major change - promoting Chester as a regional city to compete with Manchester and Liverpool in business, culture and shopping
- selective change - maintaining Chester's existing sub-regional role and extending its position as an international centre for business, tourism and as a conference centre
- reduction of growth - reducing the level of activity in the city and therefore its retail, housing and employment roles

The future of the city of Chester

In order to make suggestions about the future direction of planning in Chester, three fundamental questions needed to be addressed:

- Does the assessment of environmental capacity suggest that there are limits to advisable levels of long term development?
- Is there a way forward which involves a level of growth and activity that can take place within Chester's environmental capacity?
- What are the guidelines and the principles on which this 'way forward' should be based?

Environmental capacity

The overall conclusion was that there is considerable scope for change and controlled growth in Chester without damaging the things that make Chester special (Fig. 5). However, a number of 'pressure points' are identifiable, where any change or growth cannot take place without a substantial commitment to other planning or managerial measures. Controlled growth will require major initiatives, with early implementation of projects that will: radically upgrade the existing infrastructure; require the reuse or redevelopment of previously developed and central area sites; and focus on maximising the future use of the existing urban area, further improving its quality.

An evaluation of the scenarios shows that none of them would allow Chester to continue to grow at an unchecked rate in the future. For example, the trend and selective change scenarios, which are similar in their housing and employment needs, mean that Chester's environmental capacity would be breached in the early part of the next century. The evaluation demonstrates that environmental capacity is based on three changes that interrelate. These are: the physical change in the size, or spread, of the city; the physical effect on existing buildings of growth or decline; and the activities that are generated because of changes at the periphery or the centre. There are opportunities, however, to trade off and manage networks of elements that will postpone the point at which Chester reaches capacity, but this would require investment in infrastructure. This is especially true of the transport network.

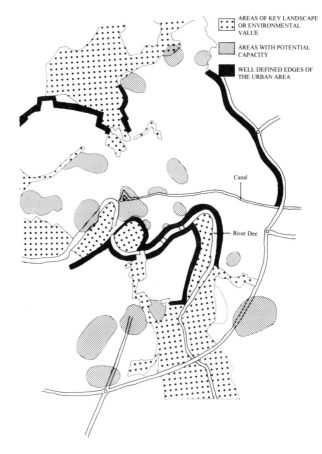

Fig. 5. The environmental capacity of Chester.

Source: Building Design
Partnership, 1994.

The way forward

So what is the way forward for Chester? In the light of the above analyses it is worth remembering that the scenarios tested were deliberately devised to examine the effects of a range of planning options. They were not selected as the only choices. The challenge for the local authorities is to establish whether or not a different scenario can be devised, after seeing the implications of those already tested. What is certain is that the council needs to commit to a strategy that will set the direction for Chester over the next 30 years. Such a strategy will need to gradually shift some proportion of long term needs away from the city, but allow it to retain its sub-regional role. This requires planning for the release of available development sites with great care.

Guidelines and principles

The environmental capacity study demonstrated that, if Chester's development is

254

to be sustainable, there are a number of guiding principles, or elements, that should be considered in planning the city's future. These elements range from broad strategic planning issues to more detailed assessments. It is important that these matters are given equal weight as they all contribute significantly to the delicate balance of Chester's special characteristics. They include:

- a city-wide view
- a development strategy
- urban design
- historic fabric
- transport
- the pedestrian city

A city-wide view

A primary conclusion of the study was that there is a connection between the size, scale and urban form of Chester, and its special qualities. Therefore in addition to the usual issues of land availability and local site planning, these elements should inform the choice of extent and location of development sites.

There is also a relationship between the activity that takes place at the edge of the city and the impacts and effects of that activity on the central area. It is important that the future strategy should not isolate the central area from the periphery of the city. The boundary between Chester and its surrounding countryside should be carefully considered. There are a number of key edges beyond which the urban area should not be allowed to extend.

There is a point beyond which the compact nature of the city and its relationship with the countryside would become damaged. Chester's suburban neighbourhoods need to retain and improve their identities, their contact with the historic heart of the city and their relationship with the countryside or substantial green areas. Reasonable physical gaps need to be maintained to protect surrounding settlements from loss of identity through merging with Chester's urban area.

Development strategy

A further conclusion of the study is that Chester has considerable scope to accommodate new development within certain limits. A number of pointers for the location of development were identified, including new housing in the south-western and north-western sectors of the city, major transport initiatives (including a western by-pass and increased Park and Ride provision) and new business areas on the southern edge and in the central area of the city. Scope also exists for major renewal and redevelopment initiatives, especially in the north-west quadrant of the city centre.

Urban design

It is fully recognised that Chester's townscape and landscape qualities demand protection and, where appropriate, enhancement. An approach to urban design that addresses these qualities is essential when considering changes to the city's built environment, particularly in the central area. Such an approach is not capable of being pre-determined, particularly within a study such as this. However, an assessment of issues, using the capacity framework, revealed a number of areas which demand particular attention. It was suggested that the following elements should be taken into consideration: urban grain, plot sizes, street patterns and frontages, skylines and important views, and open space.

Historic fabric

The historic fabric is an intrinsic part of the character of Chester, with regard to both its listed buildings and archaeology. It is important to prevent the demolition of listed buildings, and to ensure that any alterations to either listed buildings, or those with some townscape merit, do not cause damage or downgrading.

The number of buildings that are vulnerable, or at risk, should be monitored closely, and measures should be introduced, aimed at reducing the number of buildings that are not in use or under-used. A commitment to the preservation of archaeological remains is necessary, and the evaluation of potential archaeological sites should continue whether or not there is pressure to re-develop a site, or a particular part of the city.

Transport

The growth of the city has a significant effect on the transport network. This effect ranges from new roads to stricter measures for parking enforcement. It is necessary to build a western by-pass to alleviate traffic congestion in the south-west of the city. The contribution that an additional highway route could make to the transport network needs to be considered, if industrial expansion in the west of the city is to continue.

Commitment is needed to an improved public transport system. This should include improving the quality of bus services within the central area, and improving the quality of bus services to and from the Park and Ride sites. In addition to bus services, consideration should be given to developing a light transit railway that can service those parts of the city that are under pressure at the moment, or are likely to be corridors of development in the future.

The pedestrian city

The freedom to enjoy Chester in a traffic-free environment enhances the experience of visitors to the city. It is, therefore, necessary to implement the current proposals for pedestrianisation. With growth in the local and regional population, and in the number of visitors, it will also be necessary to further extend the pedestrianised area in conjunction with carefully located new shopping and cultural facilities.

Future of the environmental capacity approach

The Chester study was the first attempt to undertake systematic research to define the environmental capacity of a historic city. Allied research has been undertaken in other European cities, for particular issues. For example there have been attempts to define the capacity of cities such as Heidelberg and Venice in terms of accommodating visitors, in both a physical and perceptual sense. The essence of the capacity approach, however, is that it looks at the interrelationship between the physical environment and demand pressures, across all activity sectors. So, what is the future role of environmental capacity studies?

It has become increasingly clear that local government and the planning process have a major role in seeking sustainable land use and development patterns. Guidance at the European level (Commission of the European Communities, 1992) and at the national level (DoE, 1993) is putting increased emphasis on the need to develop, and use, more rigorous tools for assessing environmental issues as a basis for producing development plans. In our view, environmental capacity assessment has emerged as one of these tools. It has been shown to be a useful starting point in helping to set the strategic direction for the development plan process - it is not, however, a substitute. To be effective, such assessment has to be based on a systematic and comprehensive inventory of the local environment, and a structured method must be applied consistently across historic towns and cities (Grigson, 1995). Decisions in historic cities in the UK already take place within a strong statutory planning framework. An environmental capacity approach, however, allows additional rigour by:

- providing an understanding of the interrelationship of issues fundamental to strategic planning, through its concern for cumulative and indirect effects
- putting emphasis on the longer term perspective, and hence seeking to give advance warning of potential problems
- including a major role for perception studies, and the identification of the future roles that a city could fulfil
- giving a firmer basis for strategic land allocations than the rather sterile debates and bargaining procedures that precede agreement on structure plan housing guideline figures.

The usefulness of different forms of indicator was vigorously debated during the study. The emphasis in an environmental capacity approach is on indicators which have thresholds that can be identified as guidance to capacity levels. So indicators such as those based on the perception of residents and visitors will necessarily be unique to a particular place. In terms of quantitative indicators, however, there is merit in authorities responsible for historic cities focusing their data collection on a few common indicators which will have comparative use between cities, as well as over time, for a given city. Networks such as the English Historic Towns Forum, and the European Sustainable Cities and Towns Campaign, have an important role in the co-ordination of research and in information exchange.

The stock of irreplaceable cultural capital in our historic cities lends weight to the more widespread adoption of the environmental capacity approach. Indeed PPG15 (DoE, 1994) refers to 'the capacity of historic towns to sustain development' as one of the topics on which structure plans should provide guidance to influence the approach taken by a subsequent local plan. It is possible that a simplified form of the method could be devised for use in smaller historic towns, and pilot studies are being discussed with English Heritage.

The case for extending the use of the environmental capacity approach to other forms of town and city is less clear cut. On first sight the concept appears to be eminently transferable to other forms of free-standing settlements (i.e. compact cities), particularly those which experience visitor pressures. However, it would be easy to abuse the approach by arguing for arbitrary development limits in areas where environmental resources were of local, rather than national, importance. We recommend that pilot studies be undertaken in these different types of town to assess the applicability and usefulness of the approach.

In conclusion, we believe that the concept of environmental capacity has a wide application to historic cities. It has been shown in the Chester study to provide useful insights, in advance of development plan preparation. Its potential application to other forms of towns and cities remains to be tested. It need not be seen as a restrictive device. It raises the profile of environmental issues (both natural and cultural) in decision- making and improves understanding of longer term influences on an urban system.

References

Building Design Partnership in association with MVA Consultancy and Donaldsons (1994) *Chester: The Future of an Historic City*, for Cheshire County Council, Chester City Council, and English Heritage, Chester.

Clark, R. and Stankey, G. (1979) *The Recreational Opportunity Spectrum: A Framework for Planning, Management and Research*, Seattle.

Commission of the European Communities (1992) *Towards Sustainability: A European Community Programme of Policy and Action in Relation to the Environment and Sustainable Development*, COM(92)23, Brussels.

Department of the Environment (1993) *Environmental Appraisal of Development Plans: A Good Practice Guide*, HMSO, London.

Departments of the Environment and National Heritage (1994) *Planning Policy Guidance: Planning and the Historic Environment, PPG15*, HMSO, London.

English Nature (1992) *Strategic Planning and Sustainable Development: Consultation Paper*, English Nature, Peterborough.

Grigson, W.S. (1995) *The Limits of Environmental Capacity*, House Builders' Federation and Barton Willmore Partnership, London

Jacobs, M. (1991) *The Green Economy: Environment, Sustainable Development, and the Politics of the Future*, Pluto, London.

Ove Arup and Partners in association with Breheny, M., Donald W. Insall and Associates, DTZ Debenham Thorpe (1993) *Environmental Capacity and Development in Historic Cities*, for Cheshire County Council, Chester City Council, Department of the Environment and English Heritage.

Ove Arup and Partners and Building Design Partnership with Breheny, M. (1995) *Environmental Capacity: A Methodology for Historic Cities*, for Cheshire County Council, Chester City Council, Department of the Environment, English Heritage, Chester.

Caitríona Ní Riain, Ben Croxford, John Littler and Alan Penn

City Space and Pollution Dispersion: *A Modelling and Monitoring Exercise*

Introduction

How well does a particular geometry of city space affect pollution dispersion? This is a question that assumes some significance in the search for sustainable urban forms. It has been argued that the compact city may reduce travel and hence vehicle emmissions, but there are also suggestions that it may result in overcrowding, traffic congestion and air pollution, affecting the quality of life. It is thus important to understand the relationship between pollution dispersion and urban form. The geometry of a city contributes to the determination of its own climate both on a city-wide and a street scale. The implications for monitoring and modelling wind field and pollution dispersion in the urban environment are such that it is difficult to generalise for pollution movement in cities, or even different spaces of the same city. The varying relief of an urban environment means it is difficult to make meaningful air quality measurements which can help with decision-making, and it provides a highly demanding modelling challenge. Yet the benefits to be gained from a good, well-tested model extend to policy-makers, urban designers, transport planners, environmental engineers and, ultimately, to the city-dwellers and workers.

The complex topographical structure of a city, and the structure of its urban boundary layer (Fig. 1) mean that the dominant forcing terms of flow and diffusion of pollutants in the urban canopy layer are the geometry of the space, the wind profile and stability conditions in the urban boundary layer - all mutually dependent variables. Atmospheric stability governs the interaction between the city and boundary layer and influences the wind profile. The wind profile above, and in, a city is determined by the meso-scale and micro-scale topography of a city, and influences atmospheric stability conditions. The city's activities in terms of heat production and radiation from surfaces also determine atmospheric stability conditions over a city which, in turn, influence the vertical dispersion of pollutants from a city.

In many cases, such as that of Mexico City, the micro-scale geometry of the city spaces, the geographical location and the city's economic activity, all contribute to the air quality problems. As geometry is a dominant forcing term of flow and diffusion, modelling the urban environment must include adequate provision for the complex geometries of a city and, ideally, should be able to take into account both the meso- and micro-scale effects.

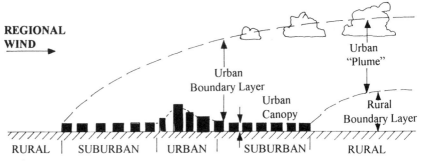

Fig. 1. A diagram showing the two layer nature of the urban atmosphere.

After Oke (1987)

Because of the difficulties in modelling the flow and diffusion fields in the urban environment, a model is not a regular addition to a routine urban pollution monitoring programme, although its value as an integral part of such studies is very important. 'Contrary to the common belief that environmental point measurements are the "real world", it should be firmly stated that a well-tested and well calibrated simulation model can be a good representation of a three-dimensional real world, its dynamics, and its responses to possible future perturbations' (Zannetti, 1992). Even in urban environmental research, models are often 'validated' against other models of different theoretical backgrounds as opposed to full scale measurements, e.g. computational fluid dynamics (CFD) modelling exercises are usually accompanied by wind tunnel studies. A good model can help to determine the most suitable positions for pollution sensors within the urban space and relative to other pollution sensors, so that meaningful data can be extracted from a pollution monitoring network. It can give an insight into the dynamics of the urban climate, and assist with the interpretation of results.

Although the obvious solution to the pollution problems of a city is to minimise the sources of pollution, this is not usually the economically feasible option. Efforts have been made to locate potential air pollution climates and give guidance towards the siting of major industrial pollution sources (Manes *et al.*, 1984, for example). There is a good case to be made for designing cities to facilitate dispersion. However, Oke (1988) warns of the difficulties in designing streets purely for the general comfort of their citizens. There is a subtle trade-off in street design which aims to maximise ventilation, dispersion of pollutants and solar access, while not compromising shelter and urban warmth. Oke sets out guidelines based on relationships between these factors and urban geometry towards finding a 'zone of compatibility'. But with so many governing factors of complex interrelationships, it seems that a comprehensive model would be highly desirable to aid the urban planner who must also be sympathetic to socio-economic needs.

Most models intended for use in the urban environment are sharply application-specific, and very few techniques can explicitly model the three-dimensional (3-D) geometry of the city and its spaces in either low or high resolution. By and large, models which consider the two-dimensional spread of pollutants in a city are probably saying more about pollution levels above the urban canopy layer, i.e. above street level, than in spaces relevant to human exposure.

In this chapter some aspects of urban modelling and techniques which consider the 3-D geometry of the urban space within the urban canopy layer will be discussed. Preliminary results of a monitoring and modelling collaboration show how qualitative modelling of flows in street networks can serve to enhance understanding of: (a) the importance of the 3-D shape of city spaces in the dispersion and movement of pollutants; (b) how monitoring strategies fit into the urban climate; (c) how modelling can also assist in interpretation of the results; and (d) the difficulties of combining modelling and full-scale measurements.

Modelling urban spaces

Many theories and techniques have been applied to the problem of modelling the built environment. Comprehensive descriptions of the theory, operation and scope of a diversity of dispersion and meteorological models can be found in Szepesi (1989) and Zannetti (1992), who also give details of commercial and freely available Environmental Protection Agency models. Here we will consider only those with proven capabilities in handling the complex topography of a city beneath the urban canopy.

The Canyon problem

The arrangement of street blocks separated by canyons in a city presents a difficult case to model; both the air-flow and pollution dispersion are heavily driven by the 3-D geometry of the space. Many pollution dispersion modelling applications do not require the third dimension; however, it is advantageous for the purposes of:

* assessing long term exposure of occupants of naturally ventilated buildings (residential and commercial)
* designing naturally ventilated buildings in urban areas
* designing air-intake locations for air-conditioned buildings

The difficulty when modelling urban pollution dispersion is that local, site specific information is required on climate - wind speed, direction, stability and mixing heights are sufficient for Gaussian dispersion models, while physical and computational fluid dynamics (CFD) models require wind profile and turbulence levels as well. These data are frequently unavailable for the site, or inappropriate - for example, it may be located in inappropriate flow conditions, either generally, or for a particular modelling application. Usually, simplified relations such as the log law or power law expressions (Aynsley *et al.*, 1977) are used to 'scale down' data from one or two sources, usually located from well above the average building height to street level. Maryama and Ishizaki (1988) found, from wind tunnel studies, that in the urban canopy region the log law does not apply. This is borne out by Rotach (1995), who measured velocities at several points above and within a street canyon. The flow is largely geometry-driven, and cannot be approximated to a single wind vector which drives a plume of pollutants in one horizontal direction.

The flow regimes in parallel series (Oke, 1988) and isolated canyons (Hunter *et al.*, 1992) are well documented. For winds perpendicular to the orientation of the canyon, a vortex structure is observed if the height to width (H/W) ratio is greater than 0.3 (Fig. 2).

(a) Isolated roughness flow

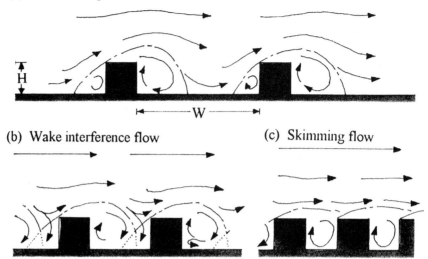

(b) Wake interference flow

(c) Skimming flow

Fig. 2. The flow regimes associated with air flow over building arrays of increasing H/W ratios.
After Oke, (1988).

The nature of the vortex changes with an increasing H/W ratio, modified by the height to length (H/L) ratio, and in very deep canyons two vortices (upper and lower) have been observed (Lee and Park, 1994). This has considerable implications for canyon ventilation and pollution dispersion, since much pollution is generated in city canyons by traffic at low level. The rate of entrainment of pollution out of a canyon is a function of canyon geometry, wind speed at roof level, wind turbulence in the canyon, turbulence generated by vehicles and the connectivity of the streets. Therefore pollutant concentration in a street canyon cannot be considered to follow a Gaussian profile, and Gaussian plume models such as the widely used CALINE4 (Benson, 1992) are of limited value in this situation. Additionally, Rotach (1995) showed, from eighteen months' monitoring of wind velocity, turbulence and temperature above and in a Zurich street canyon, that the wind profile in a canyon is also dependent on atmospheric stability. For low wind speeds, Ca *et al.* (1995) postulate that vortex stability and position in the canyon are also heavily influenced by heat conduction from the surfaces.

Street canyon modelling

De Paul and Sheih (1985) measured ventilation rates at different points in street canyons using tracer gas for winds perpendicular to the canyon. Their results supported the vortex theory, showing higher concentrations on the windward side of the street. They proposed a semi-empirical formulation for the prediction of pollutant concentrations in street canyons, with the intention of augmenting the accuracy of larger scale city-wide models. Berkowicz *et al.* (1995) also produced a semi-empirical model for the prediction of pollutant concentration in street canyons, which is being incorporated into the Danish Operational Street Model but, as yet, its performance seems to be strongly weather dependent.

The complexity of flows in street canyons and street blocks, and the number of influencing factors, has meant that canyon computer simulation has been largely dominated by Eulerian-type models. In these, the domain to be modelled is divided into small volumes or cells onto which a grid is imposed, and numerical solutions for the fluid (e.g. air) variables are found for each cell. The solution usually involves employing some form of differencing scheme (usually the finite difference method) to numerically solve the equations of motion for a fluid (Navier-Stokes equations) in their various forms. These can be coupled with models for more detailed phenomena in the flow (for example turbulence models, such as the k-ε model as used by Hunter *et al.* (1990/91) for canyon modelling, and pollutant transport models, such as the K-theory based model used by Lee and Park (1994)), or for the change in vortex structure with heat convection from the canyon surfaces (Ca *et al.*, 1995). A steady-state solution for the two-dimensional Navier-Stokes equations using a large eddy simulation (LES) model, and coupling with solutions for heat conduction from the internal surfaces, showed the vortices moving about the canyon, depending on the position of the sun in the daytime and the buoyancy of vortices at night with release of heat from the thermal mass of the canyon. However, for reasons of computational economy and simplicity, canyon modelling studies have been largely two-dimensional.

Dabberdt and Hoydysh (1991) argued that street canyon pollutant concentrations are not independent of surrounding streets and therefore cannot be modelled in isolation. Using an atmospheric boundary layer, wind tunnel model of an urban city centre block array, they discovered that contributions from adjacent streets to the overall mid-block pollutant concentration of a street canyon can reach 20% of the total, depending on the direction of the wind. Modelling complex city shapes in 3-D has, until relatively recently, been the domain of wind tunnel studies, but with increasing computing power, Lagrangian models (for example that of Schorling, 1994) and LES-type models are emerging as a more flexible option, albeit with similar uncertainty on the specification of the boundary conditions. For example, Murakami *et al.* (1990/91) obtained very good correlations for the time-dependent flow and diffusion fields between a k-ε turbulence model with an LES model and wind tunnel visualisation studies for a built-up urban block complete with tower block.

The benefits of computational fluid dynamics (CFD) models in modelling the urban environment below the urban canopy include: relative flexibility in terms of the variables it can model; the resolution, scope and quality of data which can result from a carefully constructed and well controlled model using a well validated code; and, of course, the ability to model topography-driven flows. However, in offering approximate solutions to exact equations, much information is required as input, on which much uncertainty is inevitable. Additionally, the solution of differential equations which are too complex to solve by analytical techniques requires discretisation of the equations to enable the variables to be solved for finite volumes, or cells, into which the computational domain is divided. As a result, further approximations must also be made, which is unnecessary with wind tunnel or Lagrangian models. Ideally cells should be sufficiently small so that the variables (e.g. temperature and pressure) should not vary significantly within the volume. Given that each variable is stored to memory, for each cell face in the domain, for successive iterations through the solution, the computer hardware requirements would be too demanding to give the 'perfect' solution. Therefore, sensible decisions on the model construction, location of the boundaries, grid generation and other assumptions must be made, particularly if the computational domain is very large. The result must be judged very critically. In commercial practice, CFD simulations are used to substantiate scientific intuition and, in research, they are usually validated against either real-world measurements or other simulation techniques. As with all other simulation techniques, CFD modelling must be exercised with caution but is very useful for 'what if' scenarios.

Monitoring and modelling exercise in Central London

In order to understand better the flows governing pollution dispersion for the specific case of Central London, a short joint study was proposed between the Research in Building Group at the University of Westminster and the Unit for Architectural Studies of the Bartlett Graduate School at University College London (UCL). Both groups study pollution in Central London, but with different areas of expertise and application. The monitoring work, and subsequent data analysis, were carried out by the Bartlett, using their carbon monoxide (CO) monitoring network, while the modelling work was carried out by the Research in Building Group. The objective of the study was to model and visualise the flows in a street network, to provide some insight into monitored results of the same network which consistently showed a relationship between relative CO concentrations and prevailing wind direction (Croxford *et al.*, 1995; Croxford and Penn, 1995).

Study area details

The area of the study is centred around UCL (Fig. 3); this area has the form of a square grid, 45 degrees off a north-south orientation. Eight streets were monitored, four with a north-east/south-west orientation and four with a north-west/south-east orientation. The roads have varying traffic loads from the Euston Road at 50-60,000 vehicles per day to Huntley Street, with less than 5000 cars per day (Camden Council estimates).

Fig. 3. A map of the UCL area that was used for the study, the spots denote exact sensor positions.

Modelling methodology

The code used was FloVENT (developed by Flomerics Ltd and Building Services Research and Information Association [BSRIA]) with k-ε turbulence modelling and the steady-state option. The domain was divided into finite computational volumes using a Cartesian grid generator (body-fitted mesh generation is unavailable), but, given the inherent uncertainties in the boundary specifications, it was considered that this was of sufficient accuracy to generate a 'picture' of the bulk flow movement through the street channels, which could then be considered in the light of the measurements. Therefore, this study is of a qualitative nature only.

For a steady-state model of the urban wind field in a section of a city, care has to be taken when choosing meteorological inputs as one is taking a 'snapshot' in time of a rapidly fluctuating situation. The meteorological wind data which were input to the model were in the form of hourly averages. CO and wind measurement in the street were in the form of six-minute averages. Therefore, there are likely to be some small inaccuracies introduced by the averaging process. However, persistent phenomena, which are more a function of the spatial geometry than the fluctuating climatological factors, should be identifiable on both the model and the monitored data.

A distribution of the wind speed and direction during the monitoring period was taken from Westminster City Council's weather station located on top of a 60m tower block in the Marylebone area of London, about 2000m from the area under investigation. The average building height and density in this area are very similar to that of the UCL area being monitored; therefore similar winds were expected. Fortunately, the prevailing wind direction for the time period of the study was from the south-west, which was parallel to some of the streets under study (Fig. 3) and perpendicular to the others. The average wind speed was quite low, $2.6ms^{-1}$ at a height of 65m, which may lead to inaccuracies in wind speed predictions at low levels, as poor correlations have been reported between CFD models and measurements at low speeds. This information was used to generate a logarithmic wind profile for an urban area.

A preliminary series of tests on a less complex geometrical arrangement (the average block height of 24m was similar to that of the study area) was conducted to investigate sensitivities of the model to boundary conditions (inlet, outlet and free stream boundary conditions) and their locations relative to the street blocks, and to investigate sensitivity to variations in resolution and domain size.

UCL area model

A large area model (408x470x500m) of the segment bounded by Tottenham Court Road, Torrington Place, Gordon Street and Euston Road was constructed (Fig. 4). The simulations were first tested with a domain height of 500m, and then reduced to 200m. This enabled higher resolution simulations to be run for a domain of height 200m with the adjusted free stream boundary pressure. Velocity and turbulence profiles were taken from the block array tests (although it is expected that, even by this method, turbulence was probably vastly underpredicted - a future turbulence monitoring programme, soon to commence for the Marylebone area of Central London should provide much more accurate information for future improved models). The boundaries in the vertical plane were simulated as pressure boundaries, with a lower pressure opposite the profile plane, to give the prevailing wind direction and slightly higher pressures on either side so that the flow was not totally 'forced' in the prevailing direction, which gives slightly more (intuitively) realistic street flow conditions. These boundary conditions were also sensitivity tested. Full scale simulations of the wind for the Euston area geometry (Fig. 4) were constructed for two orthogonal wind directions, south-west (Fig. 5, wind flowing from left to right) and south-east (Fig. 6, wind flowing from bottom of page to top). The time taken to construct, run to solution convergence, and test large models did not permit other wind directions to be modelled for this study.

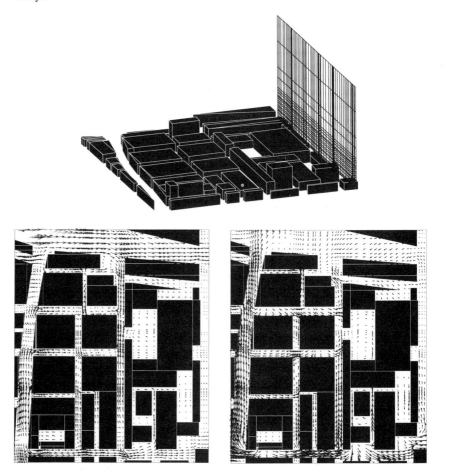

Fig. 4. UCL Area model looking north; 3-D geometry with grid in y-z plane.

Fig. 5 (left). UCL Area Model Simulation (x-y plane slice at z=3.75m). Wind blowing from south-west (left to right).

Fig. 6 (right). UCL Area Model Simulation (x-y plane slice at z=3.75m). Wind blowing from south-east (bottom to top).

Monitoring programme

Several roads in the area surrounding University College London were monitored during August. The prevailing wind data come from a weather station mounted on the roof of the second tallest university building (39m).

The CO measurements are presented as scattergrams which look at relative differences in pollution between closely situated streets, looking especially at the effects of wind direction. The wind direction is grouped into octants centred around each of eight points of the compass and then these categories are used to 'split the CO data'. In this way it is possible to see trends free from general temporal differences or differences due to different traffic densities. The way to interpret these graphs is to look at the regression line as the mean of all the points in the graph. Points above or below the line correspond to relatively more or less CO at that time on one street with respect to the other street.

Combined modelling and monitoring results

The simulations confirm the existence of vortices in street canyons for perpendicular wind directions, the structures of which depend not only on the H/ W ratio of the canyons, but also on the connectivity of the street canyons, indicating that canyons should not be considered in isolation. Narrow, asymmetric street canyons will produce either very strong vortices or no vortices at all, depending on the wind direction. Those that do not form vortices appear to act as 'drains' for larger flow channels (Fig. 7).

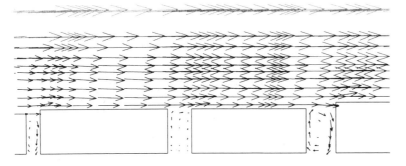

Fig. 7. UCL Area Model, detail showing vortex arrays of differing structures (y-z plane, slice detail taken at position of sensor).

Fig. 8 shows the CO concentration measured on two parallel streets approximately 600m apart. The height to width ratio of Tottenham Court Road is 0.71 and that of Upper Woburn Place is 0.55. The main point is that the sensors are on different sides of the road. The graph shows that when the wind is coming from the NE, Tottenham Court Road experiences generally lower CO concentrations than Upper Woburn Place, and the converse is true when the wind is from the SW. This is what would be expected if vortices were forming in these two streets.

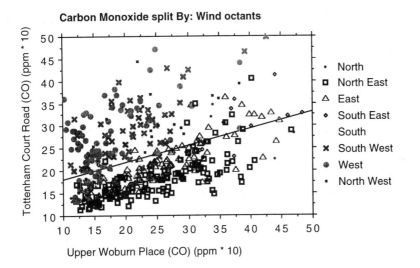

Fig. 8. Tottenham Court Road (NW/SE) vs. Upper Woburn Place (NW/SE), sensors on different sides of the road.

267

Fig. 9 (simulation) shows that when the wind is blowing from the south-east a shallow vortex is formed in Tottenham Court Road, in the plane in which the CO sensor was located, consistent with the simulations of Hunter *et al.* (1990/91) for canyons of low H/W ratio (<1). Clean air is sucked into the canyon on the leeward side and back across the road and up the windward side of the street. So when the sensor is on the leeward side it reads 'clean air', and on the windward side it reads 'dirty air' charged by the pollution blown across the road.

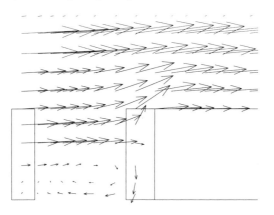

Fig. 9. UCL Area Model (detail): x-z plane slice through Tottenham Court Road at position of CO sensor.

Fig. 10 shows results from two parallel streets which are perpendicular to the previous example. Differences can be seen in relative pollution, with a NW wind producing generally lower levels on the southerly side of Euston Road and NE and E winds producing relatively higher than average concentrations. Euston Road is a wide and busy road with a height to width ratio of 0.69 which seems to experience a vortex with a NW wind, that makes the sensor on the southerly side of the street register 'clean air'. With a wind from the east and NE, higher values could indicate a vortex or perhaps just that the wind is blowing pollutants along the road.

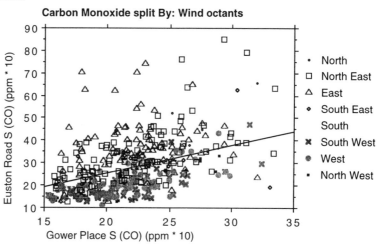

Fig. 10. Euston Road (SW/NE) vs. Gower Place (SW/NE), both sensors on the southerly side of the road.

Gower Place has a height to width ration of 1.5 and had a CO sensor on both sides of the street which worked for the entire monitoring period. Fig. 11 shows little or no vortex effect with different wind directions. This may be explained by referring to the simulations (Figs. 4 and 5) which show first, that the tall building at the SW end of the street may be inducing anomalous wind effects and preventing the formation of vortices, and second, that the courtyard off Gower Place may also prevent vortex formation by drainage effects.

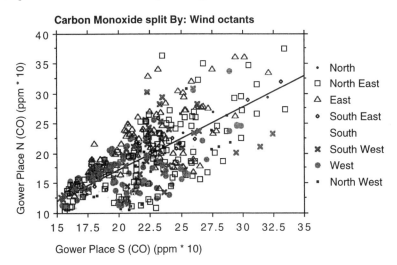

Fig. 11. Gower Place (SW/NE) measurements on both sides of the street.

Conclusion

In this chapter the authors have shown a reasonable qualitative accordance between computer simulation and monitoring. The model, though crude, proved adequate for highlighting persistent flow conditions caused by the geometrical arrangement of streets and buildings. The corroboration of a large scale street model could not have been possible without the spatial distribution of sampling points afforded by a new generation of cheap, accurate pollution monitors, which were also able to highlight the significant effect on pollution of very localised wind effects. These wind effects are primarily generated by the geometry of the streets, in particular the height and width of the street canyon, or the presence of tall buildings which disturb the flow conditions. Under certain conditions vortices form in street canyons which generate radical differences in pollutant concentrations. The difference in pollutant concentrations on the same street, under different wind directions, for example, on Euston Road, can be as much as 5 parts per million (ppm) between certain E and NW winds.

The evidence for the formation of vortices on streets, at times when the wind is blowing perpendicularly to the street, appears strong. This was confirmed by CFD modelling of the street network of the area, which illustrates the benefit of a combined monitoring and modelling programme. Results showed that street wind velocity, as predicted by network modelling of streets as open flow channels, depended not only on wind speed and direction and H/W ratio, but also on the connectivity of the streets. This suggests that some pollutant exchange can occur between streets when turbulence induced by traffic is low - for example, during queuing and idling - as well as by vertical entrainment out of the canyons. Large buildings can have an effect on the wind flows and pollutant dispersion for an urban area, even at low prevailing wind speeds, and produce anomalous flow conditions which can lead to counter-intuitive results of pollution levels for a street. CFD modelling can be used to visualise these flow conditions, which cannot be measured easily.

As pollution is primarily flow-driven, it makes sense to use a model which can handle modelling flow conditions in complex topography. However, owing to connectivity considerations, streets should not be modelled in isolation, but as part of an interconnecting network. This is very computationally intensive with CFD, but future developments in Lagrangian particle modelling may ease the load.

Although large inaccuracies are inevitable with such a crude single-zone bulk flow model, none the less, it served as an interesting qualitative complement to the measured data, and provides a good base for further refinement, testing different conditions and consideration of other influencing factors such as heat convection from surfaces.

The use of combined monitoring and modelling of networks of streets can help towards improvement of monitoring strategies, in terms of siting pollution monitoring instruments in locations which are more representative of pollutant levels and normal flow conditions, as well as increasing awareness of pollution 'hot-spots'. Although these may not be indicative of the pollution being experienced by the majority of the population, some people may have to live or work in these areas. This can be designed against by architects, urban designers and transport planners who consider buildings and streets as parts of a whole environment, influencing and influenced by the urban space and its climate. By providing a whole picture of an urban space and its ventilation patterns, changes in emissions loading (traffic levels), as well as changes in the geometry of the space, can be investigated to give an indication of the impact of a change of strategy on the air quality of the space and the adjoining spaces it influences.

The authors wish to thank Mr David Vowles at Westminster City Council for providing weather data for this project and CO data from one of their NDIR monitors (next to which one of the CO sensors was placed) for checking the CO sensors for consistency. Our thanks also to EPSRC for funding *Effects of the Street Grid Configuration on Pedestrian Exposure to Vehicular Pollution: Civilising Urban Traffic* (Grant No. GR/J 50613) project.

References

Aynsley, R.M., Melbourne, W. and Vickery, B.J. (1977) *Architectural Aerodynamics,* Applied Science Publishers Ltd, London.

Benson, P.E. (1992) A review of the development and application of the CALINE3 and CALINE4 models. *Atmospheric Environment,* **Vol. 26B, No. 3,** pp.379-390.

Berkowicz, R., Palmgren, F., Hertel, O. and Vignati, E. (1995) Using measurement of air pollution in streets for evaluation of urban air quality - meteorological analysis and model calculations, *Proceedings of the 5th International Symposium on Highway and Urban Pollution 95,* Copenhagen, 22-24 May, 1995.

Ca, V. T., Asaeda, T., Ito, M. and Armfield (1995) Characteristics of wind field in a street canyon. *Journal of Wind Engineering and Industrial Aerodynamics,* **57,** pp.63-80.

Croxford, B. and Penn, A., (1995) *Pedestrian exposure to urban pollution: exploratory results,* Air Pollution 95, Porto Carras, Greece, 25-27 September 1995.

Croxford, B., Hillier, B. and Penn, A. (1995) Spatial distribution of urban pollution, *Proceedings of the 5th International Symposium on Highway and Urban Pollution 95,* Copenhagen, 22-24 May, 1995.

Dabberdt, W.F and Hoydysh, W.G. (1991) Street canyon dispersion: sensitivity to block shape and entrainment, *Atmospheric Environment,* **Vol 25A, No. 7,** pp.1143-1153.

De Paul, F.T. and Sheih, C. (1985) A tracer study of despersion in an urban street canyon. *Atmospheric Environment,* **Vol. 19, No. 4,** pp.555-559.

Hunter, L.J., Watson, I.D. and Johnson, G.T. (1990/91) Modelling Air Flow Regimes in Urban Canyons, *Energy and Buildings,* **15-16,** pp.315-324.

Hunter, L.J, Johnson, G.T and Watson, I.D. (1992) An investigation of three-dimensional characteristics of flow regimes within the urban canyon. *Atmospheric Environment,* **Vol. 26B, No. 4,** pp.425-432.

Lee, I.Y. and Park, H.M. (1994) Parameterization of the pollutant transport and dispersion in urban street canyons. *Atmospheric Environment,* **Vol.28, No.14,** pp.2343-2349.

Manes, A., Setter, I. and Decker, D.N. (1984) Potential air pollution climates and urban planning, *Energy and Buildings,* **7,** pp.139-148.

Maryama, T. and Ishizaki, H. (1988) A wind tunnel test on the boundary layer characteristics above an urban area. *Journal of Wind Engineering and Industrial Aerodynamics,* **28,** pp.139-148.

Murakami, S., Mochida, A. and Hayashi, Y. (1990/91) Numerical simulation of velocity field and diffusion field in an urban area. *Energy and Buildings,* **15-16,** pp.345-356.

Oke, T.R. (1987) *Boundary Layer Climates* , Methuen, London.

Oke, T.R. (1988) Street design and urban canopy layer climate. *Energy and Buildings,* **11,** pp.103-113.

Rotach, M.W. (1995) Profiles of turbulence statistics in and above an urban street canyon. *Atmospheric Environment,* **Vol. 29, No. 13,** pp.1473-1486.

Schorling, M. (1994) Computation of ambient concentration distributions due to vehicle emissions. *The Science of the Total Environment,* **146/147,** pp.445-450.

Szepesi, D. (1989) *Compendium of Regulatory Air Quality Simulation Models,* Akadémiai Kiadó, Budapest.

Zannetti, P. (1992) Numerical simulation of air pollution: an overview, *Ecological Physical Chemistry, Proceedings of 2nd International Workshop,* Milan, 25-29 May (eds. Bonati *et al.*) Elsevier Science Publishers Ltd.

Part Five
Implementation

Implementation
Introduction

The move towards the compact city is now entrenched in policy throughout Europe. In Part 4 attention was drawn to the fact that, in the UK as elsewhere, policy, and therefore implementation, have raced ahead of research, whilst the outcomes of many policies and measures are still not fully understood. Part 5 is also set within this context. It examines attempts to *implement* the compact city, comments on various policy outcomes and evaluates the dynamics of different solutions. The chapters in Part 5 further the debate about the implementation of the compact city (either 'actual' or 'virtual'), by giving an insight into examples of implementation.

The chapters offer a diverse range of work, each dealing with a different aspect of implementation. However, many of the themes being addressed are common. The focus is on specific solutions, but behind these solutions are a number of shared areas of discussion. There are fundamental questions about the *agencies, methods, scale* and *legitimacy* of implementation which are, as yet, unanswered. The contributions indicate, either implicitly or explicitly, that decisions need to be made about these broad issues if the compact city is to have a chance of success.

The first area of discussion focuses on the appropriateness of different agencies to implement the compact city. Several of the authors concentrate on the role of planners, and the planning system. Pratt and Larkham, for example, illustrate how the planning system could be developed to accommodate aspects of the compact city and provide a 'New Jerusalem', Breheny *et al.* examine how local authorities, through the planning system, are implementing UK policy designed to concentrate development in urban areas, and Sherlock and Burton suggest that the planning system could do more to reconcile the problems of high density urban living.

Planners alone, however, cannot bring about the massive changes needed to make the sustainable city a reality. The cooperation, in policy development and implementation, of other local authority departments (Pratt and Larkham), developers and landowners (Burton and Matson), public service providers (Burton and Matson), businesses (Thomas and Cousins), local management agencies (Johnson) and urban residents (Johnson) is also required. Furthermore collaboration between these agencies is crucial, and partnerships and local participation which focus on issues specific to each locality are needed.

The second area for discussion addresses the measures that can be used to implement the compact city and manage its effects. Drawn into this debate are discussions about the effectiveness of policies, financial incentives, education, management techniques and design. Burton and Matson, for example, advocate the use of planning controls and policies, tax incentives, investment and urban management. The chapters indicate that it is critical that the range of methods is not limited and that the search for new ways of implementation continues.

The third, and perhaps the most developed, debate concerns the scale of implementation, or the level at which to tackle the compact city. The following chapters advocate a range of levels of implementation ranging from the national, to regional, to the social city region, the social city, the local authority and the neighbourhood. Whilst it is likely that all these levels have their role to play, the advocacy of such a range of scales does highlight the need for a new commitment to the co-ordination of levels of implementation.

The final issue relates to how implementation, by any agency or method, and at any scale can be evaluated as successful, or deemed to be 'legitimate', or 'just'. Many of the contributions concentrate on local, and in particular, community, acceptance to define success. Johnson, for example, believes that solutions to the problems occurring in high density areas should be formed within the community, as there is likely to be a greater acceptance of locally derived solutions. Sherlock also emphasises the need for initiatives to raise the quality of life, and thus be favourable to local residents. However, some measures which are essential if the compact city is to be successful, for example reduced car use and ownership, may not be popular. To overcome such difficulties it is likely that public opinion will have to be changed. This is most likely to come about through education aimed at increasing awareness of the wider issues of sustainability. This need for awareness applies equally to those implementing the compact city (Pratt and Larkham), and those living within it.

Resolving the conflicts raised in these four areas of discussion would bring 'successful' implementation of a sustainable urban form much closer. However, addressing these conflicts requires a new commitment. The chapters in Part 5 provide insight, examples, and advice on how the practical steps needed to fulfil this commitment can be made.

Richard Pratt and Peter Larkham

Who Will Care for Compact Cities?

There certainly is a lead to be taken [in sustainability]. That lead should not only be taken in the form of guidance for the planning profession in practice, it should also be taken in the academic institutions where planning professionals are taught. If we do not grasp the nettle now, the repercussions in future years could be disastrous. (Moore, 1995, p.27)

Planned Utopias and lessons from history
In the UK, from time to time, planning has been asked to provide the gateway to the New Jerusalem. There has been a continuing Utopian strand of town planning from Ebenezer Howard through to the creation of the postwar planning system (Hardy, 1991). An understanding of this history should have important lessons for current challenges, which include sustainability and what has been suggested as its key urban corollary, the 'compact city'.

Whilst not yet at the same feverish pitch of the discussion of 'ribbon development' during the 1930s, the current language about quality in town and country does share some characteristics with the rhetoric of that time (Ashworth, 1954; Bedarida, 1979; Cherry, 1988; Hague, 1984; Hardy, 1991; Ward, 1994). The 1929 Labour Government had attempted to establish more strategic policies through the setting-up of three committees, namely the Committee of Inquiry into National Parks (under Addison), the Chelmsford Committee on Rural Development and the Marley Committee on Garden Cities and Satellite Towns. The containment of urban England became a major issue of the 1930s. It is further worth recalling that the Council for the Preservation of Rural England had been founded in 1926, and greatly informed these debates as it still does today (as the Council for the Protection of Rural England). Recalling 'a sense of patrician disdain for the bargain basement environmental quality of nascent consumer capitalism', Hague (1984) analysed the social forces that combined to facilitate the passing of the 1932 Town and Country Planning Act. This Act led to Town Planning Schemes covering 3.64 million ha. by 1933, extending to

10.72 million ha. in 1939. The 1935 Restriction of Ribbon Development Act followed. As the country moved into the Second World War, two other significant reports were commissioned, the first under Sir Montague Barlow to investigate *The Distribution of the Industrial Population* and the second under Lord Justice Scott to investigate *Land Utilisation in Rural Areas*.

Historical parallels are useful if they are treated carefully. All that is being argued here is that, just as in the 1930s people looked to a 'planning system' to deliver the New Jerusalem (Hebbert, 1983; Bedarida, 1979), so in 1990s similarly ambitious objectives are being established with respect to 'sustainable development'. In this context, attention has already been drawn to the limitations of the town planning system (Hall *et al.*, 1993). But from whom do planners seek assistance in responding to such ambitions?

Planners are concerned to identify the physical pattern of settlement which would best be able to support sustainable development. Yet, throughout its history, planning has never had to rely entirely on physical configurations to deliver improvements in living conditions. Other factors have also been significant, including economics, amenity and aesthetics, together with the general issue of devising and implementing relevant policy. Planners are generically able to co-ordinate policy, with those in cities concerned with the management of area-based policy (Roberts, 1995). The ability to reconfigure the space economy has severe limitations, which have been established historically.

The direction of industry and commerce to specific locations was last discussed in the UK during the Second World War. Informed evidence and opinion to the Barlow Commission was, at that time, divided with respect to the recommendation that the disadvantages of concentration could be remedied or greatly reduced by good planning (Barlow Report, 1940). Regarding decentralisation, including the development of new towns, the Federation of British Industry strongly opposed state-directed industrial relocation, although it would accept a policy of discouragement from some areas and encouragement towards others. Those in favour of state controls on industrial location included the Trades Union Congress, the Council for the Preservation of Rural England, the Garden Cities and Town Planning Association and the Town Planning Institute. The Commissioners gave emphasis to evidence from local authorities, amongst whom views were far from unanimous. Those authorities supporting some generally limited powers of state control included London County Council, Manchester, Leeds, Liverpool, Durham, Cumberland, and even Birmingham (although with less enthusiasm) (Cherry, 1988).

After the war, and during the relative economic boom of the 1960s, the policy of Industrial Development Certificates was used in an attempt to steer development away from the South East and West Midlands. The Thatcher years were characterised by the philosophy that the selective removal or reduction of state regulations from specific locations would attract investment to them. This *laissez-faire* rationale lay behind Enterprise Zones, Simplified Planning Zones and even the de-regulatory culture of Urban Development Corporations. So are we now seeing a fundamental shift in political philosophy which countenances much tighter land use regulation of the city edge and open land adjacent to the motorway system? Could this be extended to the role of economic development? At the point when the very concept of local economy is challenged (Lovering, 1995), as a result of the much wider network of linkages that even small firms support, the concept of economic locality is re-emerging via vague concepts of compactness.

The compact city hypothesis

A necessary preface to the compact city argument is that, for much of the postwar period in the developed world at least, cities have been rapidly expanding. Decentralisation became, arguably, different in kind from earlier phases of suburbanisation, and there was a leap-frogging out of developed areas, over various barrier zones, into ever more rural areas (Cheshire, 1989). The conventional view developed that processes of desuburbanisation, or counter-urbanisation, were dominant in contemporary and future urban development and form. Volumes with eye-catching titles appeared, exploring this theme: *Can Cities Survive?* (Pettengill and Uppal, 1974) and *The Mature Metropolis* (Leven, 1978) being examples.

Three major themes are evident in current debates on compactness as a desirable urban form. Probably the longest established, and most common, is that a contained and compact city has a corollary of rural protection (McLaren, 1992). In the UK this line of reasoning is most clear in the twentieth century legislative restrictions on sprawl, from the 1935 Restriction of Ribbon Development Act to the still-current popularity of green belts. A second, more recent theme is that compactness promotes key socio-economic indicators of 'quality of life' including social interactions and ready access to services and facilities. This theme is visible in current moves towards planning 'neo-traditional' urban forms, 'urban villages' (Urban Villages Group, 1992) and, in the terms promoted by the Department of the Environment, 'vitality and viability' (DoE, 1994b). This theme is that compactness will necessarily result in a reduced need for transportation, thus less energy expenditure and less pollution emissions. The third theme is the focus of UK government initiatives including the report, *Sustainable Development: The UK Strategy*, and Planning Policy Guidance Note 13 (DoE, 1993a; 1994a) together with considerable academic research and debate (Breheny, 1995).

One of the key problems with the compact city hypothesis is that it thus brings very diverse concepts together under a potentially misleading banner. Moreover, these concepts vary from polemics based on rather Utopian ideologies through to minutely detailed empirical research, and there is also a marked trend towards computerised forecasting and urban modelling. This diversity has led to considerable differences in opinion over how far and how fast compactness should be encouraged, although there is considerable agreement over the desirability of compact form *per se*; compare, for example, the politically driven and very influential EC *Green Paper on the Urban Environment* (Commission of the European Communities, 1990) and the similarly influential report for Friends of the Earth by Elkin *et al.* (1991). Further, there is little agreement over the practical solution to encouraging or enforcing compactness. Should it be radical or incremental? Should existing urban areas be reshaped, or should compactness instead be sought in new developments and new settlements? Moore, for example, poses a series of significant, yet unanswered, questions in response to Hertfordshire's consultation draft structure plan which proposed to 'remodel' existing settlements to make them both self-sufficient and self-sustaining. He asks:

... 'remodelling' therefore becomes sustainable - and vice versa? How exactly do you remodel an existing settlement without tearing it down and starting again? Is it therefore a practical proposition? Should others be seeking to do the same? What happens to the local population affected by the 'remodelling' process? (Moore, 1995, p.26).

Reviewing contributions to a recent edited book, Breheny suggested that there was some consensus on some issues, including some which might address Moore's concerns:

- urban containment policies should continue to be adopted, and the decentralisation process slowed down;
- extreme compact city proposals are unrealistic and undesirable;
- various forms of 'decentralised concentration', based around single cities or groups of towns, may be appropriate;
- inner cities must be rejuvenated; and
- mixed uses must be encouraged in cities, and zoning discouraged. (Breheny, 1992a, p.22).

Why planners?

These confusions over issues of sustainability, and the role and shape of the compact city, suggest that a holistic policy approach is required. At all levels, from local to national, it would seem the town planners have a *prima facie* claim to this role.

Welbank, then President of the Royal Town Planning Institute, suggested that 'planning is being asked to fight the battle of "sustainable development" with no weapons and with very little strategic direction' (Welbank, 1992). Despite this pessimistic view, it was the closely related issues of uncontrolled growth versus quality of life which brought planning as a professional activity into being. Those issues are still operative, albeit if somewhat changed in their nature and extent. Further, recent important commentaries (Van der Ryn and Calthorpe, 1991; Roseland, 1992) develop the idea of sustainability and community 'on the local and regional scales at which most traditional planning occurs' (Beatley, 1995a, p.340).

In general terms, Rees (1995) and Beatley (1995b) have argued for the primacy of the role of planners in guiding the overall transition from worldwide growth to sustainability.

Planners, by the very nature of their profession, are uniquely positioned to play a leadership role in this transition. In this increasingly fragmented and specialized world, planning is the one academic discipline and professional pursuit that explicitly attempts to be holistic or at least integrative at the level of society as a whole. At its best, planning provides a context in which the specialized knowledge of other disciplines comes together and begins to make unified sense. (Rees, 1995, p.355)

Others have suggested that the attraction of the whole field of sustainability for planners is that it allows them to regain some professional integrity where planning has been fighting for recognition and status for at least one decade

(Perman, 1995).

Yet, at present, the planning profession is concerned with a number of activities which have not yet been subjected to testing for sustainability, for example conservation or development control. Other policy areas are being considered through environmental appraisal, including plan-making, implementation and review. But other areas of concern will make a major contribution to assessing the validity of the concept of the compact city - including economic development, urban regeneration and renewal, housing, transport and infrastructure. Planners already have significant influence in these areas, but what adjustments to this influence need to be made if the compact city hypothesis is to be operationalised? Planners also have considerable experience in understanding the constraints upon implementing the compact city hypothesis, particularly in the fields of urban form and design. The remainder of this chapter examines two examples of planning concerns relevant to the compact city hypothesis, suggesting how the role of planning may be developed.

The example of suburban conservation

Conservation is a policy area currently high on the social and political agenda (Larkham, 1992, Ch.2). It places a severe test on the legitimacy of planning through its direct interference in the usual processes of development; the prolongation of normal cycles of building and area decay, dereliction and replacement; and the alteration of financial interests in property through increasing or lowering individual and social use and hope values via identification, designations and grant aid (cf. Lichfield, 1988; Scanlon *et al.*, 1994). As conservation is now such a well developed aspect of planning, and many of these concerns will also relate to sustainability in general and the compact city in particular, will conservation planners be well placed to deal with the practical aspects of introducing compactness?

In the UK, various types of suburb are rapidly becoming the most common type of conservation area to be designated (cf. Pearce *et al.*, 1990). It is likely that it will be in these suburbs that the compact city will first bite; but there will inevitably also be development implications in historic town cores. Breheny (1992b) has already identified a key contradiction between the compact city concept and existing suburban values and qualities of life. He suggests that, for the UK at least, it is unlikely that further urban growth can be accommodated entirely within existing urban boundaries. Research has suggested that, particularly for the South East region, only 55% of the new building necessary in the present decade can be accommodated as 'urban infill'; the remainder would have to be suburban expansions, new settlements or expanded villages (Tym and Partners, 1987; Bibby and Shepherd, 1991). Public resistance to increased suburban densities may even lower the 'urban infill' proportion (SERPLAN, 1988). Breheny (1991; 1992b) suggests that the compact city view, at least as proposed by the EC Green Paper, ignores the realities and popularity of suburban development and the suburban way of life, and does not suggest how to convert existing suburbs into the desired high density, diverse, culturally rich cores. He concludes that:

> The more we debate these issues of sustainability, the more we seem to
> throw up complications and contradictions. None of these contradictions
> of the compact city deny that the proposal has merit. What they do suggest

is that the issue is complex and needs careful analysis and extensive debate. This implies that in the short term the problem may seem to become more, not less intractable. This is bad news for planners, who are under immediate pressure to respond practically to the sustainability problem. (Breheny, 1991)

There is a relevant current debate in Australia where the pejorative term 'sprawl' has been used to press the case for 'urban consolidation' (cf. Kirwan, 1992). However, counter-arguments are suggested by research on suburban land use and density (Harrison, 1970; McGloughlin, 1991) which shows that, because only a small proportion of urban land is used for residential purposes, it would require tremendous increases in residential density to achieve even modest reductions in city size (Troy, 1992, p.240). Troy draws attention to the likely problems for urban infrastructure if 'urban consolidation' does occur. Water and sewerage systems, road networks and facilities for education, amenity and recreation would all require massive investment and redevelopment, while 'redeveloping inner areas to higher densities involves the destruction of development, much of which is structurally sound and could be refurbished...' (*ibid*, p.241).

In Birmingham, clear conflicts are present in planning actions in the suburb of Hall Green, which is a part of a large expanse of inter-war suburbia in the south east of Birmingham. School Road itself was constructed mainly by a single developer and consists of semi-detached houses, a public house, a parade of shops and a group of almshouses. The issues surrounding designation of this common development form as a conservation area even led to a feature article in *The Times*:

> Birmingham's aim is to wrap this Arcadia in aspic by means of a conservation order, and all the signs are that it will manage to do so ... If it does, then this may be the very first development of the period to be thus protected in this country. In practical terms it would mean that nothing in the designated area of about 150 homes could be added to or altered unless strictly in the style of the original. ... One immediate result of that would be to prevent any more of the bay windows disappearing as the softwood rots and the owners look for a cheaper replacement. ... School Road happens to be an excellent example of the genus, and the whole city has become so sensitive about conserving what is good that it is now doing so long before a desperate rearguard action is required. (Franks, 1988, p.11)

The justification for designation, recalling that UK conservation areas must possess 'special' interest, is that this area is unusual since it has remained largely unchanged since development: no infilling, few extensions or other alterations, and most buildings retain original period features. The designation has been well received by most locals, although professional planners and conservation groups outside the city have expressed surprise.

Public resistance to increased densities is currently evident in another part of Hall Green, of a similar semi-detached character. Here, several speculative developers had acquired planning permission to develop small estates of between six and twelve houses on 'backland' sites in the early 1990s. These were previously open sites including tennis courts and nursery gardens, and parts of private back gardens which had been purchased from the owners. Such infill development is a common house builders' strategy to overcome the lack of identified residential development sites. In 1995 a major petition-signing campaign was organised in the majority of the district's shops, and through the local free newspapers; the resulting petition was handed to the city's planners and politicians, but development pressure remains high. The local people were concerned about their own amenities, overlooking from the new houses (some of which were very close to existing properties) and increased traffic. Schools and other infrastructure would, it was argued, be unable to cope with this influx.

The key issue surrounding the compact city versus suburbia conflict is thus a variant of the NIMBY (Not In My Back Yard) phenomenon. Increasingly, societal pressure drives the designation and retention of suburbs for reasons of conservation, and militates against increasing residential densities. Where 'densification' has occurred in low density mature suburbia, it is perceived as unsatisfactory for a variety of reasons (some of which are explored in Whitehand and Larkham, 1991; Whitehand *et al.*, 1992). Yet, largely on the grounds of energy savings in transportation, many would suggest that suburbia is a significantly unsustainable urban form: sprawl should be stopped, suburbs torn down and development contained closer to city cores. Thus public conservationism and theoretical sustainability are in direct conflict.

A further conflict arises in those city cores, many of which retain key historic structures and layouts. The EC Green Paper suggested that the compact city vision:

> offers density and variety, the efficient, time- and energy-saving combination of social and economic functions; the chance to restore the rich architecture inherited from the past. (Commission of the European Communities, 1990, p.19)

Yet major ethical and practical problems in retaining and reusing some of this rich architecture already exist, as the heated debate on 'facadism' shows (Barrett and Larkham, 1994). If development pressures are increased through compacting pressures on the suburbs and the already burgeoning 'edge cities' (Garreau, 1991) then yet more historic buildings will be at best altered for new uses, at worst demolished, and inevitably their settings will be altered for other new construction. All this has happened in recent upswings of development pressure.

The example of economic development

As clearly powerful as the new set of guidelines contained in Planning Policy Guidance Notes 6 and 13 (DoE, 1993b; 1994a) may be, it shares with all land use regulatory control systems an essentially negative control character. This suggests that gains for sustainability must await the pace of commercially driven demand for changes to existing land use. The rapid reshaping of existing settlements to new, more compact urban forms is thus unlikely. However, for planning to be able to strengthen its commitment to sustainable development, it must seek much stronger relations with other aspects of local government and control. In the UK, the economic development function of local government is a prime candidate for such links. This function is regulated by Part III of the 1989 Local Government and Housing Act. Several authors have recently addressed the issue of economic development and the environment (Daly and Cobb, 1989; Gibbs, 1991; 1993; 1994; Haughton and Hunter, 1994; Jacobs and Stott, 1992; Local Government Management Board, 1993).

In the past, the economic development function of local authorities when confronting substantial job losses could largely be described as promoting inward investment at any cost. In the late 1970s and 1980s, the metropolitan counties began to set other agendas, including a more equitable distribution of employment opportunities. Local authorities which allocate resources to the economic development function are required, under the 1989 Act, first to consult widely, but specifically among the local business community, and secondly to produce an annual strategy statement. Recently, some of these statements have begun to make explicit reference to the goal of sustainable development.

The statement produced for Birmingham in 1994 is a useful example (Birmingham City Council, 1994). The 1994/7 strategy document contains fourteen strategic aims and policies as follows: three are concerned with developing skills and employment; one with regenerating local areas; four with encouraging development and investment; one with encouraging the regional economic role of the city centre; one with participating in the implementation strategy; and, lastly, four are concerned with improving business performance. It is within this last group that a specific strategic aim deals with sustainability. This is referred to in terms of encouraging the achievement of a sustainable economy. It makes cross-references to the City's *Green Action Plan* (Birmingham City Council, 1993), the requirement of the 1990 Environmental Protection Act to monitor for the environmental appraisal of commercial activities, and the British Standard 7750 applications from local firms (concerning the environmental duty of care). It stresses that 'interdepartmental collaboration is essential'. It specifically refers to the activity of the city in raising awareness among local firms, undertakes to assist firms by better signposting of legally enforceable environmental requirements, and to assist in the introduction of European eco-management and audit schemes into local industry. In addition waste minimisation and recycling, energy-saving, clean technologies, and derelict land reclamation are all stated objectives.

Despite energetic work by the UK Local Government Management Board (LGMB, 1993; 1994), there are clearly many more opportunities to assist the remodelling of the spatial economy along more sustainable lines. This brief review of Birmingham's plan confirms the general impression that environmental statements concerned with the economy focus upon industrial processes with reference to energy and waste, the use of recycled land, the impact of legislation and product life-cycle analysis.

Conclusions

This chapter has argued for closer involvement of UK planners in sustainability issues, through the policy development and implementation of the other departments of local government. In particular, a familiarity with the techniques and objectives of those concerned not only with environmental protection in its various forms, but also with economic development, seems to be an imperative.

The instruments through which planners hope to modify spatial behaviour are extremely long term ones. It is relevant that the urban area is rebuilt at only about 1% of area per year. Current government planning guidance in Planning Policy Guidance Notes 6 and 13 (DoE, 1993b; 1994a) can have only very long term effects. The absence of tangible benefits could well undermine confidence in the ability of the planning system to deliver sustainability. The absence of immediate 'feel-good factors' arising from new planning guidance could result in jeopardising the momentum of environmental policy unless a more integrated approach is adopted.

Although planners have several decades of experience in conservation planning, this is still often a fringe activity of planning departments. Planners are still far from resolving the contradictions inherent in conservation. Conservation has little relevance to standard theories of planning (Plant, 1993). Nevertheless, these contradictions have largely been successfully ignored. The public popularity of conservation planning remains high. This suggests that planners could cope with the contradictions of the compact city. There may, however, be a fundamental disagreement if operationalising compactness does imply a radical reshaping of suburbia - but it need not do so. And if conservation has tested the legitimacy and popularity of planning, then the painful decisions involved in reshaping cities for compactness will do so to an even greater extent. The experience of planning for conservation could thus be useful.

The planning and creation of a more compact local economy, particularly in terms of work travel and service travel, would self-evidently make a contribution to reducing traffic-generated energy consumption. It could reduce urban atmospheric pollution and assist urban regeneration by bringing higher quality city centre jobs within reach of the inner city population. In addition, inducements to firms would have to be considered in a general shift of taxation policy and practice away from taxing employment towards taxing resource consumption. The miles travelled by a firm's employees in getting to work should no longer be treated as externalities. A revision in accounting procedures should require firms to acknowledge their use of the environmental resource. This could mean some form of negative company tax for eco-miles saved. It would, in effect, be some kind of variation on the theme of carbon tax. But implementing this new local economy is a function both of economic and of physical planning.

At what level would this policy intervention be pitched? The social city region seems most appropriate (Breheny and Rookwood, 1993). Regional planning, land use and transport are currently influenced by regional planning guidance. Yet the published Regional Planning Guidance notes are demonstrably inadequate. However, in the UK, the Government regional offices have been charged with many new tasks of integration, including the bidding for administration of the Single Regeneration Budget. To introduce any degree of compactness in the future, city planning would require stronger regional guidance and planning, closer co-operation between regions and their individual local authorities, together with the development of suitable incentives through government action.

The local level will be particularly significant in effecting compactness. It is here that the public will come into contact with the decision-makers. Planning has learned much about public consultation and involvement since the poorly handled comprehensive clearance and redevelopment schemes of the 1950s and 1960s (cf. Esher, 1981). Reshaping cities for compactness will be at least as controversial, even if incremental (rather than radical and rapid) change is sought.

The public must be educated and persuaded to support this policy direction, even at the cost of losing the indiscriminate use of the private car. Thus the lessons of the past could be used in implementing compactness; and issues of sustainability in general, and compactness in particular, must be embedded in planning education and training.

References

Ashworth, W. (1954) *The Genesis of Modern British Town Planning: A Study in Economic and Social History in the Nineteenth and Twentieth Centuries*, Routledge and Kegan Paul, London.

Barlow Report (1940) *Report of the Royal Commission on the Distribution of the Industrial Population*, Cmd 6153, HMSO, London.

Barrett, H. and Larkham, P.J. (1994) *Disguising Development: Facadism in City Centres*, Research Paper 11, Faculty of the Built Environment, University of Central England.

Beatley, T. (1995a) The many meanings of sustainability. *Journal of Planning Literature,* **9 (4)**, pp.339-42.

Beatley, T. (1995b) Planning and sustainability: the elements of a new (improved?) paradigm. *Journal of Planning Literature,* **9 (4)**, pp.384-95.

Bedarida, F. (1979) *A Social History of England 1851-1975*, Methuen, London.

Bibby, P. and Shepherd, J. (1991) *Rates of Urbanization in England, 1981-2001*, HMSO, London.

Birmingham City Council (1993) *The Green Action Plan: The Environment in Birmingham*, City Council, Birmingham.

Birmingham City Council (1994) *Economic Development Strategy for Birmingham 1994/7*, City Council, Birmingham.

Breheny, M.J. (1991) *The Contradictions of the Compact City*, paper presented to the ACSP/AESOP Conference, Oxford.

Breheny, M.J. (1992a) Sustainable development and urban form: an introduction, in *Sustainable Development and Urban Form* (ed. M.J. Breheny) Pion, London.

Breheny, M.J. (1992b) The contradictions of the compact city: a review, in *Sustainable Development and Urban Form* (ed. M.J. Breheny) Pion, London.

Breheny, M.J. (1995) The compact city and transport energy consumption. *Transactions, Institute of British Geographers* **NS 20 (1)**, pp.81-101.

Breheny, M.J. and Rookwood, R. (1993) Planning the sustainable city region, in *Planning for a Sustainable Environment: A Report by the Town and Country Planning Association* (ed. A. Blowers) Earthscan, London.

Cherry, G.E. (1988) *Cities and Plans: The Shaping of Urban Britain in the Nineteenth and Twentieth Centuries*, Edward Arnold, London.

Cheshire, P. (1989) The future shape of towns, in *British Towns and the Quality of Life,* Papers from the 90th Anniversary Conference of the Town and Planning Association. TCPA, London.

Commission of the European Communities (1990) *Green Paper on the Urban Environment*, EUR 12902 European Commission, Brussels.

Daly, H.E. and Cobb, J.B. (1989) *For the Common Good: Redirecting the Economy Toward Community, the Environment and a Sustainable Future*, Beacon Press, Boston, Mass.

Department of the Environment (1993a) *Sustainable Development: The UK Strategy*, Cmnd 2426 HMSO, London.

Department of the Environment (1993b) *Town Centres and Retail Developments*, Planning Policy Guidance Note 6 (revised), HMSO, London.

Department of the Environment (1994a) *Transport*, Planning Policy Guidance Note 13 (revised) HMSO, London.

Department of the Environment (1994b) *Quality in Town and Country*, HMSO, London.

Elkin, T., McLaren, D. and Hillman, M. (1991) *Reviving the City: Towards Sustainable Urban Development*, Friends of the Earth, London.

Esher, L. (1981) *A Broken Wave: The Rebuilding of England 1940-1980,* Allen Lane, London.

Franks, A. (1988) The street they froze in time. *The Times,* 15 July, p.11.

Garreau, J. (1991) *Edge City: Life on the New Frontier,* Doubleday, New York.

Gibbs, D. (1991) Greening the Local Economy. *Local Economy.* **6 (3)**, pp.224-39.

Gibbs, D. (1993) *The Green Local Economy*, Centre for Local Economic Strategies, Manchester.

Gibbs, D. (1994) Towards the sustainable city: greening the local economy. *Town Planning Review,* **65 (1)**, pp.99-109.

Hague, C. (1984) *The Development of Planning Thought: A Critical Perspective*, Hutchinson, London.

Hall, D., Hebbert, M. and Lusser, H. (1993) The planning background, in *Planning for a Sustainable Environment: A Report by the Town and Country Planning Association* (ed. A. Blowers) Earthscan, London.

Hardy, D. (1991) *From Garden Cities to New Towns: Campaigning for Town and Country Planning, 1899-1946*, E & FN Spon, London.

Harrison, P.F. (1970) Measuring urban sprawl, in *Analysis of Urban Development*, Proceedings of the Tewkesbury Symposium, University of Melbourne.

Haughton, G. and Hunter, C. (1994) *Sustainable Cities*, Jessica Kingsley/Regional Studies Association, London.

Hebbert, M. (1983) The Daring Experiment: social scientists and land use planning in 1940s Britain. *Environment and Planning B*, **10**, pp.3-17.

Jacobs, M. and Stott, M. (1992) Sustainable development and the local economy. *Local Economy* **7 (3)**, pp.261-72.

Kirwan, R. (1992) Urban consolidation. *Australian Planner,* **30** March, pp.20-25.

Larkham, P.J. (1992) Conservation and the changing urban landscape. *Progress in Planning* **37 (2)**, pp.83-181.

Leven, C.L. (1978) *The Mature Metropolis*, D.C. Heath, Lexington, Mass.

Lichfield, N. (1988) *Economics of Urban Conservation*, Cambridge University Press, Cambridge.

Local Government Management Board (1993) *Greening Economic Development: Integrating Economic and Environmental Strategies in Local Government*, LGMB, Luton.

Local Government Management Board (1994) *Local Agenda 21 Round Table Guidance Notes 3: Greening the Local Economy,* LGMB, Luton.

Lovering, J. (1995) Creating discourse rather than jobs: the crisis in the cities and the transition fantasies of intellectuals and policy makers, in *Managing Cities: The New Urban Context* (eds P. Healey *et al.*) Wiley, Chichester.

McGloughlin, B. (1991) Urban consolidation and urban sprawl: a question of density. *Urban Policy and Research*, **9 (3)**, pp.148-56.

McLaren, D. (1992) Compact or dispersed? dilution is no solution. *Built Environment,* **18**, pp.268-84.

Moore, A. (1995) Time to make sense out of sustainability. *Planning* **1102**, pp.26-27.

Pearce, G., Hems, L. and Hennessy, B. (1990) *The Conservation Areas of England,* English Heritage, London.

Perman, R. (1995) Review of C.C. Williams and G. Haughton (eds) (1994) Perspectives towards sustainable environmental development. Avebury, Aldershot. *Regional Studies,* **29 (5)**, pp.426-27.

Pettengill, R.B. and Uppal, J.S. (1974) *Can Cities Survive?* St Martin's Press, New York.

Plant, H. (1993) *The Use and Abuse of Conservation Area Designation Powers by Local Planning Authorities in the West Midlands Region,* unpublished MA thesis, School of Planning, University of Central England.

Rees, W.E. (1995) Achieving sustainability: reform or transformation? *Journal of Planning Literature,* **9 (4)**, pp.341-61.

Roberts, P. (1995) *Coordinating the Planning of Metropolitan Regions: Making Progress Towards Strategies for Sustainable Development,* Paper presented at the Annual Conference of the Institute of British Geographers, Newcastle upon Tyne.

Roseland, M. (1992) *Toward Sustainable Communities*, National Round Table on the Environment and the Economy, Ottawa.

Scanlon, K., Edge, A., Wilmott, T. *et al.* (1994) *The Economics of Listed Buildings*, Discussion Paper 43 Cambridge: Department of Land Economy, University of Cambridge.

SERPLAN (1988) *Housing Provision in the South East: A Report by W.S. Grigson*, RPC 1230 SERPLAN, London.

Troy, P. (1992) Defending the quarter-acre block against the new feudalism. *Town and Country Planning,* September, pp.240-43.

Tym, R. and Partners (1987) *Land Used for Residential Development in the South East: Summary Report,* Roger Tym and Partners, London.

Urban Villages Group (1992) *Urban Villages: A Concept for Creating Mixed-Use Urban Developments on a Sustainable Scale,* Urban Villages Group, London.

Van der Ryn, S. and Calthorpe, P. (1991) *Sustainable Communities,* Sierra Club Books, San Francisco.

Ward, S. (1994) *Planning and Urban Change,* Paul Chapman, London.

Welbank, M. (1992) Opening address to the Annual Conference of the Royal Town Planning Institute, Birmingham.

Whitehand, J.W.R. and Larkham, P.J. (1991) Housebuilding in the back garden. *Area,* **23 (1)**, pp.57-65.

Whitehand, J.W.R., Larkham, P.J. and Jones, A.N. (1992) The changing suburban landscape in postwar England, in *Urban Landscapes: International Perspectives* (eds J.W.R. Whitehand and P.J. Larkham) Routledge, London.

Harley Sherlock

Repairing Our Much Abused Cities: *The Way to Sustainable Living*

Introduction

> People came together in cities in order to live. They remain together in
> order to live the good life. (Aristotle)

From ancient times until the latter half of the twentieth century, cities were
indisputably the very essence of civilisation, although Aristotle's reason for their
continuing existence was clearly not the only one. They probably came into
being in the first place when interdependent craftsmen found that they could
better serve their separate agricultural villages by working together in a central
location. But they eventually became centres of power capable of defending
themselves and exercising power over their rivals. In medieval Europe they became
oases of semi-freedom within the feudal system.

In England, feudalism was actually brought to an end by London's support
for the barons against the King in 1215; and it is ironic that the comparatively
stable form of government that followed Magna Carta made strongly defended
towns no longer necessary. This reduced the power of English towns in comparison
with the city states of mainland Europe; but it allowed them to expand beyond
their defensive walls, while their European rivals were constrained by their
fortifications. Thus Paris, which
remained a fortified city until 1870, had twice the population density of London
- and still does! (Mogridge, 1985).

If fortifications were no longer a curb on the expansion of English towns, the
distances that people could walk, or goods could be carried, ultimately were. It
was not until the 1860s that the railways started carrying people to work rather
than just carrying fuel and raw materials to urban factories at the centres of
population. However, as soon as it did become possible to live remote from
one's place of work in the smoky city, the better off were quick to do so. In
London the Great Northern Railway advertisements posed the question 'Why

live in London when you could still work in the city and live in the Muswell Hill countryside?'. The trouble was that as soon as people moved in large numbers to Muswell Hill the countryside moved to Potters Bar! The dream of living in the country and working in the city became - and still remains - a nightmare, as new suburbs continuously leapfrog those that preceded them. It also contributed to urban degradation, as those whose influence might have improved the residential environment no longer had a direct interest in such improvement. The result in most towns was, inevitably, fine civic centres surrounded by inner city slums and an outer ring of leafy suburbs.

Ebenezer Howard's *Garden Cities of Tomorrow*, published in its original form in 1898, condemned the large conurbation and proposed instead clusters of small, comparatively dense, garden cities of 30,000 people, with everyone living within walking distance of their place of work, but with trams or railways connecting each city to its neighbour from which it was separated by about two miles of open countryside. London rebuilt in such a fashion would take up four-and-a-half times its present area; and it must be doubtful whether, even in Howard's day, space could have been found to rehouse a major part of the population in garden city style. It would certainly be near impossible now, especially in the south-east of England.

The New Town at Letchworth (started before World War One) followed Howard's principle of community ownership of freeholds; and Welwyn, built in the 1920s and 30s, followed some of his ideas on layout. But new housing before World War Two was, in fact, almost exclusively suburban. It was usually in the form of sprawling ribbon development; although, following the Tudor Walters Report in 1918, some public sector suburbs were developed in garden city style. The inner city slums remained almost untouched.

The housing disaster
With the end of World War Two, and with up to a third of the stock of inner city housing derelict, both the need and the opportunity existed for rehousing much of the urban population. Howard's ideas had been kept alive for fifty years by the Town and Country Planning Association; and they were adapted by the wartime coalition Government, and by the Labour Government which followed it, to become the programme of satellite towns designed to relieve the shortage of housing in the large cities. The New Towns were designed for populations more than double those of Howard's garden cities, and they were built to a very much lower density. There was no question of everyone being within walking distance of the town centre, and they were heavily dependent on good local bus services. Milton Keynes, one of the last generation of New Towns, was designed to accommodate 200,000 people and was built to an even lower density in order to cater for near-universal car ownership (which it did successfully). But the result is less a 'city' than an out-of-town shopping centre surrounded by suburbs. And it is so land-hungry that it could never be a model for the rebuilding of south-east England. London's population, if re-housed Milton-Keynes-fashion, as a single conurbation, would require two-and-a-half times the present area of the capital. Re-housed as thirty-three cities of 200,000 people (with intervening countryside like Ebenezer Howard's cluster of cities), it would require eleven times the area of London.

The other, and more important, aspect of postwar housing was of course that of re-building within the cities themselves. Although the Danish planner Steen Eiller Rasmussen argued strongly for the retention of the friendly 'English' urban street, such streets were seen by most people as bomb-damaged, bug-ridden reminders of the 1930s slump. And architects preferred the 'ville radieuse' of Le Corbusier: tall buildings with 'streets in the sky', long-distance views, fresh air, and with parkland between the buildings. The London County Council's pioneering estate at Roehampton was greatly admired and quickly emulated. But its success was a lot to do with its close proximity to Richmond Park; and when similar estates were built in more humdrum surroundings, it was found that the views did not make up for the loss of the street community and of the children's freedom to play outside their own front doors. Even more disastrously, with the inevitable revolt against family living in high-rise estates, came a revolt against urban living itself, particularly against urban housing densities, which became associated with tower blocks rather than with Georgian terraces. If it had not been for the almost total lack of new urban housing during the 1980s, many of our towns and cities might by now have been suburbanised beyond redemption: with communities scattered, populations reduced, and local facilities closed through lack of custom. This would have been (and still could be) a worse urban disaster than the housing policies of the 1960s.

The transport disaster

If tower-block housing represents one of the twin disasters of the postwar urban environment, the other is clearly the gradual domination of city streets by traffic. As more people take to their cars, life is made increasingly unpleasant for pedestrians and cyclists; public transport declines further, and it becomes more difficult than ever for people to get around or to get goods collected or delivered. The Government's Buchanan Report published in 1963 made it clear that for cities to work socially, environmentally and commercially in the age of the motor car they had to be completely rebuilt - with vehicles and pedestrians at different levels - or there had to be draconian traffic restraint. Both the Government and opposition of the day accepted these alternatives. But when public opinion and economic restraint ruled out the rebuilding option, the politicians ducked the issue of rational traffic restraint and opted instead for 'restraint by congestion': the policy that still prevails now, more than thirty years on, in spite of its obvious failure.

Table 1 demonstrates very clearly the deteriorating efficiency of London's roads. In 1956 they were able to carry 404,000 people to central London every day. They now carry only 251,000, as the effect of road-widening and more sophisticated traffic signalling has been far outweighed by the switch from buses to private cars. This has been allowed to happen in spite of Buchanan's warnings in 1963, and in spite of the GLC's evidence to the Greater London Development Plan Inquiry (1971) which showed that only 10% of commuters to central London arrived by car, but that they accounted for almost 70% of rush hour traffic. It is hardly surprising that, as a result of the lack of any rational road policy, railways and underground services in 1988 became so overcrowded that some stations had to be temporarily closed on safety grounds.

Dispersal versus concentration

Partly, no doubt, because of the twin failures of urban housing and urban transport,

291

it was fashionable in the 1970s to assume that there was no future for towns and cities in the compact European tradition. Rayner Banham, the architectural critic, used to maintain that the only community that mattered was the dinner party community of like-minded people who simply needed to be connected by a motorway. Even urban historian Gordon Cherry, in 1972, seemed to welcome the shift away from the radial transportation system that supported the compact city. He foresaw instead a rectangular transport grid covering a whole region, with the specialist activities that once went on at the centre of the old style city dispersed to a number of centres located at junctions of the circulation system. Plenty of Cherry's contemporaries admired the continuing urban tradition in mainland Europe, and the investment - especially in public transport - that made it possible in the late twentieth century. But many of them concluded that Anglo-Saxon devotion to private transport made better-planned-but-endless suburbia the most likely future for this country.

Table 1. People to Central London, 7-10am, by mode of travel.

Source: London Transport, Economic Planning and Development Division

	1956	1964	1972	1980	1988	1994
Cars/Cycles	144,000	176,000	185,000	211,000	177,000	165,000
Bus/Coach	260,000	191,000	195,000	113,000	101,000	86,000
Total Road	404,000	367,000	380,000	324,000	278,000	251,000
Tube/BR	748,000	849,000	823,000	717,000	879,000	738,000
Grand Total	1,152,000	1,216,600	1,203,000	1,041,000	1,157,000	989,000

At the Rio Summit in 1992, however, John Major committed his Government to reducing our contribution to global pollution. And, as part of that commitment, the Department of the Environment published *Planning Policy Guidance 13 (PPG13)*(1994), calling, amongst other things, for a new attitude to land use planning which would reduce the need to travel. This would be achieved by bringing traffic-generating facilities, like large retail stores, back into the towns where people live, and where they are more easily reached on foot, by bicycle, or by public transport. PPG 13 also called for an increase in urban density which, in the long run, would make our cities more compact, and get us at last building new communities where - as with Ebenezer Howard's original garden city concept - most of the necessities and pleasures of life are within walking distance. The switch in Government thinking away from the general acceptance of car-oriented dispersal should not be underestimated. But it has to be recognised that a great deal of dispersal has already taken place, and that stopping this trend, let alone reversing it, is not going to be easy. Already we have suburban commercial centres poorly served by public transport, and business parks - remote from the community - which can be reached only by car. Furthermore some local administrative offices have been moved to out-of-town locations; and the trend to move hospitals out into the country is still going on. The latter may suit the car-borne administrators who make such decisions; but it certainly is not in the interests of a considerable number of those (the elderly) who need hospital treatment, or need to visit those who do. It is ironic, and in no one's interest, that the health service should be making more work for itself by adding to atmospheric pollution through encouraging those who run or use the service to reach it by car. Even the Government's most welcome turn against out-of-centre retailing is in danger of becoming a case of closing the stable door after the horse has bolted.

The point has been well made that polluting our planet is nothing less than stealing from our grandchildren, and that 'sustainability' means living now in such a way that we do not threaten future life. It has also been pointed out that, in the name of equity, we cannot keep global pollution under control by asking the 'third world' not to emulate our lifestyle. If, as seems likely, the planet cannot accommodate everyone in the world consuming resources at the rate we do, then we clearly have to reduce our consumption of energy. And as the Government has pointed out, the best way of doing this is to reduce our need to travel. And the best way to reduce travel is to live in compact cities where everything is close at hand.

Although there may be isolated pockets of overcrowding in some areas, our cities generally suffer not from overcrowding but from loss of population. And bringing back people and commerce will help them to emulate the higher density cities of mainland Europe - which are made attractive, to residents and traders alike, through the variety and diversity of activities which a compact city can provide. European cities particularly demonstrate the advantages of a mixture of land uses in urban areas. For example, the fact that there are usually people living in central business areas means that, unlike the City of London, such areas do not become 'dead' in the evening and at weekends when the offices are closed.

But can the compact city, with its social, commercial and environmental advantages still provide us with the sort of housing we want? It certainly cannot provide the typical semi-detached suburban house and garage; but it can provide a modern equivalent of our equally loved Georgian streets and squares. The fact is that, although many of the Georgian and Victorian streets demolished after World War Two were overcrowded, the tower blocks that replaced them were usually built to the same density in terms of space provided. When, in the 1970s, rehabilitation became an acceptable alternative to redevelopment, the typical tower block density of 360 people per hectare was often attained, usually with space standards in excess of those customarily provided in new buildings.

Fig. 1 shows a typical Georgian terrace converted in the late 1970s for the London Borough of Islington. It provides two family homes compatible with modern living. The lower dwelling has its entrance, living rooms and garden at basement level, with bedrooms at ground floor level. The upper dwelling uses the original front door, but is otherwise on the upper floors, with the rear mansard roof removed to provide a roof garden adjacent to the kitchen/dining room. Fig. 2 shows a hypothetical variation on a 1970s new-build estate, with a wider frontage and shallower depth than the original, thus making it suitable for 'street' housing, with one car per dwelling, or two cars for every three dwellings if the two upper floors provide two small dwellings instead of one large one.

To accommodate the cars, the street is wider than normal for an access road, taking up much of the space which, in a typical development, would be used as front gardens. But it is designed along the lines of a Dutch Woonerf (street for living in), with trees and shrubs, not only to minimise the impact of parked cars, but also to form a chicane to keep speeds down to little more than walking pace.

The point about both examples is that they illustrate housing densities of about 360 people per hectare, as compared with the maximum permitted density of 250 people per hectare applied by most London boroughs. There are of course endless arguments about the best way of measuring densities; but the development control density (site curtilage plus the lesser of 6 metres or half the width of the road) is, whether we like it or not, the one used by planning authorities. And the fact that 250 people per hectare is an absurdly low maximum for urban areas has been well demonstrated by Rob Scott of planning consultants Llewelyn-Davies. At the Town and Country Planning Association in April 1994 he showed many slides of well known Georgian and Victorian terraces, and pointed out that the one thing they all had in common was that they exceeded the maximum permitted density by almost 50% and would, therefore, not now have received planning permission!

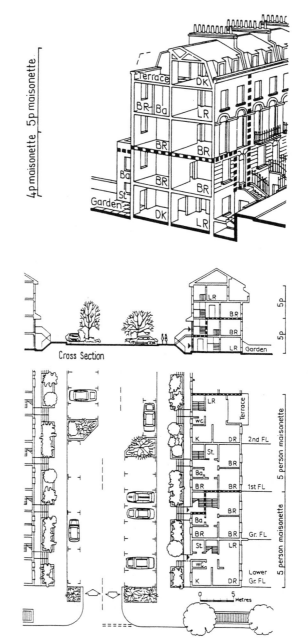

Fig. 1. Georgian houses converted into two maisonettes. Development control density 360 people per hectare.

Adapted from Cities Are Good For Us, Sherlock 1991

Fig. 2. Modern equivalent to Fig. 1. 360 people per hectare. One car space per dwelling.

Adapted from Cities Are Good For Us, Sherlock 1991

A claim often made by those who think the compact city has no future is that, while the better off may be prepared to suffer difficulties with car parking for the sake of living in a fine Georgian terrace, everyone else actually wants to move out of the inner city area. But this cannot be true - at least of London. In fact house prices for all types of property in the private sector are higher in Inner London than they are in the suburbs; and the few council conversions described in Fig. 1 which have had time to go through the full right-to-buy (and sell) process have sold at figures between £150,000 and £200,000. Certainly there must be many people stuck in social housing in an area they do not like and would leave if they could. But this is a criticism of their housing conditions rather than a reflection on urbanism. Indeed a recent Rowntree report (Page, 1993) emphasises the need for housing associations to avoid building new social housing in suburban situations where isolation is all too likely for those without cars, and where services are less easily provided than they are in inner city locations.

It seems therefore that, to prevent global pollution in the twenty-first century, most of us will have to live in cities. But it also seems that we need not, as a consequence, suffer in terms of our social or physical environment. In fact our quality of life should be enhanced provided that we can tame the motor car. Although Fig. 2 shows that, in the case of new housing developments, it is possible to accommodate one car per dwelling at densities up to 350 people per hectare, this is impossible in existing streets. A report by Llewelyn-Davies published in 1994 suggests that in most existing streets 200 people per hectare is about the highest density achievable. But do we need one car per dwelling in urban areas? There has been much talk about discouraging car use, and it is interesting to note that in Germany, where car ownership is higher than in Britain, cars are used less, especially in cities, where a cheap, clean and efficient public transport system is always available. But there seem to be many car owners in Britain who can only just afford to keep their cars on the road. For them the high cost of public transport (double the European average) virtually forces them to use their cars regardless of enjoinders not to do so. Nevertheless, cars should not be necessary in cities, as New Yorkers will confirm - especially if, as in New York, hire cars for journeys outside the city are cheap and readily available at a moment's notice.

In London, with things as they are, and with public transport comparatively expensive, it is clear that single people and couples without children would still make noticeable savings by foregoing car ownership, and using public transport instead, even after allowing for taxis and hired cars for journeys that are inconvenient by public transport (Table 2). Two able-bodied pensioners, with free travel in London and reduced fares elsewhere on the railways, would save almost £2,000 per annum, making the car, for them, an expensive and unnecessary luxury. For families with small children, however, cars will always be useful for carrying the inevitable clobber. But are they essential? With less traffic on the roads, and with a safer and more pleasant pavement environment, many local journeys - like the trip to school - could again be made on foot. This would give pedestrians safety in numbers, return streets to their role as meeting places and places for children to play and, incidentally, help to reduce the now high level of obesity in children. Furthermore, if the Government is successful in getting food retailing back into the towns, and closer to where people live, shopping could again be part of local community life. The Secretary of State for the Environment, John Gummer, when he launched his campaign for revitalising London's riverside, said that because of our obligations to prevent global warming, it was important to build urban homes so that more people could do without cars (*Independent*, 7th June 1995). We could go further and emulate Bremen and Amsterdam where people can live in car-free areas provided, of course, that they do not have a car themselves.

Table 2. Comparative car and public transport costs, 1995 for a couple without children living in Inner London, annual car mileage of 5000.

By private car

One partner to work by car (1000 miles at 48.85p per mile*)	£ 488
One partner to work by zone 1 & 2 travel card	£ 552
Both partners Inner London leisure (1000 miles at 48.85p per mile*)	£ 488
Both partners travel elsewhere (3000 miles at 48.85p per mile*)	£ 1,466
	£ 2,994

By public transport

Both partners unlimited work & leisure, zones 1 & 2 (£552x2)	£ 1,104
Both partners travel elsewhere (3,000 miles at 11.2p per mile **x2)	£ 672
Allowance for taxis and hire cars	£ 750
Saving	£ 468
	£ 2,994

*AA's 1995 total of car owners standing and running costs for 1100 to 1400 cc car doing 5000 miles per annum is 48.85 pence per mile excluding the cost of parking/garaging. This cost increases with engine size but decreases with greater mileage. At 10,000 and 15,000 miles per annum it drops to 30.52 and 26.17 pence per mile respectively. But such mileages are unlikely for people living and working in Inner London. (Source: AA Technical Services - Motoring costs 1995)

**BR's average fare paid per mile at 1995 prices is 11.2 pence. The lowest generally available fares average at 7.9 pence per mile, but such fares do not apply at peak travel times, so this lower figure has not been used. (Source: BR Annual Report 1995)

Conclusion

The compact city which reduces the need to travel must be an important part of any serious attempt to reduce global pollution and must therefore, at least at this stage of our evolution, be more sustainable than other ways of living. But our compact cities could also become the best places to live and work. For this to happen we need to take advantage of their ability to provide a concentration and diversity of activities; we also need to replace their unsatisfactory tower-block housing, not with an imitation of 1930's suburbia, but with a modern equivalent of our Georgian streets and squares; and we need to become less dependent on the private car. Just as our cities were once oases of freedom in a feudal world, so if we were to drive out the cars and bring back the people, our cities could now become oases of civilised living in the maelstrom of traffic congestion elsewhere.

Residential streets, shopping centres and commercial districts could then once again become proper places rather than mere thoroughfares; and we could all have the necessities and pleasures of life close at hand. As more people opted for city living rather than car-dependent dispersal, we would increase our chances of leaving behind us an unpoisoned planet for our grandchildren to inherit.

Harley Sherlock is the author of 'Cities are Good For Us' obtainable from Transport 2000, London.

References

Buchanan, C. (1963) *Traffic in Towns*, HMSO, London.

Cherry, G. (1972) *Urban Change and Planning*, Foulis, Yeovil.

Department of the Environment (1994) *Planning Policy Guidance Note 13: Transport,* HMSO, London.

Greater London Council (1971) *Greater London Development Plan*, GLC, London.

Howard, E. (1898) *Garden Cities of Tomorrow*, Attic Books, Powys.

Llewelyn-Davies (1994) *Providing More Homes in Urban Areas*, in association with the Joseph Rowntree Foundation and Environmental Trust Associates, SAUS Publications, Bristol.

Mogridge, M. (1985) Transport, Land-use and Energy Interaction. *Urban Studies* **22.** pp.481-492.

Page, D. (1993) *Building for Communities*, Joseph Rowntree Foundation, York.

Sherlock, H. (1991) *Cities Are Good For Us,* Transport 2000, London.

Tony Burton and Lilli Matson

Urban Footprints: *Making Best Use of Urban Land and Resources - A Rural Perspective*

Introduction

Cities place an enormous burden on the countryside. They consume land, demand water and construction aggregates, produce waste and provide a focus for commuters. Unless we understand and tackle the problems which emerge as a result of these pressures we will never get to the root of many of the countryside's problems. A key focus for any rural campaign must be to reduce the 'footprint' that our cities place on the countryside.

We also need to look more creatively at the way cities can relieve pressure on the countryside. They are the best form of living in terms of reducing society's impact on the environment and we are not making as good use of them as we might. Cities lie at the heart of the agenda about environmentally sustainable development.

What are we doing to our land?

England is a small and crowded island and land is one of its most important, yet vulnerable, resources. As we know, in the countryside we are not protecting and managing land as well as we might. The same is true in the cities. And things are getting worse:

- 300 people move out of the cities every day (Fig. 1)
- we create almost as much derelict land as we reclaim each year
- an area of rural land the size of Bristol is urbanised every year, and at current rates of loss, one fifth of England will be urbanised by 2050
- There are 1,500,000 dwellings unfit for habitation in England and more empty homes in the country than there are houses in East Anglia

These trends are understandable. People's aspirations and increased mobility make the countryside an increasingly attractive choice. But we cannot all move out! Nor can we give up on the decades of investment in the cities. The distinction between town and country is becoming blurred and we are wasting scarce resources. Yet with a new commitment to improving the urban environment we could not only improve the lot of city dwellers but also take pressure off our increasingly vulnerable countryside.

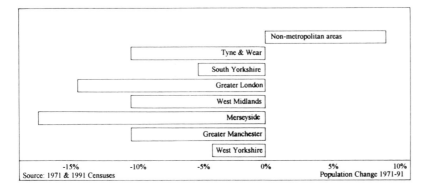

Fig. 1. Urban out-migration.

Source: 1971 and 1991 Censuses

Many of the conflicts in rural areas over new housing development, roads and commercial development are the result of urban pressures which could better be met in urban England. The countryside cannot carry the weight of the continuing dispersal of people and jobs from our cities. We need to bring a new approach to city life and provide a positive alternative to those leaving for the countryside - a high quality urban environment in which to live.

Cities and sustainability
Cities lie at the heart of the agenda about environmentally sustainable development. All serious commentators recognise that cities are the most environmentally sustainable way of housing people and providing factories, offices, shops, leisure facilities and many of the other things society wants. Cities can absorb development better than the countryside. They use less resources, save land, reduce car dependence and can improve the local environment.

We can meet society's needs and aspirations without destroying the countryside. We have to. It is impossible to accommodate everyone who wants to move to the countryside without destroying the assets which attract people in the first place. A new direction is needed which champions the cause of the city as a complement to protecting the beauty of the countryside.

We can encourage this new direction by helping celebrate the good things about city life, as well as tackling the bad. Cities are very different places from the countryside. They offer a different way of life. They are compact. You can walk from place to place. A car is not a necessity. The environment is dominated by architecture and built design. They are places for people to meet, and their rich cultural facilities offer varied opportunities for leisure. Cities are good places to be and we need to celebrate them.

We can make better use of our cities without building over playing fields and wild space or returning to tower blocks. Many fear that urban development means 'cramming' cities at the expense of a high quality environment and therefore dislike calls to increase the density of development. These fears need to be recognised and understood because they can be overcome. Playing fields and

299

open spaces need to be better protected. They are essential to a high quality urban way of life. Even if we built on every playing field or threatened patch of urban countryside we could provide only a tiny fraction of the new development which is needed. And at a huge cost! It need never be argued that we have to sacrifice important open spaces to meet the demands of development. There are better alternatives.

The spectre of tower blocks is another fear. But it is not a necessary result of higher density urban living. Tower blocks offer few environmental advantages and often accommodate fewer people than the housing they replaced. Higher density housing need not be in tower blocks and it can be an attractive place to live. Low-rise development and conversions can provide the bulk of the housing we need. Families can still have gardens, street trees can be protected, and if we reduce the huge area of urban land devoted to roads and cars we can free up extra space for improving the street environment. We should not sell our cities short. There is much more scope to adapt the existing urban fabric to our needs and re-invigorate the suburbs than is often assumed. But it needs a new commitment from planners, developers and the Government.

Planning ahead

Planners need to review their approach to encourage mixed development at higher densities and remove obstacles, such as minimum density policies and parking standards, which obstruct the refurbishment and conversion of existing buildings to better uses. Businesses and property investors should recognise the economic value of underpinning long-standing investments in the town centre. The public and community groups need to press policy-makers harder, highlighting the problems, drawing attention to the opportunities and celebrating the positive things about city life.

Central Government needs to provide a much stronger lead. It is remarkable that there is no national planning guidance for our major urban areas despite the fact that this is where most people live and most planning decisions are made. The Government should plug this gap in our planning system. It should also provide the financial carrots and sticks necessary to complement planning policies, and steer development away from greenfield sites towards brownfield ones. Private owners hoarding land against the public interest should be stung by new financial penalties. Local authorities should be provided with the resources and mechanisms necessary to overcome problems of dereliction and land ownership in regeneration schemes.

These are some of the ways forward. They provide both a vision and practical steps which can be put into effect tomorrow. The campaign to improve our urban areas is a challenging one. But it could not be more important. The future not only of the countryside but of the quality of life and environment of us all depends on whether we seize the opportunities provided by our cities to tread more lightly on the environment.

The Government · refine planning controls, policies and tax incentives so as to encourage builders and businesses to focus on urban areas · allow local authorities to do more to tackle vacancy and dereliction · issue a national statement of planning policies for cities and sustainability · provide more funds · set national and regional objectives for reducing the rate of loss of countryside to new building · discourage those who hoard vacant land and buildings

Local Councils · plan positively for every part of urban England · remove obstacles (e.g. restrictive parking standards, maximum density policies) to the better use of urban land · support community based solutions · help bring development to where it is needed · protect networks of open space · improve local leisure provision · safeguard town centres · provide employment, shopping and other facilities in suburban areas which do not have them · provide pedestrian priority and car-free areas

Developers, landowners and commerce · underpin the benefits of past investment in town centres · contribute to the management of urban spaces and provision of public facilities for both economic and environmental reasons · respond to the opportunities provided by government regeneration initiatives · refurbish and convert as alternatives to new-build · release vacant land · avoid car-based development

Public services · improve urban public transport · provide high quality local health care and education · tie future strategies more closely to land use plans

People · press local councils and your MP for new policies and funds to improve the urban environment · prepare community strategies for your neighbourhood · highlight areas of dereliction and decay and opportunities for enhancement and development · demand a positive response · celebrate the positive aspects of city life

Fig. 2. What can be done ?

makes the best use of scarce land resources · increases the cost effectiveness of public transport · reduces the loss of countryside · provides a positive alternative to building which damages landscapes and habitats · maintains urban populations · supports urban facilities and services · reduces the need for car travel · is more energy efficient · provides opportunities to live without a car or be less dependent on it · reduces length of journeys · improves the local environment of the vast bulk of the population · tackles the problem of urban dereliction · provides homes where people live · revitalises vacant buildings · returns unfit homes to active use · supports existing business investments · makes positive use of empty offices and vacant industrial land · improves town centres · supports existing infrastructure

Fig. 3. The benefits of urban development

This chapter summarizes arguments drawn from the CPRE's *Urban Footprints* leaflet, which is available from CPRE Publications, 25 Buckingham Palace Road, London, SWIW OPP.

Michael Breheny, Adrian Gurney and James Strike

The Compact City and the Need to Travel: *The Implementation of UK Planning Policy Guidance*

Introduction

In addressing the question of sustainable development, many governments around the world have identified planning systems as an appropriate device to deliver at least some of the objectives of environmental protection and enhancement. In turn, the link between land use and transport is seen as a crucial issue because of the particular concern with fuel consumption and emissions. Thus, much of the debate - both academic and political - about sustainable development has focused on the question of the degree to which land use planning can help to reduce reliance on the private car and promote greater use of other modes. A consensus view seems to have emerged which argues that policies to achieve greater urban compaction are more likely to reduce car use, and hence reduce pollution. Although this remains controversial, it is a policy stance that has been adopted in many countries.

The UK Government, along with a number of other western governments, has responded to this debate with a range of policy initiatives. The fullest statement of the Government's aims is contained in the UK Strategy for Sustainable Development (UK Government, 1994), produced in response to the Rio Earth Summit of 1992. This highlights the role of the planning system and the need to derive policy that relates land use and transport.

The most specific statement on this relationship is in *Planning Policy Guidance 13 (PPG13): Transport*, published in March 1994 (Department of the Environment, 1994). PPG13 has been described as one of the most radical postwar statements of planning policy in the UK. It has introduced a major change in policy at national level with an increased emphasis on the interrelationship of land use planning and transport as a means of: reducing the growth in length and number of motorised journeys; encouraging alternative means of travel which have less environmental impact; and hence reducing reliance on the private car.

A major concern following the introduction of such a profound policy change is the degree to which new policies are being adopted by local authorities. Thus, the Department of the Environment (DoE) and Department of Transport (DoT) commissioned Ove Arup and Partners, together with the University of Reading, to carry out research into the implementation of PPG13 by examining its influence on local authority policies and decisions, and the difficulties encountered both by local authorities and private developers.

The study aims and methodology are explained in the next section. This is followed by sections explaining the findings of the first phase of the project. These are organised into: general responses; findings relating to specific policy areas; and details of the integration of policies into planning documents and procedures. Each of these sections is organised around questions that the project is intended to answer.

Study aims and methodology

Study aims

The purpose of the research is to:

- report on the response to the PPG by local authorities, business and developer interests;
- evaluate the impact of the guidance on development plan policies, development control decisions and private sector investment plans and decisions;
- assess the effectiveness of the approaches being adopted to deliver the package of policies set out in the PPG, including efforts at monitoring of effectiveness; and
- identify areas of difficulty or misunderstanding and make recommendations to improve the delivery of the policies.

A two stage approach was adopted to the study methodology. The first stage involved the collection of information on responses to PPG13 from a variety of sources. The second stage, which is yet to be completed, will explore further the issues and questions raised during the research. This paper provides a summary of the methods used, and information obtained, during the first stage.

Study methodology

Information on responses to PPG13 was obtained from four separate sources. Firstly, a questionnaire survey was issued to all local authorities in England. This was addressed, in most instances, to the Chief Planning Officer with a request that responses should reflect the views of the authority, rather than individual officers. The questionnaire sought general responses to PPG13, as well as more detailed information on the development of individual policy areas. An examination of PPG13 identified 24 policy areas, which were separated, for ease of presentation, into those which were primarily 'land use' policies and those with a more directly 'transport' policy focus.

The questionnaire was sent to all 409 local authorities in England and 245 were returned, a response rate of nearly 60%. A higher response rate was achieved from county councils and London borough councils, than from metropolitan borough councils, district councils and national parks. There was also some variation in response rate from authorities in different regions, with the highest response rates in the South East, North West and West Midlands and the lowest in the South West and East. This may partly reflect regional differences in interest and awareness of PPG13, but also other factors such as resource availability and workload within local authorities.

The second method of collecting information was a review of recently produced development plans and transport policies and programmes (TPPs). A sample of 44 out of 75 development plans adopted or placed on deposit between March and September 1994 were reviewed. The review process examined the extent to which PPG13 policies were incorporated into plans, either in the form of plan objectives, as part of the plan strategy, or through specific policies and proposals. A parallel review was conducted of all 1995/6 TPPs published in July 1994, to identify how PPG13 policies are being taken forward through local authorities' transportation spending programmes.

Thirdly, group discussions were undertaken with representatives from business and development sectors, planning authorities and specialist interest groups. These served to raise issues to be explored and tested throughout the study, rather than provide a definitive impression of the response of different sectors to PPG13. Nevertheless, some interesting and varied views did emerge at this early stage.

Finally, a review of appeal decisions was conducted in order to investigate the ways in which planning inspectors have interpreted the guidance contained in PPG13. The review examined the 55 appeal cases between March 1994 and March 1995 which involved PPG13 considerations, based on information from the COMPASS database.

The next section presents the findings from these four research sources, in the context of the key research questions.

General responses

Awareness of PPG13

It was necessary at the outset to determine how far officers and members, and individual businesses and developers are aware of the changes in policy in PPG13, and to determine the importance and relevance to their own policy-making.

The research found that PPG13 has been one of the most widely discussed of the guidance notes with extensive coverage in the technical press and at conferences. Local authority officers and the relevant representative organisations (including those covering the business/developer sectors involved in the group discussions) are well informed.

However, only just over 30% of authorities have thus far involved members in discussions to consider PPG13. Only 15% have involved business, development or specialist interest groups. In the majority of local authorities, members of committees other than Planning and Transport may be unaware of how PPG13 considerations would be relevant to decisions on, for instance, education or waste management. Furthermore, in the majority of authority areas, local businesses and developers may be unaware of how changes in policy as a result of PPG13 could be affecting their own proposals.

It appears that the implementation of PPG13 has provided a stimulus for some local authorities to alter their working arrangements in order to implement policies of land use and transport integration. Nearly 20% of authorities have altered their working arrangements within or between local authorities since PPG13 was published, though fewer have involved working with other interests such as transport operators or specialist interest groups. Clearly, many authorities may have been engaging in joint working and cooperation between authorities prior to the publication of PPG13, so that changes are not needed.

The group discussions suggested that there are major differences in the awareness of PPG13 between different business and development sectors. It would appear that developers in the housing sector are more aware of PPG13 and its implications than development interests in the commercial sectors. Within the business community, those in the retail and leisure sectors seem better informed than those in the manufacturing and office sectors. During discussions it was suggested that these differences may relate to the extent to which operators in different sectors have a 'bank' of existing planning permissions with which to 'cushion' themselves against the immediate impact of PPG13 policies. Also, some sectors may be more innovative, and some more conservative, in their operations. Those in the retail business sector, with a small stock of existing permissions and greatest competitive pressures, seem to be most aware of PPG13 and its implications.

General changes reflecting PPG13

The second research question addressed the extent to which changes in general policy stance have already taken place in response to PPG13. The policy stances of both local authorities and development and business interests were addressed.

A majority of local authorities (65%) consider that existing policies are at least partly in line with PPG13. However, only half of the development plans adopted or deposited between March and September 1994 explicitly mentioned PPG13 objectives among the aims of planning policies. In fact, nearly two thirds of local authorities (63%) recognised the need to amend planning policies in the light of PPG13, and a similar proportion have already agreed that changes will be incorporated into the development plan.

In contrast, the inclusion of PPG13 type policies within current TPPs is better established, partly because of the shorter time-scales involved in adoption, and also because many authorities with responsibility for TPPs were already pursuing schemes consistent with PPG13 objectives. Accordingly, fewer of these authorities (32%) perceive a need to review TPPs in the light of PPG13.

It seems likely that many development and business interests will resist changes in their own investment policies or business plans for as long as possible. Most will attempt to continue with existing strategies until either users or customers change expectations (for instance of car parking facilities), or until existing permissions are used up and no other forms of investment or business opportunities are available. However, there have been some changes in the retailing and house-building sectors, with some operators developing and exploiting niche markets (such as town centre 'metro' stores or town-houses and apartments).

Perceived problems and suggested solutions

Another aim was to discover if there are any general barriers to change, and if there are, what actions are required to overcome them, either by organisations, or by others? Both the local authority questionnaire and the group discussions gave an opportunity to expand on the general problems perceived in implementing PPG13, and to consider possible solutions.

The group discussions were set up to provide an opportunity to consider the issues raised by PPG13 in greater depth with individuals who have some involvement in considering the implications of the PPG. Four discussion groups were arranged to cover business interests, developer interests, local authorities and specialist interest groups.

The business interest group expressed concern that such a major change in direction required a commitment by government to coherent national transport policy (including major investment in public transport), plus a fundamental change in business working practices (such as just-in-time deliveries). Specific problems mentioned included the likely variation in time-scale of implementation, with policies affecting some businesses and some areas earlier (for instance where existing planning permissions will run out sooner than elsewhere). In terms of initiatives there was a suggestion that greater emphasis was needed on restructuring existing areas (including suburbs and business parks), rather than on controlling incremental change (where only marginal benefits were expected by the group, even in the medium term).

The developer interests group emphasised that the need was for coherent landuse and transport policy at the national level feeding into regional plans, and use of fiscal measures to encourage the change in travel behaviour across the whole population. Specific problems mentioned included the strong investor resistance to use of contaminated land (because of the uncertainties of liability), as well as mixed development (because of different time-scales of reinvestment). The possible initiative of taxing new development in areas where public transport cannot be provided was seen as a way of directing funds to where they can be used to encourage development of difficult urban sites, while still allowing for choice.

The local authority group shared the view that changes via planning are important in the medium to long term, but must be matched by other changes (e.g. to improve energy efficiency in homes) if progress in sustainability is to be made in the short term. Particular opportunities were considered to rest with the regional planning guidance notes which would bring together the PPG principles to apply to different conditions in each region - the balance of policies will be different in each region because the sum of concerns will be different; not all PPG13 policy issues will be usable in every area. Initiatives such as restructuring of urban areas, planning at the neighbourhood level, and even new settlements were expected to receive increased attention.

The specialist interest group shared the concern that there was need for consistency in application of PPG13 issues (including in appeal decisions) if developers and local authorities were to have the confidence to pursue the major changes in policy required. There was also concern that some areas could be detrimentally affected by, for instance, increased densities if concentrated in the poorer urban locations. However, initiatives that were linked to urban revitalisation, or concentrated leisure and service provision in appropriate rural settlements, were welcomed.

Table 1 provides a summary of the main barriers to implementation and the initiatives or solutions suggested by respondents and discussion group members to overcome these barriers. Drawing from the discussions and questionnaire returns, there were three groups of actions which were suggested for priority consideration.

Problem	Affected	Suggested Solution	Activator
1. Competition			
1.1 Fear of losing competitive edge if investing in PPG13 locations	B/D	Assurance of long term commitment to policy	Government LAs
1.2 Fear of losing attractiveness compared to other areas if changing policies	LAs	Need for regional policy (eg consistent parking standards)	Government
2. Existing Commitments			
2.1 Preference for continuing investment in current locations	B/D	Need for hypothecated tax to finance alternative locations	Government
2.2 Backlog of commitments preventing changes taking place	LAs	Changing conditions on outline permission or renewals	LAs
3. Conflicts With Other Policies			
3.1 Other PPGs (2,3,4,6,7) seeming to limit PPG13 opportunities (eg public transport corridors and Green Belt)	LAs, IGs B/D	Clarify priorities between PPG or suggest stages in assessment	Government
3.2 Concerns about local economy/unemployment, need for investment	LAs	Clarify which PPG13 issues are relevant by region (see also 1.2)	Government
4. Lack of Clarity on Impacts			
4.1 Limited understanding of travel impacts of different development solutions	LAs	Need for research and demonstration projects	Government, LAs, Professional Institutes, B/D, Consultants
4.2 New transport policy areas (eg revised parking standards): lack of understanding of impacts or mechanisms	LAs B/D	Need for research	Government, LAs, B/D, Professional Institutes
5. Urban/Rural Locations			
5.1 Lack of available urban sites	LAs	Research into availability	Government, LAs
5.2 Additional costs of urban sites (land costs, assembly, congestion, management, public transport provision, contamination)	B/D	Need for hypothecated funding from non-urban site development (see 2.1)	Government
5.3 Fears of rural decline in more remote areas	LAs, IGs	Research into availability of brown-field sites and potential for public transport provision	Government, LAs, B/D, IGs
6. Implementation			
6.1 Some important means of implementation lacking (eg because of public transport deregulation)	LAs	Need to bring major elements into planning process (trunk roads, public transport provision)	Government, LAs

Problem	Affected	Suggested Solution	Activator
6.2 Need of major fiscal changes to alter perceptions (compare energy prices, altering energy/ growth relationship)	B/D LAs	Research into thresholds for fuel pricing, road pricing etc; and implementation	Government, Professional Institutes
6.3 Inconsistency in major decision-making (eg burden of proof with authority)	B/D LAs	Review of appeal decisions and use research findings (see 4.1 and 4.2)	Government

*Table 1. PPG13 -
Perceived problems and
solutions.*

(B/D = Business/Developer Interests; LAs = Local Authorities; IGs = Interests Groups)

Firstly, a firm framework of policy, particularly at regional level, would address the following specific concerns:

- that there should be long term commitment which would assure those investing in PPG13 proposals (e.g. development of urban sites) that they would not be disadvantaged by a later change in policy;
- that there should be consistency in adoption of these changes so that those adopting PPG13 policies (e.g. lower parking standards) would not find themselves at a competitive disadvantage in the future; and
- that there should be a framework for prioritising between different policy solutions involving consideration of PPG13 and other concerns (e.g. access needs of regeneration areas).

Secondly, a programme of research and demonstration projects would address the lack of knowledge that is hindering development of policies and proposals and their consistency of application:

- the current lack of understanding of the characteristics of trip-making from various kinds of development and how these might be affected by location and changes in parking, public transport provision etc.; and
- the need to understand the thresholds at which adoption of different land use changes (e.g. density, housing-employment balance, settlement size) will affect the propensity to travel and modes used.

Thirdly, an agenda of complementary measures would provide a set of specific powers and provisions that will work together with PPG13 to change the context of investment decisions and lifestyle habits. The concerns expressed included the following:

- that there are specific elements of transport provision which are not subject to planning or local authority control or influence, but which are essential elements in devising PPG13 solutions (particularly trunk road investment and public transport provision);
- that particular fiscal measures (such as fuel pricing, road pricing) which are able to alter the perceptions of travel costs are needed to change travel behaviour; and
- that urban development should be made attractive to developers by offsetting

the additional costs (land values, land assembly, contamination) perhaps by a differential taxing system (e.g. by use of 'hypothecated funding' from a tax on non-urban sites).

Specific policy areas
Importance and difficulty of policy areas
The research also aimed to find out if local authorities, developers and business interests have views on which policy issues raised by PPG13 are likely to be most important in bringing about changes, and if there are policy areas which are considered to be particularly difficult to implement.

The questionnaire provides the main source of information on specific policies, and is augmented by points raised in the group discussions where relevant. The land use policy areas and transport policy areas are presented separately (see Fig. 1 and Fig. 2). The questionnaire grouped them separately for ease of understanding - so direct comparison about importance or difficulty cannot be made across the tables: the figures represent the proportion of local authorities that mentioned a specific policy area as important or difficult. Respondents were not asked to rank the policy areas.

With regard to the perceived importance of policy areas, there are similar patterns in both the land use and transport figures. There are six policy areas in each of the groupings which are mentioned by at least half of the respondents as being important - from retail in existing centres to a range of local facilities at the neighbourhood level (Fig. 1), and from public transport provision to traffic management and calming (Fig. 2).

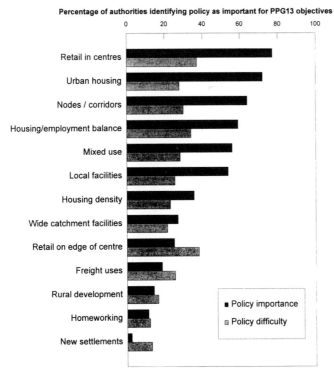

Fig. 1. Perceived importance and difficulty of landuse policies.

Percentage of authorities identifying policy as important for PPG13 objectives

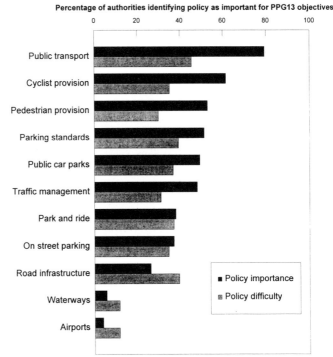

*Fig. 2. Perceived
importance and difficulty of
transport policies.*

Percentage of authorities identifying policy as difficult to implement

The remainder of the policy areas were identified as important by less than 40% of respondents, in some cases because they would only be relevant to a restricted number of authorities (e.g. small-scale development in rural areas, airports, waterways or shipping). It is possible to gauge from the discussion groups some of the reasons for these differences in perceived importance in relation to those policy areas which are of general application.

For policy areas of greater importance, it may be that some will be considered important in principle as a means of reducing travel. It is likely that concentration of employment and other travel intensive uses at public transport nodes and corridors (Fig. 1) and public transport provision (Fig. 2) are acknowledged largely because they are elements of sustainable development policy. Other policy areas may be considered important because they are currently the focus of particular attention. For instance, concerns about the future of town centres may have raised the importance of retail development as a policy issue, and similarly with mixed uses in central areas (Fig. 1). It is also possible that some policy areas have been mentioned more often because these areas are ones where the authority has already been able to achieve results - as for instance in housing provision in existing urban areas (Fig. 1) or cycle and pedestrian provision (Fig. 2).

For the other policy areas it may be that some particular difficulty limits the perception of importance. There may, for example, be conflicting evidence on the usefulness of actions - for instance the increase in density of housing required to change travel characteristics, or the appropriate size of new settlement, or how far new technology and home working will change the amount of travel (Fig. 1). There are also policy areas that are controversial by nature, suggesting limitations to the likely scale of change achievable; for instance, raising local housing densities, developing new settlements (Fig. 1), or controlling on-street parking (Fig. 2). Other policy areas will be dependent on the availability of specific local opportunities, such as rail infrastructure for freight villages, edge of town centre sites for retailing developments (Fig. 1), and edge of town sites for park and ride schemes (Fig. 2).

With regard to difficulty, it is of interest that for all the policy areas perceived as less important, the mentions of difficulty as shown in Figs 1 and 2 are close to, or exceed, the measures of importance. For the policy areas perceived to be of greater importance there are also concerns about difficulty of implementation: for instance, the perceived lack of power to improve public transport provision, or the difficulties in getting developers to invest in mixed development.

Progress in policy development

Following an assessment of the importance of policy areas, the research sought to establish what progress had been made in developing these policy areas, and also to find out if new policy areas were being taken forward sufficiently to provide a balanced strategy.

Figs 3 and 4 show, for land use and transport policy issues, the correlation between perceived importance of policy and the extent to which authorities have progressed with policy development. The vertical axis measures perceived importance of policies. The horizontal axis shows the proportion of local authorities that have developed the policy areas (to the extent of deciding on criteria to use in developing policy or selecting sites; and also identifying specific policies, proposals or sites).

In general, for both the land use and transport policies, the most progress has been achieved on the policies perceived to be most important, and the least progress on those considered less important. It is possible that there is an element of self justification in these responses, although questions regarding progress were separated on the questionnaire from those on policy importance. However, there are two specific conclusions that can be drawn from these correlation diagrams.

First, there are some policy areas that despite their perceived importance are less well progressed than might be expected. Concentrating employment and other travel-intensive uses at public transport nodes and corridors (Fig. 3) is a new policy area for many authorities. The review of development plans suggests that the majority of new plans are encouraging employment-intensive uses in town centres; but under 30% of plans are explicit in relating this to transport considerations, and there is little mention of other nodes, or corridors. Public transport provision (Fig. 4) is the policy area considered most difficult to implement. The group discussions revealed both a concern at a perceived lack of power vested in local authorities to ensure appropriate level or coverage of services, and unwillingness on the part of developers to commit themselves in a perceived policy vacuum except at certain rail nodes. Similarly, progress with revising car parking standards (Fig. 4) is slow. Specific requests were made in questionnaire responses for more guidance on parking standards: less than 20% of new development plans reviewed had considered revisions, and less than 25% of TPPs indicated that a review is to take place. The lack of progress in these closely related policy areas, which are central to the PPG13 policy changes, must be considered significant.

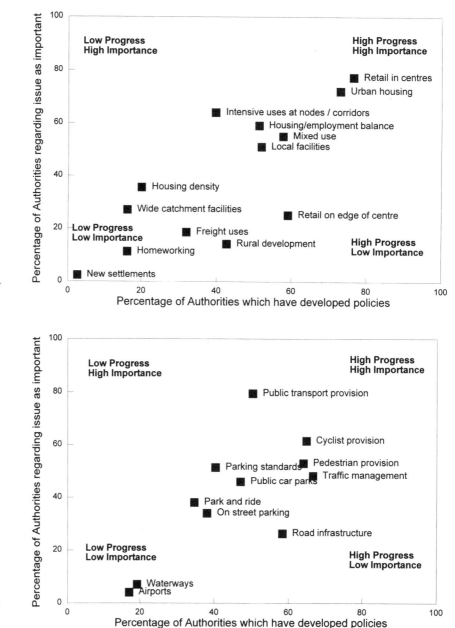

Fig. 3. Policy development: Landuse issues.

Fig. 4. Policy development: Transport issues.

Second, there are also some policy areas, which if considered of greater importance than perceived by local authorities, will need particular efforts to bring them higher up the policy agenda. For example, adopting policies for increasing housing densities and for concentrating facilities with wide catchment areas (e.g. colleges, hospitals) at public transport nodes both require major long term restructuring of existing urban areas. Progress in policy development at present is slower than would be expected from even the currently modest perception of their importance. New settlements are lowest in terms of perception of importance and progress on policy development (Fig. 3). Since the date of the survey in April 1995 there has been renewed debate about their potential role in meeting housing needs and the requirements of sustainable development. If this debate results in greater interest in new settlement solutions there will need to be considerable work in reformulating thinking in this area.

Integration of policy and monitoring

This section examines the general progress made by local authorities in implementing PPG13 through planning policies and transport investment programmes. From the questionnaire returns it is clear that the importance and high profile of PPG13 ensured that the majority of planning authorities have submitted reports to Committee on the implications of PPG13. There are, however, variations between types of authority, with county councils most advanced in this respect.

Development plans

Because of the time-scale involved in development plan preparation, there has been limited opportunity for published development plans to exhibit the direct influence of PPG13. A review of plans produced up to September 1994 suggests that in some cases PPG13 type policies have been developed prior to the publication of the PPG in relation to both the land use and transportation issues. However, it is rare for the interrelationships of land use and transport policies to be examined specifically in the justification of policies. Thus, long standing planning policies such as urban containment of housing development can be seen as being a PPG13 type policy, but treatment within development plans seldom mentions reducing the need to travel as a justifying principle for this policy.

Most structure plans and unitary development plans (UDPs) display several characteristics in their treatment of PPG13 issues which distinguish them from the majority of local plans. Integration of land use and transportation planning is most advanced in structure plans and Part I of UDPs. Structure plans and UDPs also have greater coverage and depth of transport policies than local plans, with the exception of policies relating to car parking standards, which are largely dealt with in local plans.

In the majority of plans, transport issues continue to be considered largely within the transport chapter. Half of the plans reviewed mentioned support for public transport, particularly structure plans and UDPs. Treatment of transport issues in relation to land uses throughout the plan is less common and is more advanced and explicitly stated in relation to certain land uses such as retail, compared to others such as employment or housing.

There is little evidence in plans published up to September 1994 that strategies for the location of development or transport provision were significantly altered as a result of PPG13. Some planning authorities argue that the fundamental nature of PPG13 will require a reconsideration of the development plan which is beyond the scope of the current review, and will be addressed fully in the next plan cycle.

Transport policies and programmes

In general terms, county councils, metropolitan boroughs and London boroughs have been covering the full range of PPG13 transport issues in the current round of TPPs. There is, however, variation in how far changes in policy direction have been adopted, and how far integration between transport and land use policy has been progressed.

All of the metropolitan and London boroughs and a majority of county councils have submitted package bids which present cases for funding based on wider cooperation between authorities and transport operators to achieve strategic development and transport objectives, and with particular emphasis on public transport and cyclist provision. All TPPs cover public transport issues, but financial commitments range widely depending on the role of the authority and the opportunity for specific investment in, for instance, light rapid transit; and many authorities are looking to private sector developer provision.

Some authorities, particularly the county councils, have developed, or are currently developing, integrated transport strategies or transport plans which are being used as the long term framework for developing annual TPP bids and structure plan policy. These strategies represent an important attempt to integrate, at the strategic level, land use and transportation planning.

Appeal decisions

The research also looked at how PPG13 considerations are influencing appeal decisions. A search of the COMPASS database identified 55 cases between March 1994 and March 1995 which included PPG13 considerations. The majority of these concerned retail developments. One third of cases were allowed on appeal (compared to half of all cases over the same period), confirming that the more controversial applications (e.g. retail) are more likely to be dismissed.

Table 2 shows appeals classified by type of location, whether the appeal was allowed or dismissed, and whether the overall consideration of PPG13 issues was in line with the decision. In virtually all cases where the appeal was allowed, PPG13 issues supported the appeal. The picture is less clear in the case of appeals which were dismissed. Dismissal was the result in thirty seven cases, where PPG13 considerations supported dismissal in only twenty three, suggesting that fourteen cases were dismissed despite the fact that PPG13 issues alone did not support dismissal. The suggestion, then, is that non-conformity with PPG13 is more likely to result in dismissal of an appeal than conformity is likely to result in an appeal being allowed. This is confirmed by Fig. 5, which shows that in eight cases, despite the Inspector concluding that there were positive PPG13 benefits from the proposal, dismissal was the result.

| | **Allowed Appeals** | | **Dismissed Appeals** | |
| | | PPG13 | | PPG13 |
Type of Location	No. of Cases	Supporting Approval	No. of Cases	Supporting Dismissal
Centre or Centre Edge	3	3	3	0
In Town	10	10	14	10
Edge or Out Town	5	4	20	13
Total	18	17	37	23

Table 2. Appeal decisions involving PPG13, March 1994 - March 1995.

There are some PPG13 issues on which Inspectors have been unable to come to firm conclusions. Fig. 5 suggests that in over 10% of PPG13 issues considered the Inspector was unable to be certain of the effects being argued. Change in journey length and in levels of emissions were the effects where conclusions were often not reached. Fig. 6 shows the range of PPG13 issues considered by Inspectors, and whether the conclusions reached were in line with the appeal decision. Reduction or limitation in journeys represents one third of all PPG13 considerations, and where firm conclusions are reached these are influential in the Inspector's decision. In contrast, the reduction or limitation of emissions is mentioned less often, and even less often is it influential. The policy issue most likely to influence the decision, if relevant, is the availability, or otherwise, of alternative sites. Whether there is an alternative site better suited to meeting PPG13 objectives is more easily tested and is more firmly within the traditional framework of planning considerations than other issues.

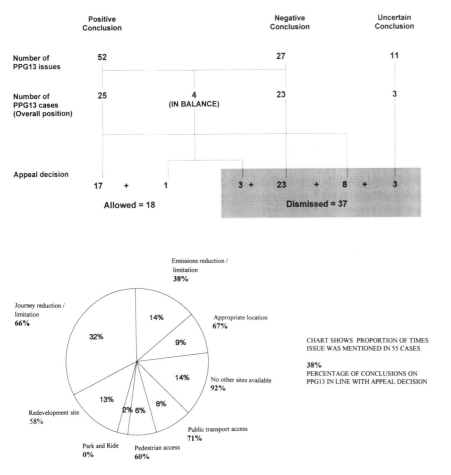

Fig. 5. PPG13 issues in appeals.

CHART SHOWS PROPORTION OF TIMES ISSUE WAS MENTIONED IN 55 CASES.

38%
PERCENTAGE OF CONCLUSIONS ON PPG13 IN LINE WITH APPEAL DECISION

Fig. 6. Range of PPG13 issues.

Monitoring

An essential aspect of any new policy development is appropriate monitoring. So the research aimed to find out if the effects of PPG13 policies and proposals were being monitored. Furthermore, if monitoring processes were not being established, it aimed to find out what additional work would be required to put them in place.

The questionnaire survey indicated that little consideration is being given to this aspect of policy development. With the exception of urban housing, the monitoring of change is being undertaken by 20%, or less, of authorities. Lack of consideration of monitoring is also apparent from the review of TPPs. With regard to development plans, county councils are more advanced in making reference to targets and monitoring, particularly of transport issues.

As with general policy development, there are three policy areas where lack of progress is particularly marked in contrast to the importance ascribed by local authorities. These policy areas are: employment- and travel-intensive uses at public transport nodes and corridors; public transport provision; and car parking standards. The particular need for assistance on these aspects is, therefore, further emphasised.

However, the generally low response in setting targets and monitoring suggests that this is an area requiring further consideration over the full range of policy issues. This is especially important if progress in implementing PPG13 is to be assessed in the longer term.

Conclusions

The study has provided a greater understanding of the general responses to PPG13, including extent of awareness of the PPG, how much change is thought to be needed in existing policies and proposals, and what general barriers are thought to hinder progress in implementation. It has also been possible to examine specific policy areas to get an impression of which are considered most important, which are most difficult to implement, and which are currently being progressed furthest in terms of policy development. And finally it has shown how far PPG13's objectives have been integrated into planning documents and the appeal process, and how far local authorities have set up targets and monitoring for the individual policy areas.

The study does suggest that PPG13 is having an impact on policy development particularly on those issues considered by local authorities to be most important. However, there are two major aspects that need to be explored further. Namely that local authorities consider that there are difficulties in implementing some of the most important policy changes (e.g. public transport provision), and that the development sector will resist PPG13 policies that appear to go against the 'grain' of the market.

The main conclusion of the study is that PPG13 does not need urgent revision, but that supplementary action needs to be taken if progress is to be made in implementation: regional planning guidance needs to take into account some of the concerns expressed by providing a framework of priorities in each region and placing PPG13 policies in context; advice is needed to enable consistent and appropriate revision of parking standards; research is required to provide a body of information on the impacts on journeys and emissions of changes in location, parking and public transport provision; and guidance is needed on targets and means of monitoring.

This chapter has outlined the findings from the first stage of this research. The next stage must address the crucial questions these findings have raised. More generally, however, there is a need for greater understanding of the broader issues - how far appropriate policies are being developed, why some priorities are being pursued and others not, why certain difficulties are of greater importance, and what could be done to overcome them.

References
Department of the Environment and Department of Transport (1994) *Planning Policy Guidance 13: Transport*, HMSO, London.

UK Government (1994) *Sustainable Development: The UK Strategy,* HMSO, London.

Jim Johnson

Sustainability in Scottish Cities:
Two Case Studies of Local Management

Introduction

Strong arguments are emerging through academic and political debate that the compact city is the most sustainable urban form. But many of the claims made about the compact city are controversial, and the counter- arguments draw attention to the dangers of increasing densities and activities within cities; of particular concern are traffic congestion, pollution, loss of urban open space and overcrowding.

This controversy about density and sustainability emphasises the importance of empirical study of existing examples of urban form. Whilst new 'green' residential developments may capture the headlines, real progress in devising more sustainable ways of living must be made in existing housing areas. It is arguable that one of the most energy efficient decisions that we could make would be to stop building new housing and concentrate instead on making the best use of the existing stock. This paper will focus on two contrasting mixed use areas, one of which, the Old Town of Edinburgh, is a classic example of high density housing interspersed with institutional and cultural buildings, and the other, South Dennistoun in Glasgow, is an area of traditional Scottish inner city housing.

South Dennistoun, Glasgow

South Dennistoun lies about 1.5 km east of the city centre. It is a densely built up area covering some ten hectares. It is an 'island' bounded to the north and west by Duke Street and Bellgrove Street, both major traffic arteries, and to the south and east by a railway cutting. To the north of Duke Street lies another much larger area of tenement flats and terraced housing mainly in private ownership. To the east and south are pockets of industrial and warehouse buildings, the few remaining remnants of what was, up to the 1950s, a prosperous manufacturing area (Fig. 1).

South Dennistoun consists of four-storey stone tenement flats, built in the second half of the 19th century, of typical Glasgow design (Worsdall, 1979). The terraces form hollow squares enclosing communal back courts, used for drying clothes and refuse disposal. The only access to the back courts is through a passage or 'close' connecting street and back court, off which stairs rise to the upper floor flats. These closes now have doors so that strangers are kept out of the communal areas. Each stair leads to two or three flats on a floor, the flats originally varying in size from one room to three. Densities of over 400 people per hectare are possible when such areas are fully built-up and occupied.

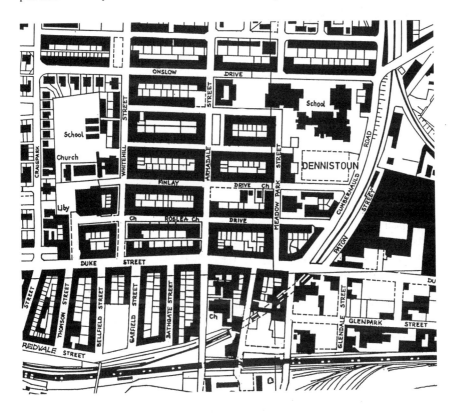

Fig.1. The Dennistoun area of Glasgow. The study area lies between Duke Street, Reidvale Street and the railway line.

Originally built by private landlords for renting, flats of this type in Glasgow were sold off individually from the 1950s onwards, so by the late 1960s the South Dennistoun area contained a mixture of private rented and owner-occupied flats, mostly in a state of neglect due to the threatened demolition of the south side of Duke Street to create an urban expressway. Sporadic demolition was taking place as tenements became structurally dangerous. The area was written-off for demolition and redevelopment by the city planners. But local residents had different ideas and their fight, coupled with political and economic changes, lifted the threat of road widening in the early 1970s. The problem then was how to organise and finance the rehabilitation of the tenements. The residents' action group formed itself into a community based housing association to take advantage of generous support and funding for social housing from the Housing Corporation and the City of Glasgow. Thus in 1974 Reidvale Housing Association (RHA) was set up, controlled entirely by local people. RHA acquired most of the flats and organised a tenement by tenement programme of rehabilitation, retaining the original population as far as possible. The external structure was overhauled and the interiors were virtually rebuilt with new bathrooms and kitchens, and rewiring was done to bring them up to modern standards. Twenty years later the rehabilitation is complete and the Association is finishing off its development programme by building new flats on some of the gap sites.

Demographic profile

The 1991 Census gave a total population of around 2,200 (this has now increased due to the completion of some new-built schemes). 28% of households have dependent children (just above the Glasgow figure of 25%). 82% of households (just over 1,000 dwellings) rent from RHA, with the remainder equally split between owner-occupation and private rental. RHA estimates that around 75% of its tenants are on some form of housing benefit. Unemployment in the Dennistoun Ward (considerably larger than South Dennistoun) is 13.2% (Glasgow 19%), with males under 19 at 24%.

Accessibility of jobs and services

Although much of the east end of Glasgow is an area of high unemployment, anyone living in South Dennistoun is well placed to reach jobs almost anywhere in the city by public transport. Local jobs are mainly in shops, catering, hospitals or education. RHA is itself a major employer of those involved in building and maintenance, with 18 local contractors being used regularly.

Local shopping used to be excellent with a wide variety of food and local needs shops in Duke Street. However, the building of a large new indoor district centre 1 km to the east has drained the life from Duke Street. Many of the grocers, supermarkets and other food shops have gone, leaving only small newsagents and general stores, charity shops, off-licenses, hot food carry-outs and all too often, voids. Of course for those who are mobile, a variety of shopping is available either at the new centre or in the city. But the less mobile, the poor and the elderly are handicapped by this decline in local services.

Public transport, car ownership and traffic

Duke Street is a major east-west bus route taking about ten minutes to the city centre. Suburban rail stations at Bellgrove Street and Duke Street, situated at either end of South Dennistoun, give connections to the east, the north and the city centre and thence on to the extensive suburban rail network.

Only 17% of households in South Dennistoun own cars (Glasgow 34%). This is a reflection both of the relative poverty of most residents and the easy access to public transport. Even so, parking space is a problem due to the density of housing. RHA have closed and 'calmed' many of the side streets in South Dennistoun to prevent their use as 'rat runs'. This has been very successful in creating safe streets where traffic is confined to slow-moving and service vehicles. However, the surrounding streets are heavily congested.

Recreation space

As originally designed, South Dennistoun had no open space apart from the back courts and the streets. Although most of the demolished areas have now been developed with new housing, one substantial space in the middle of the area has been left and developed as Reidvale Adventure Playground. Run by volunteers, it has controlled access to the playground and a building with indoor play space, offices, kitchen and storage. The encouragement this playground gives for creative play transforms the opportunities for children, in what is otherwise a grim environment.

All the enclosed tenement back courts have been improved by RHA with the cooperation of surrounding tenants. They have paved or grassed drying greens, planted shrubs and trees, and installed proper enclosures for dustbins. The involvement of tenants in design, and the restricted access, have ensured that damage has been kept to a minimum and the areas can provide a pleasant seating area for parents and young children. They are textbook examples of 'defensible space'.

Crime
Statistics are not available for the area but RHA's view is that crime, particularly burglary, is relatively low in South Dennistoun, primarily due to the natural surveillance provided by the community. Being busy night and day, Duke Street is also considered relatively safe.

Quality and demand for housing
The housing is of good quality being either rehabilitated or new-build. RHA has a cyclical maintenance programme and undertakes all repairs within 24 hours of reporting. Taken together, with the attractive communal backcourts, the safe streets within the area, and rents which are lower than equivalent accommodation provided by other public landlords, it is not surprising that the area is very popular with tenants, with a high demand and a long waiting list.

The old town of Edinburgh
The Old Town is an area of some 112 hectares focused round the Royal Mile which connects Edinburgh Castle and the Royal Palace of Holyrood. From the 16th century there was a tradition of high density living in flatted tenements (17th century stone buildings nine storeys high, still exist) with all classes in close proximity using a system of vertical segregation (Fig. 2). The Old Town was abandoned by the bourgeoisie in the late 18th century after the city expanded by the building of the New Town to the north. The population soared to 45,000 in the mid-19th century, living in terribly overcrowded squalor. This was relieved in the latter half of the century by carving new streets through the worst slum areas and building larger 'Improvement Trust' tenements, usually between four and five storeys high, with shops at street level. The general arrangement of these tenements was similar to those in South Dennistoun although their external appearance was far more ornamental.

The housing was intermixed with the remaining national and local institutions - the Supreme Courts, National Library and Museum, St Giles Cathedral, City Chambers and University - and with industry (much of it noxious) such as brewing, printing, wholesale food markets and transportation.

A century of slum clearance and industrial decline saw the population drop to 25,000 by 1901 and 3,000 by 1981. At that point the Old Town seemed to be in terminal decline, only set to become a Scottish historical theme park for tourists. Such housing as remained was predominantly public sector. However, by the mid-1970s, determined action by local groups fought off a threatened six-lane expressway bisecting the Royal Mile. Housing renewal commenced in the blighted areas, and in the early 1980s the city council began an attempt to revive the social and economic life of the Old Town. Since then population decline has been arrested. New mixed use redevelopments are filling the gaps left by departed breweries. Whole streets are being targeted for building renovation, and street improvements aimed at reducing the impact of traffic are being undertaken.

Fig. 2. Five-storey tenements lining Edinburgh's Royal Mile.

The Old Town has a strong cultural identity, being the focus of both the official Edinburgh Festival and the Fringe. It houses a number of art galleries, libraries and museums, and has theatres, cinemas and the city's concert hall in immediately accessible surrounding areas. In summary, the Old Town is a vibrant inner city area with a wide mixture of building uses and a substantial and growing residential population.

Demographic profile

At the 1991 Census, the population was 6,363, including 1,730 resident and non-resident students. Only 8.5% of households have dependent children (Edinburgh 28%). The unemployment rate in the Old Town is 15%, the fourth worst ward in the city (Edinburgh 8%) with male unemployment running at 21%.

	Old Town %	Edinburgh %
Owner-occupation	44	66
Private rental	25	10
Housing association	17	4
Public authority	14	20

Table 1. Tenure breakdown.

Accessibility of jobs and services

Employment is split between large organisations such as local authority and courts administration (to which some 12,000 commute into the Old Town every day), visitor attractions - Castle, Palace, museums etc. - and small scale retailing and catering, serving both the above and local residents. Thus there is a wide range of jobs available in the Old Town. However, it is naive to expect all residents to work locally. There is evidence of some misfit between jobs and the skills that are locally available - many manual jobs in brewing and transportation are now based elsewhere in the city.

Tourism puts pressure on local service shops. There is a proliferation of tartan, souvenir and woollen shops to the detriment of those selling food and other necessities to residents. The local community frequently voices the wish for a local supermarket with choice, competition and competitive prices. As in South Dennistoun it is fair to say that those who are fit, mobile and affluent can buy food from shops in nearby areas but the poor and elderly are handicapped.

Public transport, car ownership and traffic

A variety of bus routes are available in the western part of the Old Town but the eastern end around Holyrood is poorly served with only one unreliable minibus. At present the residential population is too thinly spread, particularly in the eastern area; it is hoped to build it up with new development on old industrial sites. The Old Town is adjacent to the main rail station with easy access to other cities, but Edinburgh has no suburban rail network.

30% of households own a car (compared to 54% in Edinburgh as a whole); even so, parking on the streets in competition with other users presents a severe problem, especially during the Festival. The area is crossed by three major north-south city traffic routes and also carries east-west traffic despite efforts to dissuade through-traffic in this direction. Current efforts in Edinburgh to restrict traffic on some key roads in the city centre (e.g. the Royal Mile, Princes Street) inevitably throw additional load on other routes. One such east-west route, Cowgate, passes through the Old Town in a deep valley, the canyon effect exacerbated by tall buildings either side. This leads to both danger to pedestrians and high levels of pollution which are currently being monitored.

The admirable traffic calming initiatives for residential areas such as the Dutch 'Woonerf' cannot be applied in mixed use areas, particularly where tourism is involved. Service vehicles to shops and pubs, and public transport cannot just be wished away even if restrictions are placed on non-essential traffic such as tour coaches.

Recreation space
Despite being adjacent to two major public parks the Old Town is poorly served for smaller, green recreation areas where children can play. The only two spaces of any size within the area are both churchyards of great historic and cultural value and thus limited in their use. Because of the density of development in the Old Town there are none of the semi-private backcourts which perform such a valuable role in South Dennistoun.

Crime
Police records indicate that the Old Town has a relatively low crime rate. Offences are mainly opportunistic (shoplifting, car theft), but there is a high perception of the threat of crime, particularly affecting the many old people in the community. This is caused primarily by the very 'liberal' liquor licensing hours allowed in Edinburgh. Generally speaking Old Town pubs are allowed to stay open until 1.00 am and pubs with 'entertainment' licenses (which include discos and clubs) stay open until 3.00 am or later. Given the large number of licensed premises in the Old Town (120 pubs and restaurants; one for every 53 residents!) this leads to crowds of mainly young people in various states of intoxication roaming the streets in the early hours of the morning, disturbing sleeping residents and carrying out acts of minor vandalism. Drunken violence erupts periodically, though the targets are usually other young people rather than innocent bystanders.

Quality and demand for housing
The quality of housing is generally good. The last pockets of substandard housing were upgraded in the late 1980s and housing associations have been active in converting and rehabilitating much of the older property. The Old Town Renewal Trust, set up in 1991 to lead the revitalisation of the area, has also focused funds on improving property in certain key streets, much of it tenements in multiple owner-occupation.

Demand for housing in the area is high. The Old Town Housing Association (community based) has around 200 houses which are in great demand. Over 300 applications for housing were received by the Association in 1994/95 although only 17 new tenancies were allocated in the year. Although the local authority and the funding agency, Scottish Homes, believe the Old Town is generally unsuitable for family accommodation, the Old Town Housing Association has many families on its waiting list.

Private sector demand is buoyant too. From being a 'red lined' area for mortgages in the 1970s and early 1980s the Old Town is now seen as an attractive area for ownership with prices up to £80,000-£90,000 for a good two-bedroom flat on or near the Royal Mile.

Urban management

Both case study areas are successful, in that they are good places to live, and meet many of the criteria for sustainability - good public transport, access to jobs (if there are any), an intrinsically energy conserving form of housing (which could easily be upgraded by improving insulation standards and introducing combined heat and power), defensible open spaces and natural surveillance of streets, proximity of entertainment, educational and cultural opportunities. They offer little support for the view that high densities can create an 'alienated community' (Breheny and Rookwood, 1993, p.155). Their problems, such as traffic and pollution, fragility of local shopping and, in Edinburgh, the disturbance to residents from late night revelry, are partly only solvable at national level (e.g. restraint on vehicle usage) but can be alleviated by intensive local urban management. Both South Dennistoun and the Old Town of Edinburgh are currently being held up as examples of good practice in urban regeneration. It is not an accident that both have dedicated local organisations managing their improvement programme.

Although RHA is funded only to improve and manage the housing in its area, the Association has always taken a wider view of its role, believing that improved housing conditions alone will not be enough to turn round an area in decline. It acquired a redundant school annexe for conversion to its own office, invited a local medical practice to join it and, using Urban Aid, produced a suite of community rooms. The garden was laid out as an attractive miniature public park focused around a specially commissioned sculpture. Members of the management committee and association staff are active in other local organisations. Most importantly, RHA is a grassroots organisation. One third of its tenants have become members of the Association, which gives them the right to elect (or become) members of the management committee. RHA has done all it can to empower the local community to achieve its aspirations.

High density urban living requires a level of communality in living habits if it is to work successfully. Even when there is a long tradition of high density living, as in Scotland, there are inevitable tensions and conflicts between neighbours and between generations. RHA has to intervene in extreme cases, but the Association's advantage is that it is embedded in the local community and guided by local committee members; it is not applying city-wide rules in a bureaucratic and perhaps arbitrary way.

The Edinburgh Old Town Renewal Trust (EOTRT) is a very different organisation, albeit equally committed to its area. It was set up in 1985 by the city council as part of its efforts to revive the Old Town, initially as a committee for its 'conservation and renewal'. In 1991 additional funding was received from the Local Enterprise Company (which has an economic development and training role) and the committee was transformed into a Trust, managed by a Board including representatives of the local residential and business communities. It has a wide ranging remit:

> To achieve long term sustainable improvements in the environment and economy of Edinburgh's Old Town, by promoting a productive balance between the interests of residents, businesses and visitors. This balance is

to be established through active partnership between the local community and developmental bodies. (EOTRT, 1995, p.10)

This involves much networking and co-ordination of a range of 'partners' in the local authorities, public funding agencies, such as Scottish Homes and Historic Scotland, and private sector developers, investors and agents. The Trust focuses investment in the Old Town through an annually updated Action Plan which highlights development sites and addresses issues of economic development (principally tourist related), and community welfare.

Whilst it cannot claim such strong grassroots as RHA, its ability to network at various levels, political and official, can pull together valuable inter-professional and inter-agency groups to deal with problems in a holistic way. For example the Trust's board is advised by a 'Quality of Life' Group in which staff from the trust meet with residents, and representatives of the city Housing and Recreation Departments, the Old Town Community Development Project, the police, the Health Board, a local doctor and others, to discuss issues such as public safety, pollution, health promotion, and the availability of fresh food in local shops.

Conclusions

The case studies demonstrate that high density mixed use areas can be both popular and sustainable but require intensive local management. So can we draw up a specification for an ideal management agency?

Firstly, it must be rooted in the local community, understand its various aspirations and be responsive to them. There are many forms it could take with varying degrees of democracy. A standard pattern should not be imposed.

Secondly, it must take a holistic view of the area, look for solutions unhampered by professional or departmental blinkers. It is notable that the professional staff of organisations such as RHA and EOTRT come from a variety of backgrounds or have 'dropped out' of traditional local authority departments. They prize flexibility of thought and action above all.

Thirdly, it must understand that local problems can often only be solved by action on a wider scale. The problem of traffic in Duke Street or the Royal Mile can only be alleviated by city-wide planning or a change in national priorities. Late night disturbance in Edinburgh could be alleviated by better links between planning and licensing legislation, but it ultimately hinges on commercial pressures from the big brewers and national attitudes to the consumption of alcohol. Local agencies should not be afraid to campaign on such issues.

Fourthly, the need for co-ordinated action by various departments and agencies can be facilitated by a consensual 'vision' for an area, expressed through an Action or Management Plan, to which the public agencies and the local community all subscribe.

Effective as both RHA and EOTRT are, they understand the limits of their power. The organisations that fund them can withdraw support if they fail to deliver or 'go native'. EOTRT has neither statutory powers nor statutory recognition. It is a truism that significant moves towards more sustainable living patterns will only come through political will and political action. It is perhaps less obvious that a political restructuring to allow devolution of control to a more local level is also a pre-requisite. The present reform of local government is a missed opportunity to give some statutory recognition to local management organisations. Moves by some local authorities to decentralise and provide inter-departmental area offices is a step in the right direction but the concern is too often with the local delivery of services rather than a move to an integrated and holistic approach to the management of the area.

References

Breheny, M. and Rookwood, R. (1993) Planning the sustainable city region, in *Planning for a Sustainable Environment* (ed. A. Blowers) Earthscan, London p.155.

Edinburgh Old Town Renewal Trust and Edinburgh District Council Planning Department (1995) *1995 Action Plan Review*, EOTRT, Edinburgh.

Wordsall, F. (1979) *The Glasgow Tenement : A Way of Life*, W. and R. Chambers Ltd, Glasgow.

Louise Thomas and Will Cousins
A New Compact City Form:
Concepts in Practice

Introduction

> Accessibility to facilities should be the guiding factor in moving towards
> more sustainable forms of development rather than development *per se*
> (Town and Country Planning Association, 1990, p.4).

In the chapter presented earlier in this book, entitled *The Compact City: A
Successful, Desirable and Achievable Urban Form?*, the hypothesis explored
was that the 'compact city' as proposed by Friends of the Earth (Elkin *et al.*,
1991), the Council for the Protection of Rural England (CPRE, 1993) and in the
Commission for the European Communities' (CEC, 1990) *Green Paper on the
Urban Environment* is an inappropriate urban form for the future. There we
suggest that its failure stems from its inability to meet and satisfy economic
demands and energy efficiency measures, as well as its lack of popular and
political support.

In order to perform as cities ought to - as the focus of diverse and often
conflicting pressures - the compact city proposal appears to have a long way to
go yet. However, the basic aspirations of the proposal are praiseworthy, and
should be considered the prerequisites of any new urban form. Essentially, these
are: compactness in scale, accessibility for all on foot, by bicycle and by public
transport, and greater respect for wildlife. Research has shown that more
'decentralised concentrations' of development may provide a settlement pattern
which is not only more environmentally sustainable, and more in tune with popular
aspirations, but could also meet the demands of economic forces, and hence win
political favour.

In this chapter we will present what we believe to be a new compact city
form, where it is possible to achieve the positive attributes of the compact city,
without resorting to draconian or 'Maoist' urban design and planning measures
(Gordon and Richardson, 1989).

328

Compactness

From the outset we must be clear about what we mean by 'compact'. What features define 'compactness' in an urban area? Is it the scale - the distance or time travelled to cross it? Is it 100 miles across, or just one mile? Or is it the capacity - how much and what kinds of things can be fitted into it? What is the intensity of its compactness? Is it home to two million people or is it a settlement of 5,000 inhabitants? Or is it containment - defined by the strict edge of the form?

Dantzig and Saaty (1973) refer to the different attitudes to compactness voiced by very many urban planners and 'master-builders' at a variety of scales and capacities; these include Broadacre City, the Garden City, and La Ville Radieuse. The solution offered by Dantzig and Saaty is the Compact City designed to overcome environmental degradation, huge conurbations, and the destruction of lives spent commuting around rapidly disintegrating 'non-cities'. It seeks to deal with the four dimensions of space and time, and the benefits of living in neighbourhoods of 5,000 inhabitants, by simply stacking whole communities of people into large multi-storey structures. This theoretical form would require the city of San Diego (in 1970 population 1,318,000) to be compacted from its area of 4,262 square miles into a structure occupying just nine square miles. While the application of this concept is clearly inconceivable, it illustrates the inherent danger of models which seek to compute efficient relationships between scale, capacity and containment to a point where human values are forgotten.

An alternative solution to the potentially conflicting need for compactness and accessibility is to be found in the work of Peter Calthorpe (1993). His Transit Oriented Developments (TODs) aim to reshape suburban sprawl into walkable settlements served by public transit. Andres Duany and Elizabeth Plater-Zyberk (1991) also promote more locally compact and liveable settlements as a panacea to energy and land consuming sprawl, currently pervading many of America's states: these settlements are known as Traditional Neighbourhood Developments (TNDs).

The components of these quite similar proposals of compact urban forms are typically:

- A development area approximately 5-10 minutes' walk (about 400-600m) from the centre to the edge, within which there is a fine grain of different land uses (see Fig. 1).
- The central area is the focus of the community's activities, with a public transport stop, several shops, restaurants and services, some small businesses, a community meeting hall, a local library and perhaps a crèche facility, plus a small public square or green. Towards the edge of this core area, there may also be a primary school.
- Residential development in this central area is high density low-rise apartments or town houses. Just beyond that, lower density terraced or row-style houses would predominate, all still within 5 minutes of the centre, and also within 2-3 minutes' walk of a local playground.
- Up to 1 mile from the central public transport stop, there would be lower density single-family housing, public recreation space, parklands with water balancing ponds, and protected natural countryside.

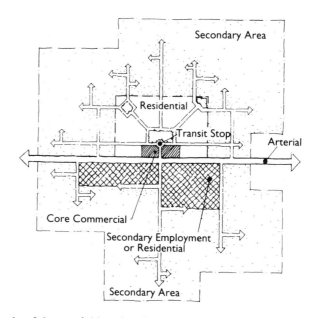

*Fig. 1. A TOD and
secondary area.*
Source: Calthorpe (1993)

The scale of these neighbourhoods or TODs is compact and aims to provide as many daily needs as possible within minutes of most inhabitants' homes. However, these models are limited in their application; the fact that they address issues of suburban sprawl means that the predominant land use is residential, and other land uses are controlled to fit both the image of these neighbourhoods, and the overall percentage of land that they may occupy.

Furthermore the provision of a public transport system - light rail or bus services - which will enable clusters of these developments to function, is not always integral to the development process; the car will continue to be the lifeblood of each place until public transport arrives in town. It is difficult to envisage how these car drivers will, even then, be tempted to leave their cars at home, to use buses and trains.

Nevertheless, the case for decentralised concentration is strong (see Owens and Rickaby, 1992; Rickaby *et al.* in Breheny, 1992). Ebenezer Howard's Social Cities provide a useful metropolitan-scale social city form, comprising 'town clusters' with 'each town in the cluster being of different design from the others, and yet the whole forming part of one large and well-thought-out plan' (Howard, 1985, p.102). All of the diversity of the city can be found in an area more geographically dispersed than the traditional nineteenth century city. This conceptual 'regional' city form may be regarded as a model structure which could enable decentralised concentrations to become more urban and powerful than just a collection of small settlements. A city form which combines the best attributes of the compact and walkable city with the spatial flexibility to accommodate the diverse needs of economic forces must surely be a step forward. We would suggest that this is possible through both physical compactness and 'virtual' compactness.

In this period of great angst and optimism about all things 'virtual', it is important to define our concept of 'virtual' compactness. Graham (1995), in his report on the current relationship between the Internet and the city, provides a useful glossary: ours is not a 'cybercity', where the public realm may be explored not on foot but by mouse, nor is it about synthesising the city into a series of computer functions which may be performed in the privacy of your own home - 24 hours a day. Virtual compactness refers to 'magic carpet' transportation which will whisk you off to the destination of your choice, foreshortening travel times and distances so that travel becomes a kind of cybernetic experience - and the city feels compact (North, 1993). This of course does not preclude the Internet from being woven into the urban fabric of our new compact city - but it will not be needed as 'an electronic *antidote* to the depressing reality of real urban life' (Graham, 1995, p.200).

The physical footprint of this city form therefore does not need to be a traditional mass of development; instead it may be exploded into fragments, each one operating like a city 'district' to create the diversity of a traditional city. What holds this city together is not its inability to move, or a tight 'green' belt - several sizes too small. Instead it is the interdependency or synergy between its parts that is this city's 'glue', while the lines of communication both real and virtual, either physical or electronic, keep this city structure in tension.

The new compact city

A unique opportunity to put these ideas into practice has arisen to develop a strategy for growth in an area of North Kent. This is unusual as it provides an opportunity to examine land use and transportation issues on a far greater scale than is often the case in Britain, and the size of this area demands a response to issues of both accessibility and compactness.

Kent Thames-side sits in the heart of the 'Thames Gateway' - an area which has been the subject of lengthy public consultations and subsequent regional planning guidance by the Government in RPG9a (DoE, 1995). Originally known as the East Thames Corridor, the Thames Gateway lies east of London, running on either side of the River Thames from Docklands to Tilbury in Essex, and to the Isle of Sheppey in Kent, as illustrated in Fig. 2. Within this area there are two potential growth centres; one is identified at the Royal Docks and Stratford, in East London; the other is Kent Thames-side. Kent Thames-side runs from North Dartford in the west, to the North Kent Marshes, east of Gravesend, and is bounded to the south by the A2 motorway and the banks of the River Thames in the north, as indicated in Fig. 3.

Kent Thames-side is a partnership formed between Blue Circle Properties, a major landowner in the area, Dartford and Gravesham Borough Councils and Kent County Council, to take up the challenge of regeneration. The launch by David Curry, Minister of State for the Department of the Environment, in September 1995, of the Kent Thames-side Group Consultation Document, *Looking to the Future,* marks the start of the transformation of an area covering approximately 28 square miles.

The proposed 'social city' of Kent Thames-side is a mixture of existing places and new proposals, comprising mixed residential, commercial, retail and education land uses, in addition to an extensive public open space network. Fig. 4 indicates the centres of the key districts in Kent Thames-side, each of which acts as a specialist district and the flavour of each is indicated. At each end of this 'city' are the towns of Dartford and Gravesend. Between these lie the existing largely residential and industrial villages and communities of Greenhithe, Stone,

Swanscombe, Northfleet, and Knockhall. Linking all of these new and existing places will be a seamless public transport network of heavy rail lines, with loops of light rail and guided bus services. The new development proposals are shown in Fig. 4.

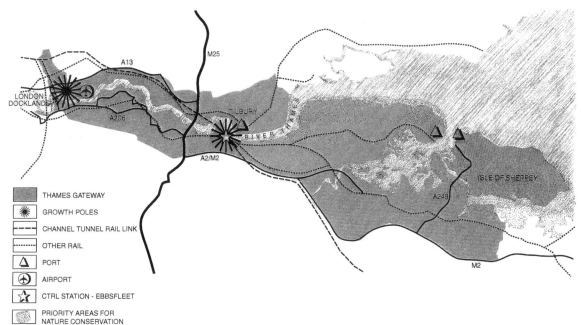

Fig. 2. The Thames Gateway.

Source: David Lock Associates (1995)

At the hub of this public transport system and Kent Thames-side, and the key to its success, is Ebbsfleet - the International and Domestic Passenger Rail Station on the Channel Tunnel rail link. From here it will be possible to catch high-speed trains to Europe, to Central London, to towns and other cities in North Kent, as well as around the new and existing areas of Kent Thames-side. The opening of the Station in 2002 will indicate the start of a new era in rail travel which has the potential to topple the car from its pedestal. Ebbsfleet also has an important role as the flagship of the new development proposals, providing an excellent location for new business and residential developments in an urban setting, within a few hours' of Paris and Brussels. The proposed new districts in this area are:

- A district comprising the London Science Park at Dartford, the University of Greenwich and Littlebrook Lakes Business Park. This is being promoted by Dartford Borough Council, The University of Greenwich, the Wellcome Foundation and South Thames Regional Health Authority. This mixed use proposal has been described as the first in a new generation of science parks, one which does not act as an isolated 'park', but that is integrated with nearby Dartford town centre. It includes a research and development centre, higher education facilities and student residences, a forum for business innovation as a catalyst for new scientific and manufacturing collaboration, plus a range of housing, shops and restaurants, all well served by public transport.

- Crossways Business Park, begun in the mid-1980s, which will be, by the time of its completion, the largest mixed use business and distribution centre in the UK, combining the facilities of Thames Europort (a freight ferry terminal), several hotels and restaurants, as well as office accommodation in the vicinity of the Queen Elizabeth II Bridge, on the M25 motorway.

- Greenhithe Waterfront, which will be a mixed use urban village, with a fine grained business quarter linked to Crossways Business Park, a variety of houses overlooking the marina with regular riverbus services, and new riverside walks to the existing Greenhithe Village.

- Swanscombe Peninsula, which will be the home of culture in Kent Thames-side, and in its dramatic position provides an excellent location for a new theatre, symphony hall, and an environmental observatory. Two urban villages will sit astride a new canal system, and the existing marshes will be protected in a new nature conservancy park.

- Northfleet Embankment which will be a predominantly residential area with some mixed uses, and the atmosphere of a high density European city. A promenade of hotels, cafes, shops, offices and parks will be the focus of local activity.

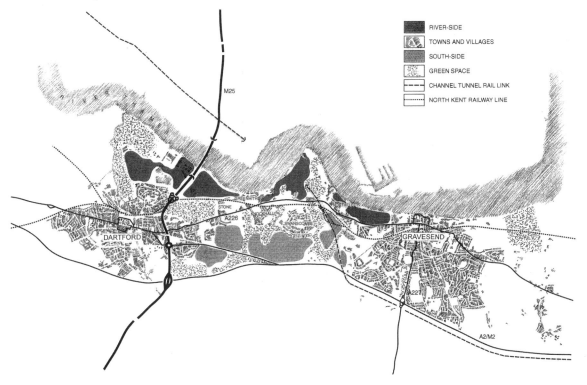

RIVER-SIDE
TOWNS AND VILLAGES
SOUTH-SIDE
GREEN SPACE
CHANNEL TUNNEL RAIL LINK
NORTH KENT RAILWAY LINE

Fig. 3. The extent of Kent Thames-side.

Source: David Lock Associates (1995)

- Bluewater Park regional shopping centre. This is in a former chalk pit and will become the core of high quality retail activity, with a multiplex cinema, fitness centres and restaurants extending its life well beyond normal shop opening hours.
- Eastern Quarry which will be a more suburban garden city district, where the houses built in the huge redundant quarry will be at lower densities, and surrounded by informal gardens and tree-lined avenues.

It is likely that the range of activities and places to be found across this social city will rival the diversity of the traditional city, in addition to responding directly to economic, environmental, social and political issues. Returning to the basis of the failure of the 'compact city' as outlined in our previous chapter, we believe that Kent Thames-side will emerge as a fine example of a 'new compact city form' for the following reasons.

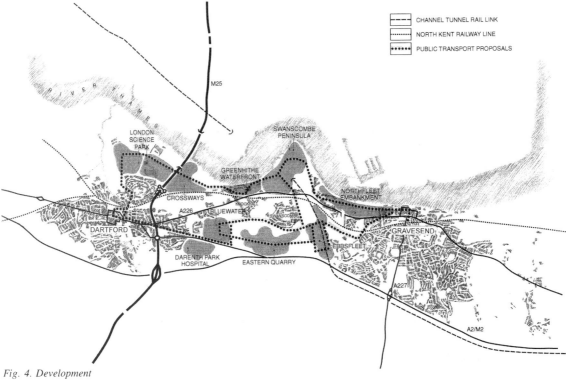

Fig. 4. Development proposals.

Source: David Lock Associates

(1995)

Economic demands

Across Kent Thames-side, it is possible to identify a range of commercial accommodation for a cross-section of uses - varying in size and location. There is a place for both the large-scale distribution industry, the commercial office space in a landscape setting of the 1980s, and the rediscovery of very cosmopolitan urban areas with easy access to Europe, enabling employees to go out at lunchtimes and 'pollinate their thinking' (Garreau, 1991). 'Tomorrow's companies' will be spoilt for choice (RSA, 1995). The new employment and economic profile of Kent Thames-side has the potential to redress the balance between housing and jobs in the area, and cut the numbers of commuter trips to London and the rest of Kent, reducing the cost of employment and increasing the leisure time of people living in the area. This new home-work relationship may also be influenced by telecommunications or 'dematerialising technologies', whereby for some employers their location and accommodation could be quite different, and far more attractive and accessible than previously possible, for example, overlooking the Thames on Greenhithe Waterfront.

The viability of economic development is already acknowledged in *The Thames Gateway Planning Framework* (DoE, 1995) in which the growth centres of Royal Docks, Stratford and Kent Thames-side are identified. Many of the development proposals for Kent Thames-side have already secured investment and are under construction. Having witnessed the fortune of London Docklands, the emphasis is on steady and responsive growth. The launch of the Kent Thames-side Consultation Document will also attract wider investment attention to the area.

It is also possible to compare Kent Thames-side to a 'technopole'; Castells and Hall (1994) have defined this phenomenon as the result of three forces: regional development, reindustrialisation and synergy. This is borne out in the following ways:

- Regional development - the regional context of Kent Thames-side's emergence as a growth centre, together with its large footprint.
- Reindustrialisation - the rejuvenation of North Kent as a centre for employment after decades of gradual decline, along with its ability to become the centre for new and innovative work practices.
- Synergy - the powerful relationships between the seemingly unrelated fragments of the city, generated in a climate of collective initiative.

Environment
Travel

> All cities have been shaped by the state-of-the-art transportation device of its time. (Garreau, 1991, p.106)

The implications on travel of this new compact city form have already been described above, in which the scale of individual city 'districts' is geared to pedestrian and cyclist access to local facilities. The slightly overlapping nature of the districts means that there are good local routes from one area to another. The rail based public transport system centred around Ebbsfleet avoids what Gordon and Richardson (1989) have described of the BART system in San Francisco. There they claim that the radial form of the rail network encouraged greater sprawl, as the perpetual extension of each line was easy and inevitable. However, the loops and feeders of the public transport in Kent Thames-side present a planned and holistic approach, which it would only be possible to extend with strategic planning. As an indication of the quality of this proposed service, the time taken to travel from Greenhithe Waterfront to Ebbsfleet (about 3.5 miles) would be about eight minutes, with trams running at least every ten minutes.

The relative development intensity around the stops and station of the public transport system means that ridership thresholds will already be in place in new development areas; there is little danger that rail will not have a direct impact on North Kent. As the CEC states, 'outright prohibition of the car is rarely the answer' (1990, p.44), therefore development strategies which manage demand for car parking to attract investment, and also to feed public transport and use land effectively, will be an appropriate course of action for many areas.

Building stock

The fragmented and diverse shape and sizes of development footprints to be found within Kent Thames-side enable a wide range of energy efficiency measures to be introduced. Blue Circle Properties, as the primary investors and developers of this new city, have commissioned David Lock Associates to develop 'Environmental Standards' for future development. This commitment to high standards at this early stage of the 'city's' life is important as it grasps the opportunity to implement such standards on a large scale for Britain. While these standards apply to fundamental strategies for land use and transportation planning, they also combine the lessons of 'green' buildings and layouts, and as such will act for the investors as both a leading-edge marketing tool, and also as a means of securing products worthy of long term investment.

Green space

A significant area of the land within Kent Thames-side has been worked as quarries; in some places these have been used as landfill sites, with many redundant factory buildings. The reclamation of this damaged or derelict land is the basis for much of the new development, with areas of more attractive landscape preserved. Proposals exist to generate electricity from the methane being produced from the many landfill sites. The pockets of development fit the topography of this 'moonscape' in North Kent, but also allow special green places to be left undisturbed. The Kent Thames-side vision for the area also promotes a wide range of green spaces and water features, some for public recreation, and others as nature areas. Natural boundaries also occur at the limits of its geographical area, the River Thames to the north, and in the west, east and south land is within the metropolitan green belt.

Social and political concerns

The word 'compact' has two definitions which are of interest to us; one is a physical attribute and is the basis of the current debate, while the other signifies an agreement, and the meeting of minds. As a collaborative initiative between the local authority, other public bodies and Blue Circle Properties, the Kent Thames-side Consultation Document represents a 'compact' city with many views of the local population already incorporated, but its publication also invites further public response. The positive changes to the area within Kent Thames-side address issues that are most frequently of popular concern: housing, jobs, new facilities, accommodating growth without destroying wildlife areas, and improving transport. The emphasis throughout the transformation of Kent Thames-side will be on creating a better image for the area, and making the most of its attributes, so that liveability, variety and economic success remain important to the investors, the residents and the local politicians.

Conclusion

Of course, Kent Thames-side remains as yet largely untried and untested; but it appears to be able to satisfy many of the demands made of it, and the concept is supple enough to be able to reshape itself as new ideas and priorities emerge. We believe that there are many indicators to suggest that Kent Thames-side as a functioning new 'city form' is economically, environmentally, socially and politically feasible, and as such is a 'sustainable' or durable model. However, it is inevitably difficult to assess how it will actually perform and, just as important, how it will be perceived.

Fig. 5 shows the three potential identities of Kent Thames-side. From the outside, and as a marketing concept, it can be seen as a single element. However, within this element there are three distinct areas:

- Riverside - where both the new and existing developments address the River Thames;
- Towns and Villages - where the core of the existing villages and settlements lie; and
- Southside - where the primary growth poles of the region will be located.

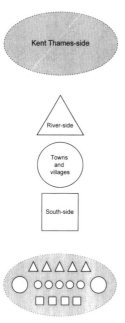

Fig. 5. Perceptions of Kent Thames-side.

Source: David Lock Associates

We envisage that the individual qualities of these three areas will provide a coherent identity to each and also to Kent Thames-side. A final, third image would be that of the residents of Kent Thames-side from inside the area; this concerns the 'knowledgeability' of Kent Thames-side as a whole and also the extent to which new development projects are seen as individual districts, sitting in either Riverside or Southside. All of the 'city districts' have the potential to be very distinctive, with local topography, land uses and outlook securing their role in the social city. However, with the vision for Kent Thames-side unfolding over a 25 year time-scale, the challenge will be to maintain a balance between these individual identities and the united image of the whole, and to promote the relationships which will enable these components to function as districts in the new 'social city'.

References

Breheny, M.J. (ed.)(1992) *Sustainable Development and Urban Form*, Pion, London.

Calthorpe, P. (1993) *The Next American Metropolis. Ecology, Community, and the American Dream*, Princeton Architectural Press, New York.

Castells, M., and Hall, P. (1994) *Technopoles of the World. The Making of 21st Century Industrial Complexes*, Routledge, London.

Commission of the European Communities (1990) *Green Paper on the Urban Environment*, EUR 12902 EN, CEC, Brussels.

Council for the Protection of Rural England (1993) *Sense and Sensibility. Land Use Planning and Environmentally Sustainable Development*, CPRE/CAG Consultants, London.

Dantzig, G.B. and Saaty, T.L. (1973) *Compact City. A Plan for a Liveable Urban Environment*, W. H. Freeman, San Francisco CA.

Department of the Environment (1995) *The Thames Gateway Planning Framework*, *RPG9a*, HMSO, London.

Duany, A. and Plater-Zyberk, E. (1991) *Towns and Town Making Principles*, Harvard University Graduate School of Design/Rizzoli, New York.

Elkin, T, McLaren, D. and Hillman, M. (1991) *Reviving the City: Towards Sustainable Urban Development*, Friends of the Earth, London.

Garreau, J. (1991) *Edge City: Life on the New Frontier*, Doubleday, New York.

Gordon, P. and Richardson, H.W. (1989) Gasoline consumption and cities, a reply. *Journal of the American Planning Association*, **55**, Summer, pp.342-46.

Graham, S. (1995) Cyberspace and the city. *Town and Country Planning Association Journal*, August 1995, pp.198-201.

Howard, E. (1898/1985) *Garden Cities of Tomorrow* (new edition) Attic Books, Eastbourne.

Kent Thames-side Group (1995) *Kent Thames-side, Looking to the Future*, Consultation Document, Dartford, Kent.

North, B.H. (1993) *A Review of People Mover Systems and Their Potential Role in Cities*, Proceedings of the Institution of Civil Engineers of Transport, 100, pp.95-110.

Owens, S. and Rickaby, P. (1992) Settlements and Energy Revisited. *Built Environment*, **18 (4)**, pp.247-52.

Royal Society for the Encouragement of Arts, Manufactures and Commerce (1995) *Tomorrow's Company. The Role of Business in a Changing World*, London.

Town and Country Planning Association (1990) *Commission of the European Communities Green Paper on the Urban Environment, A Response from the Town and Country Planning Association*, 5 October 1990.

Conclusion

Mike Jenks, Katie Williams and Elizabeth Burton

A Question of Sustainable Urban Form: *Conclusion*

The title of this book, *The Compact City: A Sustainable Urban Form?*, was posed as a question. It would be reasonable to ask, having started with a question, if a positive answer has now been given. The preceding chapters have presented a wide ranging debate based on new thought, research and experience. As is the characteristic of almost all knowledge, when some questions are answered, a host of others are raised; this book is no exception. What has been established is that the compact city concept is complex, and the issues multi-layered. On the face of it there is nothing new in that, however, there are some clear and important indications from which a consensus might emerge, and from which future directions can be drawn.

That there is a need for sustainable development is not in doubt. The ecological imperative, which addresses global warming, the consequences of profligate energy consumption and the use of non-renewable resources has long been established, and is endorsed by governments worldwide. What is now emerging is a strong desire to act, and to act specifically in relation to cities; for it is cities which are seen as the main contributors to unsustainability, and thus are the locus within which significant solutions can be found. Yet the arguments remain largely theoretical, and the impacts of any action to achieve compact city goals seem, at best, uncertain. Here the solutions remain partially unresolved, but the debate has certainly moved on. There are some discernible common threads, and the balance of discourse is beginning to move away from theory and into the realm of practical policies, and of urban forms that could contribute to achieving a more sustainable future.

Urban form

Strong arguments have been presented for two extremes, centralisation and containment, and dispersal and low density development, both of which assert a link between urban form and sustainability. But there is no consensus. Concentration in city centres is claimed to reduce journeys and improve the quality of life, but the balance of evidence in this book suggests that it may not. The counter-arguments, coming predominately from Australian experience, claim that low densities can be sustainable (or at least no more unsustainable than compact urban forms) and that the quality of life within them is much higher. In achieving sustainability the arguments both for and against these positions do not appear to provide conclusive evidence of anything other than marginal gains resulting from changes in urban form alone, unless it is associated with variations in behaviour and lifestyle.

The exodus of population from cities in the developed world is an uncomfortable fact for the proponents of high density, compact city living. Yet there is evidence that some groups, such as childless couples and young households, appear to prefer urban living. The debate has yet to explore the full consequences of the dynamics of changing lifestyles emerging in the last years of the 20th century, and the different choices between compact urban and suburban living that individuals may aspire to at different stages in their lives. It seems improbable that the exclusive promotion of either urban form would reflect reality, or be an achievable goal.

The consensus emerges around ideas that are more inclusive. The possibility of the intensification of urban areas begins to fulfil some of the aims for promoting high density compact living. At the same time it is recognised that a policy of compaction would be unlikely to satisfy the demand for certain types of homes, and that new development will be necessary in locations other than urban areas. Here the arguments for compromise, for decentralised concentration, and more autonomous settlements begin to provide answers. This requires a regional perspective beyond that of the city. However, it is clear that such solutions depend heavily on the way that transport systems evolve in the future.

Transport

The urban form that appears to provide the most efficiency for transport, and reduced car journeys, is that of decentralised concentration, but the savings are not great. Certainly they would not be sufficient to achieve the sort of reductions in greenhouse gases that would satisfy the environmental lobby. Areas of concentration, whether decentralised or within the compact city, do provide proximity and accessibility to services and facilities, giving a chance of success for a modal shift from the car to cycling or walking. However, it is largely accepted that, however convenient, this will not encourage the majority to give up their cars. What may be gained in reduced car-use for short journeys, will make little overall difference when longer, often leisure oriented journeys are considered. It is in this respect that the decentralised concentration model, if linked by good public transport, may make some gains.

It is, however, clear that some urban forms enable urban residents to undertake more sustainable travel patterns, whilst others almost force unsustainable actions. The growth of out-of-town facilities for essential requirements such as food and household goods is now seen as both unsustainable and inequitable, as it discriminates against those without access to a car. Progress will be made if such unsustainable forms are discouraged in the future.

There is also some agreement that, while urban form *per se* might make some contribution to reducing emissions, the likelihood is that more significant savings will come from more advanced technology to make personal transport eco-friendly.

Such solutions may prove to be more effective than the restructuring of towns and cities, and would certainly be quicker to implement, but they rely on the support of governments and industry. Benefits may also come from changes in behaviour, encouraged by education and awareness campaigns, and enabled by public transport and, perhaps, by more compact urban forms.

Quality of life

A common theme throughout the book concerns the quality of life of urban residents. It is the quality of life that might be offered by the various solutions to sustainable urban form that is crucial in making them attractive and achievable options. In democracies particularly, where choices are open, desired changes in lifestyle will be a matter of education, enablement and persuasion. Key arguments were made that noted the distinction between global benefits and potential local disbenefits, and of the responsibilities to the wider public interest of citizens as opposed to the wants of individuals. Few are likely to accept changes unless there is an alternative that gives as good or better a quality of life, or unless there are good and persuasive reasons to do so. There are clear arguments to suggest that the compact city needs to provide an environment where people will want to live, and which provides the services, facilities and transport that will encourage them to change to more ecologically sustainable lifestyles, particularly in relation to the use of the car.

The provision of such environments will require investment, and it is likely to depend on private sector finance, as much as, or even more than public sector funds. The need to ensure that obstacles to higher density and mixed used development are removed is essential if they are to be economically viable. Examples from Scotland show that this is no pipedream, as they would appear to be both popular places to live, as well as being economically and socially viable.

An achievable goal?

Over the broad span of the work presented in the book, there are indications of a number of ways forward. If the compact city, or urban form in general has any role to play in a sustainable future, then it has to be not only theoretically valid, but achievable in real terms. The chapters in this book offer a range of solutions to the most pressing questions concerning implementation.

Firstly the question of the overall approach to future development is addressed. The consensus seems to be that a 'balanced' approach is necessary; in the context of sustainable development, however, the term balanced is all too often used to disguise a lack of commitment to any particular option. But here it means a commitment to the most appropriate type of development in a particular location. A number of forms are emerging as sustainable, and future development should follow the combination of these forms which is most sustainable in a given local, regional or national context. It is therefore likely that a flexible approach will be needed.

Where new development is required the decentralised concentration approach has attractions. Practical models are beginning to emerge such as Transit Oriented and Traditional Neighbourhood Developments, Urban Villages, or even the 'virtual' compact city. But central to these initiatives will be the requirement to make urban areas attractive to prospective and existing urban residents. Clearly the market will continue to demand homes and businesses in a variety of locations.

Thus it is important that, income permitting, people have a choice about where they live and work.

The second question addresses how achievable the compact city is, when it is largely to be brought about by the intensification of existing towns and cities. There is not, unfortunately, a clean slate from which to start, but a legacy of existing built form which embodies historical, social, economic and cultural values. Therefore the line between acceptable compaction and overcrowding needs to be understood, and it will vary from place to place. The indications are that, if it can be done acceptably, positive benefits and some gains in sustainability will be possible.

Implementation of intensification needs to be sensitive not just to the ecological imperative, but also social and economic needs. If development is not acceptable to those who are affected by it, it is unlikely to be sustainable. Even at the broadest level there are clearly differing views on lifestyle between outlooks from the UK, Europe and Australia, just as there are variations in views about how to achieve sustainability. So compact city solutions cannot follow a standardised pattern; there are not going to be 'blanket' solutions. There may well be common themes, and common technical solutions, but there is not one overall answer. Instead solutions will need to take on board the qualities of a specific locality. In some areas the built environment may require preservation and enhancement, in others open space may need special protection, elsewhere open land may be seen as having a downgrading effect, and thus be ripe for intensification. Understanding differences and responding to them is a key to providing solutions that have the potential for success.

Following on from this argument is the question of where urban compaction should take place. Counter-urbanisation trends and derelict land figures have shown that many cities in Europe are not suffering from being too compact, but the opposite; many cities, or parts of cities are dying. Clearly in these cases urban intensification is often seen as part of the process of urban renewal, which benefits existing residents and puts a halt to further decline by encouraging people back into the city. But it is also clear that in many areas further compaction would lead to a breach of a 'capacity' of some type, and these areas have to manage any increases in activity or development carefully so that benefits can be gained without the related disbenefits.

Finally, sustainable urban forms will only be achievable if they are underpinned by a supportive policy background. Such a background appears to be one which commits to global sustainability goals, but leaves room for local solutions to be formulated and implemented. There is a large role for policy. This will not be straightforward, and it certainly cannot solve all the problems. The difficulty is that, while much can be done by ways of attraction and persuasion in the market to encourage people to return to cities and to accept higher density living, there will be many issues in the public interest that will be deeply unpopular - yet will be imperative if significant sustainability gains are to be achieved. This may involve policies to restrain car-use, to remove obstacles to high density and mixed use development, the release of land for development, and also investment in public transport.

Conclusion

This book presents a considerable amount of work which, because of the complexity of the issues, crosses many disciplinary boundaries. It has also begun to bring this work together, and to show some ways of resolving the conflicts outlined in the Introduction. Some advances have been made but there is still considerable scope for further research to continue the search for a sustainable urban form and to find solutions to many of the problems that have been raised.

One thing, however, is certain. The book has shown the pressing need, in the developed countries, to act in a way that reduces the conspicuous consumption of resources, and that demonstrates the viability and attraction of city living in all its guises. If the developed countries, which have less than a third of the world's urban population, fail to solve their urban problems, then the message to the other two thirds living in the developing world would indeed justify scenarios of ecological catastrophe. The search for the ultimate sustainable urban form perhaps now needs to be reoriented to the search for a number of sustainable urban *forms* which respond to the variety of existing settlement patterns and contexts that have been identified. A great deal has been achieved in a very short time and the drive towards finding sustainable solutions is still gathering momentum. But as the millennium approaches, much more remains to be done.

Index